A

BOOK

The Philip E. Lilienthal imprint
honors special books
in commemoration of a man whose work
at University of California Press from 1954 to 1979
was marked by dedication to young authors
and to high standards in the field of Asian Studies.
Friends, family, authors, and foundations have together
endowed the Lilienthal Fund, which enables UC Press
to publish under this imprint selected books
in a way that reflects the taste and judgment
of a great and beloved editor.

The publisher and the University of California Press Foundation gratefully acknowledge the generous support of the Philip E. Lilienthal Imprint in Asian Studies, established by a major gift from Sally Lilienthal.

A GARLAND OF FORGOTTEN GODDESSES

A GARLAND OF FORGOTTEN GODDESSES

TALES OF THE FEMININE DIVINE
FROM INDIA AND BEYOND

Edited by Michael Slouber

UNIVERSITY OF CALIFORNIA PRESS

University of California Press
Oakland, California

Library of Congress Cataloging-in-Publication Data

Names: Slouber, Michael, editor.
Title: A garland of forgotten goddesses : tales of the feminine divine from India and beyond / edited by Michael Slouber.
Description: Oakland, California : University of California Press, [2021] | Includes bibliographical references and index.
Identifiers: LCCN 2020021296 (print) | LCCN 2020021297 (ebook) | ISBN 9780520375741 (cloth) | ISBN 9780520375758 (paperback) | ISBN 9780520976214 (epub)
Subjects: LCSH: Hindu goddesses. | Hinduism—Doctrines.
Classification: LCC BL1216 .G37 2021 (print) | LCC BL1216 (ebook) | DDC 294.5/2114—dc23
LC record available at https://lccn.loc.gov/2020021296
LC ebook record available at https://lccn.loc.gov/2020021297

28 27 26 25 24 23 22 21
10 9 8 7 6 5 4 3 2 1

CONTENTS

List of Illustrations vii
Preface ix
Acknowledgments xiii
Introduction 1

PART ONE. Demons and Battle

1. Bhadrakāḷī: Slaying the Demon in the Backwaters 19
Noor van Brussel
2. Cāmuṇḍi and Uttanahaḷḷi: Sisters of the Mysuru Hills 43
Caleb Simmons
3. Kauśikī: The Virgin Demon Slayer 61
Judit Törzsök
4. The Seven Mothers: Origin Tales from Two Early-Medieval Purāṇas 83
Shaman Hatley

PART TWO. Miracles and Devotees

5. Svasthānī: Goddess of One's Own Place 117
Jessica Vantine Birkenholtz
6. Kailā Devī: The Great Goddess as Local Avatar of Miracles 143
R. Jeremy Saul

7. Bahucarā Mātā: She Who Roams Widely 171
Darry Dinnell
8. Rāṣṭrasenā: Hawk Goddess of the Mewar Mountains 193
Adam Newman

PART THREE. Tantras and Magic

9. Rangda in the *Calon Arang*: A Tale of Magic 217
Thomas M. Hunter and Ni Wayan Pasek Ariati
10. Tvaritā: The Swift Goddess 245
Michael Slouber
11. Kāmeśvarī: Visualizing the Goddess of Desire 263
Anna A. Golovkova
12. Avyapadeśyā: Indefinable Kālī 283
Olga Serbaeva

Glossary 301
List of Deities and Characters 313
Primary Sources 323
References 327
List of Contributors 341
Index 345

ILLUSTRATIONS

MAP

1. Distribution of goddesses in southern Asia / *8*

FIGURES

1. Bhadrakāḷī / *18*
2. *Bhadrakāḷī Māhātmya,* a Sanskrit work in the Malayalam script / *20*
3. Cāmuṇḍi and Uttanahaḷḷi / *42*
4. *Beṭṭada Cāmuṇḍi,* a ballad in the Kannada language and script / *44*
5. Kauśikī / *60*
6. *Haracaritacintāmaṇi,* a Sanskrit work in the Devanagari script / *62*
7. Sapta Mātaraḥ / *82*
8. *Devī Purāṇa,* a Sanskrit work in the Bengali script / *84*
9. Svasthānī / *116*
10. *Svasthānīvratakathā,* a Sanskrit work in the Newar script / *119*
11. Kailā Devī and Cāmuṇḍā / *142*
12. *Śrī Kailādevī Itihās,* a Hindi work in the Devanagari script / *144*
13. Bahucarā Mātā / *170*
14. *Śrī Bahucarā Ārādhanā,* in the Gujarati language and script / *172*

15. Rāṣṭrasenā / 192
16. *Ekaliṅga Māhātmya,* a Sanskrit work in the Devanagari script / 195
17. Rangda / 216
18. *Calon Arang,* a Middle Javanese work in the Balinese script / 218
19. Tvaritā / 244
20. *Tvaritāmūlasūtra,* a hybrid Sanskrit work in the Ranjana script / 246
21. Kāmeśvarī / 262
22. *Nityākaula* and *Ciñciṇīmatasārasamuccaya,* hybrid Sanskrit works in the Newar script / 265
23. Avyapadeśyā Kālī / 282
24. *Jayadrathayāmala,* a hybrid Sanskrit work in the Devanagari script / 284

PREFACE

You hold in your hands the first anthology of goddess narratives available in translation. Twelve Hindu goddesses make up this "garland"—not a literal string of flowers such as those offered to goddesses in temples, but rather a curated collection of exciting but largely overlooked tales and rare visualizations offered to the reader in the hopes of fostering deeper understanding and inspiring future scholarship. The narratives include legends about defeating demons and negotiating roles with other goddesses, lore about devotees and miracles, and Tantric visualizations from little-known but highly influential scriptures.

We seek to reinvigorate the study of Indian goddesses by making available fresh primary sources for the reader to analyze directly. Each of the narratives presented here is historically significant, yet they are among thousands of other overlooked stories that languish in archives all around South and Southeast Asia. The voices in these narratives have much to teach us about the ornate diversity of Hindu goddesses, the interplay of local and larger transregional traditions, and the ways religion adapts to changing times. Sourcebooks are plentiful in almost every area of the humanities, yet goddess studies has, until now, lacked an anthology of this kind. As none of these sources were previously available in translation and many remain unpublished, the volume also makes original contributions to scholarship.

The selections span a range of dates, languages, and genres: from the sixth-century Sanskrit *Skanda Purāṇa*, to the early medieval Tantras, medieval place legends, and modern song lyrics and devotional booklets targeted at pilgrims. The chapters are grouped into three categories: tales of demons and battle, miracles and devotees, and Tantras and magic. These include sources from Bali in the far southeast of monsoon Asia, from the Kathmandu valley of Nepal, and from various parts of India: the northeastern states of Bengal and Arunachal Pradesh, the southwestern states of Kerala and Karnataka, Gujarat and Rajasthan in the northwest, and Kashmir in the far north.

Our choice to frame these sources and goddesses as "forgotten" calls for an explanation. After all, over half of the selected goddesses are the focus of living local traditions, actively worshiped by millions of devotees in their respective areas. In those cases, the "forgetting" cannot apply straightforwardly to the Hindu public. And yet the sources themselves are, for the most part, no longer widely known; both insiders and outsiders may be interested in learning more about the little-known histories of these twelve fascinating goddesses. The "forgetting" that we wish to highlight also pertains to modern scholarship and curriculum design for courses on South Asian religions. When goddess traditions are included in such courses, sometimes only particular mainstream viewpoints are conveyed to students, and often only through the filter of secondary sources.

The need for a collection of diverse primary sources in English with which to introduce Hindu goddess traditions inspired this book. And it is not that such sources were entirely unavailable until now. However, most are scattered in volumes that present them with the scholar's own analysis—which is often brilliant but leaves little scope for readers to be active participants by practicing their own analysis and critical thinking. Literature is a marvelous tool in such a situation, since stories are universal ways of bringing cultural and moral values to life. Almost everyone grows up with cultural narratives, be they fictional or historical, religious or secular, family stories or national myths, for entertainment or for more serious educational purposes. The current collection serves as a reminder that a rich store of unstudied Hindu goddess lore is available in manuscripts and printed books, as songs, and in dramatic traditions from India and beyond.

"Forgetting" or neglecting the diversity of Hindu goddess traditions is not only an academic phenomenon but ties in with processes that have been actively shaping goddess worship in the Indian cultural zone for over two thousand years. We refer to these processes as "Sanskritization" or "Brahminization": connecting local deities and traditions with orthodox pan-Indian mythology and ritual practices. This pervasive and long-standing trend serves, on the one hand, to unite a myriad of deities under the banner of a more universal religious configuration that transcends regional differences. On the other hand, standardization and simplification may also occlude the beautiful and intricate depth, besides the local character, of Hindu goddess traditions. Claiming that a local goddess is none other than the Mother of the Universe who readily grants miracles to her devotees can attract huge masses of pilgrims to a previously little-known local shrine. And yet that fame may, in some cases, also result in changes to long-standing local traditions and the rejection of practices such as animal sacrifice and deity possession that high caste authorities regularly deem unacceptable. Such conversations and debates over identity and ritual have been shaping Hinduism for thousands of years and continue to influence our understanding.

As a verb, "forgetting" typically implies an unintentional failure to remember. But it can also imply a deliberate process of actively minimizing or marginalizing, such as when authorities seek to transform a goddess's character, or the rituals associated with her, in the interest of making a text or a site more appealing in the face of changing trends in religion. Responding to the conference panel that inaugurated this book project at the American Academy of Religion meeting in 2016, Rachel Fell McDermott raised the question of whether all of this forgetting is necessarily regrettable. This book contends that while changes in religion over time are not inherently regrettable, earlier texts and forms are intrinsically worthy of our attention. Knowing the trajectories of the goddesses in this book enriches the present with the depth and nuance of the past. As works exploring what it means to be human, and what it means to be divine, they have the power to touch our lives and, sometimes, to transform us. Let them be forgotten no more.

This book aims to represent diverse traditions and a broad geographical area. Given that the volume is limited to twelve subjects, however, gaps in coverage are inevitable. It lacks representatives from the Tamil- and Telugu-speaking regions of India that are so rich in goddess traditions. We could have included any number of other Hindu narratives from places like Trinidad, Malaysia, Fiji, or Japan. Oral narratives of India's scheduled castes and tribes are also conspicuously absent, given that such communities make up approximately 25 percent of the country's population. Despite these deficiencies, the selected subjects are fascinating and represent an array of genres, regions, languages, and time periods.

The original conference panel that inaugurated this book project was based on an open call for contributions. The editor recruited the remaining authors through dialog with about thirty scholars from all around the world (based in India, Korea, Germany, Thailand, Indonesia, Canada, Switzerland, Finland, France, and the United States). We share a common goal, best summed up in this sentiment from the Rāṣṭrasenā narrative (chapter 8): "Wanting to benefit the community, a knowledgeable person helps them to remember what they have forgotten. By remembering, they will all reap the fruits of a successful life, just as I did."

Michael Slouber
30th of September
Bellingham

ACKNOWLEDGMENTS

Producing this volume was a collaborative effort of many individuals, each of whom was in turn mentored and inspired by their predecessors. My own principal guides include Robert Goldman, Sally Sutherland Goldman, Alexander von Rospatt, Somadeva Vasudeva, Harunaga Isaacson, and Alexis Sanderson. The contributors themselves, with their expertise and labor, have gifted us access to these wonderful sources in many different languages. Several contributors include their own words of dedication and thanks in the first notes of their chapters.

I am grateful to the editors and production team at the University of California Press for helping to bring this book to fruition. The peer reviewers the press selected offered detailed and thoughtful suggestions that significantly improved the book. Thanks also to my colleague and chair Kimberly Lynn for supporting my initial idea for this book in 2015. Rachel Fell McDermott offered numerous helpful suggestions as discussant at the conference panel mentioned in the preface. Shaman Hatley, aside from contributing a chapter, offered sage advice at every stage. My colleague Jonathan Miran pointed me toward John Renard's *Tales of God's Friends: Islamic Hagiography in Translation*, which provided a fine model of an anthology of diverse primary sources like this one. Many thanks are due to the artist Laura Santi, who created the vibrant line drawings that enrich each chapter. The choice to include samples of the original scripts was inspired by Subashree Krishnaswamy and K. Srilata's delightful small volume *Short Fiction from South India* (2008). As a book prepared by the editor entirely with free and open-source software, many generous people have indirectly contributed by making their code, fonts, and troubleshooting advice freely available.

Financial support for the artwork and indexing were provided by Western Washington University. Students in my Fierce Goddesses of India course read most of these chapters and helped me improve it in countless ways. And finally, I thank my wife Corinne Robinson Slouber for feedback and support throughout this process.

Introduction

Much of the world rarely questions the idea that God is male. The notion that God is female may even strike some readers as radical. But in India goddesses are everywhere. They are the bedrock of ancient religious traditions that extend back thousands of years. Goddesses are honored in, though not central to, the oldest scripture from India, the *Ṛg Veda*. Some scholars even find continuities between certain early historical nature goddesses linked to fertility, such as *yakṣiṇīs*, and artistic representations going back even further—to the dawn of human civilization as we know it—in artifacts from the third millennium BCE Indus Valley civilization.[1]

Whatever their origins, India's goddess traditions proliferated and became central to religious and narrative literature there from late classical times (after ca. 600 CE). The stories in this book offer fascinating case studies of alternative imaginings of gender, devotion, and power. This is not to say that Hindu goddess traditions are necessarily examples of feminist spirituality; of the twelve goddess tales translated here, some envision female power and agency in thought-provoking and potentially inspirational ways, some are patriarchal in character, and many are ambiguous in how they portray female power. All offer studies in how the feminine divine has been construed and reckoned with in the religious imagination of Hindus.

FORGOTTEN GODDESSES

The book styles these twelve selected goddesses and their stories as "forgotten" in multiple senses. For some of them—the Seven Mothers, Rāṣṭrasenā,

Tvaritā, and Avyapadeśyā—their former glory, expressed in the translated sources, has waned to the point that a relatively small number of people still actively worship them or know of the ancient accounts translated here. Others, such as Bhadrakāḷī, Cāmuṇḍi, Svasthānī, Kailā Devī, Bahucarā Mātā, and Rangda, enjoy popular living traditions with millions of followers; in these cases "forgotten" certainly does not imply a lack of significance.

What unites all of these goddesses is that they are rarely mentioned in surveys of Hindu goddesses. In this sense, they have been forgotten by many of the authorities who speak for and about Hinduism to cosmopolitan audiences. Two other goddesses featured here have not yet been mentioned: Kauśikī and Kāmeśvarī. They are closely linked to Durgā and Tripurasundarī, respectively, and so each is honored as the Great Goddess by tens of millions of Hindus in vibrant living traditions. Durgā and Tripurasundarī are in no sense forgotten figures. However, our understanding of their early histories and transformations over time is rudimentary. The rare and largely forgotten sources translated here add depth and nuance to their better-known collections of traditional lore.

The types of sources selected for this book are also poorly represented in scholarship on Hindu goddesses. As described later in the introduction, the late-classical religious development of esoteric scriptures called "Tantras" is central to the rise of goddess traditions as we know them in southern Asia. Yet these prolific early sources have been largely ignored in American scholarship on goddesses. Several of our selections belong to the popular classic narrative genre called "Purāṇas" (ancient lore). While the Purāṇas have been relatively well studied, research on Hindu goddesses has tended to focus on a small number of popular Purāṇas readily available in printed editions. The well-studied *Devī Māhātmya* (Glorification of the goddess), for example, is an important piece of the puzzle mentioned frequently throughout this book.[2] But it is only one among many dozens of influential goddess scriptures from the first millennium, most of which have not even been published, let alone translated and studied in depth. Several contributors have done painstaking research to access and read unpublished manuscripts in order to uncover the fascinating stories of the goddesses Bhadrakāḷī, Kauśikī, the Seven Mothers, Svasthānī, Rāṣṭrasenā, Tvaritā, Kāmeśvarī, and early Tantric views of Kālī (here called Avyapadeśyā, "the Indefinable One"). Popular living traditions also possess fascinating but understudied archives of oral lore, songs, performances, and devotional booklets marketed to pilgrims. The chapters on

Cāmuṇḍi and her sister Uttanahaḷḷi, Kailā Devī, Bahucarā Mātā, and Rangda draw on such undervalued sources to help show how these goddesses are significant to a broad range of Hindus today.

Given the intricate and multifaceted religious history of Indian civilization (and Indian-influenced civilizations farther afield), it is important to understand some of the major religious currents that have affected goddess traditions. Knowing the structures of religious history discussed in the following sections will help the reader come to a deeper understanding of the tales themselves.

THE DEVELOPMENT AND SPREAD OF HINDU GODDESS TRADITIONS

Thomas Trautmann offers a useful framework of developments in Indian religious history, summarized here.[3] The historical period in Indian religions begins with the Vedic religion, which flourished among the Indo-Aryan speaking tribes of northern India from around 1500 to 500 BCE. At this time, the primary religious mode—at least so far as can be discerned from textual records—consisted of worshiping a pantheon of sky-dwelling and earthly gods, and a handful of goddesses, through recitation of hymns and offerings of food in a sacred fire. These food offerings consisted of various grains and dairy products, as well as livestock. The central importance of food offerings for strengthening the relationship between humans and the gods led Trautmann to characterize it as a *religion of sacrifice*. The stamp of the Vedic sacrificial religion is evident in the present book; for example, the goddess Uttanahaḷḷi of Mysuru is described as a seven-tongued goddess of fire, who, like the Vedic fire god Agni, is hungry for offerings (chapter 2). And it is also visible in the tale of Bahucarā, in which the goddess confronts demons who threaten the performance of Vedic sacrifices (chapter 7).

After around 500 BCE, religions such as Jainism and Buddhism rose to prominence and emphasized quite different values and ways of being religious. In contrast to prominent ideals in Vedic society of the time, they taught that violence, attachment to material things, and seeking pleasure in marriage and family life are obstacles to salvation. For these religions, at least in their early phases, the direct path to liberation lay in renouncing family and society, withdrawing into isolation or becoming part of an alternative community of nuns or monks, practicing meditation in order to tame one's desires, and otherwise living an austere life. The immense growth of *religions of renunciation* under the Mauryan dynasty led to their ideas becoming commonplace in Hinduism and all subsequent religions founded in India. The earliest Upaniṣads of the Vedic tradition are some of the first texts to show similar concerns, though this class of Hindu texts did not develop a full-fledged focus on renunciation until centuries after the rise of Buddhism and Jainism. The imprint of values from the religions of renunciation is apparent throughout this book in several forms. The great Hindu god Śiva himself, frequently regarded as the consort of most of the goddesses in this book, is usually portrayed as an austere renouncer. When the Svasthānī tale extols the religious benefits of restricting food intake, sleeping on the ground, and conquering the senses (chapter 5), or when ascetics (sādhus) play such an important role in the Kailā Devī tale (chapter 6), the values of renunciation live on.

After the fall of the Mauryan empire, which is to say, starting from around 200 BCE, new religious values developed that emphasized personal *devotion* to a particular supreme God or Goddess, or to various sorts of enlightened beings in Buddhism and Jainism. In early devotional Hinduism, the high God was typically a form of Viṣṇu or Śiva; only later did goddess worship emerge in the written record, with similar massive movements of devotion, often to a singular almighty Goddess such as Durgā or Kālī. The names for these movements are derived from the names of the deities they identify as sovereign; followers of Viṣṇu became known as Vaiṣṇava, followers of Śiva are Śaiva, and followers of any of the numerous figures honored as the premier Goddess are called Śākta after the generic name for divine power, which is always gendered feminine: *śakti*. These terms are used frequently throughout this book.

A core idea of devotional religion is that finding favor with one's personal deity does not depend on rituals, as it did in the Vedic sacrificial religion, or upon renunciation of family and social life, as it did in the religions of renunciation. Rather, a feeling of pure devotion in one's heart toward the supreme deity is enough for salvation, as taught in early devotional classics such as the *Bhagavad Gītā*. The values of devotional religion are central to most of the goddesses in this book, as is plainly visible in the various narratives of savior goddesses who entered the world to fight demons and restore order, such as Bhadrakāḷī, Kauśikī, and the Seven Mothers (chapters 1, 3, and 4).

Starting around 500 CE, Hindu Tantric religious cults developed within the Śaiva sects, and within a few centuries followers of Viṣṇu, followers of the goddesses, and Buddhists developed their own Tantric corpora, as did some lesser-known religious traditions.[4] The adjective "Tantric" has been applied to a wide variety of texts and practices. In Asia, some use it to refer to strange magical practices and transgressive rituals. In the United States, many think it refers exclusively to sacred sexuality. Neither is characteristic of the Tantric tradition as a whole, although both are present in some contexts. The Tantric tradition referred to here is an important initiation-based religious movement that purportedly was based on secret teachings of divine figures. It has had an indelible impact on the religions of Asia and left us thousands of scriptures (Tantras), most of which remain unpublished and unknown to scholarship. The Tantras are critically important to understanding the history of Hindu goddess traditions.

Central to early Tantras is the power of mantras and *vidyā*s (gendered masculine and feminine respectively). Tantric practitioners repeat these sacred utterances both to accomplish spiritual salvation and to gain worldly powers such as rainmaking or the attainment of godlike longevity and power. In practice, such sacred sounds were regarded as ways of ritually evoking a deity's presence or even causing divine possession. A Tantric *vidyā* is not only a sacred sound or spell but is considered to be the deity herself embodied as sound. It is thus perceived as a powerful living force, a link between the human and the divine.

All these religious developments—the Vedic sacrificial religion, renunciation religions, devotional movements, and the Tantric traditions—were composite affairs that intermingled in interesting and complex ways over the course of time. The Tantras encompassed elements of each of the prior three religious developments but also introduced unique deities, beliefs, and practices. Some might have worshiped a goddess like Kāmeśvarī (chapter 11) by following long-standing devotional practices, such as offering flowers and fruit to an external image of her. However, the Tantric devotee would normally show devotion through an intense sort of meditation in which one builds a detailed image of the goddess in the mind and proceeds to worship her mentally and by reciting her *vidyā*, usually silently. Far from being a form of daydreaming, Tantric visualization involves intricate and highly controlled techniques to enter altered states of consciousness wherein extraordinary visions of the goddesses may occur.

Goddesses began to rise to prominence in mainstream literature in the early medieval Tantric age. A goddess such as Kālī first came to be regarded as the supreme mother of the universe in esoteric Tantras such as the voluminous

Jayadrathayāmala (chapter 12), rather than in the Purāṇic narratives of popular Hindu devotion, where she is portrayed as a manifestation of Durgā's wrath. In this volume, the translated sources on Tvaritā, Kāmeśvarī, and Avyapadeśyā Kālī (chapters 10, 11, and 12) are all from unpublished early Tantric scriptures, while the chapters on Kauśikī, the Seven Mothers, Rāṣṭrasenā, and Rangda (chapters 3, 4, 8, and 9) show significant influence from Tantric traditions. Other goddesses, such as Bhadrakāḷī and Bahucarā Mātā, have important Tantric dimensions to their cults not reflected in the translated stories.

The early Tantras have been unfairly neglected in scholarship on Hindu goddesses. While a small number of orthodox Hindu texts have been the subject of an appreciable number of books and dissertations, the vast and largely unpublished archive of Tantric literature continues to languish, rarely even acknowledged. A concerted movement to change this situation began in the early 1980s, especially with the pioneering work of Alexis Sanderson, which is ongoing and has been expanded upon by many of his colleagues and pupils. Most notable in this respect is the scholarship of Diwakar Acharya, Mark Dyczkowski, Dominic Goodall, Harunaga Isaacson, Marion Rastelli, and Somadeva Vasudeva, among others. Several of the contributors to this volume—namely Anna Golovkova, Shaman Hatley, Olga Serbaeva, Michael Slouber, and Judit Törzsök—share the project of making the significance of the early Tantras better known to students and scholars of goddess traditions and Indian religions in general.

The final two relevant developments in Indian history are the immense growth of Islam in southern Asia over the past thousand years and the presence of European colonialism in the past several centuries. Islam was first brought to India by Arab merchants who came by sea as early as the seventh century CE, but it was not until large-scale empires under Muslim leaders arose in northern India that significant numbers of Indians began to convert. Tensions between Hindus and Muslims have marred the past century of South Asian history. However, religious identities tended to be more fluid and complex before colonial times, as demonstrated with historical evidence in the volume *Beyond Turk and Hindu: Rethinking Religious Identities in Islamicate South Asia.*[5] Muslims are among the devotees of the goddess Bahucarā in Gujarat, for example (chapter 7). When the Kailā Devī narrative (chapter 6) speaks of protecting icons of the goddess from Muslim iconoclasts, it does so with a particular figure in mind: the infamous eleventh-century warlord Mahmud of Ghazni, who was in no way typical of Muslims in India. The

Muslim-led empires of medieval north India were composite affairs, with bureaucracies and militaries composed of both Hindus and Muslims. Armies of the sultans, and later those of the Mughals, sought victory in battle for political and material gain, just as Hindu armies fighting each other had long done. With few exceptions, these were not battles between religions.

The story of colonial interactions with Hindu goddess traditions is particularly fascinating, and it is seldom flattering to Europeans. The behavior of Victorian-era Britons visiting or stationed in India was often driven by racism and reflected a sense of Christian superiority.[6] European colonialism does not directly impact any of the stories told in this book; however, indirect impacts may be noted in shifting practices. The fact that animal sacrifice—the practice of butchering livestock as food offerings to the deity—was once acceptable nearly everywhere but in some areas is now uncommon and illegal (see the Bahucarā, Kailā Devī, and Rāṣṭrasenā chapters) may be partially due to strong disapproval of such rituals on the part of colonial Christian rulers, as Masakazu Tanaka argues in "Sacrifice Lost and Found."[7] On the other hand, other factors have contributed to shifting tastes. Animal sacrifice is primarily associated with particular Śaiva and Śākta deities, whereas Vaiṣṇavas usually view it as unacceptable. Animal rights campaigns and the orthodox high-caste orientation of contemporary Hindu nationalist culture have also contributed to the trend away from animal sacrifice.

GEOGRAPHY

The fixed boundaries of modern nation-states often skew our understanding of the spheres of influence of a given culture or religion. Hinduism is most closely associated with India, but it also spread to, and was in turn influenced by, a large number of other Asian countries. Map 1 shows the spread of the goddesses in this volume all over southern Asia. Starting around the third century BCE, mariners established trade networks between India and Southeast Asia. Sustained relations led most of Southeast Asia to incorporate features of Indian civilization into their own cultures. The story of Southeast Asian influence on India is less well understood and is the subject of ongoing research.[8]

Religion was one of the principal elements of Indian culture adopted in Southeast Asia. Tantric forms of Hinduism and Buddhism spread early on, as well as devotional forms of religion and the Indian epics. Indonesia, the location of the chapter on Rangda, is home to over seventeen thousand islands

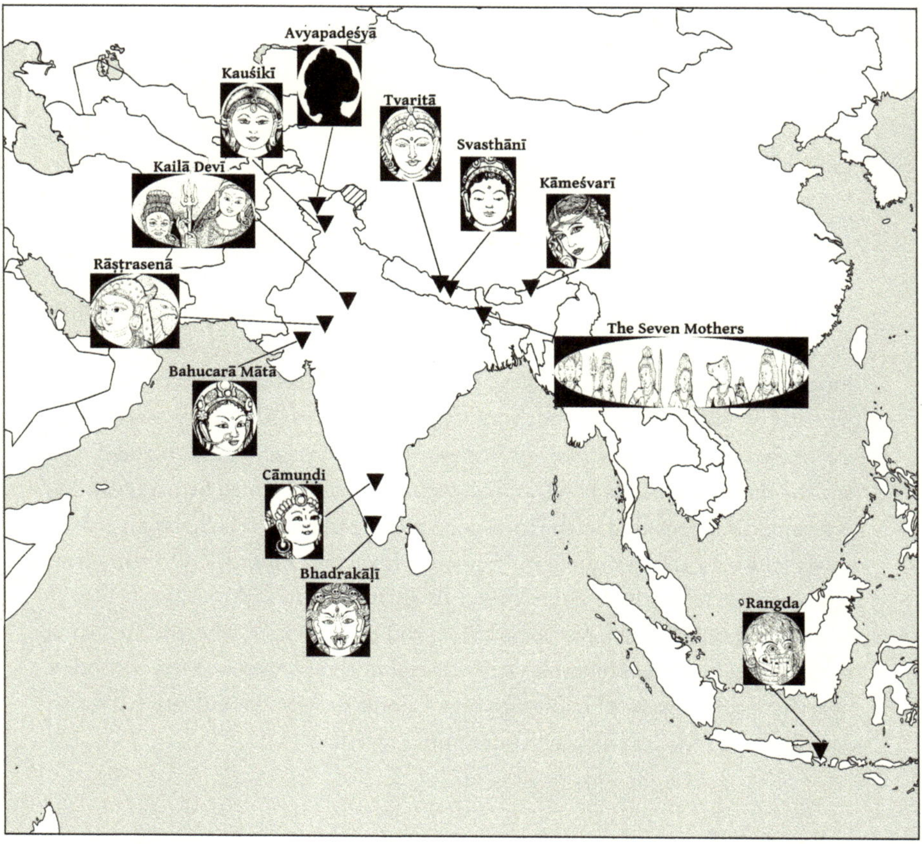

MAP 1. Distribution of goddesses in southern Asia

and about 270 million people. Its name literally means "Indian islands," referring to the influence of Indian religion and culture there. It is natural, then, to find the goddess Durgā as a prominent figure in eastern Java and Bali, as seen in the *Calon Arang* tale in chapter 9. Other Southeast Asian nations, such as Thailand, Cambodia, and Malaysia, were also heavily influenced by Indian civilization, as were places farther afield.

THOUSANDS OF GODDESSES OR ONE?

The fluid nature of Hindu discourse on the divine often confuses new learners. By all accounts, numerous goddesses and gods populate the Hindu pantheon in every phase. In the past, this often led outsiders to categorize Hinduism as polytheistic: a religion with many gods. But the idea that religions can all be categorized on the basis of having one God or many gods is misguided, oversimplifying a complex matter. From the earliest scriptures, Hindus have approached the divine differently, claiming that it is *both one and many*; the two concepts are not mutually exclusive. This idea especially came to the fore with the rise of the devotional religious movements previously mentioned, and continued to be prominent thereafter. Devotional forms of Indian religions tend to regard a particular deity as foremost while acknowledging that lesser divine figures also exist in some sense. Often the other figures are regarded as creations or emanations of that one supreme deity.

As described previously, the two most common groupings in the Hindu religion were the Vaiṣṇavas and Śaivas, who worshiped either Viṣṇu or Śiva as the highest divinity. Classical Sanskrit texts tended to lump goddesses under one or the other of these labels as mere consorts of the male god. But with the emergence of purely Śākta religious movements—which is to say, the idea of one supreme Goddess to rule them all—there was rapid growth in movements concerned solely or chiefly with goddesses. Because the goddess traditions of Tantric Śaivism were the most prolific, all of these goddesses tend to be conflated as different forms of Śiva's consort. While the Goddess is subordinate to Śiva in some of the first Tantras, she transcends even him according to many subsequent Tantric movements, such as the Trika, Yāmala, Śrīvidyā, and Krama schools discussed in chapters 3, 4, 11, and 12, respectively. In this way, the multitudes of local goddesses could stake their claims to supremacy by linking themselves to preexisting structures of Śaiva Hinduism.

There is thus a pragmatic dimension to the claim that all the goddesses are one. It is not simply a philosophical position. This sort of monism ("one-ism") also has practical implications for the lives and identities of Hindus on the local level. Consider, for example, the goddesses of the royal city of Mysuru, who are intimately associated with the hill and hillock near the city. As local goddesses (*grāmadevatā*), they most likely originated as fierce mothers who protect the territory they govern. The primary sister of the pair is Cāmuṇḍi, a name most commonly associated with a fearsome form of the goddess Kālī. However, at some point the association shifted, and she became identified with the qualities and mythological deeds of the regal Durgā. The local narrative states that Cāmuṇḍi is the true identity of the goddess of pan-Indian fame, and that her feat of fighting and slaying a buffalo demon happened on the very hill that stands next to the city of Mysuru. Such a claim raises the status of Cāmuṇḍi, and of her town as a place of pilgrimage, for Hindus from all over the subcontinent. She is no longer one among thousands of local goddesses worshiped since time immemorial; she is now the Mother of the Universe, who chose to bless the lucky inhabitants and visitors of this lovely south Indian city.

These same dynamics applied to most of the goddesses in this book, though with varying results: some rose to prominence for a time, only to be plowed back into the soil of obscurity via subsumption under more well-known figures like Kālī and Durgā (e.g., Tvaritā, Kāmeśvarī, and Avyapadeśyā in chapters 10, 11, and 12); some rose to popularity precisely because of their claim to pan-Indian fame, which saved them from obscurity (e.g., Uttanahaḷḷi, Kailā Devī, and Rangda in chapters 2, 6, and 9); and some continually balance their transregional and local identities as both goddess of place *and* supreme Mother of the Universe (e.g., Cāmuṇḍi, Svasthānī, and Bahucarā in chapters 2, 5, and 7).

THE BOTANICAL IMAGERY AND STRUCTURE OF EACH CHAPTER

English and many Indian languages share the metaphor that imagines an anthology of literary works as a flower garland. Classical Indian poets and scholars saw garlands everywhere; they spoke of the ocean as garlanded with waves, musical compositions as garlands of musical notes, and even the alphabet as a garland of phonemes. The book's title is not only a tribute to this metaphor in Indian literature; the image also aptly describes the mechanism of religious change that each goddess undergoes throughout her history. She often starts as a local deity or the focus of a Tantric sect, here represented by the symbol of an individual flower. Her popularity then grows and her status is raised by the claim that she is really a form of a more famous pan-Indian goddess. This process of linking a local goddess with a transregional one is like the string of a garland that holds the individual parts together while also subsuming the individual identity of each flower under the unified whole of the garland.

Each chapter is arranged to foreground the translated source. Preceding each translation is a brief introduction providing the essential minimum context about the goddess and source, including the region, date, and themes to look for in the text. Further context is withheld until after the translation, in order to encourage readers to engage with the source and try their hands at analysis first, without the influence of the scholar's essay.

These essays, called "The Goddess in Context," are intended to deepen and clarify the reader's understanding, and are divided into sections called "Seed," "Flower," and "Fruit," in keeping with the botanical imagery of the book as a garland. The origin and early precursors of the goddess are explained in "Seed." Her flourishing or high point in popularity is described next in "Flower" (indeed, the English word flourish is derived from a Latin root that means "to flower"). This often corresponds to the period of the text translated. And finally comes "Fruit." Please note that "fruit" is used in this historical analogy in its *botanical* sense. The fruit is the final step in a plant's reproductive cycle; it is not meant in the human-centered agricultural sense of a product for consumption. So, when we speak of the "fruit" era of a particular goddess's development, we mean what comes after her period of flourishing. Some of the goddesses in this volume are virtually forgotten, and so the fruit section is about their waning popularity or absorption into a new and more widely known identity (as a fruit sets seed). Others are still very much part of living local traditions that are currently expanding their sphere of influence; they are still flourishing. All the goddesses offer fine case studies of the dynamics of religious change in the world's oldest continuous goddess tradition.

Following the "Fruit" section is information on the nature and specifics of the translated source, including full bibliographical details, and then a short list of suggestions for further reading and notes for the whole chapter.

TECHNICALITIES

Bibliographical References

Citations to published sources are referenced with a concise author-date system in the endnotes; full details of each source are provided in the reference list. Primary sources are referenced by title; the section "Primary Sources," just before the reference list, includes the editor and year for published primary sources and archival details for unpublished sources.

Translation and Epithets

Since the book is designed to appeal to a general public readership, the editor requested that the contributors make their translations as readable and jargon-free as possible. Whereas strict scholarship often demands an exactingly literal translation and brackets for any words not in the original, here we intentionally dispense with such conventions in order to make the texts more inviting and comprehensible to our readers.

The huge diversity of names and epithets of Hindu goddesses and gods can be bewildering and a potential barrier to learning. For example, when we are meant to envision the Goddess as the wife of Śiva, an Indic text may call her Pārvatī, Umā, Gaurī, or any of hundreds of other common epithets. Or, just as commonly, she may be referred to by any of the names of her alternative forms, such as Kālī or Durgā. She also might have a name calqued on the name of her male counterpart (e.g., Bhavānī, Śaṅkarī, Raudrī). In general, we have defaulted to calling her either Pārvatī or the name of her main identity highlighted in each chapter, unless the text in question explicitly speaks of her as the Great Goddess (Mahādevī), in which case we also use that honorific. The same plethora of names and epithets applies to other deities too, such as Śiva, and these have likewise been flattened in the translations by defaulting to the name Śiva for the husband of the Goddess.

An advantage of this artificial simplification of names and epithets is that readers new to Hinduism are not overwhelmed by unknown names and words. However, the disadvantage is that much of the rich cultural flavor that these names and epithets add to the primary sources is lost in translation.

Capitalization of Goddess

Hindu thealogy (discourse on the nature of goddesses and gods) comes to identify goddesses as both local deities with unique forms and identities, and as manifestations of the principal Goddess who generated the entire universe. Given that Indian scripts do not have a convention analogous to capitalization, we have opted to default to "goddess" and to reserve the capitalized form for cases where the goddess is described as singular and supreme (e.g., the Great Goddess, Mother of the World). Such a convention becomes blurry in situations where individual local goddesses are being spoken of in the singular or addressed directly as *the* Goddess. Instances of the word "goddess" occurring as part of a proper name or at the beginning of a sentence are, of course, capitalized without regard to this distinction.

Languages, Scripts, Transliteration, and Pronunciation

The book features translations and studies involving seven languages (Sanskrit, Newari, Middle Javanese, Malayalam, Kannada, Hindi, and Gujarati) and numerous regional writing systems. Each chapter showcases samples of the diverse regional scripts these sources are written in. Because fonts that are accurate to period manuscripts are unavailable, these are approximations.

Maintaining a coherent policy of transliterating words from so many languages into the Latin script was challenging. Understandably, readers may be more familiar with rendering Indian words without diacritical marks, as in "Kali," "Shiva," "mandala," and "chakra." Scholars generally favor the more consistent and accurate approach of using diacritical marks according to international standards for each language in order to retain the one-to-one correspondence between a letter and its sound that Indian scripts can offer. In English, for example, the vowel "a" is regularly pronounced five or more ways. This and other ambiguities of English spelling lead to a variety of mispronunciations of Indian words. Chakra (*cakra*) is frequently mispronounced "shah-kra" instead of the correct "chuck-ra" and mandala (*maṇḍala*) becomes "mahn-dah-la" instead of "mun-duh-la." To avoid this sort of confusion, Indian scripts employ a larger number of letters, but they generally stand for single sounds. Readers can use the following abbreviated pronunciation guide to approximate the correct pronunciation of any word in this book:

- *a* is what linguists call a schwa, as in "alone" or "up"
- *ā* is reserved for the sound "ah," as in "father" or "honor"
- *i* is a short vowel sound, as in "fit" or "India"
- *ī* corresponds to English long "e," as in "neat" or "tree"
- *u* is short, as in "pull" or "wool"
- *ū* is long, as in "boot" or "rude"
- *ṛ* is a vocalic r sound corresponding to "trip," or in some areas of India like "brook"
- *e* is what we call long "a" in English, as in "cake" or "gate"
- *ē* is a slightly longer variant of the above distinguished in south Indian languages
- *ai* is the long "i" in English, as in "bike" or "nine"
- *au* is a diphthong, as in the English words "house" or "town"
- *ṃ* is a sign that nasalizes the vowel before it. It can be pronounced like the consonant "m" for simplicity

- *ḥ* indicates a sound approximated by an "h" followed by a fragmentary echo of the previous vowel
- *c* is equivalent to "ch" in English, as in "chunk"
- *ṭ*, *ḍ*, and *ṇ* are retroflex sounds similar to the English consonants, but with the tongue touching the roof of the mouth
- *ś* and *ṣ* are both pronounced like "sh" in English. The latter is articulated with the tongue touching the roof of the mouth
- *ḷ* is a retroflex "l" distinguished in south Indian languages

We have omitted diacritics for modern geographical names (place-names, rivers, and mountains) and names of historical people; however, we have retained them for the names of deities and for geographical names that are no longer in use.

Notes

The notes included at the end of each chapter annotate both the translation and contextualizing essay. Notes provide additional context and clarification, technical information about the translation, and references to prior scholarship.

Glossary, List of Deities and Characters

The glossary in the back of the volume clarifies non-English words and technical terms and concepts in both the translations and essays. The list of names following the glossary serves the same purpose for the names of deities and other characters in the stories.

ADVICE TO THE READER

The fact that you made it this far in the introduction means you are already equipped with important background knowledge. The chapters of each unit are arranged in approximate order of accessibility, so we recommend that you read them in order. Important names and terms from earlier chapters are also often useful to know for the later, and sometimes more difficult, chapters. Make use of the glossary and list of names; these are tools we have carefully prepared to help you navigate these sources.

Read the brief introductions that open each chapter carefully, as they contain essential facts and tips to orient you to the story. Likewise, read each narrative slowly, trying not only to follow its logic but also to think about the purposes it was designed to serve for its intended audience. The notes at the end of each chapter are often useful, explaining cultural aspects and technical details in the translation, as well as providing references to further reading. After finishing the story and wrapping up your own notes on it, read the translator's essay to get a more complete understanding of the passage you have just read and analyzed.

Excellent audiovisual material is widely available on the internet and can deepen understanding of these sources. For example, one can view vivid photos of women performing the Svasthānī *vrata* in Sankhu (chapter 5) by executing an image search. Likewise, the Rangda chapter can be enriched by video clips of contemporary Rangda-Barong performances in Bali. And the Bahucarā chapter is well paired with documentary material on the Pāvaiyā/Hijra communities.

NOTES

1. For recent scholarship that cautiously accepts the idea of continuity of nature divinities between the Indus Valley civilization and historical traditions, see Padma (2013, 262), Onishi (1997), Haberman (2013, 48–49), and Shaw (2006).

2. The *Devī Māhātmya* has long been regarded, on weak grounds, as centuries older than the evidence supports. See Yokochi (2004, 21–23n42). Several contributors to this volume draw heavily on Yokochi's scholarship, the importance of which has been underappreciated in South Asian goddess studies.

3. See Trautmann (2011, 102–15).

4. For abundant evidence that the early medieval period was dominated by Tantric Śaivism, see Sanderson (2009).

5. Gilmartin and Lawrence (2000).

6. For excellent and accessible overviews of the goddess Kālī in the colonial imagination, see the chapters by Cynthia Ann Humes and Hugh Urban in *Encountering Kālī* (McDermott and Kripal 2003).

7. Tanaka (2000).

8. See, for example, Acri, Blench, and Landmann (2017).

PART ONE

Demons and Battle

FIGURE 1. Bhadrakāḷī, by Laura Santi

CHAPTER 1

Bhadrakāḷī

Slaying the Demon in the Backwaters

NOOR VAN BRUSSEL

The first tale comes from the far southwestern state of Kerala, a subtropical paradise with white-sand beaches, coconut palm trees, alluring and mysterious backwaters, and fragrant hills that have produced sought-after spices for thousands of years. A rich maritime tradition with trading links all over the Indian ocean has made Kerala's culture one of the most cosmopolitan in India.

The narrative consists of two chapters translated from *The Glorification of Bhadrakāḷī* (*Bhadrakāḷī Māhātmya*), a Sanskrit text of the "regional Purāṇa" type, which mixes local narratives and perspectives with transregional myths and themes. It tells the tale of the demon Dārika and his destined death at the hands of the fierce goddess Bhadrakāḷī. In this way, it is part of an enduring motif in Hindu myth and art: that of demons being slain by fearsome goddesses. While the text in its current version likely dates to the fourteenth to sixteenth centuries, the first reference to a fierce goddess battling a demon called Dārika already appears about one thousand years earlier, in the Tamil epic *Cilappatikāram*. The Hindus of Kerala developed the Bhadrakāḷī narrative into a multifaceted framework of legends, rituals, songs, and performance traditions.

The tale is arranged using what classicists call ring composition: it is framed as a conversation between two sages, Mārkaṇḍeya and Śivaśarman, who discuss the tale of a king named Candrasena, who himself goes on to hear from the sage Sutīkṣṇa the main tale of Bhadrakāḷī and the demon Dārika. Thus, it is presented as a story within a story within a story. This should not deter readers, as the main story starts rather quickly and is presented as a coherent whole.

As you read, think about how and why the story humanizes the demonic characters and the attitude of the main demon Dārika toward gender. Also pay attention to the theme of hunger and gorging, on the part of both the demons and the allies of the goddess. What cultural meaning might the gruesome descriptions of violence and death hold for the audience?

ഭദ്രകാളീ മാഹാത്മ്യ ൏

അഥാതഃ സമ്പ്രവക്ഷ്യാമി ഭദ്രകാള്യാഃ സമുദ്ഭവം. അദ്ഭുതാനി ച
കർമാണി മത്തഃ ശൃണു മഹീസുര. രുദ്രസ്യ തനയാ സാധ്വീ ഭദ്ര-
കാളീ മഹേശ്വരീ. ഭദ്രാണി ജഗതാം ദേവീ യാനി യാനി സനാത-
നീ. കർമാണി ചക്രേ കല്യാണീ കല്യാനി സുമഹാന്തി ച. താനി
താനി ശൃണു ശ്രീമൻ ശിവശർമൻ ദ്വിജോത്തമ. കാശ്മീരനാമ്നി
നഗരേ രാജാഭൂദ്ധാർമികോ ബലീ. ചന്ദ്രസേന ഇതി ഖ്യാതശ്ചന്ദ്ര-
ബിംബമുഖഃ സുഖീ. സ്വസൈന്യൈരന്വിതോ ധന്വീ രഥാരൂഢോ
മഹാരഥഃ. ദണ്ഡകാരണ്യമാപേദേ മൃഗയാകർമകർമഠഃ. സിംഹ-
വ്യാഘ്രാദി സത്വാനി ഹത്വാ ഹത്വാ ചരൻ വനേ. ദദർശ പുരതഃ
കഞ്ചിദ്വൽമീകം ഭൃശമുന്നതം. തസ്യാന്തീകസ്ഥിതേ വൃക്ഷേ ദ്വൗ
ഗണ്ഡൗ ഗിരിസന്നിഭൗ. ലോഹശൃൺഖലയാബധ്വാനിഷ സാദശി-
ലാതലേ. മന്ത്രിഭിസ്സഹിതഃ കൈശ്ചിദക്ഷൈർദീവ്യന്നനന്യധീഃ. വി-
ജഹാര ചിരം വീരശ്ചന്ദ്രസേനോ മഹീപതിഃ. തസ്മിന്നവസരേ തൗ
ദ്വൗ ഗണ്ഡരാജൗ മദോത്കടൗ. പാദഘാതേന വൽമീക മുന്നതം
തദ്ബഭഞ്ചതുഃ. തതോ ഭവത് താലതരുപ്രമാണയാ തനുശ്രിയാ
കശ്ചന ധൂമധൂമ്രയാ. പ്രവൃദ്ധകോപാധികരക്തലോചനഃ കൃതാ-
ട്ടഹാസഃ പുരുഷോ॑തിഭീഷണഃ. ദ്വാഭ്യം സ പൃഥുദീർഘാഭ്യാം കരാ-
ഭ്യാം കരിണാവുഭൗ. ഗൃഹീത്വാ ഭക്ഷയാമാസ ലീലയാ വിഹസൻ
മുഹുഃ. അഭിദുദ്രാവ രാജാനം മന്ത്രിണശ്ച മഹാബലഃ. തേ ചഭീ-
താഃ പലായന്ത സ ച താൻ അന്വധാവത. സന്ത്രസ്താശ്ചന്ദ്രസേ-
നാദ്യാഃ ധാവന്തോ ദണ്ഡകേ വനേ. സുതീക്ഷ്ണസ്യാശ്രമം പ്രാപ്യ
പ്രണേമുസ്തം മുനീശ്വരം. കുതോ ഭവാന്മഹാരാജ കോ॑യം ത്വാമ-
നുധാവതി. കുതസ്താവദിയം ഭീതിരുത്പന്നാബ്രൂഹിതത്വതഃ. **രാ-
ജാ** പാഹി പാഹി മഹായോഗിൻ ഏഷ കശ്ചന പൂരുഷഃ. ഗജാ-
ഭ്യാം ഭജ്യമാനാത്തു വൽമീകാദയമുത്ഥിതഃ. ഭക്ഷയിത്വാ ഗജേന്ദ്രൗ
തൗ ഭൂയോ॑സ്മാനനുധാവതി. ഭക്ഷയിഷ്യതി നഃ സർവാന്മഹാഭീ-
ഷണവിഗ്രഹഃ. അസ്മാത് ത്രായസ്വ നോ ബ്രഹ്മൻ ശരണം ത്വാ-
മുപസ്ഥിതാൻ. **സുതീക്ഷ്ണഃ** മാ ഭൈഷീർമാനവാധീശ മഹാഭൂ-
താദിതോ॑ധുനാ. അഹം തു വാരയാമ്യേനം വിജ്ഞാതം ദിവ്യച-
ക്ഷുഷാ. ഭോ ഭോ മഹാഭൂത മഹാനുഭാവ ത്വം ഭദ്രകല്യാഃ ഖലു കി-

FIGURE 2. *Bhadrakāḷī Māhātmya,* a Sanskrit work in the Malayalam script. Font “Noto Serif Malayalam” © The Noto Project Authors.

THE GLORIFICATION OF BHADRAKĀḶĪ

Mārkaṇḍeya said, "O Brahmin, listen to me! I will now tell you of the origin of Bhadrakāḷī and her extraordinary deeds.[1] The great goddess Bhadrakāḷī was the chaste daughter of Śiva. O Śivaśarman, glorious best of the twice-born, listen to these excellent, noble, and great deeds the noble and eternal goddess performed for the worlds. In the city of Kāśmīra, there was a king named Candrasena, whose face was like the moon. He was strong, righteous, and full of happiness. This great warrior, armed with a bow and skilled in the art of hunting, mounted a chariot and entered the Daṇḍaka forest with his army.[2] Traveling through the forest killing many tigers, lions, and other creatures, he suddenly saw some kind of an enormous anthill up ahead. He bound his two mountain-like elephants to a nearby tree with an iron chain and sat down on top of a rock. There, the heroic king Candrasena passed the time playing dice with his ministers, paying no attention to anything else.

"Suddenly, his two gigantic elephants, in a frenzy, destroyed the anthill with kicks of their feet. Then, a terrible creature the size of a palm tree arose from it. It had a splendid body, gray like smoke, with eyes bright red from anger, laughing grotesquely. The creature grabbed both elephants with his two large hands, and devoured them in a second, laughing as if it was just for fun. Next, the beast ran toward the king and his ministers. Trembling with fear, they ran away, and he chased them. Terrified, Candrasena and the others fled further into the Daṇḍaka forest and finally reached the hermitage of Sutīkṣṇa.[3] They bowed before that supreme ascetic, and Sutīkṣṇa said: 'Where do you come from, great king! Who is chasing you? What gave rise to such terror? Tell me truthfully!'

"The king said, 'Save us, great yogi! Some kind of creature arose out of an anthill when our elephants destroyed it. After devouring two bull elephants, he came after us. This huge and terrible creature will certainly destroy us all. O Brahmin, protect us! We have come to you for refuge.'

"Sutīkṣṇa said, 'O lord of people, do not fear this huge creature henceforth. I will stop him, as I perceive him with my divine eye.' Addressing the demon, he said, 'Hello, great and noble demon! You must certainly be a servant of Bhadrakāḷī. O wise one, pardon this act of the king, done out of ignorance. I salute you.'

"Thus, after hearing the excellent words of the ascetic Sutīkṣṇa, the demon bowed and left out of reverence to Bhadrakāḷī. Candrasena then questioned that best of sages Sutīkṣṇa: 'Who is this Bhadrakāḷī? I really want to hear about the one whose powerful demon-servant is capable of devouring two bull elephants. Her power is surely immense. Please tell me her story.' Sutīkṣṇa said, 'I will tell you everything, king Candrasena. Listen to this account of the blessed origin of Bhadrakāḷī!'

———

"'A long time ago, when a big war arose between the gods and the demons, the venerable Viṣṇu joined the army of the gods and smashed the skulls of all the demons with his discus.[4] When the lineage of demons was completely eradicated, four grief-stricken young demon women hid in the underworld. Together, they made the firm decision to take revenge. Among them was one named Dānavatī and the virtuous Dārumatī. Both were prominent, married demon women and faithful to their husbands. They hastily remarked: "The two of us will appease Brahmā by practicing a severe form of religious austerity.[5] For, if only us women of good family survive, this surely would mean the end of our race!"

"'On the splendid coastline of the western ocean there was a sanctum of Śiva named Gokarna, auspicious for all living creatures.[6] So the two of them proceeded there, and entered that prosperous temple, so well liked by all the gods. They bathed in the water of that sacred place, and then performed fierce austerities. They suffered exhaustion and insomnia, without support of any kind, although they were free of anxiety. They honored their ancestors and, sitting down in the middle of five sacred fires, undertook a terrible vow that implied total control over the five senses. In this auspicious state, they maintained their vow for forty days. Then, the honorable god Brahmā appeared before their eyes. He said, "O ladies, you both cherish a wish for a worthy son to augment the lineage of Daitya demons. You may ask for that boon now." So, they both asked for that boon from Brahmā, the granter of wishes, and after granting them, the lotus-born god disappeared again.[7]

"'Then the ladies descended into the underworld, where they greeted their husbands, and after a while both of them were with child.[8] Ten lunar months later, two sons were born. Dānavatī gave birth to a nameless son they called Dānava (demon). Dārumatī gave birth to the victorious Dārika, yet many bad omens appeared at his birth: frightful jackals with frenzied faces cried out in all directions, winds gray with dust circled around their bodies. The clouds rained blood and big trees fell; the earth with its mountains, forests, and oceans shook. The three fires of the Vedic priests were blown out.

"'Having turned into proper youths, the princes named Dārika and Dānava gradually learned from their mothers about Hari and the other gods, and the annihilation of their own lineage. They also heard about Brahmā granting wishes, and so Dānava and Dārika traveled to the distant city of Gokarna and performed excellent austerities. In the hot season, Dārika stood in the middle of five fires; in the cold season, he stood immersed in water; in the rainy season he stood exposed to the elements, with a vow to take only air as food. He hung from the branch of a tree with his head down, heated by the smoke rising up from a big fire, and at other times he assumed a difficult position touching the earth with only one foot. Nevertheless, the venerable Brahmā did not appear. The god thought, "This is a villain preparing for the destruction of the world." Dārika's eyes reddened with anger toward Brahmā, and seizing his sword, he said: "I will cut off my head and sacrifice that." The moment the sword touched his throat and one drop of blood fell on the surface of the earth, Brahmā appeared. And the god said "O, great hero, when one drop of your blood falls from your throat onto the earth, a thousand excellent demons will be born from it. Through my power, they will be equal to you in courage, heroism and strength. Tell me this: What other boon should I give you?"

"'Dārika said, "Give me the ability to not be killed by men, demons, or gods. I will not be opposed by Śiva, Viṣṇu, or Indra. Give me the strength of one thousand elephants and Brahmā's staff, for the sake of my victory in war. Furthermore, present me with the two spell-goddesses, Māyāvatī and Tāmasī as well![9] Give me all of this, O Brahmā!"

"'Brahmā said, "O hero, so be it! All this, whatever you desire, I give you gladly because of your terrible penance. I ask you, though, lord of the Daityas, why do you make no stipulation for women? Have you forgotten that the boon is about invincibility in battle?"

"'Dārika said, "What?! This is ridiculous, Brahmā! Will women slay me? As soon as they lay eyes upon me, they run away! The gods would laugh at such a wish when they hear of it. Not only do we not desire the boon, even more modest demon descendants do not wish for it. Hence, we do not seek invincibility with respect to women."

"'Brahmā said (*to himself*), "Oh, he has become arrogant then, for sure!" (*Aloud*) "A divine woman will slay you, and the two mantras will not help you in battle, nor my staff."

"'Dārika said, "Neither a divine nor a human woman, nor a dryad, nor a demoness—no woman would be able to kill me, Brahmā. Go away."

"'Addressed like this with such pride, Brahmā the Creator gladly vanished. Dārika, on the other hand, entered the underworld. After bowing down to his mother and father and his elder brother Dānava, he told them about the boons he obtained for the sake of his people, who had been tormented by the gods. This made his whole family happy.

"'Then, he called upon Maya to have him construct a royal palace. The wise and honorable Maya, the architect of the demons, constructed such a palace on the shore of the western sea. It was a splendid residence with thousands of bejeweled temples, penthouse apartments, busy crossroads with terraces, shops, and carriages. There was a network of spacious stables as well: for donkeys, cows, big buffaloes, horses, and elephants. The residential areas were dense with the fragrance of musk imported by tradesmen arriving from abroad. All dwellings in the king's residence were filled with of piles of rubies, coral, emeralds, topazes, pearls and other gems. It had silver oval-shaped ponds, and pinnacles made of jewels on the ridge of the roof. It was richly endowed with parks, ramparts, and bejeweled archways, as well as halls full of precious stones, silver and gold. The palace was a true delight for the eye with its golden appearance and sporting halls, while the grounds around it abounded in temple gates and ritual platforms, pleasure hills, pools of lotuses, and beautiful ponds. There were various kinds of trees: bulletwood, plantain tree, palm tree, mango tree, chaste tree, sandal tree, jasmine and coral tree, and those groves were inferior to none with their hundreds of impeccable pools, their rims glittering, decorated with garlands of areca nuts, and curved vines wriggling up like snakes. It was beautiful with thickets of yellow amaranth, various kinds of magnolia trees, cobra's saffron and mangosteen, and woods of mangrove date palms and fan-palms, while other areas grew hundreds of screw-palm trees, date trees, royal banana plants, and lines of rice and sugarcane as far as the eye could see. Such a residence was constructed by Maya, and in charm it put to shame even the residence of Indra.[10]

"'At an auspicious moment, Dārika, the best among his people, entered the pleasing fortress and upper rooms accompanied by his entourage. He rewarded the great Maya with ornaments, such as bracelets and other types, and after sending him away, he caused the royal drums to be struck. Subsequently all the enemies of the gods, greatly delighted and proud, abandoned their mountain hideouts and arrived at Dārika's dwelling. The great demons, both old and young, amounting to ten billion all together, arrived in alliance at the kingdom of that lord of demons. They anointed Dārika out of recognition of his success. Some were appointed as generals in the demon king's army, others took on the position of counselor to the king, others still cultivated his friendship. Then Dārika mounted his chariot and, joined by his great forces, he cruelly set out with the desire to conquer heaven. The great hero approached the capital city of the gods, Amarāvatī, accompanied by his many soldiers, whose hands were gleaming like fire with their sharp, powerful weapons: spears, arrows, slings, bows, hammers, and swords; malicious three-pointed tridents, lances, maces, axes, spears, sickles, chains, and others. The demon Dārika, red with anger, swiftly reached the city of Amarāvatī with his army, and terror spread in Indra's palace because of the sounding war drums.'"

Thus ends the first chapter of the story on the origin of the Honorable goddess in the *Mārkaṇḍeya Purāṇa*.

Summary of Chapters 2–4

Dārika sacks Indra's city, capturing all its treasures and heavenly women. Then he destroys the remnants of Amarāvatī and returns to his stronghold to marry the daughter of Maya, Manodarī. Meanwhile, his troops continue to distress and destroy the universe, thus calling the fury of the gods upon them. After coming together to discuss the matter with Brahmā, the gods decide to transform into six mother goddesses: Brāhmī, Māheśvarī, Kaumārī, Vaiṣṇavī, Vārāhī, and Indrāṇī. However, even these mother goddesses are not able to stop the demon army, and they have to flee from the battlefield. The gods then decide to take up the matter with the mightiest one among them: Śiva. Upon hearing about the chaos and violence, Śiva becomes very angry and decides to take action.

Chapter 5: Bhadrakāḷī on the Battlefield

"Sutīkṣṇa said, 'Thereupon, Śiva manifested himself in his destroyer form, with a body as tall as Mount Kailash, laughing loudly. His third eye that had burned the god of love and the three cities, located on his wide and prominent forehead, grew unsightly with terrible dense fires, sparks, and flames.[11] And then, out of the fire of the eye on Śiva's forehead, Bhadrakāḷī suddenly manifested herself. Deafening the universe with her loud, crude laughter, her body resembled a black cloud, like the great Añjana Mountain.[12] She had thousands of faces and arms, and a hundred thousand eyes, gleaming cruelly like unsightly gems. As she came down in all her terror, born from the fire of the eye on Śiva's forehead, Mount Kailash shook vehemently. The mighty lions resting in its caves were confused. The oceans were agitated, the sharks and sea monsters in it disturbed. The seven mountain ranges shook. The elephants guarding the four directions, their ears filled with the terrible sound, shrieked and shook their heads. When Pārvatī, trembling with fear, saw that all-pervading, enormous form, she tried to calm her down.'

"'Pārvatī said, "Hey, Caṇḍikā, my daughter, Cāmuṇḍā, blessed Kāḷī, daughter of Śiva—give up that form of yours that terrifies the world. You will become the foremost among the mothers—the seventh mother! You will bear the name Cāmuṇḍā, the great Kāḷī."'[13]

"Sutīkṣṇa said, 'When Pārvatī addressed her thus, her eyes full of loving tears, Bhadrakāḷī gave up that terrible form of hers and bowed down before her mother. She now had one face, three eyes, and sixteen arms with various weapons. She wore golden earrings and jewels on her head, a diadem, bracelets, a hip girdle studded with gems, arm rings, and much more. Śiva then summoned his daughter, made her sit in his lap and spoke.

"'Śiva said, "Daughter of mine, as I have a black throat, so you too will be the dark-throated one: Kaṇṭhekāḷī! You will have a black form thanks to the darkness of my notorious black throat.[14] Moreover, you came forth from my angry form, dark and fierce, so you shall be called the black-colored Bhairavī."'

"Sutīkṣṇa said, 'And after he had named her Kaṇṭhekāḷī, Śiva gave her a garment made of elephant skin.

"'Kaṇṭhekāḷī said, "O father! You are the moon-crested supreme lord of the universe. Tell me what I need to do."

"'Śiva said, "Slay this great demon king called Dārika! He induces fear in the three worlds, and possesses the power of twelve thousand elephants. He is a sorcerer and a foe of the whole universe, terrorizing it with all sorts of weaponry. Destroy him completely and then present yourself to me again."

"'Kaṇṭhekāḷī said, "Father, please, may your power also be mine, just like my body resembles yours. Give me weapons, a vehicle, an army, the whole lot, so that I can kill our mortal enemy."

"'Śiva said, "Take these weapons—a curved sword, trident, discus, hammer, and lance—O daughter, and capture Dārika. I, the ruler of the *kūḷi* hordes, will offer you my huge force of 660 million spirits as your helpers, O Kālikā. Also, somewhere to the north of Mount Kailash, rests Vetālī. My spirit servant Kauṇḍika will show her to you. Make her into your vehicle—mount her and go to the city of the enemy. May good fortune be with you."'

"Sutīkṣṇa said, 'After saying this, Śiva equipped her for war. Kaṇṭhekāḷī accepted this and subsequently set out. Keeping Kailash to her left, she journeyed north, passing through three forests, before she entered the Mahākāla forest, where Nandimahākāla and Vetālī lived.[15] Kauṇḍika showed her where Vetālī was resting, hungry and thirsty. Bhadrakāḷī respectfully said to her: "Wake up!"

"'Vetālī said, "Auspicious lady, I am hungry and thirsty! I cannot carry you, Great Goddess. My stomach is hard to fill. Would you be able to do so? If you do, I will carry you and your forces on the battlefield of the demons."

"'Bhadrakāḷī said, "When we go to Dārika's fortress, I will present you with two-hundred million demons on the war-fest that is soon to occur."'

"Sutīkṣṇa said, 'Hearing this, Vetālī was thrilled with delight and got up quickly to prepare herself. She bathed in the water of the ocean and adorned herself with mineral mud. Then she made a garland with flowers and creepers from the trees in the forest and tied it around her hands, head, hips, and neck. Then she put Kāḷī on her neck and on her back she carried the armies. The ghosts beat the war drums while bellowing fierce lion-like roars and howling from their throats. The six mothers, who were hiding in the bushes of creepers, heard this and joined the armies. They praised lovely Cāmuṇḍā: "Cāmuṇḍī is chief! The mothers were only six in number, but now the sages declare that there are seven." Then Caṇḍikā's armies surrounded the city of the enemy. They filled the caverns of the chief mountain ranges with the sounds of long horns and war drums and covered the area with yak-tail whisks and umbrellas. Thousands, tens of millions, and hundreds of thousands more spirits surrounded Dārika's home. They placed general Nandimahākāla in front, and Maheśvarī and her other mother goddesses took position at the city gate in the north. Immediately, Caṇḍikā called the great demon Dārika to war. When he heard this, Dārika, who was napping on the rooftop of his mansion, woke up quivering. Confused, he said: "What is all of this?" and sent forth a messenger. Frightened out of his wits, the messenger arrived at the city gate. There, Nandimahākāla violently drew him near. He beat him up and restrained him by tying a large piece of wood to his neck. The messenger dragged the piece of wood with him, and arrived like this back on Dārika's territory. Mentally suffering from fear and distress, he lamented his grave discomforts. Full of contempt for the enemy, the messenger spoke.

"'The messenger said, "Good king, rescue this forlorn man! The enemy chained an immense piece of wood to me and then let me go. I could not count the armies of the enemy, O demon! But among them I saw a mighty female form. She is called Kāḷī, a fearful and black figure, with three eyes shining in her face, so high it grazes the clouds. She has large fangs, and a tongue lolling from the cavern that is her gaping mouth. Moreover, she has sixteen club-like arms that are both broad and lengthy. Her earrings are made of elephants, and she has hair that waves and moves in every direction. Her garment is made of elephant skin, and with the shrill roar coming out of her throat she pierced the ear canals of the guardian elephants that were roving about. Such a woman is standing on the edge of the battlefield, carrying a multitude of excellent weapons: a barbed dart, sword, trident, arrows, a bow, mace, missiles, skull-club, and lance. She surpasses the splendor of a thousand autumnal suns in brightness."'

"Sutīkṣṇa said, 'After hearing out the messenger, the lord of demons gave his ministers the order to fight this goddess. His eight ministers, namely Karaṅka, Kṛpāṇa, Bāṇa, Sthūṇa, Jayandhara, Tāmrākṣa, Dhūmrākṣa, and Dhūmra, supervised tens of millions of troops. Surrounded by a fourfold army consisting of an infantry, a division of chariots, one of horses, and one of elephants, it seemed as if Death itself had appeared. Some soldiers were carrying shield and sword, others a bow and arrows, some were bearing maces, others had weapons like hammers and lances, others had shield and knife, some carried axes, others had clubs in their hands, still others carried lances, spears, barbed darts and knives. Thus there were various kinds of warriors attending to the ministers. The space between heaven and earth was thick with gold dust, produced by the friction between the various ornaments they carried. Laughing, the goddess observed those armies of the eight ministers, protected by many clever generals, as they approached for battle.

"'Then an unequaled, tumultuous, terribly violent, and hair-raising battle began between the two armies. Rains of missiles and arrows covered the space between heaven and earth. The whole earth was deafened by loud and cruel laughter. Blood that poured out of mutilated throats, severed by swords, soiled the battlefield. Rushing and stammering streams of blood flowed forth in every direction from the wounds of the mountain-high elephants that had perished. Like duckweed, the hair of hundreds of corpses was flowing in these streams, with waterfall-like torrents of missiles. A host of ghouls and ghosts feasted on blood, flesh and brains, as headless corpses danced around and horses were slashed to pieces and sunk into the reddish water of the river of arrows. As agreed upon beforehand, Kāḷī gladly gave her vehicle Vetālī 200 million demons to devour. The multitudes of *kūḷi* hordes eagerly began to dance, clapping with their palms stretched out, scratching open their foreheads with their fingernails, garlands of entrails swaying and hanging down from their throats, and with the most terrible sounds coming from their throats.

"'Then the goddess struck minister Karaṅka in the throat with her trident and threw him down to the ground to quickly kill him. She annihilated Kṛpāṇa with a sword, Bāṇa with an arrow, Sthūṇa with a club and Jayandhara with a hammer. She destroyed Dhūmra with a discus, Dhūmrākṣa with a smoky comet-like weapon, and Tāmrākṣa with a copper lance. When finally she had killed these eight ministers and their armies too, Bhadrakāḷī stood firm, surrounded by her companions and radiating the splendor of victory.'"

Thus ends the fifth chapter of the story on the origin of the Honorable goddess in the *Mārkaṇḍeya Purāṇa*.

Summary of Chapters 6–9

After Bhadrakāḷī had thus demonstrated her power, all kinds of gods, sages, and powerful men gathered to see the final battle between the goddess and the demon king. They came together and praised the goddess extensively, invigorating her for the coming battle. Dārika, in the meantime, took leave of his wife and with great pomp departed for battle himself. He ridiculed the goddess, telling her that women are weak and unfit for battle, whereas he was in charge of a powerful army with hundreds of thousands of demons. Thanks to his wielding of the staff of Brahmā and his ability to procreate via blood drops touching the earth, he seemed too powerful for the goddess also, so she saw no option but to flee. Then Durgā appeared and told the goddess she would try to obtain a pair of secret mantras from Dārika's wife, Manodarī, which were helping Dārika to stay in power. Durgā disguised herself as a Brahmin mendicant girl and with a ruse managed to deceive Manodarī. The kind woman revealed the pair of mantras to Durgā and later on had to admit to her husband that, although unwillingly, she had contributed to his downfall. With the pair of mantras being revealed, Bhadrakāḷī returned to the battlefield and managed to destroy the staff of Brahmā. Dārika now realized that his end was near and he went into hiding. The goddess and her army destroyed his city, while Vetālī devoured his army. Seated on the shoulders of her mount Vetālī, the goddess roamed the earth, yet she was unable to find him. She was ashamed and thought of what she would have to say to her father when she returned home from a failed mission. So the goddess decided to trick the demon. She obscured the sun with her wild bush of hair, making it appear as if night had fallen. Believing himself to be safe, Dārika left his hiding place and stepped right onto the outspread tongue of Vetālī. Seizing the opportunity, Bhadrakāḷī subsequently thrust her trident into his chest, pinning him to the ground. Bleeding like an ox, the demon king begged for mercy and briefly managed to create some doubt in the goddess's mind. However, the gods and sages that were watching urged her to show no mercy to the villain. Scolding herself for being so weak for an instant, the goddess finally decapitated Dārika, taking his head, and adorned herself with his intestines. Mad with bloodthirst, she ran back to her father. In her madness, however, she threatened to destroy the universe, so Śiva decided to place two children on her path: Nandī and Gaṇeśa. When the goddess saw them lying before her, her maternal feelings immediately took over, and she decided to suckle them at her breasts. Thus she calmed down, and the universe was saved from the terror of the demon king and of the maddened goddess.

THE GODDESS IN CONTEXT: BHADRAKĀḶĪ IN MULTIPLE LITERARY WORLDS

Throughout Hindu myth and art, we are confronted with demons dying at the hands of merciless goddesses. From the pan-Indian to the local level, narratives of battle between eternal adversaries endure, albeit taking different forms in different locations. In Kerala, a multifaceted narrative tradition developed around the goddess Bhadrakāḷī and her triumph over the demon king Dārika. This narrative, codified in the text called *The Glorification of Bhadrakāḷī* (*Bhadrakāḷī Māhātmya*), is the overarching framework onto which many local legends are woven and the fertile substrate out of which many rituals and performances arose. It is told within families, recited in temples, and sung as a ritual song (*pāṭṭŭ*) at festivals and on many other occasions, such as female Brahminical rituals.[16] Apart from that, it has also been committed to writing, in the form of Tantras, Purāṇic poetry, and many other genres. It is a tradition with many threads, weaving the regional, transregional, and pan-Indian together into an intricate and ever-transforming texture of narrative—both oral and written.

Seed: Origin of the Goddess in Time and Text

To seek the origins of Bhadrakāḷī's story, we have to go back to one of the oldest literary traditions in south India, namely the early layers of classical Tamil poetry (ca. 100 BCE–300 CE).[17] Even though the passage translated here is in Sanskrit and comes from the Malayalam-speaking region of Kerala, traditions of Bhadrakāḷī there have been influenced by Tamil culture and the Tamil language, which was spoken throughout southern India in ancient times. Relying on this body of poetry to establish history is notoriously problematic, since the poems themselves have been edited, selected, and grouped into anthologies in a process that mixes historical layers. Even so, the classical Tamil poems are the literary world in which we can discover early traces of a bloodthirsty south Indian goddess named Koṟṟavai, who influenced the warrior-goddess type in early historical south India.[18] Like Kālī, Koṟṟavai is a ferocious war goddess who dances on the battlefield accompanied by ghouls feasting on blood and gore. She is propitiated by kings in search of victory and receives their gruesome offerings during elaborate and bloody war rituals. She is furthermore associated with *pālai*, one of the seven conventional landscapes that dominate the imagery of the classical Tamil poems. The *pālai* landscape is one of drought and heat, of wasteland and war.[19] This scenery of waste is, however, intrinsically connected to the idea of regeneration, whereby war and chaos are a prerequisite for new life and order. This is the earliest image of the south Indian war goddess that we can construct, though due to the nature of the sources this image remains rather vague and incomplete.

A more detailed character emerges in later sources like the *Cilappatikāram*, a Tamil epic text that dates to around the fifth century CE.[20] This "Tale of the Anklet," elegantly translated into English by R. Parthasarathy, reflects a society marked by religious plurality, with Jain and Buddhist influences placed next to dynamic Hindu traditions and decidedly regional forms of religious devotion. In this *tableau vivant* of belief systems, Koṟṟavai is featured as the tutelary deity of groups of brigands who live in arid wastelands and who honor the goddess with possession rituals to obtain victory in battle. Over the course of the narrative, Koṟṟavai's shrine is visited by Kaṇṇaki and Kōvalaṉ, the main characters of the story, who witness such a possession ritual from the first row. The *Cilappatikāram* is also the first source to fully describe the goddess, in its "The Song and Dance of the Hunters" (canto 12):

> The goddess wore the silver petal of the moon on her head. From her split forehead blazed an [unblinking] eye, her lips were coral, bright as silver her teeth, and dark with poison her throat, whirling the fiery serpent as a bowstring, she bent mount Meru as a bow, her breasts smothered inside a bodice [made of the venomous fangs of snakes]. In her hand, piled with bangles, she bore a trident, a rope of elephant skin covered her and over it, as *anaṅku*, a girdle of tiger skin. Her radiant left foot clasped a tinkling anklet, a heroic anklet her right. She is Koṟṟavai of the triumphant sword, who stood on the head of the broad-shouldered demon with two bodies. She is the goddess adored by many as Amarī, Kumārī, Gaurī, Samarī, the one with the trident, the blue one, Vishnu's younger sister, Aiyai, the red one, Durgā. On the leaping stag with a sword in her large hand, Lakshmi with a fine bracelet, Sarasvatī, the goddess of learning, the woman shining with rare gems,

> the ever-young virgin robed in the vesture of *kumāra* whom her kinsmen, Vishnu and Brahma, came to adore.[21]

While the influence of Brahminical traditions from northern India is already clear in this fragment, it would only increase over subsequent centuries. Such a development enhanced the process of assimilating local goddesses into the metaphorical garland of Great Goddesses. In regard to Korravai, we see this process taking place quite clearly in sources such as the *Kaliṅkattupparaṇi*, a twelfth-century Tamil war poem.[22] Elaborate battle scenery and depictions of temples in extremely arid regions overflow with allusions to the Tamil victory goddess of the *pālai* region. Yet where the *Cilappatikāram* celebrates this goddess as Korravai, the *Kaliṅkattupparaṇi* consistently calls her "Kālī."[23] A clear strategy of interweaving both images becomes apparent, which ends with Korravai subsumed under Kālī in the greater Brahminical tradition.

Flower: The Goddess and Her Tradition in Full Bloom

The merging of Korravai and Kālī, each representative of a whole body of religious and literary influences, reflects the development of a multifaceted regional tradition in Kerala. While there is insufficient evidence to claim that the contemporary Bhadrakāḷī of Kerala is a direct descendant of Korravai, the described process is indicative of a transformation that must have affected Bhadrakāḷī at some point in history. The association of local goddess to pan-Indian one was not a complete transition, however, for certain elements of regional identity resisted the new mold. The regional goddess remained in perpetual motion. Bhadrakāḷī and her eternal adversary, Dārika, became the central focus of a well-developed narrative, which in turn gave rise to various interpretations and forms of rendition. As such, the goddess and the demon came to feature in a diverse body of works—oral and written, ritual performative and literary, concise and elaborate, widely known and relatively obscure—in Malayalam, Sanskrit, or a mixture of the two languages called Maṇipravāḷam. The oral-performative part of the Slaying of Dārika (*Dārikavadham*) narrative has been subject to various ethnographic studies, yet the literary texts of this narrative remain largely unexplored.[24] As I have argued in more detail elsewhere, both sides of the tradition developed in mutual interaction, and each contributes to the understanding of the other.[25] This inclusive view of the development of narratives in the south Indian region, and more specifically the region where Bhadrakāḷī is worshiped, is supported by Richard Freeman in his contribution to Sheldon Pollock's *Literary Cultures in History: Reconstructions from South Asia* (2003). There, Freeman emphasizes the strong link between the oral and written that has always existed in regional Keralite literature. These dynamics are especially clear in one specific written text that came forth from the *Dārikavadham* tradition: *The Glorification of Bhadrakāḷī* (*Bhadrakāḷī Māhātmya*).

Bhadrakāḷī Māhātmya

The *Bhadrakāḷī Māhātmya* is a narrative text found in manuscript collections throughout Kerala. It dates to between the fourteenth and sixteenth centuries and belongs to the genre of regional Purāṇas.[26] Purāṇas in general are encyclopedic repositories of myth, lore, science, and religious material composed in late classical and medieval India. Regional Purāṇas, by contrast, are similar in structure and content, yet they are textual repositories specifically for local knowledge.[27] They are united in their endeavor to express a geographically limited textual identity within a framework that appeals to a wider Indian audience. By inscribing themselves within the greater Purāṇic tradition, known for its fluidity and flexibility, they activate a discourse of enormous renown and authority, which then reflects back onto them. Within this authoritative framework, the text then allows for various other literary voices to enrich its texture. It becomes a multivocal rendition of a regional narrative, reflecting various textual traditions that contributed to the formation of the goddess. In the *Bhadrakāḷī Māhātmya*, this process provides us with good insights into the dynamics that lie behind the development of a regional, Sanskritic goddess. Originating most probably in what David Shulman called "the golden age of Purāṇic composition" in south India (fifteenth–sixteenth century CE), the *Bhadrakāḷī Māhātmya* arose at a time when Purāṇic and epic literature were highly popular.[28] Together with influences from regional and transregional literature, these texts have therefore left a specific mark on the *Bhadrakāḷī Māhātmya*'s narrative.

Pan-Indian Connections with the *Devī Māhātmya* and Epics

First and foremost, the authors of the *Bhadrakāḷī Māhātmya* sought to embed the story in the Purāṇic tradition. This is made apparent from the opening lines, where the framing narration is put in the mouth of the sage Mārkaṇḍeya, an ancient authority to whom one of the major Purāṇas is also attributed. The *Mārkaṇḍeya Purāṇa* is also the textual matrix of the most famous goddess narrative, the *Glorification of the Goddess* (*Devī Māhātmya*). Indeed, the *Bhadrakāḷī Māhātmya*'s colophons at the end of each chapter claim it to be part of this great Purāṇa. Not only does the *Bhadrakāḷī Māhātmya* thus refer to the *Mārkaṇḍeya Purāṇa* as its source; it also explicitly assumes a place that is of lesser hierarchical importance to the Purāṇa mentioned. It defines itself as a chapter, while viewing the *Mārkaṇḍeya Purāṇa*, in which it does not feature according to the extant editions, as an accommodating superior. Furthermore, this definition as a chapter also implicitly positions the regional *māhātmya* on the same level as the most studied and analyzed part of that same Purāṇa: the *Devī Māhātmya*, a text that is itself famous for its crucial role in assimilating goddesses in Hindu traditions. This purported affiliation thus endorses a clear intention to be part of one of the biggest literary traditions on goddess worship in India and to assert a place in the larger Sanskritic world. Yet in between these two formal bookends, a whole world of literary allusion, of narrative reinvention and intertextual engagement, is hidden.

The tale of Bhadrakāḷī slaying Dārika is presumably built on the mythical backbone, so to speak, of the *Devī Māhātmya*'s narrative of Durgā slaying the "blood-seed" demon Raktabīja. This narrative depicts a demon (*asura*) warrior, Raktabīja, who acquired the ability to reproduce through blood, and a goddess, Durgā, fighting the former with great difficulty. In the end, Durgā is able to defeat the *asura* only with the help of her bloodthirsty assistant Kālī, who spreads her eager tongue over the entire battlefield and absorbs Raktabīja's blood. The *Bhadrakāḷī Māhātmya*'s narrative also deals with a demon king being able to procreate through blood drops and a goddess unable to take down this demon on her own. Eventually, Bhadrakāḷī receives the help of Vetālī, a bloodthirsty creature taken from Keralite folklore. She too will absorb all blood oozing from the enemy's wounds, thereby helping the goddess to her triumph. Quite remarkable is the way in which Durgā, Kālī, and Vetālī switch places, with Kālī becoming the victorious goddess and Vetālī taking the place of the monstrous but also indispensable helper. A regional influence on the story is thus visible through the narrative.

Less pronounced but equally present are various resonances with the *Rāmāyaṇa* epic. The scenery of the frame story, for example, depicts a king named Candrasena roaming the Daṇḍaka forest and ending up in Sutīkṣṇa's hermitage. This evokes images of Rāma in that same forest. Likewise, Dārika's wife Manodarī is often confused in contemporary retellings with Rāvaṇa's wife Mandodarī. These kinds of engagements subtly connect the *Bhadrakāḷī*

Māhātmya—and by extension the goddess—to wider literary worlds. The authors aimed to create what Michel Foucault called a regime of truth and to install the regional goddess within this pan-Indian regime.[29] Yet the pan-Indian literary world is not the only one that resonates in the *Bhadrakāḷī Māhātmya*.

Transregional Connections: The *Cilappatikāram*

As touched upon previously, classical Tamil literature played a crucial role in the origins of the goddess. The fierce goddess is first described in it, connected to battle imagery and ideas of chaos and regeneration. These images continue to feed the narratives surrounding the goddess, in particular the gruesome descriptions of war as found in the *Bhadrakāḷī Māhātmya* (see translation). The somewhat later *Cilappatikāram*, however, has a special place in this transregional dialogue. Apart from its rich information on Koṟṟavai, this specific source is crucial to our portrait of the goddess for two more reasons. First of all, it contains the first literary mention of a demon called Dārika in south Indian literary sources.[30] As extant research dates the *Cilappatikāram* to somewhere between the fourth and sixth centuries, this means we can assume the cult of a goddess slaying a demon with that name is at least as old. A second interesting feature is the storyline that connects the main heroine, Kaṇṇaki, to the goddess Bhadrakāḷī and her foremost temple in contemporary Kerala: the Kodungallur Bhagavati temple. The last of the three books that comprise the *Cilappatikāram* tells of Kaṇṇaki's supernatural death in the mountain forests and of a Cēra king called Ceṅkuṭṭuvaṉ, who finds her body, takes it with him, and establishes her shrine in his capital, Vāñci. This capital then is supposed to have been located where nowadays we find the bustling temple town of Kodungallur, devoted to the fierce Bhadrakāḷī. In addition, the narrative of the *Cilappatikāram* and that of the *Dārikavadham* are woven together into one contemporary ritual performance, called *Thoṯṯam Pāṭṭŭ* (Songs of origins). This specific rendition in song form connects both narratives by stating that Kaṇṇaki was a manifestation of Bhadrakāḷī. An unequivocal link between the characters thus persists.

Regional Connections: Demonic Characters in Ritual Performances

The topic of ritual performances brings us to a final category of influence to be looked for in the *Bhadrakāḷī Māhātmya*: the regional. Apart from the strongly regional narrative of the *Dārikavadham*, which served as the inspiration for this work, there are more indications of active interaction between the Purāṇic frame of the *Bhadrakāḷī Māhātmya* and its regional context. As I have argued elsewhere, the character of the demon is playing a vital role in this conversation.[31] After all, whereas the goddess has to remain flawless and superior, and thus quite static, the very understanding of the nature of evil as circumstantial, malleable, and in perpetual motion permits the demon to be interpreted more flexibly. He thus grows beyond his role as mere adversary and is able to present a deviant perspective on the goddess that adds to her greatness. His view is one of the subaltern, so to speak: a position that allows him to be activated by discourses and strategies that add to the narrative without obscuring the radiance of the goddess.

This predilection for the demonic character is clear from the start in the *Bhadrakāḷī Māhātmya*. The opening chapter (translated here) is devoted entirely to the demon, as are the next three. Only in the fifth chapter (translated here) does the goddess herself appear. Furthermore, the demon is depicted in an overtly humane way, afflicted by flaws and emotions very recognizable to the audience. This stands in stark contrast to the archetypal way in which many demons are depicted in the great Purāṇas. The aforementioned Raktabīja of the *Devī Māhātmya*, for example, serves no other purpose than as an eternal adversary of the goddess. He is meant to challenge and die, a narrative trajectory that the *Bhadrakāḷī Māhātmya* ultimately follows but also reinvents. Some performative ritual traditions within Kerala are markedly similar in this respect. Ritual songs such as the *Kaḷam Pāṭṭŭ* feature equally humane demonic characters. Not only Dārika, but his wife, the goddess's *vāhana* Vetālī, and many more characters are depicted in a fashion that appeals to the audience.[32]

The tradition's sympathy for Dārika deserves more analysis than can be provided here, but one strand of it may derive from devotional Hinduism (*bhakti*). As Shulman argued, a notable character type developed in Purāṇic literature under the influence of *bhakti* devotionalism is the "demon-devotee."[33] Devoted to the goddess, even by means of hatred (*dveṣa-bhakti*), the demon comes to represent vices such as egotism and materialism. No longer an adversary destined to die, he becomes a personification of human flaws. His subsequent beheading then represents liberation at the hands of the goddess, one to be experienced vicariously by the audience experiencing the performed/written text. It could well be that the demon king Dārika encompasses this interplay of performance and *bhakti*, leading the audience to identify with the demon and experience a sort of spiritual catharsis at his destruction.

Fruit: Resonating Literary Worlds

In spite of the interaction of various traditions in this text and its consciously dynamic portrayal of the goddess, it remains rather unclear what exact function the *Bhadrakāḷī Māhātmya* served and in which circumstances. Some of the pan-Indian Purāṇas were, and still are, orally performed for large audiences. Recitation of the *Bhāgavata Purāṇa*, for example, still fills large halls with people eager to experience the text and receive the spiritual rewards of hearing it.[34] There is no mention to be found of such performances when it comes to the *Bhadrakāḷī Māhātmya*. It is, however, frequently encountered in libraries of all sorts, attesting to its once having been quite popular. The text clearly belongs to the heyday of the goddess in Kerala, when the tradition not only proliferated within the region but also started to profile itself within the larger transregional world. In contemporary Keralan society, however, the text has been forgotten, while the goddess Bhadrakāḷī lives on. She is a multifaceted goddess, Sanskritic, yet with performances and rituals devoted to her that contest her depiction as purely belonging to the pan-Indian traditions. She has been formed by many currents, the same ones that flow through the *Bhadrakāḷī Māhātmya*. The text thus becomes a silent witness to the complicated and multifaceted formation of a regional goddess. These currents are like seeds in the ripe fruit that came forth from a blossoming goddess tradition, attesting to a perpetual interaction of pan-Indian, transregional and regional influences. In the meantime, the goddess keeps on evolving, adapting to a certain extent in concordance with the contemporary needs and wishes of the devotees, while her portrayal in the *Bhadrakāḷī Māhātmya* slowly fades from memory.

SOURCE

The translation is based primarily on a 1925 Devanāgarī transcript held at the Oriental Research Institute and Manuscripts Library (ORIML) of Kerala University (T697). In addition, I adopted some variant readings from the Girija and Visalakshy (1999–2000) edition of the *Bhadrakāḷī Māhātmya* as published by that same institute and some of the (heavily damaged) manuscripts that I digitized in various libraries during my fieldwork trip in 2015, funded by the

Ghent University Special Research Fund. The text itself has been briefly mentioned by a few authors, for example Pasty-Abdul Wahid (2010), Freeman (2016), and especially Caldwell (2001), who translates a few short passages in her book chapter. To my knowledge, however, the *Bhadrakāḷī Māhātmya* has neither been fully translated nor fully subjected to any in-depth scrutiny. It is written in standard Sanskrit, with some apparent influence from Malayalam occurring here and there, especially in scenes that deal with local scenery and architecture or in certain characters and names (e.g., the occurrence of *kūḷi*s, Malayali demonic creatures). The text is written mostly in the classical *śloka* meter, with some verses in Vasantatilaka meter interwoven into that whole, and in total consists of 560 verses distributed over nine chapters. Each chapter ends with a colophon that describes it as being a part of the *Mārkaṇḍeya Purāṇa*, a claim that is strengthened by Mārkaṇḍeya's presence as the primary narrator of the frame story. The Purāṇa appropriately ends with an overview of the many merits it offers to its audience.

FURTHER READING

Caldwell, S. 2001. "Waves of Beauty, Rivers of Blood: Constructing the goddess in Kerala." In *Seeking Mahadevi: Constructing the Identities of the Hindu Great Goddess*, edited by Tracy Pintchman, 93–114. Albany: State University of New York Press.

Chakrabarti, K. 2001. *Religious Process: The Purāṇas and the Making of a Regional Tradition*. New Delhi: Oxford University Press.

Rohlman, E. 2011. "Geographical Imagination and Literary Boundaries in the Sarasvati Purana." *International Journal of Hindu Studies* 15, no. 2: 139–63.

van Brussel, N. 2016. "Revenge, Hatred, Love, and Regret: The Use of Narrative Empathy in a Regional Purāṇa." *Religions of South Asia* 11, no. 1: 193–213.

NOTES

1. Since the source text neglects to introduce the sage Mārkaṇḍeya, the primary narrator, until several paragraphs into the narration, the translation has taken the liberty of moving the phrase "Mārkaṇḍeya said" to the beginning. The spelling of Bhadrakāḷī reflects the convention of the source text. It is in Sanskrit but uses the retroflex "ḷ" preferred in the Malayalam script. In the Malayalam language, the goddess is known as Bhadrakāḷi (with the final vowel short). When referencing the goddess Kālī in general in the introduction, the standard Sanskrit spelling of her name is used, whereas Kāḷī is the preferred spelling in the translation in accordance with the source text. The name Dārika is also spelled Dāruka; both are used interchangeably in Kerala.

2. The Daṇḍaka forest plays an important role in the *Rāmāyaṇa*, where it is the home-in-exile of Rāma, Sītā, and Lakṣmaṇa and the backdrop for many important scenes, such as the abduction of Sītā.

3. The *Rāmāyaṇa* also features a sage named Sutīkṣṇa, who lives in the Daṇḍaka forest and meets with Rāma.

4. Here the word "demon" is translating *asura* (non-god). *Asuras* are the eternal enemies of the gods. While there are two main lineages of *asura*, the Dānava and the Daitya, all three words are often used interchangeably to indicate a demonic race of beings. For clarity, and to reflect this mixing of demonic species in the source text, the translation uses the generic "demon" in each case.

5. The phrase "religious austerity" (*tapas*) indicates various types of bodily mortification, penance, intensive meditation, and special observances, often culminating in one or another god offering the practitioner of such penances a boon as reward.

6. Gokarna is a major pilgrimage site in the modern south Indian state of Karnataka that has an important temple devoted to Śiva.

7. The "lotus-born god" describes Brahmā's birth atop a lotus that sprouts from Viṣṇu's navel, in order to create the universe.

8. The story does not explain whether the husbands continued living in the underworld after their deaths or were revived by Brahmā.

9. Māyāvatī and Tāmasī, in this context, appear to refer to spell-goddesses for deluding an enemy and causing darkness, respectively.

10. The order of the last few verses was adjusted for a more comprehensive and fluent translation.

11. This line alludes to two famous myths involving Śiva. The first, involving the destruction of the god of love, Kāmadeva, is famously retold in Kālidāsa's poem *The Birth of Kumāra* (*Kumārasambhava*). The latter myth involved Śiva destroying three magnificent cities built by the same demon architect Maya, referenced here.

12. This may refer to the tall and dark Anjaneri Mountain near Nasik in the modern state of Maharashtra. This mountain is also referenced in the Sanskrit epics, Purāṇas, and Tantras.

13. Cāmuṇḍā, Cāmuṇḍī, Caṇḍikā, and other names are all used interchangeably here to denote the great goddess Kāḷī. In other contexts they may refer to separate goddesses or separate manifestations of the great goddess.

14. Śiva's "black throat" refers to the myth of him swallowing poison to save the world from its destructive power. Pārvatī caused the poison to stay in his throat to save his life, and the poison stained his throat blue/black.

15. Nandimahākāla is the general of Bhadrakāḷī's army.

16. *Pāṭṭū* are ritual performances that embrace the singing of a narrative connected to the goddess. There are several kinds; the *Bhadrakāḷī Kaḷam Pāṭṭū* recounts the Slaying of Dārika (*Dārikavadham*) narrative to invite the goddess into a ritual depiction of her made with colored powders (*kaḷam*). For more on Bhadrakāḷī and female Brahminical rituals, see Caldwell (2001).

17. Classical Tamil poetry is often referred to as Caṅkam or Saṅgam poetry. The date range (ca. 100 BCE–300 CE) is based on the work of Zvelebil (1975), which most scholars follow.

18. See Caldwell (1999) and Mahalakshmi (2011) for further discussion of the influence of Koṟṟavai.

19. On the conventions of classical Tamil poetry and their interpretation, see Hart (1975) and Ramanujan (2011).

20. Zvelebil (1975).

21. Parthasarathy (2004, 121–22).

22. Zvelebil (1975).

23. Mahalakshmi (2011).

24. Ethnographic studies of the *Dārikavadham* tradition include those in Aubert (2004), Caldwell (1999), Pasty-Abdul Wahid (2010), and Tarabout (1986).

25. Brussel (in progress).

26. For discussion of the date of the text, see Brussel (in progress).

27. Recommended studies on regional Purāṇas include Rohlman's (2011) article on the Gujarati *Sarasvatī Purāṇa*, Chakrabarti's (2001) study of Bengali *Upa Purāṇas*, and Shulman's (1980) study of *Sthala Purāṇas* from Tamil Nadu (1980).

28. Shulman (1980, 32).

29. Taylor (2012) has argued that such a process is common in the Purāṇic genre. In her work on the *Sarasvatī Purāṇa* from Gujarat, Rohlman (2011) has written extensively on its active engagement with diverse texts belonging to the pan-Indian Sanskrit tradition, arguing that such intertextuality forms a crucial part of the text's character.

30. *Cilappatikāram* 20.50–55; for translation, see Parthasarathy (2004, 88).

31. See Brussel (in progress).

32. For more on the empathetic depiction of demonic characters, see Caldwell (2001) and Brussel (in progress).

33. Shulman (1980).

34. See Taylor (2008) for more on performances of the Purāṇas and the role of the text's list of benefits (the so-called *śravaṇaphala*) in attracting audiences.

FIGURE 3. Cāmuṇḍi and Uttanahaḷḷi, by Laura Santi

CHAPTER 2

Cāmuṇḍi and Uttanahaḷḷi

Sisters of the Mysuru Hills

CALEB SIMMONS

The next tale comes from the city of Mysuru (formerly Mysore) in the southern part of Karnataka state in south India. This lovely city, encircled by large hills and, at one time, sandalwood forests, was the capital of its own sovereign kingdom for centuries and joined the new Republic of India in 1947. Flanked by two sacred rivers, the Kaveri to the north and the Kapini to the south, the area is a landscape with deep religious significance to Hindus. The stunning royal palace of the Woḍeyar dynasty still defines the eastern edge of the city, near Cāmuṇḍi hill. This hill is held to be the site where the goddess Cāmuṇḍi and her sister Uttanahaḷḷi came together to slay the notorious buffalo demon Mahiṣa.

The story is told on the basis of two songs from the Kannada folk ballad *Beṭṭada Cāmuṇḍi,* whose date of origin is not known. The ballad is still performed by the Kaṃsāḷe musical community today. It makes allusions to the famous story of the defeat of Mahiṣa, but unlike the ancient narratives, the ballad focuses on the goddess's battle against his brother Aisāsura, who takes on the role of the demon called Raktabīja. Normally, a form of the regal Durgā is credited with slaying the buffalo demon, as in chapter 3 on the goddess Kauśikī. Here, however, the act is attributed to the beloved guardian of Mysuru, the goddess Cāmuṇḍi, and her sister goddess, Uttanahaḷḷi. The pair are place-guardians (*grāmadēvate*), a category of Hindu deities who are normally fearsome, since they serve to protect the inhabitants of a locale from evildoers.

Readers should analyze how the songs portray the femininity of Cāmuṇḍi and Uttanahaḷḷi, as well as their relationship as sisters. How does the second song set up a mythological basis for divine and royal alliances, annual rituals, pilgrimage, and other features of sacred geography? What elements of "Sanskritization" can you recognize in the songs? Recall from the preface that Sanskritization is the process by which a local or regional goddess is adapted as a form of a more famous or universal deity.

ನಾಲಗೆ ಮ್ಯಾಲೆ ನಿಂತು ಕಾಳಗ ಮಡಕ್ಕಯ್ಯ

ಶಿವನಿಂದ ವರವ ಪಡೆದ
ಬೆಟ್ಟದ ಚಾಮುಂಡವ್ವ

ಹತ್ತು ಭಾಜವಂತೆ
ಇಪ್ಪತ್ತು ಕೈಯಮಾಡು ಕೊಂಡು
ಆಯ್ದ ಮಸ್ತಾಪ ಕತ್ತಿ ಕಠಾರಿ ಹಿಡ ಕೊಂಡು
ಶಿವನತ್ರ ವರವ ಪಡ ಕೊಂಡು
ಮೈಸೂರು ಸಂಸ್ಥಾನದಲ್ಲಿ

ಮಹಿಷಾಸುರನ ಮ್ಯಾಲೆ
ಕಾಳಗವ ಮಾಡುತಾರೆ

ಮಹಿಷಾಸುರನ ಸಂಹಾರವ
ಯಾವ ರೀತಿ ಮಾಡುತಾಳೆ ಅಂದರೆ
ಐಸಾಸುರ ಬಂದು ಚಾಮುಂಡೇಶ್ವರಿಯ ಮುಂಗೈ ಹಿಡಿದಿದಾನೆ
ಚಾಮುಂಡೇಶ್ವರಿ ಕತ್ತಿಯನ್ನು ಕೈಲಿ ಹಿಡಿದಿದಾಳೆಲ್ಲ
ಐಸಾಸುರ್ನ ಹೆಕ್ಕತ್ತ ಮ್ಯಾಲೆ ಹಿಡಿದಿದಾಳೆ
ಅವನ ಒಂದು ಚುಟ್ಟು ರಕ್ತ ಏನಾದರೆ ಧರಣಿ ಮ್ಯಾಲೆ ಬಿದ್ದರೆ

ಕೋಟಿ ರಾಕ್ಷರು ಅಲ್ಲಿ
ಉತ್ಪತ್ತಿಯಾಗುತಾರೆ

ಮಾಯಕಾತಿ ಬೆಟ್ಟದ ಚಾಮುಂಡೇಶ್ವರಿ
ಮಹಿಷಾಸುರನ ಸಂಹಾರ ಮಾಡಬುಟ್ಟು
ಐಸಾಸುರನ ಸಂಹಾರ ಮಾಡುತ್ತಿದ್ದಾಳೆ
ಐಸಾಸುರ ಅನ್ನತಕ್ಕವನು
ಚಾಮುಂಡೇಶ್ವರಿ ಹಾವಳಿಯನ್ನು ತಡೀನಾರದೆ
ಕೋಣನ ಹೊಟ್ಟೆಯೊಳಗೆ
ಅವುತು ಕೊಂಡು ಕುಂತಿದಾನೆ
ಅವನ ಒಂದು ಚುಟ್ಟು ರತ್ಕದಿಂದ

FIGURE 4. *Beṭṭada Cāmuṇḍi,* a ballad in the Kannada language and script. Font "Arial Unicode MS" © Monotype corporation.

"SISTER, STAND ON MY TONGUE AND FIGHT!"

A boon was given by Śiva,
O Mother, Cāmuṇḍi of the hill![1]
With your ten shoulders and
with your twenty hands you did it!
You grabbed the sharpened sword and dagger.
A boon was given by Śiva
in the land of Mysuru.
You won the battle
against Mahiṣāsura!
[*Directed to the audience*]
After the annihilation of Mahiṣāsura
Do you know what happens?
Aisāsura comes and grabs the forearm of Cāmuṇḍēśvari.[2]
Cāmuṇḍēśvari grabs the sword with her hand.
She grabs the nape of Aisāsura's neck.
Wherever a little drop of his blood fell to the earth . . .
Countless demons
are born.
Cāmuṇḍēśvari of the hill, the maker of illusion,
has killed the demon Mahiṣāsura.
She keeps fighting with Aisāsura,
but Aisāsura is a worthy opponent.
Cāmuṇḍēśvari endures his mischief.
But inside the [dead] buffalo's belly,
he hides and plots
and countless demons are produced
from every little drop of his blood.
Then she steps on the buffalo's hoof and stands up.
She looks to the left and to the right
and thinks, . . .
"I don't have the power
to destroy all these demons.
What can I do?"
Cāmuṇḍēśvari of the hill
looks to the left and right and thinks.

Sweat is pouring all over her body.
She sighs "Ughhh" and wipes and slings it [to the ground].
She thinks "Nobody can solve this problem alone.
I need to call someone."
Tears well in her eyes
O Mother Cāmuṇḍi, who belongs to the hill
O Guru, O Cāmuṇḍēśvari of the hill,
tears well up in your eyes.[3]
Śrī Kṛṣṇa the Supreme realizes [Cāmuṇḍi's] affliction.[4]
He, who is married to Rukmaṇi, the one called Sārada,
and plays games on the seven seas,
he, the Supreme, thinks,
"Ah Rukmaṇi! I need to go![5]
Cāmuṇḍēśvari of the hill
needs a boon from me
so she can kill Aisāsura."
Śrī Kṛṣṇa, the Supreme Soul,
takes hold of Garuḍa
and leaves Nanda's ranch.[6]
Śrī Kṛṣṇa, the Supreme Soul,
comes to the Mysuru region.
Cāmuṇḍi is in Mysuru
wiping her sweat and slinging it to the ground.
Śrī Kṛṣṇa, the Supreme Soul, watches
her sweat fall to the ground
flowing like a river.
Then Uttanahaḷḷi Māri arises,
born from her sweat.[7]
Śrī Kṛṣṇa, the Supreme Soul,
gives the boon.
Immediately after receiving the boon she
is born, rising from Cāmuṇḍi's sweat and
spreading her seven hoods and sticking out her seven tongues.[8]
Look! The beautiful Uttanahaḷḷi Māri
is now standing before you!
Uttanahaḷḷi Māri grabs her by the hand and says,

"Sister, don't be afraid."
"Lady, who are you?" asked Cāmuṇḍēśvari.
"Sister, don't you know who I am?
I took birth in your sweat."
Hearing this, Cāmuṇḍēśvari was happy and said,
"Wow! Child of my sweat!
By your birth in my sweat
you are closer
to me than all of my other siblings.
You are now my sister."
"Sister, those words are too great.
What is your trouble?"
asked Uttanahaḷḷi Māramma.
"You said 'What is your trouble?'
How do I reply, Sister?
I have killed Mahiṣāsura,
but now if I strike Aisāsura
from every small drop of his blood
that falls to the ground . . .
Countless demons
are born, Sister."[9]
Mother Uttanahaḷḷi feels
fire in her belly and says,
"Sister, when I am here, why should you fear?
His blood won't fall to the ground anymore!
Fight, Sister!"
"Sister, it isn't possible."
"Ugh! Why are you worrying?
At this moment, I am spreading
my seven tongues around the hill.
Sister, stand on my
seven tongues and fight!"
"Sister, stand on my seven tongues
and fight!" says Uttanahaḷḷi
as she spreads out her tongue.
Courage comes to Cāmuṇḍēśvari of the hill.

Cāmuṇḍēśvari stands on her Sister Uttanahaḷḷi's,
the fire-starter's, tongue.
She fights
with Aisāsura.
Cāmuṇḍēśvari of the hill
looks for that buffalo.[10]
When she spots the buffalo,
he's gonna die.
Cāmuṇḍēśvari of the hill looks around the hill.
She looks here.
She looks there.
But wherever she looks
there is no sign of Aisāsura.
Then she says,
"Sister, Sister, I have
gone and circled the hill and hillocks,
and there is no sign of Aisāsura."
Uttanahaḷḷi replies,
"Sister Cāmuṇḍēśvari,
This buffalo is dead.
Thrust the trident
through his corpse-like body."
"Who are you Uttanahaḷḷi Māramma?"
Hearing words of her little sister,
Cāmuṇḍēśvari of the hill
thrusts her trident, and
the buffalo is split in two.
The real Aisāsura
comes outside.
When the true form of Aisāsura comes out,
he looks like a huge hill.
His teeth look like gigantic white radishes.
He sticks out his tongue like a monkey.
He opens his mouth like a metal pot.
He comes to grab
Mother Cāmuṇḍi.

She exclaims, "Oh no! He's coming this way!
How can I kill him?"
Then she meditates on Śiva, and
Brahma becomes aware of her tears.
He said, "Uh-oh Cāmuṇḍēśvari
is fighting the demon Aisāsura.
I gave him a wish
and he asked,
'If a drop of my blood falls to the ground
countless more like me
should be born.'
He has no fear
There is no one who can defeat him.
Agh, Cāmuṇḍēśvari!
Śiva gave a blessing to the demon.
Now death must come to Aisāsura
Agh, I must support Cāmuṇḍēśvari."
Brahma Dēva swears this
and sends the fiery lion.
Brahma Dēva sends the fiery lion.
The fiery lion comes
to Pārvatī-Cāmuṇḍēśvari
and bows [before her].
"Oh! A little lion!"
Cāmuṇḍēśvari of the hill said,
and then she sat on the lion-vehicle.
She fights
with Aisāsura.
With ten shoulders
and twenty hands she does it.
She stares at him with her burning eyes
and her lolling tongue.
Seated on her lion vehicle,
she grabs Aisāsura's long hair.
O Cāmuṇḍēśvari of the hill!
She fights him, and she kills him!

"SHE BATHES IN THE KAPINI AND KAVERI"

Uttanahaḷḷi Māramma worries and asks,[11]
"Sister, I can't bear to see your trouble.
I was born from you, but
now what should I do, Sister?"
"O little sister, you don't go far away.
I live on top of this hill.
I'm the patron goddess of Cāmarāja Woḍeyar.[12]
Once a year I go down to take *pūjā*,
but the rest of the year I live on this hill.[13]
You should live nearby."
"Tell me, Sister, where should I live?"
asks Uttanahaḷḷi.
Cāmuṇḍi says,
"Little Sister, if you live on the side of this hill
in the town of Uttanahaḷḷi,
I'll arrange an annual *pūjā* for you.
I'll make sure you get homemade offerings
I'll make *tambiṭṭu* and send it to you."[14]
Cāmuṇḍamma of the hill
blesses her like this.
Standing on the top of the hill
during the middle of the night
when stones and water melt into one,
she looks around her neighborhood and says,
"God, I need to bathe;
where should I go?"
She looks
all around the seven regions.
Cāmuṇḍēśvari of the hill
looks all around the seven regions.
In the region of Nañjalagūḍi,
which is equal to Kailash,
the Kapini river flows.[15]
Thinking that she needs a bath,
Cāmuṇḍēśvari goes to the river.

She says to the lion,
"Honorable lion, you stay here.
I am going to bathe and clean myself."
She gives her word and leaves
to go and bathe.
After killing countless demons
when she crosses into Mysuru
her right hand is covered
with the stain of their blood;
so the Mother comes to bathe
in the Kapini river.
She goes into the Kapini-Kaveri
and bathes.
She puts on a fancy white sari, and
then Cāmuṇḍēśvari of the hill
magically makes a golden comb
with a golden handle
and combs her long
knotted hair.
Cāmuṇḍamma of the hill
combs her knotted hair.
Cāmuṇḍēśvari of the hill
combs her knotted hair.

THE GODDESSES IN CONTEXT: LOCAL AND SITUATED GODDESSES OF SOUTHERN KARNATAKA

The two songs in this chapter tell the story of the sister goddesses Cāmuṇḍi and Uttanahaḷḷi. The bards recount the sisters' epic battle against demons on the hill outside of Mysuru (also called Mysore), a city in the modern state of Karnataka in south India. These songs, which are sung in the Kannada language, are part of a larger epic ballad called *Cāmuṇḍi of the Hill* (*Beṭṭada Cāmuṇḍi*), about the goddess and her relationship with the god Śiva in his local form as Nañjuṇḍēśvara, "the lord who consumed the poison."[16] In these songs, and in the epic ballad more broadly, the local traditions of these two situated goddesses seamlessly blend into the broader Indic tradition through narrative and mythic adaptation and acculturation.

Seed: Goddesses Rooted in Place

The origins of these goddesses remain largely obscure. Locals regard both as *grāmadēvate,* deities who protect specific areas that are under their care: Cāmuṇḍi is associated with Mysuru, and Uttanahaḷḷi with the village of the same name. The relationship of these goddesses to the land is apparent in their names and the way that devotees from the area refer to them. Cāmuṇḍi lives atop the large hill just outside of Mysuru, which is aptly named Cāmuṇḍi Hill (*cāmuṇḍi beṭṭa*). She has been associated with this hill since the first historical records from the seventeenth century, which mention her as either "Cāmuṇḍi of the hill" (*beṭṭada cāmuṇḍi*) or "Mother of the hill" (*beṭṭada amma*). This association continues even today as the residents of Mysuru and its surrounding areas simply refer to the hill as "the hill" (*beṭṭa*) and the goddess simply as "mother" (*amma*). Uttanahaḷḷi's connection is even more straightforward, as she shares her name with her village. The name literally means "the 'in-between' village," and this name locates her both spatially and mythologically between Cāmuṇḍi and her husband deity Nañjuṇḍēśvara in nearby Nanjangud, a relationship we see unfold in the ballad from which these songs are translated.

Flower: Classical Myth and Sweet Local Songs

The development of these local goddesses opens in full bloom with their incorporation into the broader Indic tradition and narratives of the Sanskritic deities Durgā, Kālī, and Śiva. Through these associations, the local traditions expand to engage well-known narratives that are often described by Kannada-speaking locals as "sweet" (*rōcaka*) because of how they please the senses by mixing epic battles and romantic longing and realization into one riveting plotline. The narratives themselves are complex and nuanced expressions of local traditions, culture, and practices that are situated within the broader framework of well-known myths from Hindu religious stories known throughout monsoon Asia. In particular, these songs build upon the Purāṇic narratives of the Great Goddess (Mahādevī) and her dual manifestations as the regal Durgā and the fearsome Kālī/Cāmuṇḍā. In the classical Sanskrit tradition, Cāmuṇḍā is a fierce hag goddess associated with the ghastly gang of the "seven mothers" (*saptamātṛkās*) and with the gruesome deeds of the goddess Kālī, which are perhaps best known from the telling in the Sanskrit *Devī Māhātmya* or through her prominence in Hindu Tantric traditions. For those who visit her temple atop Cāmuṇḍi hill outside the city of Mysuru and for those who hear the songs of her exploits, however, the goddess Cāmuṇḍi (aka Cāmuṇḍēśvari, "the lady/queen Cāmuṇḍā") bears little resemblance to these characterizations. Instead, in her mythology and iconography she has been transformed into the regal Durgā, specifically in her manifestation as the "slayer of the buffalo-demon" (Mahiṣāsuramardinī). The Great Goddess's manifestation as the buffalo slayer is one of the most ubiquitous images in Indic iconography, and the narrative has been told and retold in a variety of texts and contexts, with the first extended version appearing in the Sanskrit *Skanda Purāṇa*, only later to be popularized in the *Devī Māhātmya*.[17] Variations of this famous narrative form the basis for the songs translated in this chapter, and I summarize it here:

> Mahiṣa (buffalo) was a demon, who had risen to great power and had usurped from the Vedic gods the highest position in the cosmos. Through his great piety and devotion, as well as severe penances, he compelled Śiva (or Brahmā according to some versions) to grant him a wish.[18] He wanted immortality, which is the one thing the gods will not give, so he opted for what he thought would be the next best thing: to be invulnerable to all male beings. He thought that a female inherently could pose no danger to him, and so he was confident that his immortality was virtually assured. The gods, however, joined forces by emitting their inner brilliance (*tejas*) through beams of light that merged their powers together to form the Great Goddess. This goddess, who is known by many names including Durgā, Ambikā, and Mahādevī, then attacked the buffalo-demon. Their battle was fierce with the buffalo-demon shifting into different forms (lion, man, elephant) to avoid deathblows by the goddess. Finally, the demon assumed his buffalo form, and the goddess leapt upon him, striking him with her spear. The demon attempted to shape-shift again, but this time the goddess grabbed him mid-transformation and decapitated him, killing him and ending his threat to the gods once and for all.[19]

The narrative of the Goddess killing Mahiṣa is summarized iconographically in the image of Mahiṣāsuramardinī in which Durgā's lion holds down the carcass of a decapitated buffalo and the goddess thrusts her spear into an anthropomorphic demon emerging from its body. Indeed, this image is recognized in local Mysuru tradition to be none other than their own Cāmuṇḍi, and her hill is believed to be the very location upon which the demon was slain, perfectly mapping the local goddess to the pan-Indic myth.[20] Interestingly, the narratives about the fierce and ghoulish Cāmuṇḍā are not absent from the local mythological landscape. It is Uttanahaḷḷi, however, who carries out the deeds and exhibits all of the characteristics normally attributed to Cāmuṇḍā in the broader Indic traditions, particularly the story of Kālī and the demon Raktabīja (literally "blood-seed"). This story, too, is relatively well known throughout India, and I again summarize it briefly here, primarily from the narrative of the *Devī Māhātmya*:

> Raktabīja was a general in the demon army of Śumbha and Niśumbha, demons who, like Mahiṣa, had usurped the position of the gods. Raktabīja, however, proved to be one of the Goddess's greatest foes because every time she struck the demon, every drop of his blood that hit the ground would spawn another demon; therefore, with every slash of her sword or shot from her bow, her demonic adversaries grew exponentially, soon pervading the entire world. To combat the demon's special power, the Goddess instructed Kālī, calling her Cāmuṇḍā, to open her mouth wide, drink up the torrents of blood, and eat all the demons produced by the demon's blood. This strategy worked and the Goddess was able to quickly defeat the mighty demon general.

In illustrations of this scene, Cāmuṇḍā is depicted not only opening her mouth but also spreading her tongue over the battlefield in order to lap up Raktabīja's blood before it can touch the earth. As we see in the translation of the songs, Uttanahaḷḷi similarly extends her tongue for her sister to stand upon as she fights the demon. Indeed, it seems plausible that the association of Uttanahaḷḷi with this narrative is a result of the similarity of the Kannada descriptor in her name (i.e., *uttana* or "between") and the Sanskrit term *uttāna*, which is an adjective that describes something that is "stretched out."

Fruit: Negotiating Complex Identities

The blending of the local and pan-Indic traditions and myths not only created dynamic ballads such as *Beṭṭada Cāmuṇḍi*; it has also caused the identities of both Cāmuṇḍi and Uttanahaḷḷi to be forever altered—one might say forgotten—and moved further away from their local context, in which their situatedness on the hill and in the village was so important. Cāmuṇḍi, or Cāmuṇḍēśvari as she is known on most of her temples' signage, is no longer simply the "Mother of the hill"; she has become "Mother of the universe" (*jagajjanani*), associated with transcendent reality as the Sanskritic Mahādevī. Likewise, Uttanahaḷḷi has been further connected to the goddess Jvalajjihvā (flaming-tongue) or Jvālāmukhi (fire-face/mouth), names of another popular goddess. In the Kangra district of the northern Indian state of Himachal Pradesh, the goddess Jvālāmukhī is linked with other goddess sites all over India through the network of *śakti pīṭha* (goddess seats). This process of connecting local deities and traditions with pan-Indian mythology and ritual practice is often referred to as "Sanskritization." While Sanskritization can be a helpful heuristic for beginning a conversation about the development of local traditions in relationship to regional and pan-Indian concerns, it is also problematic in that it often masks the more complicated negotiations of identities, practices, and peoples. In the case of Beṭṭada Cāmuṇḍi and Uttanahaḷḷi, the processes through which their significance was broadened beyond their local sphere of influence can be traced through literature from the Mysuru court that was primarily composed to praise the local kings. In this literature, we can see that Mysuru's Cāmuṇḍi was first associated with the slaying of the buffalo-demon in 1639 CE, when she was called Mahiṣāsuramardini in the *Cāmarājokti Vilāsa* and the "Gajjiganahaḷḷi inscription."[21] During the reign of Kṛṣṇarāja Woḍeyar III (r. 1799–1868), however, the transition to Beṭṭada Cāmuṇḍi and Uttanahaḷḷi's pan-Indian and Sanskrit identity was thoroughly implemented, with Brahmin priests being assigned to Cāmuṇḍi's temple on the hill and Uttanahaḷḷi only being referred to as Jvālāmukhi/Jvalajjihvā in the epic history of the royal lineage *Śrīmanmahārājavara Vaṃśāvaḷi* (ca. 1860s). After this period, most references to the goddesses, especially those in English, all but forgot their situated histories in favor of their newer, broader identities.

The goddesses and their connection to the city and the village, however, are still very much alive in the religious and devotional imagination of Mysuru and its surrounding areas and becomes evident when speaking (particularly in Kannada) to local devotees and through performances such as those translated here. Therefore, when we talk of Beṭṭada Cāmuṇḍi and Uttanahaḷḷi as "forgotten goddesses," it is important to ask "forgotten by whom?," because for a certain segment of society their very presence is a constant reminder of their situatedness and their local identity. Therefore, it might be more accurate to speak of these local goddesses as masked rather than completely forgotten.

SOURCE

As previously mentioned, the source for the translations is the Kannada folk ballad *Beṭṭada Cāmuṇḍi*, a collection of songs that contain the mythology of gods and goddesses of southern Karnataka. The major focus of the ballad is the romantic relationship between the goddess Cāmuṇḍi and her consort Nañjuṇḍēśvara, with Cāmuṇḍi's younger sister Uttanahaḷḷi acting as the "go-between." While the precise date of the ballad's composition is unknown, it continues to be performed by members of the devotional bardic Kaṃsāḷe community today.[22] The Kaṃsāḷe community's performers sing, play music, and dance, and it derives its name from the small cymbals they carry and with which they perform. As a community, they are devotees of Śiva, specifically his manifestation as Mahadēśvara, a local Liṅgāyat saint whose temple is in the Chamarajanagar district in southern Karnataka. The Kaṃsāḷes' songs and performances are quite popular throughout southern Karnataka, where they can be seen at festivals, in cultural programs, and even on television talent shows. The songs themselves are sung by a lead singer and a choir. The lead serves as the soloist, who sings the majority of the narrative, only joined by the entire choir to repeat the refrain and to add emphasis to particularly important lines. In my translation, the soloist's lines are given in roman text, and the lines sung by the choir are rendered in italics.

This translation comprises the first two songs of the ballad, "Sister, Stand on My Tongue and Fight!" ("Nālage Myāle Nintu Kāḷaga Māḍakkayya") and "She Bathes in the Kapini and Kaveri" ("Kapini Kāvēriyōlage Stānavannu Māḍutāḷe"). The first song tells of the goddess Cāmuṇḍēśvari's battle with the buffalo-demon king Mahiṣāsura and his younger brother Aisāsura, which reframes the narratives of the Goddess's battles from the Purāṇic tradition. In these songs, Mahiṣa does not play a very large role, as the battle between him and Cāmuṇḍi is only referenced through allusions. The narrative instead focuses on the battle between Cāmuṇḍi and Aisāsura, in which we see an interesting collapse of the two mythic scenes previously summarized. In this battle, whenever the mighty demon king is struck by the goddess, every drop of his blood that hits the ground gives birth to another manifestation of the mighty demon, collapsing both the Mahiṣa and Raktabīja stories into one super myth. In addition, this song also relates the birth of Uttanahaḷḷi from Cāmuṇḍi, who, in her exasperation, slings her perspiration to the ground, which then gives rise to her sister. After a brief negotiation of their familial relationship and obligations, Uttanahaḷḷi invites her sister Cāmuṇḍēśvari to fight the demon upon her tongue so that she can drink his blood before it hits the earth. The second song takes place at the culmination of the battle. In this song we see the local situatedness of Uttanahaḷḷi and Cāmuṇḍi as the latter takes up residence atop the hill and establishes a temple and annual festival for her younger sister, thus placing these local goddesses, temples, and their festival calendars within the broader framework of Indian mythology.

In addition to live performances by itinerant bards outside the sister goddesses' respective temples, these songs can be found in a variety of media, such as CD and MP3 recordings, and have been incorporated into dramatic performances, including the play *Cāma Celuve*, written by Sujatha Akki and directed by Mandya Ramesh.[23] While many of these sources have been consulted for clarity, my translation is based on the work of P. K. Rajasekhara, who originally collected and published the songs along with an excellent introduction in 1972, as *Beṭṭada Cāmuṇḍi*. It remains the most thorough documentation of the ballad, and I have relied on this text and personal communication with Professor Rajasekhara to clarify terminology (including the titles of most songs), fill in gaps missing in the narrative, and for the overall structure of the ballad, which in its oral form is dynamic and at times difficult to contain.

FURTHER READING

Aiyar, Indira S. 1997. *Durgā as Mahiṣāsuramardinī: A Dynamic Myth of Goddess*. New Delhi: Gyan Publishing House.

Coburn, Thomas B. 1991. *Encountering the Goddess: A Translation of the Devī-Māhātmya and a Study of Its Interpretation*. Albany: State University of New York Press.

Kassebaum, Gayathri Rajapur. 1998. "Communal Self and Cultural Imagery: The Katha Performance Tradition in South India." In *Self as Image in Asian Theory and Practice*, edited by Roger T. Ames, Thomas P. Kasulis, and Wimal Dissanayake, 260–79. Albany: State University of New York Press.

Simmons, Caleb. 2014. "The Goddess on the Hill: The (Re)Invention of a Local Hill Goddess as Chamundeshvari." In *Inventing and Reinventing the Goddess: Contemporary Iterations of Hindu Deities on the Move*, edited by Sree Padma, 217–44. Lanham, MD: Lexington Books.

NOTES

Much of this translation was conducted in Mysuru while I was supported financially by the American Institute of Indian Studies and the generous donors of the Daniel H. H. Ingalls Memorial Fellowship. I owe a great debt of gratitude to them for this support. In addition, I would like to thank C. S. Poornima of Mysuru for her help with my translation.

1. In Purāṇic-style myths, deities (often Brahmā or Śiva) frequently grant wishes to devotees in compensation for their pious devotion and penance. In the classical tradition, "demons" too could propitiate gods and seek their boons. In many cases (e.g., Hiraṇyakaśipu) the demon wishes for immortality, but since this cannot be given,

demons instead seek very specific and limited conditions under which they can die. In the *Devī Bhāgavata Purāṇa*, Mahiṣāsura is given this boon by Brahmā; however, here, as in some versions of the *Rāmāyaṇa*, Śiva is the deity who grants the powers to Mahiṣāsura, who is regarded as a famous devotee of Śiva in the region.

2. Aisāsura is commonly regarded as the younger brother of Mahiṣāsura, although the songs themselves do not specify the nature of their relationship. His name may be a euphonic shortening of Mahiṣāsura and may thus suggest the conflation of their identities. This is most likely related to the popular etymology of Mysore (Kannada: Maisūru) as the city of the buffalo (*maisa* = *mahiṣa*) + *ūru* ("city").

3. "Guru" (and "Svāmi") in this context does not reference a specific teacher; instead, in southern Karnataka it is used as a respectful address, especially for male devotees of Śiva. In this case, it might also be a direct address to Śiva.

4. The term used here is Kṛṣṇa *paramātma* ("the supreme soul/self"). This might strike one as odd, since this song is a Śaiva devotional ballad, and Kṛṣṇa is an avatar (incarnation) of Viṣṇu. Nevertheless, it is common for popular songs and myths to appeal to multiple sectarian sensibilities.

5. Rukmaṇi (Sanskrit: Rukmiṇī) is the principal wife of Kṛṣṇa, and Sārada (Sanskrit: Śāradā) is another name of Sarasvatī, consort of the deity Brahmā.

6. Garuḍa is Viṣṇu's primary vehicle (*vāhana*). Nanda is Kṛṣṇa's foster father, who raised him in the village Gōkulam, which also happens to be an important neighborhood in Mysuru.

7. Māri is a common name for fearsome local goddesses in south India. These goddesses, who are often simply called Māriamman or "Mother Māri," are frequently associated with infectious diseases.

8. The ancient fire god Agni is often said to have seven tongues (flames); thus Uttanahaḷḷi's epithet Jvālāmukhi (fire-face/mouth) is subtly suggested here.

9. The term here is *kōṭi*, which literally means ten million (i.e., a "crore"). The connotation, however, is that the demons are innumerable.

10. The term used here is derived from the Kannada term for buffalo, *kōṇe*, and refers to Aisāsura and not Mahiṣāsura.

11. The Kapini (Kabini) and Kaveri are two important rivers of south India. Their confluence is in T. (Tirumakuḍalu) Narasipur in southern Karnataka.

12. The Woḍeyar dynasty has ruled Mysuru since at least the late sixteenth/early seventeenth century (tradition asserts that they established the kingdom in 1399 CE). Cāmarāja has been the most popular name in the lineage, including Cāmarāja Woḍeyar X (r. 1868–1894) and Jayacāmarājēndra (r. 1940–1956).

13. *Pūjā* is the primary form of worship in devotional Hinduism. This yearly descent of Cāmuṇḍi is a reference to the yearly celebration of the holiday Dasara, at the end of Navarātri. During this festival, the goddess is worshiped in the palace by the Mysuru kings. For more on this holiday, see Simmons (2018).

14. *Tambiṭṭu* is a rice dish that is created by combining rice and jaggery sugar and forming the mixture into a ball or mound; it is often offered to goddesses in southern Karnataka.

15. Nañjalagūḍi is another name for Nanjangud; Kailash is the Himalayan mountain in Tibet on which Śiva and Pārvatī are believed to live.

16. The name Nañjuṇḍēśvara is a reference to the Hindu myth of Śiva swallowing the poison that emerged along with the nectar of immortality (*amṛta*) during the churning of the cosmic ocean of milk.

17. On the relationship between the original *Skanda Purāṇa*'s myth cycle relating to the Goddess and that of the *Devī Māhātmya*, see Yokochi (2004, 20–23).

18. Other versions say he rose to power by consuming the gods' portion of the sacrificial offerings.

19. Some texts add that Mahiṣa was granted *mokṣa* (liberation) by the goddess before she decapitated him.

20. On the northern side of the hill near the colossal image of Nandi, there is an area known as "buffalo point/stone" (Kannada: *koṇana mūle*) that is believed to bear the marks of the mythic battle. Indeed, there are indentations in the stone that resemble gigantic foot, paw, and hoof prints. On one visit to the site I was accompanied by temple workers, who were able to retell the details of the battle, retracing the tracks of the goddess, her lion, and the buffalo. I have also been told many times in informal conversations with devotees that the hill formations themselves are the remains of the giant buffalo carcass.

21. Rao (1946, 98n73).

22. Rajasekhara (1972, xi–xii).

23. Akki (2012). There is some controversy over this play because it seems to have been based on a radio drama written by P. K. Rajasekhara several years earlier.

FIGURE 5. Kauśikī, by Laura Santi

CHAPTER 3

Kauśikī

The Virgin Demon Slayer

JUDIT TÖRZSÖK

The following tale comes from the mountainous region of Kashmir in the far north of the subcontinent. Famous for its alpine meadows, fragrant pine forests, idyllic waters, and snowcapped Himalayan peaks, it is now more often in the news as a site of political tension between Pakistan, India, and China, each of whom claim as their own part, or all, of this strategically located Shangri-la. In the past, Kashmir was also famous for its erudite intellectual and religious luminaries. The present story is translated from a collection of stories rewritten in Sanskrit by the thirteenth-century Kashmiri scholar Jayadratha.

Jayadratha called his collection of myths *The Magic Jewel of Śiva's Deeds* (*Haracaritacintāmaṇi*), and indeed most of them focus on Śiva rather than the Goddess. The selected tale is an exception, but the nondualist theological verses that introduce and conclude it pose the goddess as inseparable from Śiva. "Nondualist" refers to a philosophical position, popular in early medieval Śaiva intellectual circles, that rejects dualism; that is to say, it rejects the idea that the creator is inherently separate from the created world, or that the various deities are separate from the supreme godhead. Here the goddess Kauśikī-Durgā is presented as the embodiment of Śiva's divine energy, or *śakti*. In this respect, while the story conforms to the classical idea—prevalent after the eighth century CE—of a singular Great Goddess slaying troublesome demons, it also includes variations on this theme that make it unique.

Readers who happen to be familiar with the popular tale of Durgā in the *Devī Māhātmya* should compare and contrast it with the current story, then compare notes with the translator's own list in the essay that follows. One notable difference, for example, is that the story here presents Kauśikī as a young girl rather than a grown woman. All readers should analyze the way the story poses the goddess's youth, femininity, and power in comparison to the demons' brute strength and objectifying sexuality. It would also be fruitful to analyze how the portrayals of relational alliances in the previous chapters contrast with Kauśikī's relative independence in the present story.

॥ हरचरितचिन्तामणिः २३ ॥

ॐ नमः श्रीपरारूपिण्यै मृत्युजिच्छक्तये ।

आद्या मूर्तिरसावनुद्गतरजःशक्तेस्तव त्र्यम्बक
त्रैलोक्यैकजनन्यबाह्यविषयासङ्गा च दुर्गेति या ।
संहारेण तमोमयैकवपुषा विश्वोद्भवोद्भासिनी
सासौ पञ्चमुखोर्ध्वकल्पितगतिः स्वैरं समुज्जृम्भताम् ॥

यतस्ततो देहवतां भयमुत्पद्यते महत् ।
एका माहेश्वरी शक्तिस्तन्निवारणकोविदा ॥

कदाचिदसुरैः क्रूरैर्बाध्यमाना दिवौकसः । वैकुण्ठं शरणं जग्मुः समं कम-
लयोनिना ॥ दानवोत्पादनं श्रुत्वा तेभ्यस्त्रैलोक्यकम्पनम् । बभाषे पुण्ड-
रीकाक्षो गम्भीरमधुरां गिरम् ॥ निसुम्भसुम्भमहिषप्रमुखान्दानवेश्वरान् ।
जानीहि सर्वैरस्माभिरजेयान्ब्रह्मणो वरात् ॥ तथा हि वरमेतेभ्यो व्यतर-
त्तपसा विधिः । अष्टवर्षा कुमार्येव निहन्त्री नापरास्त्विवति ॥ तदृशी का
कुमारी स्यादिति ते बाहुशालिनः । लुण्ठयन्तस्त्रिभुवनं गणयन्ति न कंचन
॥ इदानीमस्त्युपायो ऽत्र दानवानां क्षयावहः । तमाकलय्य सर्वे ऽपि कुरु-
ध्वं समयोचितम् ॥ गौरीप्राङ्कोशतः कन्या कौशिकीत्युदिता पुरा । अष्टव-
र्षा प्रदीप्तास्त्रा शक्ता सैवात्र कर्मणि ॥ सा गौरीवचसा विन्ध्यशैलस्थित्य-
भिलाषिणी । चचाल सिंहवहना तदानीं तुहिनाचलात् ॥ अस्मिन्नेव क्षणे
विन्ध्यो वर्धमानो यथायथम् । अशेषमरुणद्व्योम निशातैः शृङ्गवेष्टितैः ॥ सू-
र्यचन्द्रगतिं रुद्ध्वा कालस्य कलनां हरन् । गतागतानि भवतामपि विन्ध्यो
न्यवारयत् ॥ विषण्णेषु समस्तेषु ततो विन्ध्याद्रिचापलात् । आजगाम म-
हादेवी दुर्गा सिंहोर्ध्ववर्तिनी ॥ तामागतां शुभाकारां पश्यता विन्ध्यभूभृता
। तदा विग्रह आत्मीयो जङ्गमः प्रकटीकृतः ॥ तस्याः कान्तिं तदा दृष्ट्वा
स तदा काममोहितः । जगाद मधुरां वाणीं पिकलोकानुवादिनीम् ॥ अहं
सुन्दरि सर्वेषां भूभृतामुपरि स्थितः । तन्मयैव समं तिष्ठ नान्यत्कर्तव्यम-
स्ति मे ॥ इति तस्य वचः श्रुत्वा दुर्गा कोपमुपागता । दृक्पाताद्दीर्घमाकारं
ह्रस्वीचक्रे महागिरेः ॥ ह्रस्वयित्वा गिरिं देवी गगनाङ्गनरोधिनम् । प्राव-
र्तयत सर्वेषां गतागतमयीः क्रियाः ॥ तस्यैव च गिरेर्मूर्ध्नि कौशिकी व्यधित
स्थितिम् । नन्दास्रुबिन्दुनोत्पाद्य पावनीं नन्दिनीं नदीम् ॥ सा नर्मदा नदी

FIGURE 6. *Haracaritacintāmaṇi,* a Sanskrit work in the Devanagari script. Font "Free Serif" © gnu.org.

HOW KAUŚIKĪ CONQUERED SUMBHA AND THE OTHER DEMONS

Oṃ Homage to the Power of the Conqueror of Death, Who Has the Form of Parā.[1]

She is the original manifestation of your Power, whose activity is yet dormant, O lord of the three mothers. She is called Durgā, the unique Mother of the three worlds, who has no attachment to external objects.[2] She illuminates the source of the universe with her unique body made of the Dark principle when she reabsorbs the world in herself. May she manifest herself, of her own accord, she who made her way above five-faced Śiva.[3]

Only the Power (Śakti) of the Great Lord is able to hinder those who produce great fear in living beings.

Once upon a time, when the cruel demons tormented the gods in heaven, including lotus-born Brahmā himself, the gods sought refuge in Viṣṇu's paradise. Lotus-eyed Viṣṇu, after hearing about the birth of the demons and how they had made the three worlds tremble, spoke to them with sweet and wise words: "You must know that those powerful demons led by Nisumbha, Sumbha, and Buffalo (*mahiṣa*) cannot be conquered by any of us, due to a boon they have obtained from Brahmā. In fact, the boon Brahmā gave them for their asceticism was that they could only be killed by an eight-year-old girl and none else. 'How could such a girl ever exist?' the powerful demons said to themselves and kept plundering the world, without respecting anyone. Now there is a way to destroy the demons. You should all understand that and do what the situation requires.

"A girl named Kauśikī was born some time ago from Gaurī's previous skin.[4] She is eight years old and has shining weapons. She would be able to perform this task. Since she wanted to take up residence on the Vindhya Mountain, following Gaurī's command, she left the snow-covered Himalaya, riding her lions. At that moment, the Vindhya was still growing, as it used to do, and blocked the whole sky covering it with sharp peaks. The Vindhya stopped the course of the Sun and the Moon, thus taking away the course of time, and prevented even you, the gods, from coming and going. When everything was thus disturbed because of the Vindhya's whim, the great goddess Durgā arrived on the back of her lions. As the Vindhya Mountain saw this beautiful girl arrive, his unstable nature became manifest. Seeing her beauty, he was so love-struck that he started cooing with a sweet sound like a dove: 'My darling,

I am above all other mountains, stay with me, that is all I need.' Hearing these words, Durgā became angry and with her mere glance, she made the great mountain short. As the goddess shortened the mountain that had blocked the sky, she made it possible for everyone to come and go at ease.

"At the top of that mountain Kauśikī took up residence, and with her tears of joy, she created a sacred and delightful river. That river, the Narmada, purifies several regions and those who drink its water will get the benefits of a *rājasūya* sacrifice.[5] There, a *yakṣa* king called Pāñcāla came to be appointed as Durgā's servant: he is strong and no demon can match his courage.[6] It is this strong eight-year old girl called Durgā who shall kill the demons headed by Nisumbha. Now here is sage Nārada, who can be very convincing. He is able to bring together the goddess and the demons."

After saying this, lotus-eyed Viṣṇu dispatched sage Nārada, who, wishing to help the gods, thus left to meet the demons. In the meantime, the demons, who were much more powerful than the king of the gods, arrived at the Mandara Mountain, with the intention to amuse themselves there.[7] They saw the great sage Nārada there, with reddish dreadlocks piled up on the top of his head, with a lute in his hand, wearing yellow clothes. Seeing him, the demons spoke: "Where are you going, sage? Tell us where Indra and the other gods are and what they are doing now!" Hearing their question, the sage seized the occasion and started speaking with a smile on his face, arousing their curiosity: "I appreciate the company of learned Brahmins, so I am always on the way to hermitages of great ascetics and to ashrams of perfected sages. When I arrived today at the peaks of the Vindhya, I saw the gods in a state of great excitement so I respectfully questioned them.[8] They said the following: 'On the Vindhya Mountain there is a girl who attracts the three worlds; she is organizing a marriage contest, that is why we have come here.'[9] Hearing their story, I said: 'There are so many divine nymphs. What is so special about that girl?' The gods headed by Viṣṇu and Indra all laughed at me and said: 'This beautiful girl is different from the nymphs and goddesses such as Rambhā, Rati, Śacī, or Lakṣmī.[10] Otherwise, who would come and strive for her? If we were to choose between, on the one hand, the sovereignty of the world, jewels, and the nectar of immortality, and on the other, only this girl, we would not hesitate. What are our lives worth if she is not ours, what is our wealth worth if she is not our beloved? A mortal who thinks only of her has already a fruitful existence. All the magic jewels in the world, all the wish-fulfilling trees, and anything that exists in the world—all that is worth just a straw. That girl alone surpasses all wealth. Without getting her, nobody can obtain happiness.' After the gods explained this to me, I left them and arrived here. And you yourselves? Tell me where you are really headed for."

After these words of the sage, the demons started speaking. "We are off to mount Meru to plunder it, to take its jewels by force." To this, the eminent sage replied again: "Are you only interested in appropriating the jewels of Meru? As you know, a woman is the most supreme of all jewels, and the one who is on the Vindhya Mountain is desired by everybody. Go to mount Meru, I do not care.[11] You can always maintain that jewels are only made of stone, if you like, you clever people." When the divine sage spoke in this way, the demons retorted: "We do want to obtain the most precious jewel in the world." After making sure to have aroused the demons' desire with his speech, Nārada left, with his duty accomplished, to the delight of the gods.

As the sage left, Sumbha, Nisumbha, Buffalo, and the other demons gave up on going to Meru and headed toward the Vindhya Mountain. When the powerful demons reached the Vindhya, they spoke to the demon Hārava, after observing each other: "A girl, even if she is charming, is not taken by virtuous people directly. A messenger should be sent to her, to inquire about her situation. She is a solitary young girl, very tender by nature. Seeing ferocious demons, she may be scared to death. There is this demon called Barbarian. He is wise and speaks with a smile, let us send him there. She shall be relieved by his gentle words and shall surely come over to us." Hārava agreed, and they all dispatched the demon called Barbarian, after explaining to him his task. Barbarian obeyed, and as he was climbing up, at only three-fourths of the Vindhya Mountain, he caught sight of her guardian Pāñcāla.

Pāñcāla had five reddish-brown knots of hair. Painted with mineral paints, he was wearing ornaments made from whatever is found in a forest and held a stick in his hand. His arms were strong and he had a prominent chin. His loincloth was black and he was covered with a lion hide. As he saw Barbarian arrive, he loudly called out: "Who are you? Why have you come here? Tell me where you are from. If you do not introduce yourself, you will not be able to go further." Hearing these words, Barbarian replied: "You tell me who you are and why you are here!"

Then Pāñcāla spoke, smiling, with a menacing frown: "If you still do not know who I am, then listen. I am the Lord of all the dangerous paths in the mountains, of all the forest regions and jungles. Nobody can match my strength anywhere in the three worlds. My name is Pāñcāla, I am the overlord of millions of *yakṣas*. There is a girl called Kauśikī living in a cave on this mountain. She has made me her servant herself, since she is very powerful."

Hearing these words of Pāñcāla, Barbarian was rather irritated and told his own story from beginning to end. Learning about the demons' intention to possess the goddess, Pāñcāla spoke, with his red hair in flames: "Who can obstruct the light of the sky? Who can block the wind? What fool could possibly desire to marry Durgā, the mother of the three worlds?[12] To put a long story short: you shall not see Kauśikī unless you beat me. For I am her servant and able to win against your kind."

After saying this, he launched his club against Barbarian's head, but Barbarian started beating him with his fist. As the terrible fight was progressing with the use of various weapons, Barbarian emitted a host of ogres from his body. Pāñcāla, invoking the goddess in his mind, took a chain and a missile, and with the chain he bound up the night-stalking ogres led by Barbarian. Then he started thinking for a second, with a rational overview of the situation: "These good-for-nothing fellows are bound and cannot do anything now. I know that if I kill them, that will be an inappropriate act, for messengers are not to be killed because of their function. So if I murder them, the goddess Kauśikī will be furious and how can I appease her then? I am her servant and the goddess commands me, I cannot just do whatever I want. I shall simply take these bound ogres and show them to her." Reflecting in this way, Pāñcāla took them and went to Durgā's home, where he showed them to her.[13]

Then the goddess asked Barbarian to tell her the whole story. Barbarian, whose mind was completely deluded and whose body was tightly bound, started speaking: "The lord of demons, who has conquered all the gods, demons, and humans and is now the ruler of the universe, has decided to choose you as his wife, O beautiful goddess. With due respect, a girl must be given in marriage. And where could one find a husband like him? So consider yourself honored to be his wife, that is what I suggest." When she heard him speak in this way, the charming goddess smiled gently, and, with a brow slightly raised, spoke these sweet words: "Indeed, a woman must have a husband and a man must have a loving wife. Which woman would not desire such a handsome man, who is also the richest in the world? All righteous men know, however, that only a father can give a girl in marriage. She may also organize a marriage contest for herself, or alternatively, she can be taken by force.[14] I do not know who my father was, so who else could give me in marriage? And I have no notion of what is appropriate, so I cannot hold a marriage contest.

Now what else can I say? The lord of demons is powerful, if he takes a wife for himself by force, what else could be more appropriate? You should go and tell him about this, Barbarian. I command you, Pāñcāla, to release all the ogres from the chains."

After these words of the goddess, Pāñcāla released them. Seeing them without the chains, Kauśikī spoke again. "These ogres who have been produced from Barbarian's body are my followers called 'the barbarians'; they are without the sins of greed and egotism. By looking at me, they have become valiant, these barbarians shall only think of me. Even those mortals who are born in their lineage shall obtain the highest good, since they will also be purified by their devotion to me." When Durgā spoke in this way, all the ogres produced from Barbarian's body started worshiping the Mother of the Three Worlds, with great devotion.

In the meantime, Barbarian, released by the great goddess, quickly went to see the demons who wished to possess her and said to them: "I have seen that young and beautiful girl. Indeed, there is nothing comparable to her in the other worlds. She is the Mother of the whole universe and shines forth with energy. Her servant, Pāñcāla, is the powerful king of the *yakṣas*." After this speech, Barbarian explained what the goddess had told him, and the demons became totally blinded as they were heading toward their fate. "We shall all go there," they said in their lust and climbed up the Vindhya Mountain by the pathways going upward. As their feet were stomping everywhere, the Vindhya was trembling like a tree hit by the storm. The gods headed by Indra honored Viṣṇu and went to the peak of the Vindhya, eager to see the fight.

The goddess, after checking what the demons did through meditation, followed Pāñcāla, and left riding her two terrifying lions. She had delicate golden ornaments and was adorned with earrings made of precious stones. She shone forth in her beauty on top of the peak of the Vindhya. The demons, looking at the Mother of the universe, all had to squint their eyes at the sight of her radiance and felt discouraged in their hearts. Among them, Sumbha was standing somewhat in front and spoke to the goddess, smiling under the spell of his own delusion: "What is the use of this meaningless fight, O pretty lady. I have conquered even great Indra himself, so do what I wish."

Hearing these teasing words of that villain, Durgā, the Mother of the Three Worlds, started speaking, while her earrings were trembling. "The virtuous do not voice their wish again and again, do they? Please think of the matter at hand." Having said this, the goddess hit Sumbha on the head with a flaming trident while he was sending terrible arrows toward her. Pierced by the goddess's trident, he fell on the ground, but he stood up again in a second, propelled by his pride and grinning widely. The goddess's luminous trident went back to her hand.[15] Sumbha then released his heavy club, more powerful than a thunderbolt. As that club of the demon merely touched her necklace, it crumbled to pieces, although her chest was tender. The goddess then threw a heavy disc at Sumbha's chest, and he fell unconscious. Seeing Sumbha in pain, Nisumbha, Buffalo, and the others attacked the goddess with various hard weapons. Dundubhi tore out a mountain several miles wide, with its countless huge trees, and threw it against the goddess's chest. As it was approaching her, terrifying as it was with its numerous mountain caves, the goddess hit it with her thunderbolt and it fell to the ground.

Then the Buffalo demon came forth with his dangling tail, shaking his neck, eager to devour her. With the tip of his horn, he slashed the stomachs of the goddess's two lions that were carrying her, and then attacked Pāñcāla, while emitting a harsh grunt. The goddess, observing that he was difficult to conquer, took her bow and covered all the other demons with arrows. But Buffalo devoured the goddess's arrows easily as if they were thousands of straws and made a terrible and frightening grunt again.

"The bow is useless," said the goddess to herself and broke off the great demon's horn with her powerful club. As his horn fell, even the Vindhya Mountain shook and the directions were filled with streams of flowing blood. Although his horn was chopped off, the Buffalo demon hurt the goddess's lions with his kicks and started hitting the goddess with his teeth.[16] Seeing this commotion, Kauśikī, as if she were tired of it, smashed Buffalo's terrible teeth by hitting it with her club. Even after losing his teeth, powerful Buffalo wrapped the lions around with his tail furiously. As Kauśikī was upset to see her lion vehicles in distress, the other demons started attacking her with harsh weapons all over. Then the goddess created the goddesses Brāhmī and the others, eight deities carrying various weapons who stood in front of the demons.

Beholding Brāhmī and the other goddesses who seemed to be shining forth with their inner power, the demon lords started laughing out loud: "You are a young girl, frightened to be alone, so give up the fight. For what else did you bring Brāhmī and the others along if not to keep you company?"

Hearing these words, the Supreme Goddess looked slightly shy and made the goddesses return to her own body. Then she began to fight as if she was celebrating a festival, all alone. All the courageous demons were confused.

Dundubhi took his terrible iron club and hit the goddess on the head, since he was much deluded by his strength and pride. The goddess became furious and pulled him by the hair with her hand, killing him with merely a kick. As all the gods saw Dundubhi die, they sounded their kettle drums and created a rain of flowers out of joy.

Angered by this, Buffalo, who was much conceited, hit the goddess on the thigh with his strong horn. The goddess, distressed, took her sword suddenly and cut the evil Buffalo's pointed horn. That strong demon, thus made hornless, started kicking her, so Kauśikī cut his feet too with the same sword. Having lost his feet, he wrapped the goddess's chariot with his tail and started squeezing her, suddenly laughing out harshly.[17] The Supreme Goddess then crushed Buffalo with her foot and pierced his neck with her trident. Seeing Buffalo dead, and the demons having fled, Sumbha and Nisumbha then faced the goddess themselves. Kauśikī observed the two villains who were ready to wrestle, and she pierced them with the tips of her nails, which were needle sharp.[18]

When the goddess thus killed the demons in the front line, all the gods became confident, seeing the destruction of their enemies. Viṣṇu, himself observing this miraculous heroic deed accomplished by the goddess, spoke to all the gods in the sky: "The demons, who had conquered us and dominated the universe without fear, came here to fulfill their desire and have now been killed by the goddess. O goddess Durgā, you are above all, for thanks to your power, even these enemies of the gods have been annihilated. So please come here, all of you, to honor this great goddess who took away our fear. It is now we who come to you in the Vindhya Mountain."

After Viṣṇu spoke thus, all of them went to see Durgā with offerings, scattering flowers for her from their cupped hands. As they saw the goddess who had killed the demons, shining forth with her energy, Viṣṇu and the other gods gave her the offerings and began praising her: "You alone are the Mother of the Universe! You alone are the supreme way! You alone are Pārvatī's splendor! You alone are the power of the Great Lord Śiva's will! The whole world, with moving and non-moving creatures, has been born from you alone and it is in you alone that they shall all be dissolved; please take pity on us. You are our savior, O great goddess Durgā. You manifest yourself as both the subject and object of speech."[19]

Lauded in this way by Viṣṇu and the other gods, the glorious goddess was contented and said the following sweet words, which took away all fear: "You have no source of fear now, and you know my power, so please do as I say, fulfilling my wish. Go home, each of you to your own paradise and stay there without fear for a long time. I shall certainly act for your benefit again and again. I have killed these demons; only Kujambha remains alive. My son, Nandin, shall kill that demon." Hearing these words of the goddess, Viṣṇu, Indra, and the other gods all bowed down happily, again and again, and went to their respective places.

> The female power of the Supreme Lord removes the pain of all. She performs all good acts—some lucky people who know this for certain shall see her true form here or there in this world.

THE GODDESS IN CONTEXT: KAUŚIKĪ IN KASHMIR

In classical India, the "Great Goddess" Mahādevī represents the emergence of the concept of an essential feminine divinity who underlies the incredible diversity of the Indian feminine pantheon. She gained prominence especially under the names Durgā and Kauśikī, worshiped in all the different regions of India and beyond. She is known everywhere as a warrior goddess, and in particular as the demon killer who annihilated two demon brothers, Sumbha and Nisumbha, as well as Mahiṣa, a demon in the form of a buffalo.

Unlike the more popular accounts that portray the Great Goddess as the united energy of all the gods, she here represents Śiva's energy (*śakti*), as her story is embedded in a work on Śaiva mythology. This Śaiva partiality is rather unsurprising in Kashmir, well known for its Śaiva Tantric traditions and the importance of its nondual Śaiva philosophy from at least the ninth century.[20] The story of Kauśikī conquering the demons is presented as an illustration of Śiva's power here, which is seen as inseparable from Śiva himself.

Moreover, according to the Kashmirian nondualist theological tradition, the phenomenal world is created by Śiva's power of will, knowledge, and action. It is not fashioned from a material separate from Śiva himself and not a mere illusion either, but it shows us the infinite freedom of the God, who is thus embodied in his own creation. Consequently, each mythological story in the collection illustrates an aspect of Śiva's power, and those who recognize this power as being the ultimate agent in this world can hope to attain final liberation, that is, complete unity with Śiva. Reading or hearing a story thus has an important theological implication, made explicit at the beginning and the end of each myth.

Seed: The Rise of the Warrior Goddess

The idea of a singular supreme warrior goddess first appears in epic and Purāṇic literature in the fourth to sixth centuries CE.[21] Her most important cult text, however, is the eighth-century CE *Devī Māhātmya*, where her most renowned stories are told.[22] Although buffalo-killing goddesses are depicted already in the Kuṣāṇa period of the first centuries CE, these predate the idea of a singular "Great Goddess" famous for her feat of slaying the buffalo demon.

Because of the pan-Indian influence of the *Devī Māhātmya* on texts and visual art, scholars have often accepted the claim that Durgā originated as a transregional deity, not associated with any locality in particular. This is contradicted by in-depth studies such as those by Yuko Yokochi, which show that the earliest sources refer to the warrior goddess Kauśikī as inhabiting the Vindhya Mountain of central India.[23] Her figure is then absorbed into the Great Goddess in the *Devī Māhātmya*, which indeed attempts to establish this warrior goddess as not just transregional but also the ultimate identity of all (regional/minor) goddesses.[24]

The development of Durgā's mythology and iconography from the early centuries to the eighth century CE suggests that Durgā and goddesses associated with her gradually lost their regional character to take up their place in a standardized medieval pantheon throughout India and beyond.[25] While a tendency toward standardization is undeniable, leaving it at that would be an oversimplification. The story of the warrior goddess and her iconography continue to change and take up new regional forms in literature as well as in art. The text translated here is only one among several sources to show that this and other allegedly pan-Indian goddesses have their local identities, and that indeed, perhaps no pan-Indian goddess exists as such, for each region provides its own myth and gives a new identity to what appears to be the same goddess.

Flower: Kauśikī's Story in The Magic Jewel of Śiva's Deeds

The author of the story translated here, Jayadratha, was active in Kashmir in the thirteenth century CE. The story comes from his work on the mythology of Śiva, *The Magic Jewel of Śiva's Deeds* (*Haracaritacintāmaṇi*). He is sometimes also said to be the author of two other works—both on poetic theory—and scholars usually regard him as the younger brother of Jayaratha, commentator on Abhinavagupta's *Tantrāloka* (Light on the Tantras).[26]

Both brothers were certainly devout followers of Śiva. Two aspects of *The Magic Jewel of Śiva's Deeds* are notable here. One is that it relates a number of local Kashmirian myths or local inflections of myths known in other, more widespread, versions. It is therefore an important source for the history of Hindu mythology as well as for Kashmirian cultural history. The other is that it introduces each myth with a particular verse of invocation that frames the narrative as illustrating concepts in Kashmirian nondual Śaivism. With these introductory verses, each story receives a sophisticated, theological interpretation, which shows the reader how that particular myth may be conducive to final liberation.

Some of the myths in the collection are not about Śiva himself but relate stories of deities associated with him or his retinue. Most goddess cults were integrated into the cult of Śiva to some degree; therefore it is not surprising to find goddess mythology in a work dedicated to Śiva.[27] The story of Durgā in particular is associated with Śiva's mythology in at least three ways. First, she is said to have been produced from the body of Śiva's wife, Pārvatī, when she discarded her dark skin to become the Fair One, Gaurī. Durgā thus represents Pārvatī's dark aspect and is also called Kauśikī, the "One Who Comes from the Sheath."[28] Second, she absorbs in her mythology the figure of the goddess Tilottamā, created by Brahmā to delude and destroy two demon brothers, Sunda and Upasunda. This beautiful goddess is admired by Śiva himself, according to the *Mahābhārata*.[29] Finally, and most importantly, the goddess in Jayadratha's story represents Śiva's power manifested as a female entity (Śakti); therefore, as the invocatory verses stress, her conquest of the demons is ultimately understood here as a manifestation of Śiva's triumph over them.

As the origin of these myths shows, some elements of Durgā's mythology go back as far as the epic. However, it is in the *Skanda Purāṇa* (end of sixth to beginning of seventh centuries CE) that the myth of the warrior goddess develops into a full-fledged form for the first time. Later, the most well-known text about Durgā, the *Devī Māhātmya*, further establishes her cult as the supreme goddess.

Given the importance of the *Skanda Purāṇa* and the *Devī Māhātmya* in the development of Durgā's mythology, it may be useful to point out a few major differences between these versions of the story and Jayadratha's narrative. Since Jayadratha's story differs from these versions in numerous details, only a few are mentioned below, without analyzing them. It would be the task of further research to analyze and understand the role of these differences, which should then also include a comparison of other mythological elements in Kashmirian and non-Kashmirian Śaivism.

1. Unlike in other versions, Śiva does not appear at all in Jayadratha's story, which is rather surprising in a collection of Śaiva myths. This may be because the gods do not have a respectable role here; they are completely helpless against the demons. For this reason, Viṣṇu directs them to Durgā, who, as mentioned in the end, is Śiva's power of Will (*icchā*).
2. Jayadratha's story makes the point several times that Durgā is an eight-year-old girl (*aṣṭavarṣā kumārī*), a detail unknown elsewhere.
3. This myth commonly involves the demon brothers Sumbha and Nisumbha, but the killing of the buffalo demon, Mahiṣa, usually forms a separate myth.[30] In Jayadratha's version, Mahiṣa is only one of several demons conquered in the army (next to Dundubhi, etc.); his killing appears much less emblematic than in the other narratives and in the iconography.
4. Here, the shortening of the Vindhya Mountain is attributed to Durgā rather than to Agastya, which would be the case in most etiological myths about the Vindhya. The Vindhya Mountain, in addition to being conceited, is also depicted as lustful. It is a rather intriguing aspect of the story. Was Agastya less popular in Kashmir? Or is there another reason why Durgā takes his role here?
5. Durgā's *yakṣa* servant, Pāñcāla (whose name itself is puzzling), is generally absent in other narratives except for a brief mention in the *Matsya Purāṇa*.[31] He looks quite tribal with his dreadlocks, body paint, and forest ornaments. He also calls himself the king of mountain paths and forests.
6. Another figure completely absent elsewhere is Barbarian (*barbara*), the messenger of the demons. A similar figure is found, nevertheless, in the *Devī Māhātmya,* called Raktabīja or "Blood-seed" for his supernatural power of regenerating a copy of himself from each drop of blood that touches the ground.[32] Barbarian is, however, very different from Raktabīja, for the *rākṣasa* ogres born from his body eventually become Durgā worshipers, thus associating Durgā worship with the non-*āryas*, as is the case already in the epic.
7. While Durgā's myth in the *Devī Māhātmya* contains a reference to her being made of the united energy (*tejas*) of all the gods (at least when she

kills Mahiṣa, the buffalo demon), it is not the case here. The gods, as previously pointed out, have a rather unrewarding role here. There is also no reference to Durgā's weapons as being given to her by the various gods, the disc by Viṣṇu, and so forth.

8. Just as Jayadratha's Durgā does not depend on the gods, she does not need helpers in the form of the mother goddesses, Brāhmī and the others. These are the same mother goddesses as those in chapters 4 and 8. As the *Devī Māhātmya* tells it, seven gods see Durgā surrounded by the demons and create female manifestations of their energy to help her, in the form of the seven mother goddesses Brāhmī (Brahmā's energy), and so forth. These mothers are reabsorbed into Durgā's body after the battle. The *Skanda Purāṇa* (64.18ff.), which does not speak of seven but of innumerable mothers (many with animal and bird faces), describes them as emerging from Kauśikī's body, who later distributes them in various countries and cities.[33] In *The Magic Jewel of Śiva's Deeds*, too, the goddess herself creates the mothers, who are not seven as in the *Devī Māhātmya*, but eight as is common in, for example, Tantric sources. However, instead of helping her, they are immediately reabsorbed into her body when she is mocked by a demon, who says that Durgā has created them to keep her company because she feels lonely. Thus, while the mothers are not omitted from the story, they do not represent the energy of the gods, and they also lose their original function. This is yet another element whose interpretation is not straightforward.

While the interpretation of the differences in the narrative is a complex task, the introductory passage, although it is rich in theological allusions, is easier to contextualize. Its main function is to stress that the Goddess in the story is the manifestation of Śiva's power; in other words, the Goddess ultimately represents Śiva himself. In this way, the introductory passage explains why a goddess story figures in the collection, while it also alludes to Tantric forms of Śiva's power, such as the goddesses Parā and Kālī, and establishes a theological interpretation of the story: only Śiva's power can save us from pain and distress.

The first invocation (which appears only in the Kāvyamālā edition) pays homage to the female power (*śakti*) of Śiva, Śiva being called here the Conqueror of Death. She is said to have the form of Parā, "the Supreme Goddess," who is one of the three main mantra goddesses of the Tantric current called the Trika. She is the only benign one of the three main goddesses and is said to conquer death herself through visualizations in which she pours the nectar of immortality into the practitioner's body. Her invocation here suggests the identification of Durgā with her, given that they are both considered to be Śiva's power (*śakti*), and this benign form is invoked perhaps to appease the violent forces of Durgā. Similarly, Parā is often invoked in connection with Tantric rituals involving some form of violence, to calm the violent forces that have been activated.[34]

The second invocation in the form of a verse refers to Durgā more directly. She is called the mother of the universe, an epithet that recurs several times in the narrative. Her body is said to be made of the Dark principle, which may have a double or triple meaning here: (1) her body is the source of creation; (2) she is born from Pārvatī's dark skin; or (3) she is identical with the black goddess Kālī, who devours and destroys the universe. The last line of the verse may refer to Śakti's position above the five-faced form of Śiva. The five-faced form may stand here for Sadāśiva, the supreme deity of the nonesoteric Śaivism of the Siddhānta school, who is also said to have produced other theological and philosophical schools of thought from his various faces.[35] The Goddess being above him may allude to the superiority of Tantric goddess cults over the Siddhānta and other schools.[36] It may also be understood to show that Sadāśiva is already a product of the act of creation; it is a manifested form, which is superseded by Śiva's Will to Create (Śakti in the form of *icchāśakti*) as well as by his transcendental, undifferentiated form (Śiva).

It is also notable that the verse is addressed to Śiva himself, who is called the Lord of the Three Mothers (Tryambaka). Although this vocative of Śiva goes back to Vedic epithets of Rudra, here it may again allude to Śiva being associated with the triad of Tantric goddesses of the Trika school.

The third introductory verse emphasizes again that the Goddess is a manifestation of Śiva's power. This verse is the only one to refer to the story itself to be told: it is only Śiva's female power, that is, the Goddess, who is able to destroy the demons. This is also what the closing verse reiterates, also mentioning that some lucky devotees may get a vision of the Goddess even in this world—in other words, even before reaching final release.

Fruit: Theology and the Kumārī Cult

The theological framing of the story is obviously an important means of adapting this myth to a Kashmirian context. The adaptation is nevertheless not only a local one. This and other stories of the *Magic Jewel* are adaptations of Purāṇic mythology into a more sophisticated literary form. Although Jayadratha's work does not belong to the most elaborate types of ornate Sanskrit poetry, its style and language are certainly more sophisticated than what is common in the Purāṇas, which targeted a relatively less educated audience. The stylistic upgrading and the theological interpretations both seem to serve the same purpose here: that of seducing a more educated, elite public.

This upgrading of the Kauśikī story also shows that the direction of adaptation is not necessarily from local/popular/vernacular to transregional/Brahminical/Sanskrit or vice versa, for here we have an adaptation of a widespread transregional myth to a local but sophisticated and Sanskritic context.

One striking element of Jayadratha's version is that Kauśikī is an eight-year-old girl. While the goddess is said to be a virgin from the earliest accounts, she is normally regarded and depicted in art as a young woman.[37] The idea that a child can incarnate a deity is certainly not new, for early Tantric texts such as the *Niśvāsatattvasaṃhitā* mention that children (*kumāra, kumārī*) can serve as oracles when possessed by a god, and that such a possession can be provoked by certain Tantric rites. Early Śaiva and Śākta Tantric texts also describe girls (*kanyā*) as female forces acting at certain levels of the universe, and some categories of goddesses are also called "girls" (in the Kubjikā tradition, for instance). Nevertheless, no account of the so-called *kumārī* worship—worship of a prepubescent girl as a goddess, such as that practiced in the Kathmandu Valley even today—seems to be available from an early period.

The divinization of prepubescent children is generally explained in the same way, namely that due to their purity, the divine can incarnate in them easily and appropriately. This explanation is given in varying ritual contexts, for the Kumārīs in the Kathmandu Valley as well as for the male child actors who play the main roles in the Rāmlīlā performances of northern India. Such an explanation may also underlie the Kashmirian Kauśikī story, although nothing of the sort is stated explicitly.

Whatever the case is, it is said in the beginning of the story that according to Brahmā's gift/curse, only an eight-year-old girl can end the rule of the demons. It is important to remark that only the demons lust after this girl, not the gods. Although Nārada speaks of the gods as desiring her too, this seems to be a made-up story he tells the demons to arouse their curiosity. The Vindhya Mountain, also attracted by her, is duly punished by the goddess herself at the very beginning of the story. As the goddess's servant Pāñcāla explains, nobody should lust after the Mother of the Three Worlds, and as the myth demonstrates, those who do so are severely punished.

While Jayadratha does not reveal any ritual aspect of the cult of this goddess in thirteenth-century Kashmir, one is tempted to speculate and see in the eight-year-old Kauśikī a prefiguration, or perhaps a mythological transposition, of the Kumārī cult, known from later sources in various regions of the north, east, and south of the Indian subcontinent.

SOURCE

The basis of the translation is chapter 23 of Jayadratha's *The Magic Jewel of Śiva's Deeds* (*Haracaritacintāmaṇi*). A Sanskrit edition of the work was published by M. P. Shivadatta and K. P. Parab in 1897, as number 61 in the *Kāvyamālā* series, and it has never before been translated into a European language. It has also received little attention from scholars, with the exception of Shibazaki's (2007) study of another story in the collection, cited in the notes. As Shibazaki notes, nine manuscripts are known to exist, and variant readings from four of these were consulted to emend the text for this translation.[38]

FURTHER READING

Shibazaki, Maho. 2007. "The Role Played by Goddesses in the *Haracaritacintāmaṇi*." *Journal of Indian and Buddhist Studies* 55, no. 3 (March): 1035–42.

Yokochi, Yuko. 1999a. "The Warrior Goddess in the *Devīmāhātmya*." In *Living with Śakti: Gender, Sexuality, and Religion in South Asia*, edited by Masakazu Tanaka and Musashi Tachikawa, 71–113. Senri Ethnological Studies 50. Osaka: National Museum of Ethnology.

———. 1999b. "Mahiṣāsuramardinī Myth and Icon: Studies in the Skandapurāṇa II." *Studies in the History of Indian Thought* 11 (May): 65–103.

———. 2013. *The Skandapurāṇa*. Vol. 3, *Adhyāyas 34.1–61, 53–69: The Vindhyavāsinī Cycle*. Leiden: Brill.

NOTES

1. This first line, a prose homage, only figures in the Kāvyamālā edition of the text (Shivadatta and Parab 1897); the manuscripts consulted (see note 38) provide either a different first line, such as "Oṃ homage to the Goddess" (*oṃ namo bhagavatyai*, MS ORLS 1510), or nothing at all (MS ORLS 599).

2. She has no attachment to external objects, since she represents the first instance of creation, the Power (*śakti*) or Will (*icchā*) to create.

3. Or "she whose way has been created above by five-faced Śiva." I read *pañcamukhordhvakalpitagatiḥ* with the two MSS cited in note 1, against the Kāvyamālā edition's *pañcamukho 'rdhakalpitagatiḥ*.

4. This sentence summarizes the story of Durgā's birth, also called Kauśikī. She is said to have been born of Pārvatī's previous, dark skin. After Pārvatī discarded her old skin or "sheath" (*kośa*), she herself came to be called Gaurī or White-skinned. The goddess who was born from her old "sheath" (*kośa*) was then called Kauśikī. For a discussion of variations on this story, see Yokochi (2013a, 23ff.).

5. The *rājasūya* is a solemn Vedic sacrifice that extends over two years and is performed by a Kṣatriya, in particular to become king. For details, see, for example, Kane (1991, 2:1214–23).

6. Pāñcāla is a puzzling name for Durgā's servant; it denotes a north Indian kingdom and its inhabitants, known already in Vedic times and situated between the Ganga and Yamuna Rivers. As a *yakṣa* king, one would think rather of Hārītī's consort, Pañcika, who is basically the Buddhist equivalent of the god of treasures and *yakṣas*, Kubera. He is, however, almost exclusively known in Gandharan art. Perhaps some synthesis of the two was invented in this episode.

7. I read *vihartuṃ* (to amuse themselves) with the two MSS from Shrinagar and the one from London (see note 38) against *vihantuṃ* (to kill or to shatter) in the Kāvyamālā edition, which would require an object in this context. The gods cannot be the object silently understood here, because they cannot be killed or shattered, and they have already been conquered and chased away.

8. I follow three MSS of the four (two from Shrinagar and one from Paris; see note 38) in reading *dṛṣṭā* for *dṛṣṭa-* and *hṛṣṭā-* for *bhraṣṭā-* in the Kāvyamālā edition.

9. A marriage contest (*svayaṃvara*) is a special occasion for a girl to choose her husband by assigning a particular task to the suitors. Only certain particular situations warrant a *svayaṃvara*; usually the father chooses the future husband for a girl.

10. Rambhā is the name of a famous nymph; Rati "Joy" is the wife of the god of love, Kāma; Śacī is Indra's wife; and Lakṣmī, the goddess of fortune, is Viṣṇu's.

11. I accept Tsuchida's conjecture of *prayāta* for *prayātu* here (1997, 5–22).

12. All MSS read "fool" (*jaḍaḥ*) instead of the Kāvyamālā edition's "man" (*janaḥ*); it seems more appropriate to call such a person a fool, and therefore this reading has been adopted.

13. I read *adarśayat*, following all MSS available to me, rather than the Kāvyamālā edition's *nyavedayat*.

14. I understand that three options are mentioned here: a girl may be given in marriage by her father; she may organize a *svayaṃvara*, in which she chooses the husband for herself by setting a task; or she may be taken by force. This understanding of three options seems to be confirmed by the goddess's subsequent words. The Sanskrit of verse 77, however, does not appear to yield this meaning easily. One should certainly read *vā* for *yā*, but this reading is only confirmed by the relatively corrupt Paris MS.

15. One could also understand that the goddess's luminous trident reached only Sumbha's hand, not his head.

16. The Kāvyamālā edition has the singular of "lion" here, but two MSS have an accusative dual, which is much more coherent, given that there are two lions in this version of the story.

17. I follow the reading of the London MS *ābādhayām āsa* for the Kāvyamālā edition's *ārādhayām āsa*.

18. Here, the Kāvyamālā edition inserts a verse not found in any of the manuscripts consulted and which seems to be spurious, intended to depict the killing of Buffalo in a less violent way, with a sword. The inserted verse can be translated as follows: "Durgā then chopped their heads off with her sword, and as they fell to the ground, the other demons cried: 'Alas.'"

19. Here, Durgā is also seen as the source of all verbal manifestation or the goddess of speech, Vāc, which is not very common in mythological contexts but is rather a Tantric idea. For the importance of Vāc in Tantric Śaivism, see, for example, Padoux (1990).

20. For a general discussion of Kashmir's place in the history of Śaivism, see Sanderson (1988, 663, 690–704).

21. For possible Tamil antecedents, see Tiwari and Basham (1985, 229–35) and Hart (1975, 23f., in Yokochi 2004, 116).

22. For this dating, see Yokochi (1999a). Previously, scholars dated the *Devī Māhātmya* to the sixth century CE, though on weak grounds.

23. See Yokochi (1999a, 1999b, and 2013a).

24. Yokochi (2013a, 151ff.).

25. See, for example, Yokochi (1999b, 66–69) and Panikkar (1997, 146ff.).

26. This identification is based on a closing verse of Jayaratha's commentary on the *Tantrāloka*, which names the two brothers and gives other details about their family. The works on poetic theory are more commonly attributed to Jayaratha. See Bühler (1877, cliii) and De (1923, 197–99).

27. This is the case at least for the Śaiva Tantric traditions that include goddess cults. See Sanderson (1988, 660ff.).

28. It is notable that this version of the story is found in the *Skanda Purāṇa*, while the *Devī Māhātmya* makes Kauśikī luminous and leaves the dark skin to Pārvatī. This reversal in the *Devī Māhātmya* may be an attempt to make Kauśikī more adapted to the pantheon of radiant divinities. On this story, see Yokochi (2013a, 23ff.). The *Haracaritacintāmaṇi* (in its chapter 22) agrees on this point with the *Skanda Purāṇa*.

29. For the whole story, see *Mahābhārata* 1.200.18–1.204.26, as well as 12.128.1–6. On the relation of this story to the development of Kauśikī's mythology, see Yokochi (2013a, 38ff and 85ff.).

30. It is related in a separate section of the *Devī Māhātmya*, while the *Skanda Purāṇa*, which considers Mahiṣa to be Sumbha's son, just briefly mentions this event as an additional exploit of the Goddess in 68.10–23. For a discussion, see Yokochi (2013a, 128ff.).

31. See Yokochi (2013a, 19ff.).

32. The same demon appears in other versions, such as in that of the *Matsya Purāṇa*, under the name Andhaka. See Yokochi (1999a, 86ff.).

33. For a discussion of this story, see Yokochi (2013a, 99ff.).

34. See, for example, *Siddhayogeśvarīmata* 24.10ab: *śāntyarthe ghṛtahomaṃ tu parayā kārayet sudhī[ḥ]*.

35. For a discussion, see Kafle (2015, 20ff.) and Goodall, Sanderson, and Isaacson (2015, 38).

36. For the hierarchy of revelation as seen by more esoteric Tantric schools, see Sanderson (1986, 1988).

37. For example in the *Skanda Purāṇa*.

38. See Shibazaki (2007, 1042). The following four manuscripts were consulted for this translation: from the Srinagar Oriental Research Library, numbers 599 and 1510; from the India Office Library, London, number 7042; and from the Bibliothèque Nationale de France, Paris, number D28. See also Tsuchida (1997).

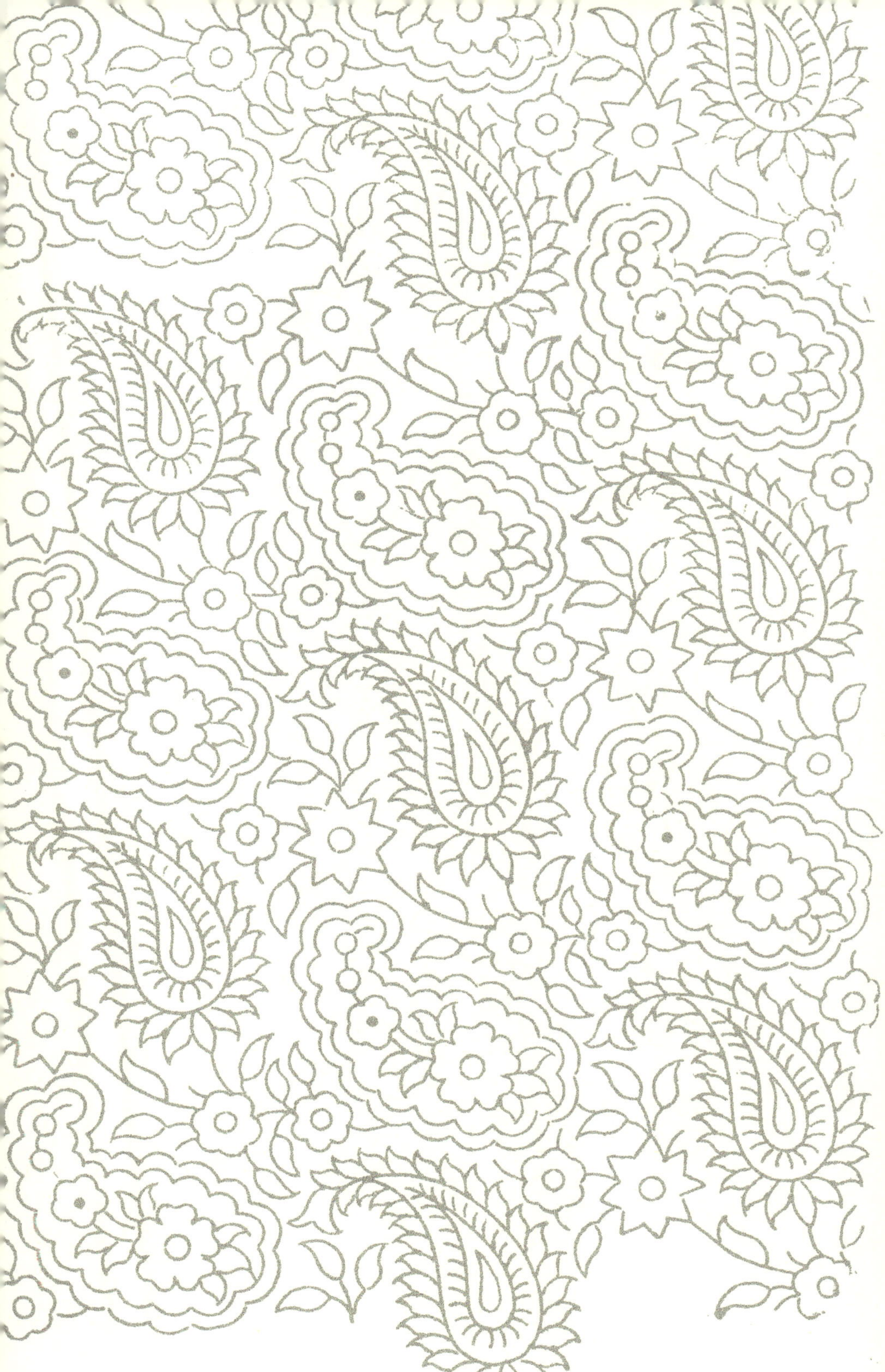

FIGURE 7. The Seven Mothers (Sapta Mātaraḥ), by Laura Santi

CHAPTER 4

The Seven Mothers

Origin Tales from Two Early-Medieval Purāṇas

SHAMAN HATLEY

This chapter presents us with two final tales for this section on demons and battle. Both are closely associated with the region of Bengal in the northeastern part of the Indian subcontinent. Now divided into Bangladesh and the state of West Bengal in the Republic of India, this larger region is united by the Bengali language and a shared culture. Home to mighty rivers such as the Ganges and Brahmaputra, it is a land of dense rain forests and rich agricultural plains, mountainous tea plantations and expansive mangrove forests where the famous, but now endangered, Bengal tigers still roam in the wild. Currently, it is also home to over 250 million people, making Bengal one of the most densely populated areas of the world.

The Seven Mothers (*sapta mātaraḥ*), whose names and identities mirror those of Hindu gods such as Viṣṇu, Indra, and Brahmā, originate from an earlier tradition of popular, largely unnamed goddesses with animal features associated with infectious disease and childhood illness. The first and briefer story, translated from the Sanskrit, is from the mid-sixth- to late-seventh-century *Skanda Purāṇa*. It localizes the goddesses' origin in the city of Koṭīvarṣa (Devīkoṭa) in West Bengal, where they battled a horde of demons led by Haimakuṇḍa. In epic style, it portrays the narration as a conversation between two sages. The second origin tale is from the earliest and most influential of the goddess-oriented Śākta Purāṇas, namely the *Devī Purāṇa*, dating a century or two after the *Skanda Purāṇa* narrative. In this case the Mothers' adversary is the formidable demon Ruru.

For the first tale readers should observe how the text serves to sanctify the city of Koṭīvarṣa as a pilgrimage destination and consider the significance of Bahumāṃsā's unique role there. Readers should compare the myths in both sources, reflect on their portrayals of gender and hierarchies of power (*śakti*), and compare the latter with the Bhadrakāḷī story in chapter 1. The essay that follows these two tales provides further context on the significance and arc of popularity of this fascinating class of goddesses.

॥ দেবীপুরাণম্ ৮৪ ॥

শক্র উবাচ ॥ ভগবন্ভগবতীখ্যাতিমরাতিক্ষয়জাং কথাম্ । সুমনাকৃষ্টিজননীং শ্রোতু-মিচ্ছামি তত্ত্বতঃ ॥ কথং স দৈত্যরাজেন্দ্রো মহাবলপরাক্রমঃ । অজয়ঃ সর্বদেবানাং ভবান্যা বধিতো বদ ॥ শ্রীভগবানুবাচ ॥ শৃণু তে কথয়িষ্যামি দেব্যাঃ কীর্তিং রুরোর্ব-ধম্ । যথা পৃষ্টস্ত্বয়া শক্র তথাহং মে নিবোধত ॥ দত্ত্বা শক্তিং স্বকায়েভো দেবদেবেন বাসব । গচ্ছধ্বং সগণাঃ সর্বে বিষ্ণুব্রহ্মপুরন্দরাঃ ॥ তদাদেশাদ্বয়ং সর্বে গতা যত্রা-সুরাধিপঃ । তথা তেন জিতাস্তস্মাৎপুনস্তত্রৈব আগতাঃ ॥ স চ ক্রোধসমাবিষ্টঃ শম্ভুং ঘাতায় আগতঃ । তং দৃষ্ট্বা সহসা শম্ভুর্গণান্সর্বান্সমাদিশৎ । যোধধ্বং দানবেন্দ্রেণ দেবানাং হিতকাম্যযা ॥ তথা স গণসংঘেন বেষ্ট্যমানো ঽপি বাসব । নির্জিত্য সহসা দেবান্শিবোপরি ব্যবস্থিতঃ ॥ এতস্মিন্নন্তরে দেবো রূপং কৃত্বা তু ভৈরবম্ । কিল বিধ্বংসয়িষ্যেতি ন চ ভীতঃ প্রহর্ষিতঃ ॥ ততস্তস্যাহবং ঘোরং সহ দেবেন শম্ভুনা । সঞ্জাতং সহ দেবানাং দানবানাং ভয়ংকরম্ ॥ কথঞ্চিৎসুপ্রয়ত্নেন বীর্যবন্তস্য বা-সব । ছিন্নং তস্য তদা কণ্ঠং ধারাসৃগ্ভূতলং গতা ॥ অসংখ্যাতা রুরোস্তত্র নির্গতাঃ কাশ্যপীতলাৎ । ভূতাধং ভূতিরুদ্ধন্তঃ কবচিনঃ সোত্তরচ্ছদাঃ ॥ সুরক্তরাগপট্টৈস্তু আপীডতো ঽপি তাডিতাঃ । বিকাশোদ্যতনিস্ত্রিংশতডিদ্ধস্তাঃ সখেটকাঃ ॥ আয়া-মিতশিরোৎকম্পবিষাণকরকার্মুকাঃ । প্রভাম্পাতালমাকাররথাঙ্ঘ্রিকরভীষণাঃ ॥ প্র-পীডিতাগ্রসংবর্তক্ষুভিতাম্বররাগিণঃ । প্রদেশিনীসনাসাক্ষিবর্তিতোষ্ঠদ্বিজাঃ মতাঃ ॥ বৈজয়ন্তীধরা রৌদ্রাঃ পরিঘাশক্তিপাণয়ঃ । জ্বলন্তাগ্নিলতাকারপট্টিশোদ্যতশক্তিভৃৎ ॥ কটঙ্কটকরাঃ কেচিৎপাশাঙ্কুশকরাস্তথা । ভল্লীকর্ণীকচন্দ্রার্ধকুঠারকরভাসুরাঃ ॥ মু-ঞ্চন্ত্যস্ত্রমহৌঘানি বল্গন্তো বলদর্পিতাঃ । ভয়ব্রীডোজ্ঝিতমনাঃ শৌর্যবীর্যবলান্বিতাঃ ॥ কেচিৎস্যন্দনমারূঢা মৃগরাজস্থিতাপরে । গজবাজিস্থঋক্ষস্থাঃ পদস্থামোঘবীর্যযা ॥ লক্ষকোটিবিভাগৈশ্চ বেষ্টিতস্তৈর্মহাবলৈঃ । ছিদ্যন্তে ভেদমায়ান্তি নিবর্তন্তে শিবায়ু-ধৈঃ ॥ বিশীর্যন্তে ঽপি বাণৌঘৈঃ সংমুখং প্রবহন্তি চ । রক্তমেদেন গৌঃ পূর্ণা তেষাং কায়োদ্ভবেন চ ॥ ততো ব্রহ্মাদয়ো দেবা ভয়ং জগ্মুঃ সবাসবাঃ । যদি স্যান্নির্জিতো দেবঃ ক্ষয়ঃ সর্বদিবৌকসাম্ ॥ এতস্মিন্নন্তরে শক্র ব্রহ্মা চিন্তয়তে ক্রিয়াঃ । স্ত্রীরূ-পধারিণী ভূত্বা সহায়ত্বং মহেশ্বরে ॥ ক্ষিপ্রং কুর্যুঃ স্বকার্যেদমেবং বিশ্বেশ্বরে রণে । তত্রোৎপাদিতবান্ব্রহ্মা স্বশক্তিং কিরণোজ্জ্বলাম্ । কমণ্ডলুকরাং দেবীং শরাসনকরাং তথা ॥ একৈকাঃ কোটিরূপেণ সর্বায়ুধধরাঃ স্থিতা । নিঘ্নন্তি ন চ হন্যন্তে পাতয়ন্তি সহস্রশঃ ॥ ব্রহ্মরূপধরা কিংতু ললনাকারবিগ্রহা । হংসস্যন্দনমারূঢা স্বকীয়ায়ুধ-ধারিণী ॥ তর্জয়ন্তী মহৌজেন দানবানাং ভয়ংকরী । তস্য ঘোরাণি কর্মাণি দৃষ্ট্বা সবিস্ময়ঞ্শিবঃ ॥ কা পুনঃ স্রষ্টঃ সুস্নেহা সদা তে প্রতিপক্ষজিৎ । তস্যাঃ শক্তিদ্বিতী

FIGURE 8. *Devī Purāṇa,* a Sanskrit work in the Bengali script. Font “Free Serif” © gnu.org.

THE "GLORIFICATION OF KOṬĪVARṢA" IN THE *SKANDA PURĀṆA*

Vyāsa spoke: "How did the Lord, the supreme deity Śiva, become leader of the Mothers? And who are these Mothers? Tell me what I ask of you."

Sanatkumāra spoke: "I will now narrate to you the auspicious origin of the Mothers. Of old, the lord Brahmā performed his evening worship on the beautiful banks of the eastern waters, tirelessly for millions of years.[1] His worship complete, the lotus-seated god then built an unsurpassed city in that beautiful land. After creating this golden city, adorned with gems, Brahmā spoke exceedingly wondrous, profound words: 'Those highly fortunate ones who will dwell in this beautiful, excellent city, partaking of their good karma, will, by my grace, become undefeatable, free of old age, and endowed with power and strength, without doubt.' After Lord Brahmā, grandfather of the worlds, spoke thus, he departed for his divine court, which was attended by no small number of perfected beings (*siddhas*).

"Next, the demons came together, led by Haimakuṇḍa. Staying in that most excellent city, they caused all kinds of torment, for those haters of the world slew Brahmins by the thousands. These lowly anti-gods broke asunder the rites of fire-sacrifice and oblation, and other rituals. Coming to know of their actions, the gods then all assembled in Brahmā's heaven and reported everything to the god. After hearing their speech and coming to know the deeds of the demons, Brahmā said 'this is impossible for me,' and came with the best of gods to the beautiful woodlands of the Himalayas in order to see Śiva. This is where fair-faced Pārvatī, who bears half of her husband's body, practiced penance.[2]

"When the gods entered there, headed by Brahmā, by the power of Pārvatī's penance every one of them rapidly became female. Then the God of gods, bearer of the trident, asked those preeminent deities, who had become women, 'For what purpose have you come?' Next, they all together first informed the benevolent Śiva about the devastation caused by the demons, and afterward said, 'womanhood is a painful condition for us. May we become men, just as we were before!' The Lord of gods then spoke to those gods, who had become women: 'Go into the demons' presence, all ye gods, having become women. For those demons, proud of their power, may be slain only by women. Having created bodies full of beauty as auspicious Mothers, afterward you will become just as you were before, O best of gods.'

"Bowing in respect to Lord Śiva once again, the deities then said the following: 'O god, create a beautiful female body of your own as well; together with her we will forcibly slay the demons, O supreme lord!' The god then created the goddess Māheśvarī, an auspicious Mother, and also, resorting to a deformed appearance, a second Mother—Bahumāṃsā ('Very Fleshy') by name, the embodiment of universal destruction.[3]

"By the command of the God of gods, afterward the lord Viṣṇu also created two Mothers: Vārāhī as well as Vaiṣṇavī. From grandfather Brahmā came Brāhmī, and from Śiva, Māheśvarī.[4] Kaumārī came from six-faced Kumāra, and Vaiṣṇavī from Viṣṇu. The goddess Vārāhī came from Viṣṇu, and Indrāṇī from the great Indra, the destroyer of cities. Possessing all powers, the auspicious goddess Bahumāṃsā, most excellent of the Mothers, the Great Spell (*mahāvidyā*), came into being from the god Śiva, who has the bull as his standard.[5] And from the bodies of all other gods emerged auspicious Mothers as well, possessing their natures and power, slayers of demons: Vāyavī, Vāruṇī, Yāmī, the mighty Kauberī, Mahākālī, Āgneyī, and others by the thousands.[6] Those goddesses went to that beautiful city and in various ways slew the demons, whose heroism was fierce, to the accompaniment of frightfully dreadful sounds. And they rendered that gilded, foremost of cities free of demons.

"With all of the demons slain, Pārvatī's husband Śiva, the God of all gods, then came to that land out of a desire to give boons to the Mothers. Seeing all of the demonic enemies of the gods slain, Śiva, god of the bull standard, was pleased and then bestowed boons upon them. He said, 'Having become Mother-goddesses, you shall be the Mothers of the world. Those who will be devoted to you, whether the best of men or fortunate women, pernicious spirits will not harm; and after death, they shall become my ageless, immortal attendants (*gaṇas*).[7] This place of yours, known as Koṭīvarṣa, shall become world-famous, freeing one of all sin. And since I am your cause (*hetu*), because you were created by me, I will remain here by the name Hetukeśvara, granting boons. I shall dwell among you as your leader. One who will worship you properly, together with me, shall, free of all sin, attain the highest destination. Since Bahumāṃsā slew the demons with a spear, this sacred bathing place shall be known by the name Pool of the Spear. And any excellent person who drinks here from the Pool of the Spear and prostrates before Bahumāṃsā shall be unassailable by all harmful spirits. The beautiful river Mandākinī shall be known here as Pratikūlā (River Contrary); she will always be brimming with blood for you.[8]

"'Myself, Brahmā, Viṣṇu, and sages rich in penance shall create holy Mother-goddess Tantras through which you shall receive the highest worship, the rites of sacrifice to the Mothers: the *Brahmayāmala, Svāyambhuvayāmala, Kumārayāmala, Sarasvatīyāmala, Gāndhārayāmala* [?], *Īśānayāmala*, and *Nandiyāmala*—these Tantras of yours, and others too by the thousands, through which men shall worship you with devotion.[9] You shall grant boons to the men performing worship. You shall become goddesses who bestow divine powers, possessing the divine powers of yoga. Those women who always worship you, secretly, shall become queens of yoga, lovely women of divine valor.[10] And the leaders of my retinue, Chagala (the Goat) and Kumbhakarṇa (Pitcher-ears), shall by my command remain with you as door guardians. This excellent place, Koṭīvarṣa, dear to the Mothers, shall become the foremost divine cremation ground, bestowing bliss upon those who worship here.'[11]

"Having obtained these boons, the Mother-goddesses, Mothers of the world, prostrated before the Lord of the gods with devotion and rejoiced, extremely excited. From that point on, all of them dwelt in Koṭīvarṣa together with Śiva, granting freedom from danger to the entire world. Thus did the divine Lord Śiva become leader of the Mothers, O Vyāsa, which is what you had asked me.

"A person who would ever recite or hear this tale of the origin of these queens of the world, paid homage by Brahmā, Indra, Śukra, and Vāyu, attains the world of heaven upon death."[12]

THE TALE OF THE SLAYING OF RURU IN THE *DEVĪ PURĀṆA*

Narrated by Viṣṇu to Indra, chapter 83 recounts the origin of Ruru and his ascent as king of the anti-gods (*asura*) or demons.[13] Brahmā, Viṣṇu, Indra, and Bṛhaspati once went to Mt. Kailash to see Śiva and Pārvatī. While the divine child Skanda was playing, his mount, a peacock, pecked Brahmā's swan, which cried pitifully. Brahmā then struck the peacock with a staff and it let out a great cry. On hearing this, the Goddess was filled with sorrow. The cry of the peacock and the Goddess's compassion together took on life as the powerful and terrible Ruru (Howl), who blocked Brahmā's path. Ordered by Śiva, Ruru devoutly sings a hymn of praise to Brahmā, who blesses him to become ruler of the Seven Worlds. While departing, Ruru gazes at the Goddess, and Śiva prophesies that she will slay him. He enters the netherworlds (*pātāla*), where over time he becomes ruler of the anti-gods and thence conquers the earth and the gods. They approach Viṣṇu for succor. Though Viṣṇu defeats Ruru's army, the king of the anti-gods uses his powerful magic, and Viṣṇu and the gods are forced to flee into Śiva's presence. The gods sing a long hymn in praise of Śiva and the Goddess, naming her as the supreme *Śakti* who pervades the cosmos; they beseech her to slay Ruru. Composed by the gods, this hymn offers protection from all danger, removes even terrible sins, and bestows merit equal to the Vedic horse sacrifice.

Chapter 84: The Origin of Brahmāṇī

Indra spoke: "O Lord Viṣṇu, I wish to hear the story that made the Goddess famous and captivates those of good disposition—the tale of the gods' enemies' destruction as it really happened. Tell me how the Goddess, Śiva's consort, slew the mighty and courageous Ruru, king of the demons, whom none of the gods could defeat."

The blessed Lord Viṣṇu spoke: "Listen! I will narrate to you the Goddess's famous deed, the slaying of Ruru. O Indra, hear from me just what you requested. The God of gods Śiva bestowed his power (*śakti*) upon our bodies, O Indra. He then said, 'Viṣṇu, Brahmā, and Indra—let everyone depart to attack Ruru, together with my attendants (*gaṇas*).' By his command we then all went where the king of demons was. He defeated us, and we returned again to Śiva's place. Filled with rage, Ruru came to slay Śiva. Seeing him, the god immediately commanded all of his attendants, 'For the good of the gods, do battle with the lord of demons.' And yet, though surrounded by the horde of Śiva's troops, O Indra, Ruru rapidly defeated the gods and confronted Śiva.

"In the meantime, Lord Śiva took on his terrible (*bhairava*) form. Thinking, 'I shall surely slay him,' he was overjoyed, not afraid. A horrific battle then arose between Ruru and the god Śiva, terrifying for both gods and demons. O Indra, somehow, with great effort, Śiva cut the throat of the powerful Ruru, and a stream of blood fell to the ground. Countless warriors emerged there from Ruru's blood, from the surface of the earth, fully accoutred."

There follows a description of Ruru's innumerable blood-born warriors, who carry lethal weapons, ride chariots, lions, elephants, and so forth, and who surge forward irrepressibly under fierce attack.

"Then Brahmā and the other gods, together with Indra, became afraid, thinking, 'If the lord is defeated, then all the heaven-dwelling gods will perish.' In the meantime, O Indra, Brahmā pondered courses of action, and thought, 'The gods should quickly take on female form and give aid to the great Lord Śiva; thus would they fulfill their duty to the lord of the universe in battle.'[14]

Brahmā created his own *śakti* there, a goddess blazing with radiance, holding a waterpot and bow. Heavily armed, each goddess stood with innumerable attendants; they slaughtered, but were not slain, felling demons by the thousands.[15] For her part, the one with Brahmā's form had a playful appearance, mounted on a swan and bearing her own characteristic weapons, terrifying the demons with powerful threats.

"Seeing her terrible deeds, Śiva was astonished and said, 'O creator, who is this very dear one who ever defeats your enemies? I will create for her a second unconquerable *śakti*.'"

Thus ends chapter 84 of the *Devī Purāṇa,* in the "Slaying of Ruru" cycle, entitled "The Origin of Brahmāṇī."

Chapter 85: The Origin of the Seizers

Lord Viṣṇu spoke: "Beholding the battle of Brahmāṇī with the demons, Śiva also contemplated the supreme *śakti* for the purpose of creation. 'Mutually protecting each other, they will do battle and conquer'—thinking thus, the lord of the gods created Māheśvarī, his own female embodiment. He first contemplated the goddess situated in the lotus of his heart, purely radiant like a hundred moons, mounted on a broad-shouldered bull bearing a trident and skull-staff. She shone brightly and her speech was grim: 'Slay! Seize! Chop up!' All the enemies fled after seeing her, sick with fear.

"Overjoyed, the six-faced Skanda also contemplated the radiant female power (*marīcinī*) within himself. He produced the powerful Kaumārī, seated on a peacock, fierce, bearing a spear and bell, bent by the weight of a mighty spear.[16] She filled the directions with a trumpeting sound like the call of a swan and plunged into battle with the demons, resembling a quivering streak of lightning. O Indra, I too created the goddess Vaiṣṇavī from my own power, in accordance with the wish of the Ultimate Cause.[17] Fierce, she stands upon the divine eagle Garuḍa, best of Brahmins, wearing radiant armlets and bracelets. With fierce cries like an antelope, abundant blows of the conch, and roaring sounds of "Kill!," she was lethal to demon lords. Offering homage, Yama produced his own female embodiment, Vārāhī, with terrible, unbreakably hard staff-like tusks, mounted upon a great water buffalo, holding a noose and staff as weapons. With an exceedingly harsh sound resounding like doomsday thunderclouds, she was as difficult to look upon as the tongue of Death, resembling the pure flames of the doomsday fire. Indra too in the same way produced Indrāṇī, a goddess of his own radiance resembling molten gold, mounted upon a frenzied elephant and sparkling with a thousand eyes, holding a thunderbolt, goad, and bow in her hands.

"Heavily armed, each of them stood with innumerable attendants; they slaughtered, but were not slain. They felled demons by the thousands. They rapidly split apart the demon army with their mighty weapons. O Indra, the demon army resembled ocean waves inundating the earth, perishing and returning to perish again. The goddesses became satiated by flesh and fat, yet the lord of demons was not defeated, standing firm with his long sword and mace in hand. The gods were astonished. O Indra, afflicted with despair, fear, and doubt, headed by Brahmā, god of gods, they extolled Śiva and all the Rays of *śakti*. The goddesses said, 'Our staff-like arms have fallen upon them, yet there is no end to the demons, O lord.' Then Brahmā and the other gods became extremely perturbed, and eulogized Śiva as Kālarudra, the transcendent-cum-imminent lord of the gods.[18]

"Then, after Śiva heard the speech of the *śakti*s and of Viṣṇu, a great rage arose in him, and from the rage emerged fire. Bright flames emerged from the fire, blazing sideways, upward, and downward. In the middle of that mass of flames stood the *śakti* of Kālarudra, resembling billions of suns, ready to give aid to Śiva. She is the dreadful-looking Kālarātri, seeming to devour the entire world, with fangs, reddish eyes, and a sound like doomsday thunderclouds.[19] The goddess has in her [eight] hands the *vajra* and goad, together with a staff, noose, sword, mace, and spear. She also carries the trident as her weapon.

"Gesturing menacingly all around, she stood before the god of gods and spoke briskly: 'What shall I do, lord of the gods?'

"Then the god, delighted, spoke to the unconquerable one: 'If you love me, O goddess, you shall fell Ruru.'

"'I shall do thus, O lord of gods, just what you say!'

"Śiva then created an alcoholic drink as vast as the ocean. The goddess quickly drank this, together with the *śakti*s, and flew into a rage. The army of demons then grew again by the millions. The *śakti*s, whose desire was stimulated by the potency of that drink, requested food: 'We are hungry, lord of the gods; feed us.'[20]

"Then Śiva said to all the goddesses, whose power is unhindered: 'I offer to you Ruru; consume him as a sacrificial beast.' Then, making a terrible, cruel howl, they fell upon the powerful demon army."[21]

There follows a gory and tumultuous battle, which is inconclusive. Then, by the will of Śiva, to aid the Mother-goddesses there arise the Seizers (*grahas*): a number of powerful male warrior deities in the image of the Guardians of the Directions (*dikpālas*) and twenty-four powerful goddesses known as *yoginī*s, also arrayed in the directions, each with countless attendants. They are born from the mind of Śiva and pervade the cosmos. This tale was once told by Śiva to the Goddess at great length and then revealed by Skanda to Brahmā.[22]

Thus ends chapter 85 in the "Slaying of Ruru" cycle of the glorious *Devī Purāṇa*, entitled "The Origin of the Seizers."

Chapter 86: The Rise of Caṇḍeśvara

The blessed Lord Viṣṇu spoke: "Then those heavily-armed demon warriors with horses, elephants, and chariots were defeated by all the Seizers, who abide following the commands of Śiva. Afterward, those mighty, indomitable *śakti*s devoured the demon army, brimming with Śiva's power. Ruru, lord of demons, then entered into the netherworlds below the surface of the earth."

Ruru enters the City of Gold in the land of Citravatī, presided over by Hāṭakeśvara, one of many Śiva-like deities called *rudras*. There he is confronted by Kālarātri and Mother-goddesses of the netherworlds. Seeing them, he flees below to another realm; there too the Goddess appears menacingly. He flees from netherworld to netherworld, again and again being confronted by the Goddess and a powerful retinue of goddesses of that realm.

"Hateful, but deprived of his power and heroism, he then went to the netherworld called Ābhāsa. There lies the City of Ashes, where Ucchuṣma (Dessicating Fire) dwells together with the Ucchuṣma Mother-goddesses. Kālarātri stood there before him, extremely cruel and with cruel speech. She spoke menacingly: 'Stay put, wicked fool; Śiva the Archer is angry with you. Where could you go where I am not present? How could that be? This universe exists within my jaws, in the middle of the causal fire.'

"After hearing these ferocious words, he once again readied himself for battle. He abandoned his fear of death, took his bow in hand, and cast a powerful spell, making thousands of illusions. He seemed to create a shower of thunderbolts with his arrows and with the deep bellows of his bowstring. He made a full army replete with chariots, horses, and elephants.

"They attacked with various arrows: hollow, feathered, and gold shafted. Breaking these apart with hundreds of fierce blows, the Mother of

Mother-goddesses fell upon them.[23] She rendered the demon army deaf through the sound of her bells and *ḍamaru*-drum, . . . her eyes flashing like millions of lightning bolts.[24] After destroying Ruru's magic, she shattered his weapons. She broke his bow using arrows of indomitable power, completely disarming the proud king of demons. Śiva's queen then assailed him, bereft of power, bereft of valor. She sucked out his fat, marrow, bones, and flesh with a torrent of blood, seized both his skin (*carma*) and his head (*muṇḍa*), and then departed."[25]

Following Ruru's demise, the gods grew fearful of the gory goddesses and approached Śiva. They sang a hymn of praise to Śiva as Caṇḍeśvara, "The Grim Lord." They danced and played musical instruments, filling the entire world with song.

Thus ends chapter 86 in the glorious *Devī Purāṇa*, in the "Slaying of Ruru" cycle, entitled "The Rise of Caṇḍeśvara."

Chapter 87: Hymn of Praise to the Mothers

The blessed Lord Viṣṇu spoke: "In the meantime, O Indra, the Mother-goddesses returned in peaceful, entrancing forms resembling millions of moons, born from the eternally beneficent Śiva, lutes in hand, illuminating the world.[26] O Indra, they expressed a variety of dramatic sentiments and were accompanied by Śiva."

There follows a description of the goddesses' beauty and their wondrous dance, which shook the world.

"Seeing them, the clouds, constellations, and planets in the sky all abandoned their stations, overjoyed. Positioned in the sky above, they released flower garlands by the thousands. With the goddesses poised to commence their dance, everyone experienced the highest bliss. With varied expressions arising from the play of various dramatic sentiments, the Rays of *śakti* frolicked in this way with the *gaṇas*, *rudras*, *yoginīs*, *vetālas*, *rākṣasas*, and *yakṣas*, then paid homage to Śiva as Rudra and stood before him.[27]

"Pleased, the god then paid homage to the *śaktis*. He spoke thus to the goddesses, who are Mothers of the entire world: 'You shall be worshiped in all endeavors by Brahmā and the other gods, as well as by men. You were created by the will of the Ultimate Cause in order to protect the world. That Ultimate Cause is the supreme Śakti, who is primordial and beyond suffering.'

"O Indra, She created us—Brahmā and the other gods—and the Rudras as well. She employs us for the sake of creation, maintenance, and destruction, in due course. Just as the rays of the divine Sun dispassionately cause a lotus to open and then close again, in due course, she likewise effects the unfolding and cessation of all endeavors. She has no beginning, nor does she have a middle or end; she abides as mere essence. By the will of that Ultimate Cause, Śiva told the Mother-goddesses, 'You will be paid worship in the world of men. You will bestow upon devotees what they wish for, in accordance with their desires.'[28]

"Then, O lord, each of the goddesses was offered a hymn of praise by the god from whom she arose. Brahmā, Skanda, myself, Yama, Indra, and all the gods paid reverence to Rudra and the goddesses. The world-guardians, celestial bodies, divine serpents, and demons all paid reverence to them as well.

> 'With fearsome jeweled earrings, a shining, terrible face with knitted brows, fanged and ferocious, with grotesque garb, and exceedingly luminous, bearing a shining axe, lute, *ḍamaru*-drum, severed head, and skull-staff: I bow to the great three-eyed Bhairava, mounted on a bull.'
>
> 'Seated ever on an enormous royal swan atop a fine white lotus, pure and wide, filled with buzzing throngs of bees, . . . attended upon by clans of sages: I bow my head to Brahmāṇī, the Mother-goddess born of Brahmā, the Grandfather.'[29]
>
> 'Radiant like a hundred autumn moons, resembling ice, conch shell, and jasmine, giving off sparkling rays, seated on a white bull, bearing the crescent moon on her formidable matted locks: I bow to Māheśvarī, whose weapon is the trident, born from the body of Śiva, lord of *gaṇas*.'
>
> 'Riding on a peacock, fierce on account of her bright vermilion, with little bells sounding clamorously, holding a sharp spear in hand, her garment lit up by the rays of her abundant glow: I bow to Kaumārī, born of Skanda, who destroys enemies of the thirty gods.'
>
> 'Whose blue color resembles dense heaps of profusely-flowering linseed, who bears a mace, hammer, bow, conch, and discus, seated upon Garuḍa as her chariot, with broad lotus-like eyes: I bow to Vaiṣṇavī, who bestows abundant success, born from the body of Viṣṇu.'
>
> 'Having the face of a boar, with skin as black as dark kohl eyeshadow, shining with a short sword in hand, bearing an iron club and the death-god's noose, born from the body of Death, resounding like doomsday's

dense thunderclouds: I bow with reverence to the beneficent Vārāhī, mounted on a mighty buffalo.'[30]

'With a lustre of pure gold, resembling a meteor accompanied by tremulous lightning, resonating with the cries of great elephants, adorned with numerous ornaments, bearing a radiant goad, paid reverence by the hosts of gods: I bow to Indrāṇī, granter of boons, bestower of abundant pleasures, born of Indra.'

'Radiant like a hundred suns, wearing a garland of white skulls, having a mouth with fanged teeth and eyes as red-orange as the doomsday fire, bearing . . . a body, fond of blood, flesh, and fat: I bow to Cāmuṇḍā [Kālarātri], the one seated upon a corpse, giver of refuge and bearer of the ghastly skull-staff.'

'Who makes bees buzz, striking them with the fly-whisks of his fluttering ears, perfuming the ten directions with musk from his cheeks, who has the auspicious head of an elephant and destroys all obstacles: I bow to [Gaṇeśa], leader of the *gaṇas*, born from the body of Śiva, lord of the *gaṇas*, whose valor is manifestly evident, worshiped by all the world-guardians, destroyer of the clans of the gods' enemies, remover of supplicants' sin and suffering.'[31]

"A man who sings this hymn of praise to the Mothers, whom all gods praise, attains abundant happiness and ascends thereafter to the World of the Mothers."

Thus ends chapter 87 of the glorious *Devī Purāṇa*, in the "Slaying of Ruru" cycle, entitled "Hymn of Praise to the Mothers."

Chapter 88: Finale to the Slaying of Ruru

Lord Viṣṇu spoke: "People desiring liberation worship the Mothers by way of the Vedas and the Śaiva Tantric revelation. They are also worshiped in accordance with the Gāruḍa Tantras, Bhūta Tantras, and Bāla Tantras.[32] Beneficent, they bring all endeavors to fruition, and are like wish-fulfilling jewels. Heretics of the future—such as Buddhist proponents of the Gāruḍa Tantras—will worship them according to their own methods, devoted to their own ways, dear child. They give rewards that accord with any disposition wise people worship them with, whether they be Brahmins or even lowborn outcastes. In the ordinary mortal world, those desiring visible or unseen [future] rewards also worship them by way of the auspicious marriage rites, whether of the divine, *gandharva*, or *kiṃnara* kind.[33] Whatsoever in this world consists of the Word—whether visible or invisible, moving or inert—all of this is born of the *śaktis*, O Indra.[34] There is no doubt about this. They are declared by the infinite being, Śiva, to be the wombs of the gods, ancestral spirits, and men, O Indra.

"Creation, preservation, and destruction; bondage, liberation, and activity; heaven, emancipation, and hell: everything proceeds from them. From the cosmic serpent Ananta at the bottom of the universe up to the sphere of Sadāśiva, everything is permeated by the *śaktis*, like milk by ghee.[35] Therefore, O king of gods, you too must worship them through the offering of good deeds. Ritually worshiped in images made of gold, gilded metal, coral, painted wood, baked earth, or stone, they fulfill all of one's desires.[36]

"Hear now the merit obtained by someone who thus promulgates, listens to, or recites, with devotion, the Origin of the Mothers, the Churning of the Demon Ruru, which brims with Śiva's power: In this world he becomes completely free of all impediments, and endowed with everything wished for; and, O Indra, in the end obtains the supreme state of liberation. From merely hearing this one obtains [merit equal to] all charitable gifts, votive rites, and other rituals."

Thus ends chapter 88 of the glorious *Devī Purāṇa*, entitled "Finale to the Slaying of Ruru."

THE GODDESSES IN CONTEXT: THE RISE AND FALL OF THE SEVEN MOTHERS

Temples dedicated to goddesses known as "the Seven Mothers" (*sapta mātaraḥ*) once dotted the sacred landscape of southern Asia. Indeed, the circa sixth-century *Bṛhatsaṃhitā* of Varāhamihira names the cult of Mother-goddesses (*mātṛ*) as one of the major religious orders of the time, alongside Buddhism, Jainism, the Bhāgavatas (i.e., Vaiṣṇavism), Pāśupata Śaivism, and so forth.[37] Royal inscriptions of the Gupta-Vākāṭaka age (third–sixth centuries CE) and thereafter invoke the goddesses' protection as "Mothers of the Seven Worlds."[38] Yet their status had declined precipitously by the second millennium, and in modern times they feature, if at all, only as minor deities in the retinue of Durgā, Kālī, Śiva, or other divinities. Their mythical and ritual significance has largely been forgotten.

This chapter presents translations of two narratives concerning the Mother-goddesses written in their heyday. Both concern their origins in epic battles between the gods and anti-gods (*asura*). The first, comparatively brief, narrative is from chapter 171 of the original *Skanda Purāṇa* (sixth–seventh centuries CE). This is a "glorification narrative" (*māhātmya*) celebrating Koṭīvarṣa, a medieval sacred site also known as Devīkoṭa or Bangarh, located in the South Dinajpur district of West Bengal.[39]

The second translation is from the influential but poorly preserved *Devī Purāṇa*, which postdates the original *Skanda Purāṇa* and reflects further developments in the cult of the Seven Mothers. The *Devī Purāṇa* is, in fact, the single most important surviving source concerning early medieval Mother-goddesses, containing narratives as well as detailed material on their iconography and worship. Selected for translation are excerpts from the "Slaying of Ruru" (*ruruvadha*) cycle, chapters 83–88 of the *Devī Purāṇa*.

This tale cycle echoes other narratives concerning the *mātṛ*s' origins in battle, including chapter 171 of the *Skanda Purāṇa* and chapters 7–10 of the *Devī Māhātmya*. It also has thematic parallels with the much later *Bhadrakāḷī Māhātmya* of Kerala, part of which is translated in the present volume (chapter 1).

Seed: The Seven Mothers and Their Antecedents

The Seven Mothers have roots in a goddess type of ancient pedigree, deeply connected to the natural world and its feminized powers of sustenance, fecundity, contagion, and mortality.[40] Statuary of the popular deities known as *mātṛ*s (Mothers or Mother-goddesses) first appears in the archaeological record of the Kuṣāṇa era (first–third centuries CE), while the *Mahābhārata*, parts of which were likely contemporaneous, contains multiple narratives involving *mātṛ*s. Their natures and identities in this text seem reasonably congruent with the material record. Images recovered from the Mathura region suggest that *mātṛ*s formed a diverse category of non-elite goddesses. Frequently theriomorphic (animal headed or having other animal features) and often holding infants, *mātṛ*s were enshrined in groups of variable size alongside a male guardian figure, especially the youthful warrior Skanda. Their connection with Skanda forms the key link between the goddesses' representations in statuary, narrative texts, and the early medical literature, in which Skanda and his subsidiary deities—especially *graha*s (seizers, i.e., possessing spirits) and *mātṛ*s—are described as afflicting children with disease if not propitiated. Both nurturing and potentially dangerous, the Mothers were intimately linked with fertility and well-being, indeed with life itself, especially for mothers and infants.

Despite their connection to Skanda, there is evidence for fluidity and competition concerning the sectarian identities of the early Mothers. They were also associated with Kubera, god of wealth, and their sculpture has been recovered from Brahminical (i.e., Hindu), Jain, and Buddhist architectural contexts. They may also have been worshiped in their own temples.[41] Among the numerous, usually anonymous *mātṛ*s depicted in early statuary are several goddesses of high status who can be identified by name, such as Ṣaṣṭhī and Hārītī. By the fifth century, however, veneration of variable groups of *mātṛ*s began to give way to a new configuration: the Seven Mothers. Today they are usually called "the *saptamātṛkās*," though the plural Sanskrit expression *sapta mātaraḥ* or *saptamātaraḥ* is more faithful to period sources. In the form of this heptad, the *mātṛ*s became the focus of a pan-Indian temple cult linked closely to Śiva, rather than Skanda, which attracted considerable elite patronage. Shrines of the Seven Mothers feature in some of the most magnificent temple complexes of the fifth to eighth centuries CE, such as those of Ellora, Aihole, and Elephanta.[42] In addition to their temple cult, the Seven Mothers also became important goddesses within the initiatory traditions of Tantric Śaivism and have important connections with Tantric Buddhism as well.

The goddesses of this heptad mirror a series of major Brahminical gods—Brahmā, Śiva, Skanda, Viṣṇu, Varāha or Yama, and Indra—on whose names those of six Mothers are calqued: Brāhmī, Māheśvarī, Kaumārī, Vaiṣṇavī, Vārāhī or Yāmī, and Indrāṇī, each name having several common variants. Iconographically, these goddesses largely mirror their male counterparts. Exceptional is the seventh goddess, Cāmuṇḍā, the fierce and usually skeletal hag who is "leader of the Mothers" (*mātṛnāyikā*) and who does not mirror a male deity in the manner of the others. She alone among the seven seems to have been a major independent goddess, though there are also temples dedicated to Vārāhī. Especially in Tantric traditions, the Seven Mothers are sometimes joined by a variable eighth goddess, often Mahālakṣmī or Aghorī/Bhairavī, who in this configuration usurps Cāmuṇḍā's position. By the sixth century, the Seven Mothers were conventionally depicted in the company of two male guardian figures: the elephant-headed Gaṇeśa/Vināyaka and either Vīrabhadra (Auspicious Hero) or Vīṇādhara (Bearer of the Vīṇā-lute), prominent attendants of Śiva sometimes viewed as his own forms. In many cases, Śiva joins the Mothers as Naṭeśa, "Lord of Dance." As Michael Meister argues, this new configuration of Mothers simultaneously asserts Śiva's dominance over rival deities, such as Viṣṇu, while assimilating and containing popular traditions of *mātṛ* veneration.[43]

Flower: Mother-Goddesses in the Purāṇas and in Early Tantric Traditions

The *Skanda Purāṇa* and Koṭīvarṣa

Given the prominence of the Seven Mothers in the religious landscape of the fifth to eighth centuries CE, it is surprising how few works of period religious literature concern them directly. This may in part reflect their non-elite roots. The account of the Mothers' origin in the "Glorification of Koṭīvarṣa" episode of the old *Skanda Purāṇa* translated here is thus particularly valuable. It likely predates by at least one century the more famous origin story in the *Devī Māhātmya* of the *Mārkaṇḍeya Purāṇa,* as well as the *Devī Purāṇa*'s detailed material on the cult of *mātṛs*.[44] As its editors highlight, the original or "old" *Skanda Purāṇa* is distinct from the better-known published text by this name; the latter was in fact somewhat artificially assembled by *paṇḍits* in the colonial period from various independent medieval texts ascribing themselves to the *Skanda Purāṇa*.[45] By contrast, the original text may have been composed in the sixth to early seventh centuries and is preserved in sources that include a Nepalese palm-leaf manuscript of 810 CE. The authors had strong connections to the holy city of Varanasi and to the Pāśupata sect of Śaivism. Hans Bakker proposes that the "Glorification of Koṭīvarṣa" in chapter 171 (out of 183) was one of the final compositions included in the Purāṇa, most likely toward the end of the sixth or early seventh centuries. This tale from the *Skanda Purāṇa* has been the subject of multiple scholarly discussions, including a detailed article by Yuko Yokochi on the religious history of Koṭīvarṣa.[46]

Representations of Mother-goddesses in the *Skanda Purāṇa* seem in several respects transitional, linking their depictions in early sources, such as the *Mahābhārata* and early medical literature, with the temple cult of the Seven Mothers and their myths in later Purāṇas. As Yokochi points out, the *Skanda Purāṇa* preserves the older, Kuṣāṇa-era and *Mahābhārata* conception of countless diverse Mother-goddesses alongside the "Hinduized" Gupta-era Seven Mothers, who in fact appear within the *Skanda Purāṇa* only in the account of Koṭīvarṣa.[47] Crucially, this chapter of the *Skanda Purāṇa* is also transitional in cultic terms, for it juxtaposes the older popular worship of Mother-goddesses with their worship by Tantric initiates. In fact, embedded within the myth of the origins of Koṭīvarṣa and its presiding deities is important early evidence for Tantric Śaivism.[48]

In its final verses, the narrative implies the existence of a temple at Koṭīvarṣa dedicated to the Mothers and refers also to a body of water sacred to the goddess Bahumāṃsā called the "Pool of the Spear" (*śūlakuṇḍa*). Apparently viewed as a form of Cāmuṇḍā, Bahumāṃsā presides over the sacred site together with Śiva in the guise of Hetukeśvara, with the *gaṇa*s Chagala (the Goat) and Kumbhakarṇa (Pitcher-ears) serving as temple door guardians. We may infer from this that the temple sanctum proper contained cult images of the Seven Mothers along with Śiva, though, as Yokochi points out, Hetukeśvara could possibly refer to a *liṅga* or aniconic form of Śiva, which may have been housed in a separate shrine.[49] This iconic program seems unusual and somewhat archaic when compared to sixth- to seventh-century temples. In Kuṣāṇa-era *mātṛ* sculpture, the Mothers were often depicted with images of the young, spear-bearing Skanda or the robust *yakṣa*-lord Kubera.[50] However, from the Gupta era, Śiva himself often features as leader of the Mothers, displacing Skanda and Kubera, particularly in the form of Naṭeśa, "Lord of Dance."[51] Yet in only one extant shrine does Śiva alone appear in the Mothers' company: that of the fifth-century cliff shrine between Badoh and Pathari, in present-day Madhya Pradesh. Koṭīvarṣa's iconic program might hence have resembled that of Badoh-Pathari, the cult images being those of Śiva, Bahumāṃsā, and six other *mātṛ*s. With the exception of the early Badoh-Pathari shrine, the Seven Mothers are normally depicted in the company of multiple *gaṇa*-lords, usually Gaṇeśa and either Vīrabhadra (Auspicious Hero) or Vīṇādhara (Bearer of the Vīṇā), or with Śiva and a *gaṇa*-lord. At Koṭīvarṣa, the *gaṇa*s Chagala and Kumbhakarṇa appear instead, stationed outside the shrine proper, with Śiva himself joining the Mothers in the sanctum. This pantheon suggests a transitional picture, for although described in the *Skanda Purāṇa* as *gaṇa*s of Śiva, Chagala and Kumbhakarṇa have ties with the older cult of Skanda. Chagala is likely a name of Naigameṣa, a goat-headed deity prominently associated with Skanda, while Kumbhakarṇa or Ghaṇṭākarṇa (Bell Ears) has affinity with, and may be an alias of, Lohitākṣa (Red Eyes). These two fierce deities serve as male companions to an archaic set of seven *mātṛ*s associated in the *Mahābhārata* with the cult of Skanda. At Koṭīvarṣa, Śiva apparently displaces Skanda in presiding over a group of nine deities that seems to echo this earlier configuration, which the *Mahābhārata* refers to as the "Nine Heroes."[52]

Bahumāṃsā, the now-forgotten goddess heading the Mothers at Koṭīvarṣa, may be traced back to the Mother-goddess Lohitāyani of the *Mahābhārata,* where she is closely associated with both the Brahmaputra River and Skanda.[53] She appears to be a regional deity later brought within the orbit of Śaivism by her identification with the fierce Cāmuṇḍā (also known as Carcikā). The *Skanda Purāṇa* amply attests to this process of incorporating local goddesses: chapters 64 and 68 enumerate the names and locales assigned to the numerous Mothers, including Bahumāṃsā, who emanate from the goddess Kauśikī. This process not only brings *mātṛ*s within the orbit of Śaivism but links them together via an emergent thealogy of the Great Goddess (Mahādevī) as the source of all goddesses.[54] This rhetoric of emanation and localization appears almost as a precursor to discourse on *śakti,* as adapted into popular religion with great success from Tantric Śaivism. Through this, any and all goddesses and their sacred sites, declared *śaktipīṭha*s (seats of power), could be subsumed within the identity of the one Goddess.

The name Bahumāṃsā ostensibly means "having lots of flesh," that is, corpulent, though as Yokochi points out, this could potentially be euphemistic, referring not to the goddess's appearance but to her robust appetite for sacrificial victims.[55] While most early sources describe Cāmuṇḍā as emaciated, and she usually appears as such in statuary, at least one text describes a full-bodied Cāmuṇḍā; there are examples of statuary, though I am unaware of any that are corpulent.[56] Alexis Sanderson argues that the goddess of Koṭīvarṣa was an emaciated trident bearer seated below a banyan tree, an iconography attested in two east Indian images that may be her replicas, and in an image recovered from Bangarh/Koṭīvarṣa itself.[57] If so, the goddess of Koṭīvarṣa's influence came to extend well beyond her original sacred site.

In the course of Śiva's granting boons to the Mothers, the narrative speaks of a genre of literature called the *Yāmala Tantra*s (Union Tantras) or *Mātṛ Tantra*s (Tantras of the Mothers), which it lists by name. These texts form a branch of the scriptural literature of the Śaiva Mantramārga (Path of mantras), better known as Tantric or "esoteric" Śaivism. Their attestation here is profoundly important to the history of Tantric Śaivism, as highlighted by Sanderson, who first identified the texts in question and discussed their significance.[58] At least one of these texts survives: the voluminous *Brahmayāmala,* which heads most lists of *Yāmala*s and has been the subject of recent studies by the present author and Csaba Kiss.[59] In the *Skanda Purāṇa*'s "Glorification of Koṭīvarṣa," verses 25–33 describe the lay, that is, non-Tantric, cult of the Mothers at Koṭīvarṣa. The rituals associated with this may include pilgrimage, worship of the images of the Mothers and Śiva-Hetukeśvara, partaking of the sacred waters, and animal sacrifice (suggested by the reference to the river brimming with blood). The aims are correspondingly of the variety advanced in Śaiva Purāṇas: deliverance from harmful spirits, going to heaven, or joining Śiva's entourage of *gaṇa*s after death. Verses 34–40, however, appear to describe the cult of Mothers for those who have received Tantric initiation. Its rituals are those taught in the *Mātṛ Tantra*s or *Yāmala*s, and its aim, for men, is the attainment of magical powers (*siddhi*; literally "perfection"). For women, the secret rites promise more: the possibility of divine apotheosis as *yoginī*s, powerful and beautiful queens of yoga (*yogeśvarī*s). In the Tantric cult, the goddess Bahumāṃsā is the "Great Spell" (*mahāvidyā*), and Koṭīvarṣa is not merely a holy ford and place of pilgrimage but the best of cremation grounds—preferred locations for the esoteric rites described in texts such as the *Brahmayāmala*.

One level of this narrative's significance thus lies in its juxtaposition of a temple cult of Mother-goddesses with their Tantric worship, which seem to have coexisted in cultic centers such as Koṭīvarṣa. This features in the sacred geography of a number of goddess-oriented Śaiva Tantras, though the presiding goddess is named as Karṇamoṭī rather than Bahumāṃsā.[60] Moreover, elements of Koṭīvarṣa's divine pantheon and its sacred attractions are inscribed into the deity maṇḍala of the *Brahmayāmala*, where it is one of eight cremation grounds surrounding Prayāga in the maṇḍala's center. Fittingly, given its geographical position on the subcontinent, Koṭīvarṣa occupies the maṇḍala's northeastern portion.[61]

The "Slaying of Ruru" of the Devī Purāṇa

As the earliest and most influential among the goddess-oriented Śākta Purāṇas, the *Devī Purāṇa* is invaluable for the window it provides on the formation of popular Śāktism in the latter centuries of the first millennium. Among much else, it provides uniquely valuable material for study of Mother-goddesses, especially the temple cult of the Seven Mothers.[62] While the *Skanda Purāṇa*'s redactors were associated with the Pāśupata sect of Śaivism, the *Devī Purāṇa*'s redactors instead had close connections with Tantric

Śaivism. Indeed, the text stands out among the Purāṇas of the first millennium for being comparatively unorthodox, to the extent that one twelfth-century author, Ballālasena, explicitly rejected its authority. This reflects not only the *Devī Purāṇa*'s incorporation of esoteric and antinomian Tantric traditions, but perhaps also its broad social horizons. Study of the *Devī Purāṇa* has long been hampered by the poor condition of the text. Though it has been published twice, the printed editions have major limitations, and no early manuscript survives; parts of this Purāṇa also appear to have been lost over time. Long believed to be a composition from around the sixth century, more recent assessments of the *Devī Purāṇa* point toward its compilation somewhat later, perhaps in the eighth or ninth centuries.[63] The text certainly postdates the *Brahmayāmala*, a Tantric scripture of perhaps the late seventh to early eighth centuries that the *Devī Purāṇa* draws upon.[64]

Spanning chapters 83–88, the "Slaying of Ruru" is one of several story cycles within the *Devī Purāṇa* that culminates in the Goddess slaying a powerful anti-god. Distinguishing this cycle are the prominence of *mātṛ*s and the identity of the supreme Goddess as Cāmuṇḍā or Kālī/Kālarātri, leader of the Seven Mothers. While the frame story in chapter 83 features the pacific Umā or Pārvatī, the goddess reappears in chapter 85 in a fierce guise, born from the fiery rage of Śiva, who took on his own terrible form called Kālarudra (Dark Howler), Bhairava (Terrible), or Caṇḍeśa (Grim Lord). In the "Slaying of Ruru" the Mothers appear in their commonly attested configuration of seven—Brahmāṇī, Māheśvarī, Kaumārī, Vaiṣṇavī, Vārāhī, Indrāṇī, and Cāmuṇḍā/Kālī—emanated by the gods Brahmā, Śiva, Skanda, Viṣṇu, Yama, Indra, and Śiva/Bhairava, respectively.[65] The logic behind the Mothers' creation is opaque in comparison to similar tales, such as the *Skanda Purāṇa*'s, which intimate that the demons can only be slain by women.[66]

The devotional and iconographic content of the "Slaying of Ruru" cycle reflects connections with the temple cult of the Seven Mothers. Their visual forms find vivid description in chapters 85 and 87. Clarifying the precise pantheon envisioned, the praise hymn of chapter 87 extols nine deities: Śiva as Bhairava, the Seven Mothers, and the elephant-headed Gaṇeśa.[67] Here Naṭeśa, the dancing form of Śiva found in so many temples of the Seven Mothers, gives way to a fiercer form of the god, though he remains a dancer.[68] This may reflect the influence of Tantric cults of Bhairava and various goddesses, as one sometimes sees in eastern India from the eighth century onward.[69]

In contrast to the *Skanda Purāṇa*, the *Devī Purāṇa* tends to elevate the supreme Goddess to at least the level of Śiva, the supreme God, often according to her preeminence. The *Devī Purāṇa* has fully assimilated the doctrine of *śakti* from Tantric Śaivism, according to which the divine consists of the gendered polarities of consciousness (*śiva*) and its dynamic power (*śakti*). Manifesting in countless forms, this power is ultimately singular, concomitant with the supreme Goddess herself, who is simultaneously one and many. She pervades the universe as myriad divine powers (*śakti*), like the rays (*raśmi*, *marīci*) of the singular sun. This doctrine of *śakti* is a key strand in the formation of the Great Goddess (*mahādevī*) of Purāṇic, devotional Śāktism, as Tracy Pintchman observes.[70] The praise hymn that occupies much of chapter 83 highlights the Goddess's numerous names and forms, including Durgā, Caṇḍī, Kālarātri, Nārāyaṇī, Kātyāyanī, the Alphabet (*mātṛkā*), and Mother of the Vedas, as well as the Seven Mothers, headed by Cāmuṇḍā; the goddesses Jayā, Vijayā, Ajitā, and Aparājitā; Śiva's dual powers of Knowledge and Action; and so forth. Like the *Devī Māhātmya*, the *Devī Purāṇa* envisions each of the Mothers as the emanation or embodiment of a male deity's *śakti*. However, it is ultimately the singular power of Śiva that engenders the Mothers, for prior to the battle, Śiva imparts his own *śakti* into the gods' bodies.[71] It is this that they appear to re-emanate in creating the *mātṛ*s. While this appears to make Śiva the ultimate agent of creation, his pronouncement to the Mothers in chapter 87 overturns that idea:

> You were created by the will of the Ultimate Cause in order to protect the world. That Ultimate Cause is the supreme Śakti, who is primordial and beyond suffering.

Viṣṇu, who narrated these words of Śiva, continues:

> O Indra, She created us—Brahmā and the other gods—and the Rudras as well. She employs us for the sake of creation, maintenance, and destruction, in due course. Just as the rays of the divine Sun dispassionately cause a lotus to open and then close again, in due course, she likewise effects the unfolding and cessation of all endeavors. She has no beginning, nor does she have a middle or end; she abides as mere essence.[72]

Here the Goddess emerges unambiguously as the impetus and paramount agent of all action in the universe.

Tantric Śaiva influence on the *Devī Purāṇa*'s "Slaying of Ruru" cycle extends beyond discourse on *śakti*. In chapter 85, the *Devī Purāṇa* seems to exhibit specific knowledge of the *Brahmayāmala*, a Tantra previously introduced: the four groups of four warlike Seizers who arise in the cardinal directions mostly correspond to the *rākṣasas* occupying these positions in the *Brahmayāmala*'s initiation maṇḍala. And though not listed by name, the twenty-four *yoginīs* the *Devī Purāṇa* mentions in this context may likewise refer to *yoginīs* of its maṇḍala.[73] This is not surprising, for in another section of the text, the *Devī Purāṇa* has incorporated much of an entire chapter from the *Brahmayāmala*.[74] This passage of the *Devī Purāṇa* also includes among the Seizers the lords of four cremation grounds from the maṇḍala of the *Svacchanda Tantra* and makes passing reference to Svacchanda Bhairava, the presiding deity of this influential Tantra.[75] Furthermore, in its description of the seven netherworlds (*pātāla*) through which Ruru traverses while fleeing the lethal Goddess, the *Devī Purāṇa* reveals intimate knowledge of the cosmological teachings of the *Guhyasūtra*. The latter belongs to the highly influential *Niśvāsatattvasaṃhitā*, probably the earliest surviving Śaiva Tantra. Although presented in reverse order, the *Devī Purāṇa*'s account of the netherworlds—their names, presiding deities, cities, and divine and semidivine denizens—closely follows chapter 5 of the *Guhyasūtra*, upon which it is likely based.[76]

Despite drawing upon Śaiva Tantras, the *Devī Purāṇa*'s concerns are not esoteric; as Bihani Sarkar highlights, it devotes significant attention to civic religion and rituals of state and can in fact be read as a manual for Śākta kingship. It provides an important early account of the Nine Nights (*navarātra*) festival, integral to worship of the goddess Durgā even today, among other corporate rituals.[77] Though itself indebted to Tantric sources, the *Devī Purāṇa* observes that the Mother-goddesses are worshiped in accordance with the Vedas as well as the Tantras of Śiva, and by people of all castes; it further prophesies that heretics of the future will worship the Mothers by their own methods, giving as an example Buddhist proponents of the Gāruḍa Tantras.[78] In the *Devī Purāṇa*'s representation, worship of the Mothers was widespread, trans-sectarian, and integral to preservation of the state.

There are intriguing thematic parallels between the "Slaying of Ruru" cycle of the *Devī Purāṇa* and chapters 7–10 of the more famous *Devī Māhātmya*. Both narrate the origins of the Mothers as *śaktis* of the gods in a battle against powerful anti-gods, with a key protagonist being the fearsome Kālī or Cāmuṇḍā. While the *Devī Purāṇa* has Śiva create Kālī/Cāmuṇḍā from his fiery rage, in the *Devī Māhātmya* she emerges from the knitted brows of the supreme Goddess herself, called Ambikā (Mother) and Caṇḍikā (Fierce), among other names. Both texts link Kālī's emergence to the problem of an anti-god's spilled blood giving rise to lethal warriors, a theme that reappears in the tale of Dāruka (see chapter 1). The *Devī Purāṇa* reveals no explicit awareness of the *Devī Māhātmya*, and it remains unclear how the tales relate to each other historically.[79] While the *Devī Māhātmya* belongs to the comparatively orthodox, Veda-affirming *Mārkaṇḍeya Purāṇa*, the *Devī Purāṇa* has close ties to Tantric Śaivism as well as the popular nonorthodox goddess traditions of eastern India. Their idioms also differ: the *Devī Māhātmya* is written in a correct, unembellished Sanskrit typical of Purāṇas, while the *Devī Purāṇa*'s generally rustic language is closer in idiom to the early Śaiva Tantras. While the *Devī Purāṇa* focuses on the triumph of Kālarātri and the Mothers over Ruru, the related tales of the *Devī Māhātmya* feature a wider range of protagonists and antagonists. Their configurations of the Mothers also differ: the *Devī Māhātmya* adds to their ranks an eighth goddess, Nārasiṃhī, the *śakti* of Narasiṃha, Viṣṇu's Man-lion avatar. This group of eight is found neither in temples nor in Tantric ritual texts. Despite its popularity as a liturgical text, the *Devī Māhātmya* lacks the *Devī Purāṇa*'s deep connections to the temple cult of the Seven Mothers.

Fruit: From Imperial Protectresses to Minor Attendants

In light of their prominent worship in the fifth to seventh centuries, the decline of the cult of the Seven Mothers seems precipitous. Major shrines dedicated to them became increasingly rare after the eighth century in most regions. On the other hand, diminutive doorway panels depicting the Seven Mothers became commonplace in temple iconography, especially in central India, where they first appeared in the eighth century.[80] This is one of the many ways in which the Seven Mothers remained well-known divinities, recognizable even today, but with the greatly diminished status of attendants of Durgā and other deities, or minor guardian divinities, rather like the Nine Planets (*navagrahāḥ*). The fate of the Mothers in Nepal is somewhat exceptional, where, as a group of eight, they remain more prominently a part of lived religion.[81] After the decline of the Mothers' temple cult, Cāmuṇḍā's worship continued independently of the others, much as it probably began, as the prevalence of her images in eastern India intimates.[82] However, the ancient regional goddess Bahumāṃsā seems to have faded into oblivion, presumably induced by the sacking of Koṭīvarṣa at the beginning of the thirteenth century by Muhammad Bakhtyar Khilji, under whom the city served as a capital known as Devkot.[83]

In contrast, worship of the goddess Kālī or Kālarātri, whom both the *Devī Purāṇa* and *Devī Māhātmya* conflate with Cāmuṇḍā, continues to thrive. Living traditions centered upon Kālī are prominent in Bengal and in Kerala, whose eminent goddess, Bhadrakāḷī, has a demon-slaying form known as Rurujit, "Conqueror of Ruru." Ruru's tale nonetheless seems largely forgotten, supplanted by the story of Bhadrakāḷī slaying the demon Dārika or Dāruka, as told in the *Bhadrakāḷī Māhātmya* (see chapter 1). The latter tale, however, echoes themes from the *Devī Purāṇa*, with which it may have more affinity than the *Devī Māhātmya*. Fascinatingly, the *Skanda Purāṇa*'s "Glorification of Koṭīvarṣa" converges with the *Devī Purāṇa*'s "Slaying of Ruru" cycle as well as the tale of Dāruka in a text called *Mātṛsadbhāva* (Essence of the Mothers). This Tantric ritual manual in the tradition of the *Brahmayāmala* was composed by the fifteenth century, probably in Kerala.[84] Its nineteenth chapter transforms the *Devī Purāṇa*'s "Slaying of Ruru" into an origin myth for Koṭīvarṣa, which, it claims, acquired holiness as the place where Cāmuṇḍā, in the form of Karṇamoṭī, entered the earth to hunt down Ruru when he fled to the netherworlds.[85] The Mothers sat there with Śiva (by the name Hetuka) for crores (*koṭi*) of years (*varṣa*) while Karṇamoṭī battled Ruru—an etymology for the name Koṭīvarṣa. This chapter then briefly recounts the slaying of Dāruka by the goddess Ekavīrī (Solitary Heroine), who emerges from Śiva's forehead, and subsequently links the tales together in its account of rites concerning Koṭīvarṣa's holy water. The *Mātṛsadbhāva*'s narratives illustrate how Purāṇic tales came to be woven and rewoven together, acquiring new meanings in shifting contexts. They also attest to millennium-long links between demon-slaying Mother-goddesses and devotion at Koṭīvarṣa in northern Bengal—long after the site's demise, and in the distant land of Kerala—and between Tantric ritual texts and Purāṇic narratives.

Despite its declining fortunes, Mother-goddess veneration continued to take on new guises. While the temple cult of the Seven Mothers waned in most regions from the eighth century, Tantric goddess cults incorporating them flourished. In particular, a new deity typology closely linked to the Mothers became pivotal to Tantric worship: *yoginīs*, a variety of goddesses mentioned in the "Glorification of Koṭīvarṣa." Accounts of *yoginīs* describe them as belonging to clans (*kula*) having the Seven or Eight Mothers as matriarchs. Monumental stone temples dedicated to *yoginīs*, usually a set of sixty-four goddesses who include some or all of the Seven Mothers, appear from as early as the ninth and into the thirteenth centuries, marking the reemergence of *mātṛ* veneration in major public temples.[86] The emergence of *yoginī* temples is intimated or at least presaged by the *Devī Purāṇa*, whose fiftieth chapter describes worship of a circle of sixty goddesses who are *yoginī*s in all but name. This chapter seems to be the basis for several later lists of sixty-four *yoginī*s.[87] Popular veneration of Mother-goddesses persists to the present day in varied guises, some with direct connections to the Seven Mothers or *yoginī*s and others with even more ancient roots.

As for the *Yāmala Tantra*s mentioned in the *Skanda Purāṇa*, few of these survive. The original *Rudrayāmala* seems to have been lost; the published texts bearing this title belong to a later period. Among *Yāmala Tantra*s named in older lists of texts, it seems that the *Brahmayāmala* alone survives in manuscripts, although the text was largely forgotten by the twelfth century.[88] The text was nonetheless well known to the redactors of the *Devī Purāṇa*, who incorporated substantial material from it into chapter 119, which concerns the obscure anti-god Khaṭvāsura.[89] Traditions connected to the early medieval *Yāmala*s continued well into the second millennium in south India, where new *Mātṛ Tantra*s and some exegetical works were composed. These sources preserve notable traces of the older literature.[90] Prominent among them is the *Mātṛsadbhāva*, previously discussed; rooted in the tradition of the old *Brahmayāmala*, it weaves together both tales translated in this chapter, conflating the tale of the Mothers' victory at Koṭīvarṣa with the "Slaying of Ruru."

SOURCES

The translation of the *Skanda Purāṇa* is based on the recent edition by Yuko Yokochi, which appears in an appendix to Hans Bakker's *The World of the Skandapurāṇa* (2014). This represents a considerable improvement over the first edition by Krishna Prasad Bhattarai (1988); as Yokochi shows, the latter artificially conflates the two surviving recensions of the "Glorification of Koṭīvarṣa": the old version (recension "S") and one dating to approximately the ninth to tenth centuries (recension "RA").[91] My translation is of the earlier version. A detailed summary is provided by Yokochi and Bakker, who also translate short excerpts.[92] No full translation of this section, nor indeed of any section of the original *Skanda Purāṇa*, has previously been published.

The translation of the *Devī Purāṇa* passages is based on a provisional critical edition of the Sanskrit under preparation by the present author. This makes use of a limited number of manuscripts from Bengal and Nepal in addition to the text's two printed editions, by Panchanan Tarkaratna (1895–96) and Pushpendra Kumar Sharma (1976), which are based on distinct sources. No early manuscript of the text seems to have survived, and both printed editions are problematic.[93] Passages that remain difficult to interpret have either been left untranslated and marked with ellipses (. . .) or tentatively translated and flagged in the notes. Passages summarized rather than translated in full are set in smaller type. A full critical edition of the *Devī Purāṇa* remains an important desideratum for the study of medieval Hinduism and the history of Śāktism.

FURTHER READING

Harper, Katherine Anne. 1989. *Seven Hindu Goddesses of Spiritual Transformation: The Iconography of the Saptamatrikas*. Lewiston: Edwin Mellen.

Hatley, Shaman. 2012. "From Mātṛ to Yoginī: Continuity and Transformation in the South Asian Cults of the Mother Goddesses." In *Transformations and Transfer of Tantra in Asia and Beyond*, edited by István Keul, 99–129. Berlin: Walter de Gruyter.

Hazra, R. C. 1963. *Studies in the Upapurāṇas*. Vol. 2, Śākta *and Non-sectarian Upapurāṇas*. Calcutta Sanskrit College Research Series, no. 22. Kolkata: Sanskrit College.

Yokochi, Yuko. 2013. "The Development of Śaivism in Koṭīvarṣa, North Bengal, with Special Reference to the *Koṭīvarṣa-Māhātmya* in the *Skandapurāṇa*." *Indo-Iranian Journal* 56: 295–324.

NOTES

1. "Millions of years" loosely translates *varṣakoṭi* ("crores of years"), an etymology of the city Koṭīvarṣa. On the meaning of *pūrvodadhi*, which ostensibly means "the eastern ocean" but may instead refer to the Brahmaputra River, see Yokochi (2013b, 298n12). Koṭīvarṣa in fact lies on the banks of the smaller Punarbhava River.

2. The phrase "bears half of her husband's body" alludes to Ardhanārīśvara (the "Half-female Lord"), a deity-form in which Pārvatī and Śiva each make up half of a single body, female on the left and male on the right.

3. The masculine adjective *śubham* has been emended to the feminine *śubhām* (cf. the correct feminine plural *śubhāḥ* in 15b, and the feminine singular *śubhā* in 20b).

4. After delineating several Mothers and breaking off, verse 19 starts afresh, listing the Seven Mothers in their most commonly occurring order, from Brāhmī to Cāmuṇḍā (here bearing a more distinctive local name, Bahumāṃsā). I have substituted the more common name Māheśvarī for the text's Rudrāṇī ("of Rudra") and Śarvāṇī ("of Śarva," i.e., Śiva), to avoid confusion.

5. In Tantric Śaivism, *vidyās* ("lore" or "spell") are the mantras identified with goddesses, the epithet *mahāvidyā* ("Great Spell") thus intimating Bahumāṃsā's identity as a Tantric deity.

6. That is, Mothers who emerge from the gods Vāyu, Varuṇa, Yama, Kubera, Mahākāla, and Agni, respectively (cf. *Mahābhārata, Śalyaparvan* 45.35–36b). The thirteen goddesses listed by name in this passage hence comprise the Seven Mothers (with Bahumāṃsā standing in for Cāmuṇḍā) and the eight Mothers of the Directions (*diṅmātaraḥ*), with Mahākālī standing for Nairṛti. Īśānī (Māheśvarī) and Indrāṇī belong to both sets and are listed just once. On the *diṅmātaraḥ*, see my entry in Goodall and Rastelli (2013, 162–63).

7. Becoming one of Śiva's *gaṇas* ("group," i.e., his divine entourage), or a lord among *gaṇas* (*gaṇapati, gaṇeśvara*, etc.), is arguably the principal aim of Śaiva devotion in the vision of the *Skanda Purāṇa*. See, for instance, Bisschop (2009, 747–49).

8. The interpretation of *bhavatīnāṃ* ("yours") in *rudhiraughavatī seha bhavatīnāṃ bhaviṣyati* (33cd) is not certain. This might alternatively be understood to mean "brimming with blood, she [the river] will always here belong to you." Yokochi (2013b, 300) suggests "carrying a stream of blood owing to you," that is, on account of animal sacrifices offered to the Mothers; this is also plausible.

9. On the interpretation of this passage, as mentioned previously, see Sanderson (2001, 6–7).

10. On the subject of *yoginīs* and their powers of yoga, see Hatley (2013).

11. That is, Koṭīvarṣa is hereby declared to be one of the principal cremation grounds, part of a network of places of pilgrimage for Tantric Śaivas, who regarded cremation grounds (*śmaśāna*) as excellent places for meditation and religious practice.

12. Since Śakra is usually a synonym of Indra, this name has been emended to Śukra, a divine sage and preceptor of the *asuras*.

13. The passage from the *Devī Purāṇa* summarizes chapter 83 and translates sections of chapters 84–88. Sections that are summarized are set in the same typeface and size used for the introduction to the chapter. The subsection headings reflect chapter breaks in the original.

14. The phrase "would they fulfill their duty" is a conjecture for the corrupted reading *kuryuḥ svakāryyedaṃ*.

15. This sentence translates a doubtful verse (84.24) that may have been spliced into this position or misplaced; it is repeated again in 85.13c–14b, where it better fits the context.

16. The phrase "bent by the weight of a mighty spear" renders a conjectural emendation, *śaraśṛṅgena nāmitā* for *śaraśṛṅgāranāmitā* (as read in most sources). The word *śaraśṛṅga* (literally "arrow-horn" or "pinnacle of arrows") may refer to a particular weapon, since it is attested as an item held by a deity in several Tantras: *Jayadrathayāmala* (3.19.29), *Vārāhī Tantra* (line 14031), *Tantrasadbhāva* 10.29 and 20.167, and *Brahmayāmala* 90.71. I am grateful to Michael Slouber for making this observation.

17. "Ultimate Cause" translates *kāraṇa* and alludes to the Śākta doctrine that the creator of everything in the universe, including the other gods, is the Great Goddess.

18. Kālarudra, "Dark Howler" or "Death Howler," is probably a synonym of Mahākāla, a fierce, skull-bearing form of Śiva, here conflated with Bhairava as well as Caṇḍeśa. On the history of Mahākāla and some related deities, see Granoff (2003/2004).

19. In contrast to Bahumāṃsā's role in the "Glorification of Koṭīvarṣa," the *Devī Purāṇa* names Kālarātri, "Dark Night" or "Night of Death," as leader of the Mothers, and conflates her with Kālī as well as Cāmuṇḍā. On the early history of Kālarātri and her conflation with Kālī, see Sarkar (2017, 41–69); on their conflation with Caṇḍikā and Cāmuṇḍā, see Sarkar (2017, 70–96).

20. "Whose desire was stimulated by the potency of that drink" is a conjectural translation, because the original Sanskrit phrase appears to be corrupt.

21. "They fell upon the powerful demon army" is a conjectural translation, because the original Sanskrit phrase appears to be corrupt.

22. This statement (*Devī Purāṇa* 85.81) reveals that the redactors have summarized the tale from an unnamed older source.

23. The entire sentence "They attacked . . . fell upon them" is conjectural, as the text appears to be corrupt here.

24. The ellipsis indicates that the original text is faulty here and was not translated.

25. This is an etymological explanation of the name Cāmuṇḍā: "bearer of the hide (*carman*) and head (*muṇḍa*) [of Ruru]." Cf. *Mātṛsadbhāva* 19.60. This may be predicated on *carman* (hide) being pronouned in the vernacular as *cāma*, via Prakrit *camma*, much as *karman* becomes *kāma* in modern Indo-Aryan languages. Another explanation is that Cāmuṇḍā acquired her name from slaying the anti-gods Caṇḍa and Muṇḍa; see *Devī Māhātmya* 7.23–27 and *Devī Purāṇa* 37.87–88 (where *caṇḍa* and *muṇḍa* are given symbolic meaning).

26. The phrase "illuminating the world" is conjectural, as the original text is corrupt here.

27. This list of divine and semidivine beings encompasses important Śaiva deities—Śiva's loyal entourage, the *gaṇas*, led by Gaṇeśa, Nandin, etc.; a multitude of male Śaiva deities called Rudras, who preside over various realms of the cosmos, with diverse functions; and *yoginīs*, Tantric goddesses who are in some ways female counterparts to the *gaṇas* and Rudras—as well as *vetālas*, vampiric animated corpses; the demonic *rākṣasas*; and *yakṣas*, local deities or nature spirits.

28. The phrase "By the will of that Ultimate Cause, Śiva told the mother-goddesses" is conjectural, as the original text is corrupt here.

29. The ellipsis indicates that the original text is unintelligible here.

30. In contrast to the first narrative, here Vārāhī is not Viṣṇu's *śakti* but rather the *śakti* of Yama-Vaivasvata.

31. These two lines (*Devī Purāṇa* 87.33ab) seem to describe Gaṇeśa, but their placement raises doubt.

32. These genres of Tantric medical literature in broad terms concern countering poisons, control of spirit beings, and protection of children, respectively. Chapter 10 of this volume features material from a Gāruḍa Tantra.

33. Classical Indian tradition recognizes eight kinds of marriage, of which the *gandharva* variety refers to elopement, and divine (*daiva*) to the gifting of a bride to a priest during the performance of a sacrifice. See Kane (1974, vol. I, pt. I, 516–26). The *kiṃnara* marriage mentioned here does not feature in orthodox lists.

34. Implicit here is the Tantric Śaiva notion that all creation is sonic or vibratory in nature, emerging from the Word or Logos (*vāk*)—which is none other than *śakti*. See Padoux (1990).

35. Tantric Śaiva cosmology conceptualizes the universe as an ascending series of planes or levels (*tattva*, "ontic principle"), classically thirty-six in number; the higher *tattva*s contain various worlds. The transcendent-cum-immanent *sadāśiva-tattva* is just below the *tattva*s of *śakti* and the wholly transcendent *parama-śiva*. The Rudra named Ananta presides over the base of the cosmos.

36. The translations "gilded metal, coral, painted wood, baked earth" are conjectural.

37. *Bṛhatsaṃhitā* 59.19. Concerning the likelihood that Varāhamihira spoke of the Seven Mothers and not some other *mātṛ* group, see Hatley (2012, 106).

38. For instance, the Āmudālapāḍu plates of the Cālukya king Vikramāditya I of 660 CE refer to his dynasty as "made prosperous by the Seven Mothers, mothers of the seven worlds" (*saptalokamātṛbhis saptamātṛbhir abhivardhitānām*; *Epigraphia Indica* 32, no. 21: 175ff.).

39. Concerning the location and names of the site, see Yokochi (2013b, 295–96).

40. For a more detailed presentation on this subject, see Hatley (2012), "From Mātṛ to Yoginī," which I frequently paraphrase or quote in this section.

41. Regarding the multiple religious contexts of *mātṛ* statuary, see Joshi (1986, 15); concerning the possibility of their own temples, see Singh (2004, 390–92).

42. For a detailed study of temples and statuary of the Seven Mothers, see Harper (1989).

43. See Meister (1986, 239, 244–45).

44. A translation and analysis of this tale may be found in Coburn (1991). Concerning the date of the text, see Yokochi (2004, 21–22, 23n42); she argues for the second half of the eighth century. Concerning *mātṛ*s in the *Devī Purāṇa*, see Pal (1988, 22–59). Regarding the *Devī Purāṇa*'s dating, see Hatley (2018, 121–23).

45. See the introduction to Adriaensen, Bakker, and Isaacson (1998–2018).

46. See Sanderson (2001, 6–7), Bakker (2014, 241–60), and Yokochi (2013b, 295–324).

47. Yokochi (2004, 99–113, esp. 110–11).

48. See especially Sanderson (2014, 40).

49. Yokochi (2013b, 301).

50. Joshi (1986, 103–28).

51. See the tables in Meister (1986), which provide for the iconic programs of Gupta and early post-Gupta *mātṛ* sets, as well as later sets from central and western India (charts A and B).

52. *Mahābhārata, Āraṇyakaparvan* 217.3–11. See Hatley (2007, 57–64) and Yokochi (2013b, 305).

53. See Yokochi (2013b, 304–6).

54. *Skanda Purāṇa* 64 narrates the emergence of manifold goddesses from Kauśikī's limbs. In *Skanda Purāṇa* 68, Kauśikī assigns the various Mother goddesses that emerged from her to locales, including Bahumāṃsā to Koṭīvarṣa. See Yokochi's discussion (2013b, 99–100, 111–12).

55. Yokochi (2013b, 303).

56. The textual reference is that of the Kashmiri *Bṛhatkālottara,* in which Yogeśī, eighth of the Mothers, is visualized as emaciated and Cāmuṇḍā as full-figured. See Sanderson (2004, 267n92). On the statuary, see, for example, Hatley (2007, figure 2.7).

57. Sanderson (2009, 230–31). Perhaps the goddess's trident replaced an earlier spear, the emblem associated with Bahumāṃsā in the *Skanda Purāṇa,* as well as with Lohitāyani in the *Mahābhārata* (as Yokochi points out; 2013b, 305). On the image recovered from Bangarh/Koṭīvarṣa itself, see Bakker (2014, 255, plate 64).

58. For an analysis of the passage listing the *Yāmalas,* see Sanderson (2001, 6–7).

59. See Hatley (2018) and Kiss (2015).

60. See, for example, *Tantrasadbhāva* 19.32–33. Karṇamoṭī bears a spear as her emblem, suggesting that the goddesses are one and the same.

61. *Brahmayāmala* 3.119c–27b; see Kiss (2015, 104, 193–94). See also Yokochi (2013b, 311–13).

62. See especially *Devī Purāṇa,* chapters 90–91 and 117–18. Pal (1988) makes important observations concerning Mother-goddess worship in the *Devī Purāṇa,* although his findings require revision on numerous points.

63. Concerning Ballālasena's exclusion of the *Devī Purāṇa* from his digest, see Hazra (1984, 46). On the abridged nature of the extant *Devī Purāṇa,* see Hazra (1963, 69–71). Hazra (1963, 71–90) advances a detailed argument in favor of dating the text to 500–700 CE, favoring the latter part of the sixth century; for a critique of this, see Hatley (2018, 121–23).

64. Concerning the *Devī Purāṇa*'s adaptation of the *Brahmayāmala,* see Hatley (2018, 251–72).

65. Despite her name, the sow-faced Vārāhī is usually regarded as the female emanation of the death god, Yama (also Vaivasvata), rather than Viṣṇu's boar-*avatāra,* Varāha; she shares Yama's emblem, the staff, and his mount, the buffalo, and is also known as Yāmī/Yāmyā or Vaivasvatī. The Koṭīvarṣa narrative, however, is among the sources linking her with Viṣṇu.

66. Cf. the tale of Dārika/Dāruka, translated in chapter 1 of this volume.

67. Both printed editions confuse matters by having the opening and closing verses of the hymn extol female deities: Bhairavī (the female counterpart of Bhairava) and Gaṇanāyikā (the female counterpart of Gaṇeśa) instead of Bhairava and Gaṇeśa. Cf. Pal (1988, 40–41). These female names, though found in some manuscripts, are unlikely to be original.

68. On images of Naṭeśa in *mātṛ* temples, see Meister (1986).

69. See Donaldson (2002) concerning *mātṛ* temples of Odisha. Much earlier and in the Deccan, note the late-sixth-century Rāvaṇa-kā Kāī and Rāmeśvara cave shrines

of Ellora, where the Seven Mothers are joined by a skeletal divine couple, probably Mahākāla and Kālī/Kālarātri.

70. Pintchman (1994, 3–5, passim). Notably, this discourse on *śakti* is absent from the old *Skanda Purāṇa*.

71. *Devī Purāṇa* 84.4: "The God of gods Śiva bestowed his power (*śakti*) upon our bodies, O Indra. He then said, 'Viṣṇu, Brahmā, and Indra—let everyone depart to attack Ruru, together with my attendants'" (*dattvā śaktiṃ svakāyebhyo devadevena vāsava gacchadhvaṃ sagaṇāḥ sarve viṣṇubrahmapurandarāḥ*).

72. *Devī Purāṇa* 87.17–20c.

73. See *Devī Purāṇa* 85.68–79. On the deity pantheons and primary maṇḍala of the *Brahmayāmala*, see Kiss (2015, 16–30).

74. See Hatley (2018, 251–72).

75. Passing reference to Svacchanda Bhairava occurs in *Devī Purāṇa* 85.80.

76. Ruru's descent through the seven netherworlds is described in *Devī Purāṇa* 86.3–15, which is likely based on *Guhyasūtra* 5.1–21. One verse is nearly identical: *Devī Purāṇa* 86.3c–4b and *Guhyasūtra* 5.16c–17b. Chapter 82 of the *Devī Purāṇa* provides a more elaborate description of the netherworlds, which serves also as a prelude to Ruru's tale.

77. On kingship and the *Devī Purāṇa*, see Sarkar (2017, 180–82); on the *Devī Purāṇa*'s account of *navarātra*, see Sarkar (2017, 226–29).

78. *Devī Purāṇa* 88.1–2.

79. Hazra (1963, 71–90).

80. Meister (1986).

81. On the Mother-goddesses in Kathmandu, see Tachikawa (2004).

82. Concerning Cāmuṇḍā statuary in the state of Odisha, see Donaldson (2002).

83. On Bakhtyar Khilji's conquests in Bengal, see Sarkar ([1948] 2006, 1–36).

84. See Sanderson (2014, 50–52). I am grateful to Muralikrishnan M. V. for sharing with me his draft edition of *Mātṛsadbhāva* chapter 19. In this text's version of the myth of the Mothers, among other interesting differences, the Mothers take on children's forms (*bālarūpa*) and have neither husbands nor offspring. On the theme of the Goddess appearing as a prepubescent girl, see chapters 3, 6, 7, and 8 in this volume.

85. As previously mentioned, though the *Skanda Purāṇa* celebrates Bahumāṃsā as the presiding goddess of Koṭīvarṣa, several Tantric sources name her as Karṇamoṭī, which may be a synonym.

86. On temples of the *yoginī*s, see Dehejia (1986) and Hatley (2014).

87. On chapter 50 of the *Devī Purāṇa*, see Hatley (2014, 212–13). As Gudrun Bühnemann (2003) observes, the circle of goddesses there delineated seems to be the basis for sets of sixty-four *yoginī*s described in three texts that predate the fourteenth century: the *Agni Purāṇa*, *Mayadīpikā*, and Vairocana's *Lakṣaṇasaṃgraha* (also known as *Pratiṣṭhālakṣaṇasārasamuccaya*).

88. A number of compositions by the name *Brahmayāmala* were written in later periods, and the *Brahmayāmala* became an important locus of ascription for various short texts; see Hatley (2018, 4–7).

89. See Hatley (2018, 251–72).

90. See Sanderson (2014, 40–41, 50–52).

91. On this conflation, see Yokochi (2013b, 297–98) and Yokochi's appendix in Bakker (2014, 252–56).

92. See Yokochi's appendix in Bakker (2014, 252–57).

93. For a recent assessment of the printed editions and manuscripts of the *Devī Purāṇa*, see Hatley (2018, 256–57); for an older assessment, see Hazra (1963). Concerning the specific manuscripts used in the provisional critical edition on which the present translation of *Devī Purāṇa* 84–88 is based, see Hatley (2018, 621).

PART TWO

Miracles and Devotees

FIGURE 9. Svasthānī, by Laura Santi

CHAPTER 5

Svasthānī

Goddess of One's Own Place

JESSICA VANTINE BIRKENHOLTZ

The next four chapters tell tales that are less about amazing the audience with awe-inspiring descriptions of battle and more about relating to the concerns of the audience. They focus on the miraculous powers of the Goddess, justice in daily life, and how devotion to the Goddess can serve to uplift her votaries. The first is from the Kathmandu Valley of Nepal, home to several cities and towns that functioned as independent kingdoms in the past. It is a bowl-shaped valley surrounded by what would be called high mountains in any other part of the world, but which are mere foothills in the Himalayas, the highest mountains anywhere. Nepal is home to a broad range of landscapes and an even broader diversity of ethnic groups and languages. The native inhabitants of the Kathmandu Valley are the Newars, who until recently were the primary custodians of the written tradition on the goddess Svasthānī.

The translation is based on the oldest surviving manuscript of *The Story of the Ritual Vow to the Goddess Svasthānī*, a text that has become of central importance to Hindus in Nepal. For the past five hundred years, the tale has circulated primarily in the Newar language, although its oldest version was written in Sanskrit and it thrives in the Nepali language today. The story focuses on two women, the devout but luckless Gomā and her selfish and sinful daughter-in-law Candravatī, with a supporting role played by Navarāj, their son and husband, respectively. The trials and triumphs these characters experience illustrate the reasons and rewards for worshiping Svasthānī. Of central importance is the performance of a vow or pledge (*vrata*), which thousands of Hindu women in Nepal perform every year during the month of Māgh (mid-January to mid-February). The story frequently uses the term "twice-born" to refer to Brahmins, an allusion to their spiritual rebirth following a rite of passage into adulthood.

Readers should think about how the Svasthānī vow described here is similar to, or different from, vows in other religions or contexts with which they are familiar. After reading the commentary, readers should also consider how events in the story inform the living tradition in Nepal described in the essay. In what ways is the female-dominated Svasthānī tradition empowering for women? In what ways does it support patriarchy?

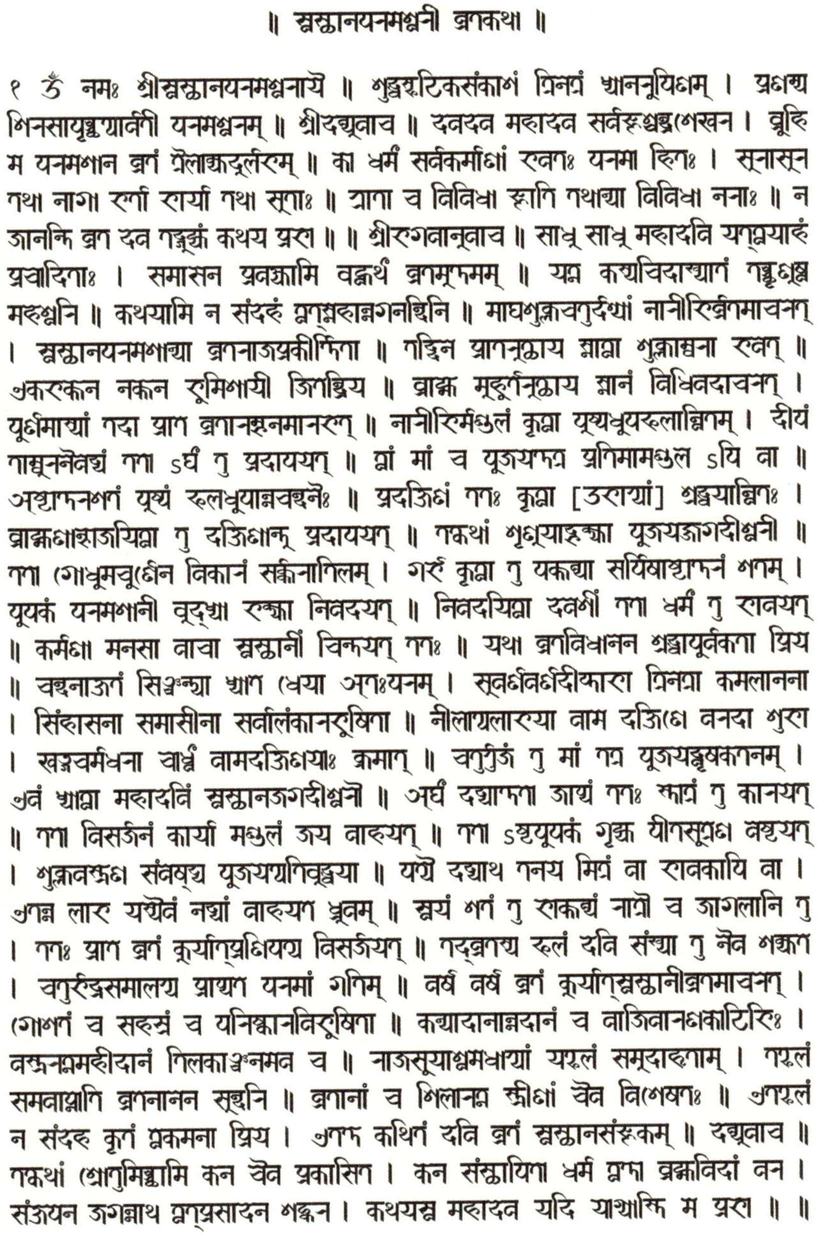

FIGURE 10. *Svasthānīvratakathā*, a Sanskrit work in the Newar script. Font "Nepal Lipi Unicode" © Nepal Lipi Online.

THE STORY OF SVASTHĀNĪ AND THE SECRET VOW

Oṃ Salutation to the radiant Supreme Goddess Svasthānī![1]

The mountain's daughter Pārvatī bowed her head with respect and questioned three-eyed Śiva, radiant as a clear crystal in his meditation form. The radiant goddess said: "O God of gods, Mahādeva! O all-knowing, moon-crested lord! Tell me, Supreme Lord, about the vow that is difficult to learn of in the three worlds. What is the most beneficial course (*dharma*) among all actions in your view?[2] Gods, demonic *asuras*, divine *nāga* serpents, husbands, wives, sons, brothers and various relatives, and various other people do not know this vow, O god! Please tell me that secret vow, my lord!"

The lord said: "Yes, good! Good, O Great Goddess! At your behest, I will succinctly narrate the ultimate vow, of which the rewards are many. Listen, Great Goddess, to that which has not been related to anyone. I will tell you because of my affection for you. Do not doubt, O joy of the mountain!

"On the fourteenth day of the bright lunar fortnight in the month of Māgh (mid-January to mid-February), women should perform the vow of the Supreme Goddess Svasthānī, which is called the king of vows. On that day, after rising early in the morning and bathing, a woman should dress in pure clothes. She should eat but one meal a day, sleep on the ground, and conquer her senses. After rising at the holy hour, one should take a ritual bath according to the prescribed rules.[3] Then, at daybreak on the day of the full moon, one should begin the preparations for the vow.

"One should make a maṇḍala with other women, and then present the guest offering along with food, lamps, and areca nut, together with flowers, incense, and fruit.[4] Then she should worship you and me in an image upon the maṇḍala, with 108 flowers, sandalwood, fruit, incense, and grain.[5] Then, after circumambulating us both, she who is endowed with devotion should feed the Brahmins and give them a donation. One should then listen to the story with devotion and worship Pārvatī, queen of the world. Then, after combining sesame and coarse sugar together, mixing it with wheat flour, and frying it in clarified butter, she should offer to the Supreme Goddess 108 pieces of bread, understanding the significance of the bread and her devotion. Having made this offering to the goddess, one should meditate on righteousness. One should concentrate on Svasthānī in action, thought, and speech. According to the precepts of the vow, O beloved, sprinkle sandalwood and whole rice on her image with devotion.

"Then one should reflect on her in meditation. Her beauty is luminous like the color of gold. She has three eyes and her face is like a lotus. She sits on a throne that is a lion and is decorated with all kinds of ornaments. In her left hand she holds a blue lotus while making the fear-dispelling gesture. She holds her right hand in the boon-giving gesture. In her other right and left hands she holds a sword and shield upraised, respectively. Such is the image of the Supreme Goddess Svasthānī. Such is also the image of Śiva. The only different feature is his vehicle, which is a bull. One should meditate on me, whose symbol is the bull, in this four-armed form. Thus, meditate on Svasthānī and the Lord of the World, O Great Goddess.

"Then one should offer water, mutter a prayer in a low voice, and recite a hymn of praise. One should then perform the conclusion, saying 'May the maṇḍala be successful.' Then one should take eight pieces of the bread and tie them with yellow thread, wrap them in white cloth, and engage in worship while thinking of one's husband. You should give these eight pieces of bread to your husband, or to a son, or to a ritual friend's son, or even to a sister's husband. If one does not have such wealth in the form of one of these recipients, the bread should then be released into a river. One should oneself eat the remaining one hundred pieces of bread and remain awake in the night. Then, in the early morning of the next day, one should bow down respectfully and thus release oneself from the objective of the vow.

"The benefits of this vow cannot even be counted, O goddess! Having achieved the four auspicious ends of human life, one will obtain final emancipation.[6] One should perform the Svasthānī vow with the intention to do the vow every year. Those who perform this vow, O beautiful, will obtain the same benefits as a gift of a hundred or a thousand ornamented cows to a Brahmin; of a gift of a daughter in marriage; of a gift of grain, a horse, an elephant, or by giving tens of millions of elephants and horses; of a gift of clothes, jewels, or landed property, and even of a gift of sesame or gold; the benefits of a sacrifice to crown a universal emperor, or a horse sacrifice. This is the crown jewel of vows, particularly for women. My dear, these are its fruits. Of this have no doubt. The vow is to be done with singular concentration. O goddess, I have now told you about this vow, which is called 'the vow of one's own place' (*svasthāna*)."

The goddess said, "I have a desire to hear the story of this vow, by whom it was made known, and by whom it was established, O greatest among the learned! Lord Śiva, ruler of the world, graciously tell me in brief, O Great God, if I am worthy, my lord!"

The lord said, "There was a place named Brahmapurī, where lived a great ascetic named Śiva Bhaṭṭa. Near his pleasant courtyard, Ganges water flowed. He had fulfilled the six duties of a Brahmin and was completely conversant with the meaning of many sacred books.[7] His wife was named Satī, and she was at all times devoted to her husband.[8] As a consequence of actions from a previous birth, the twice-born man did not have children.[9] With tears of sorrow falling from her eyes, the Brahmin woman said to her husband, 'Alas! I do not know what I did. My body is sinful from birth. I do not have any children. My birth was useless. It was in vain!' Listening to his wife's words, her husband consoled her with words of wisdom.

"Soon after this, the husband and wife were living a comfortable life when, by the power of their religious merit, a single cow approached. The cow, foremost among protectors, defecated. After seeing that cow dung emitted in a hole, an obstetric smell wafted. Having seen this transpire near their courtyard, they found a beautiful girl child who was a delight. The old husband and wife carried the auspiciously marked girl to their own dwelling. The twice-born received this child as if she was the goddess Lakṣmī, possessor and bestower of money and grains. There was a celebration with great noise of drums, conch shells, and trumpets. Then a religious ceremony was performed at the auspicious time with a recitation of the Veda by a Brahmin. Day by day, the girl grew like the moon in the bright half of the lunar month.[10]

"Meanwhile, the gods, Indra, and so forth trembled from fear of the growing spiritual power of that twice-born Brahmin. After they had all arrived at Kailash, Śiva then informed the gods, 'I grant you assurance of safety and security. Go with peace of mind, Indra. At present, Great Goddess, I will wander on the great earth.' Śiva assumed the form of a skull-bearing mendicant, and, with the pretense of begging for alms, he went to the door of the twice-born.[11] Playing a double-sided, handheld drum, he begged at the Brahmin's house, whereupon the girl child, because of her pride, did not register his words but continued to play with some flowers. Her mother heard all his words and said to the girl, 'There are heaps of grains. Grab a handful of grain, daughter!' Upon hearing her mother's words, she went in front of him bearing alms. 'I will not take these alms given by you, Brahmin girl! What foolishness!' He then issued her a curse filled with inward wrath: 'Your husband will be an old man of eighty years!' Hearing the curse, the girl, overcome with fear, cried and cried.

"Now, on the peak of Mt. Kailash, the daughters of the gods were congregated together and encircled by the guardians of the [ten] directions and other divine beings, together with Gaṇeśa, Skanda, and Brahmā, and also with Indra, Sarasvatī, Lakṣmī, sylvan *yakṣas*, celestial *gandharvas*, and horse-headed *kiṃnaras*. They made the preparations for the vow and performed that vow to Svasthānī. They assembled in heaven and performed the crown jewel among vows, O Pārvatī! Whether poor or wealthy, it leads to religious merit (*dharma*), sensual pleasure (*kāma*), prosperity (*artha*), and spiritual liberation (*mokṣa*). I said, 'They do not know this vow in the realm of the mortals, O Mother of the World! Let the sage Āśava go there for the purpose of instructing mortals in the vow!' Having received Śiva's order, Āśava departed. He who knows the true nature of everything and who is solely devoted to doing good for others, thought, 'Among the people living on earth, who is destitute?'

"Meanwhile, O goddess, the beautiful girl who was produced from the cow dung was named Gomā Bhaṭṭinī on account of having been born from cow dung. At the time to put out a call for a son-in-law, Śiva Śarma arrived, fated to do so by the curse of the mendicant. The Brahmin, who was very, very old, came to ask for the girl in marriage. The twice-born, whose hair was long and matted, was tall but his long limbs hung low. He was very weak and his limbs trembled. He was stooped over, deaf, and dressed in rags. He was in the declining time of his life. Śiva Bhaṭṭa gave his daughter to that old man because he had not found another Brahmin and, remembering the earlier curse, he feared the mendicant's curse. For this, his own relatives reproached him when the wedding ceremony concluded. That son-in-law was taken in and protected by Śiva Bhaṭṭa.[12]

"Then, Śiva Bhaṭṭa suffered a fever and aching limbs and went to heaven. The mother of that girl, who was named Satī, lived up to her name.[13] Now Gomā Bhaṭṭinī was distraught living with her husband. He was an impoverished man with matted hair and a stooped back, who was so old he tasted nothing when eating. Gomā became pregnant, and they performed the rite for the birth of a male child and the other rites.[14] Then, the satisfied old man performed the hair-parting rite.[15] But then the old Brahmin informed his wife that he would set off in order to seek alms. That twice-born, who had been away in another region for one month, was overcome by fever and chills and died in a forest.

"His wife, the Brahmin woman Gomā, lived in her own dwelling, which was desolate and unfrequented. Protection and food were provided to the Brahmin woman by the residents of the village. After some months Gomā gave birth to a virtuous son. The rite for a newborn infant was performed, followed by the hair-parting ceremony.[16] The naming ceremony was performed and the young twice-born was named Navarāj.[17] His mother performed all the rites on behalf of her son, with the help of a twice-born priest. The tonsure ceremony, marriage, and all of the other rites and ceremonies were performed for the son. Even though poverty stricken and suffering greatly, his mother always provided for him.

"In his youth, Navarāj was the most excellent of the twice-born. Properly observing the ritual procedures, his mother arranged for the marriage of her son. The young husband and wife lived in hardship together with his mother in her house. Navarāj, very sorrowful, asked his mother, 'Who is my father? Where did he go? Tell me the truth. Do not lie.' Hearing the words of her son, the greatly suffering woman cried. She said, 'O son!' and related her husband's actions. 'When you were in my womb, son, he went to beg for alms. Where he is I do not know. I know not even whether he is dead or alive.'

"Having heard his mother's words, the very pious Navarāj consoled his mother with reasons well grounded in the authoritative *śāstra* texts. 'Then I will go to that region, if you grant me permission to depart from you. Isn't the most important duty of a son the salvation of his father? He who is able but not working for the deliverance of his father does not have a proper desire for happiness. He goes to the frightful infernal underworlds, for as long as fourteen Indras.'[18]

"Having thus convinced his mother, that twice-born obtained her permission to leave. He then informed his young wife and received provisions for his journey. Having undertaken preparations for the journey in accordance with the ritual precepts, he then set off for the region to which his father had traveled. Following in his father's footsteps, he went from one village to another village, whereupon he heard from the mouths of the villagers that his father had died. He cried with great sorrow, 'Alas, woe is me! My beloved father!' He then went to the bank of the Ganges and performed the death rituals as prescribed.

"Meanwhile, the Brahmin woman Gomā Bhaṭṭinī was crying from the trouble caused by her daughter-in-law, who had left to go back to her natal home. Gomā was the most wretched woman in the vicinity. She left the village out of embarrassment. Deprived of suitable clothes and very filthy, she lived on the narrow bank by the river in a small hut made of grass that was surrounded by castor oil trees.[19] She always ate only the grains poor people eat [i.e., millet, barley] and spun thread. She thus passed the time due to the great suffering that was her karma.

"Now after some time, Āśava, the son of a twice-born, asked a cowherder nearby, 'Who is poor and needy? Who is rich?' The cowherds replied, 'Gomā, the woman who lives in the forest outside the village—her suffering is the greatest of those who suffer. There is no greater suffering.' After hearing this from the cowherder, the great sage went to the woman's dwelling. He stood at the door and called out to the Brahmin woman again and again. 'Listen to the instructions for the *dharma*, the vow of Svasthānī, which is supreme.' So he told her the instructions for the vow, which the Brahmin woman readily accepted. She received the instruction for the vow like a poor person receives a treasure. She bowed down to the most respectable sage with an extremely peaceful mind. She gave him a seat on which to sit and made him comfortable in her dwelling. She then thought how to provide the proper hospitality for him, her guest. The wretched woman thought, 'I do not have anything in the house. What can I do?' So she took some spun thread and went to buy areca nut or betel leaf. She bought betel leaf and betel nut and returned home. Oh! What a surprise! The sage had left a treasure in her house and departed. The Brahmin woman arrived home but did not find the sage there. Then filled with dejection, she began to sweep the house. Lifting up the good chair, she saw the treasure the sage had left for her. As tears covered her face she uttered sweet words. 'He came to give me not only instructions for performing the vow, but treasure too.' She received the splendid treasure with a joyful mind.

"She then performed the vow as explained by the sage. On the full moon day in the month of Māgh, she completed it according to the ritual precepts. With a desire for the return of her son, she made preparations for her son as if for a guest.[20] By the power of that vow her son returned. He stood in the door and said, 'Mother! Mother!' Hearing such very pleasing words, she realized, 'That is my son!' and grabbed a vessel of water for the purpose of washing his feet and went to him, nearly senseless with delight. Upon seeing his mother, the son made obeisance to her. She honored him with blessings and washed his feet. She then settled him inside her house. The son gave his mother a description of everything: the other region, the death of his father, the death rituals, and so forth. Beholding the fragrant room, perfumed from being filled with lotus flowers, he then said, 'Tell me mother, what is the reason for all these various flowers?' She replied, 'My son, I performed a vow with the stated desire for your prosperity.'

"Hearing his mother's words made the son of the twice-born happy. 'You are virtuous! You have fulfilled your duty! You successfully performed this vow. In this world and in the next world also, this vow is indeed the path to the Supreme. Even as in this world the vow protects righteousness (*dharma*), so in the next world it preserves it. There is no other vow comparable in this world. There is no other protector! Please tell me the precepts of this vow.' She then told him everything, the very precepts of the vow. Now it was a great festive occasion, since he would become prosperous and powerful. The mother had her son bathe as prescribed by the ritual precepts. She collected eight pieces of bread, fruit, flowers, and whole grains and, together with a mixture of whole grain, yogurt, and cooked grain, duly gave them to her son. She fed her guest, who desired to please the gods, as ritually prescribed. And then after giving him betel nut leaf with areca nut, the Brahmin woman herself ate. Then, by the power of her merit, Navarāj, the twice-born, had his mother perform the death ritual for her husband.

"At this time in their region a preeminent king died. Because the king had no son, the king's priests and ministers sought out one worthy to be made king. Navarāj possessed the auspicious signs and bore the marks of royalty. He was bathed with water from a large bejeweled earthen water jar by the trunk of a large elephant. Then they took the Brahmin and seated their new supreme lord on the elephant's back. A festive procession was undertaken with red vermilion powder and the sounding of conch shells, trumpets, and large kettledrums, as well as lutes, drums, flutes, and more. After she worshiped her son at the door, the mother went inside with him. He was then consecrated as king and placed on the throne as ruler.

"Having become king and being incredibly happy, he asked his mother, 'Mother, where is my beloved? Or did she go to her own home? By the grace of that vow—by the power of Svasthānī!—I have attained great happiness,' said the proud, dignified king. His mother declared to her son, 'Send a palanquin and bearers for her.' The chief bearer asked people, 'Who are you? Where is the wife of Navarāj?' A woman living on the bank of the river then said to the bearers, 'I am Navarāj's wife! Whatever is the young king's is certainly mine! Gomā is my mother-in-law. Let's go, bearer!' The palanquin was immediately dispatched by the king's unconsecrated wife, who was greedy for material prosperity.

"Soon the palanquin encountered showers of flowers produced as a result of a religious rite. At this curious sight, the mistress turned wicked. She became angry with the bearer, who stopped the palanquin along the bank of a river. The bearer was heartened by the sight of a group of celestial nymphs and Brahmins. [Śiva commented,] 'The bearer will become purified by means of this shower of flowers. He will have no other birth as a result of the Svasthānī vow.' After that, the bearer said, 'Let there be victory for the unconsecrated queen! Because I saw this vow, I am very thankful. My happiness is exceedingly abundant! My body, O lady, has been purified by the flowers of Svasthānī's vow.'

"Hearing the words of the bearer, she reproached him angrily, 'Hey, you sinners![21] You carried me to the water and abandoned me there! Of what sort is this Svasthānī? Who is she? What is this vow? Where is she who institutes this vow?' The Brahmin woman desecrated the fruit and scattered the flowers there.

"Then, because of that sin, Svasthānī emitted a deep, terrible roar like the thundering of clouds of destruction. The two bearers fell into the river. With the sound of that destruction the rain descended. Thus did the goddess arrive. That sinful woman was destroyed there, devastated by the sin of that insult. By the power of Svasthānī's vow, those two bearers went to heaven. But the woman's hands and feet, which were completely submerged by the flood of water, decayed. The sinful woman had fallen in the water like a mountain with its wings clipped.[22]

"Nearby was King Navarāj, whose right to rule was due to his excellence in his regular ritual practices. Just as the form of Svasthānī was previously described, so the goddess appeared to him. Svasthānī said, 'Ah, you are a minor king and your mother is my devotee. I am pleased. That which was done, was done for me. I made you king. After enjoying a prosperous kingdom here in this world, you will obtain liberation.' After giving this boon, the goddess disappeared.

"Meanwhile, the sinful woman was reduced to misery for twelve years in the frightful infernal netherworld for having insulted Svasthānī's vow. In that time, she wasted away. Then two fishermen approached. The sinful woman surfaced, entangled by the nets floated by those two fishermen. She was like a piece of wood fallen on the ground for another twelve years. Day and night, she suffered a fever, like a trial by fire.

"Now, a ceremonial performance—the best among all—was organized by Navarāj. The Brahmins, together with all the people, were invited as guests. Then the Brahmin named Kapila saw the sinful woman on the road. The twice-born Brahmin asked with curiosity, 'What is this thing made of earth ensnared in a net? What is this firewood already ruined?' The sinful woman heard his words and said, 'I am a sinful woman. I have sinned. Because I, a Brahmin woman of good family, insulted Svasthānī—because of this sin I am in this situation. How may I be liberated?' Then from the mouth of the Brahmin the sinful woman learned the instructions for the vow.

"Just as the twice-born had instructed, she performed the vow. She performed the vow with devotion in the sand with water. By the power of that vow, the sand and water became milk and bread. By merely meditating on Svasthānī and by uttering her name, the Brahmin woman was liberated from all her sins. She became even more beautiful than before. By the power of that vow, she was freed from her disease.

"Seeing this, the Brahmin was amazed. He went to the ritual ceremony as ordered by the king. The king provided hospitality to all the Brahmins who had been invited. The traveler told the story of the sinful woman to the king. After hearing the traveler's words, again a bearer was dispatched. With the noise of various musical instruments and such, and with numerous recitations of the Veda, the transformed Brahmin woman made an announcement to the people at the door and entered the king's palace. Thereupon, her heart was filled with happiness as she was seated on the throne to receive blessings. The king experienced divine happiness and then obtained liberation.

"O Great Goddess, such are the fruits of this, the most excellent vow of Svasthānī. Whoever performs this always with devotion will forever have material prosperity. Wealth, animals, and sons, as well as knowledge, life, dignity, and power: by the power of Svasthānī, one will certainly have everything. One who listens to and recites this story is great. One who recites and listens to it will be freed from all sins in the world. She will certainly not be a widow. She will obtain the auspicious state of wifehood, of having a living husband. She will abound in money and grain. She will be surrounded by sons and grandsons."

Thus concludes the story of the ritual vow of the Supreme Goddess Svasthānī in the revered *Liṅga Purāṇa*.[23]

This was completed on Thursday, the fifth day of the bright half of the month Phālgun, in the year 693 of the Nepali calendar (1573 CE). Śrī Jayantadeva is the scribe of this book.

THE GODDESS IN CONTEXT: HIDDEN IN PLAIN SIGHT

The goddess Svasthānī and the month of Māgh are synonymous for Hindus in Nepal. She is worshiped in the form of a devotional text, *The Story of the Ritual Vow to the Goddess Svasthānī* (*Svasthānī-vrata-kathā*), which Nepali Hindus recite annually over the course of the cold winter nights of Māgh. Brought out only for this yearly monthlong recitation, the text—and so the goddess herself—is wrapped up and stored for eleven months of the year, precluding her worship until the following winter.

The ritual vow (*vrata*) to Svasthānī, which the text describes as "the most secret vow," is similarly observed only in Māgh, for either the entire month or, at a minimum, on the last day. A *vrata* is a votive rite that Hindus perform to honor a deity with the aim of earning the deity's blessing in support of achieving a specific goal or fulfilling a particular desire. The central elements of these vows are (1) stating one's intention to undertake the vow; (2) fasting for a designated period of time (most commonly for a day); and (3) telling or listening to the *vrata-kathā*, the story of the ritual vow. There are many different kinds of *vrata*s that one may choose to observe: *vrata*s to particular deities on particular days of the week; *vrata*s dedicated to other deities; and *vrata*s for specific holidays or for specific reasons, such as healing or in thanks for healing that has already occurred. Most *vrata*s are performed voluntarily, though Hindus consider some compulsory, such as Tīj, which high-caste women in Nepal and north India perform to ensure the long life and health of their husbands, or in the case of unmarried girls, in the hopes of attaining a good husband. Many *vrata*s are rooted in Sanskrit literature such as the Purāṇas and Dharma-śāstras, but there are also folk *vrata*s that circulate orally. Women and girls, as the primary caretakers of their family's earthly and spiritual well-being, are the primary performers of *vrata*s, especially folk *vrata*s, though men also perform the more formal, Brahminical type.[24]

The *Svasthānī-vrata-kathā* (hereafter *Svasthānī Kathā* or SVK), however, demonstrates that many *vrata*s in fact concurrently meet several of these criteria, and that some deviate from them in one or more ways. The Svasthānī *vrata*, for example, is performed to a specific deity but also often for a specific reason; often the reason is related to family and health, but also nowadays for success in school. It is performed mostly by women, but also by men. It originated as a local rite but expanded to incorporate many Sanskritic elements. Both its ritual fasting—in this case eating one meal per day—and the *kathā* recitation span a month's duration, in contrast to the one- or two-day duration of most *vratas*.[25] It is also noteworthy that the SVK describes the Svasthānī *vrata* as a "secret vow," though what is meant by this is not explicitly explained in the narrative or its framing apparatus. The primary suggestion is that the Svasthānī vow is one that Śiva, for reasons unknown, has kept secret until now. This underscores the divine origin of the practice and hints at its potential potency. It could also betray the presence of Tantric influences in the tradition that privilege secrecy.

The text and ritual have historically been celebrated only among Hindu communities in Nepal; Svasthānī's foray into Indian Hinduism has begun only within the last decade.[26] As a goddess worshiped almost exclusively in the private sphere of the home and only once a year, Svasthānī has largely escaped attention from scholars of both Nepali culture and Hinduism more broadly.[27] Even among her devotees and observers, neither the text nor the ritual has inspired regular local artistic representations (until the nineteenth and, more so, twentieth centuries), acknowledgments in inscriptions, or ethnographic descriptions, nor has either otherwise been mentioned in historical documents, even in passing, as is common with so many of Nepal's numerous goddesses.[28] The SVK manuscript corpus is our only historical documentation and source for Svasthānī and her devotional tradition. This lack of outside documentation stands in stark contrast to the sheer volume of extant manuscripts—more than seven hundred have been cataloged and are preserved in Nepal's archival collections.[29] These are striking paradoxes given her ubiquity in Nepali Hindu homes and the profound influence the annual recitation of the *Svasthānī Kathā* narratives has had in shaping Nepali Hindu identity.[30]

Seed: The Origin of Svasthānī in Sixteenth-Century Nepal

The earliest surviving record of Svasthānī and her tradition is an SVK manuscript from 1573 CE, written on eight palm-leaf folios in the Sanskrit language. Her tradition originated and matured during a period of great cultural efflorescence among the Newars, the indigenous inhabitants and rulers of the Kathmandu Valley and its environs. The Newars today are one of the largest and most culturally prominent of Nepal's numerous ethnic groups. They have historically been the primary custodians of the SVK tradition, as evidenced by the fact that the SVK was transmitted almost exclusively in the classical Newar language for the first two centuries of its history. Following Prithivi

Narayan Shah's invasion of the Kathmandu Valley in 1769 CE, the Nepali-speaking Parbatiya (or hill) Hindus became dominant socially, religiously, linguistically, and politically, and they remain so in modern Nepal.[31] The SVK was translated into the Nepali language in 1810 CE for the use of these non-Newar, Parbatiya Hindus, who also claim the SVK as their own tradition.[32] While the ruling Parbatiya Hindu elite tried to suppress all things Newar, the growth of the SVK tradition, in both the Newar and Nepali languages, suggests they did not always succeed. Svasthānī's history from the sixteenth century to the present day is well documented through the SVK's textual and narrative developments.

Flower: A Thriving Women's Religious Tradition

The *Svasthānī Kathā* translated in this chapter is based on the oldest-extant SVK manuscript, from 1573 CE. The story focuses on two women, the ever-devout but luckless Gomayaju (which Nepalis frequently shorten to Gomā, as done here) and her selfish and sinful daughter-in-law Candravatī, with a supporting role played by Navarāj, their son and husband, respectively. The trials and triumphs these characters experience illustrate the reasons and rewards for worshiping Svasthānī. This foundational narrative constituted the whole of the SVK in its earliest iterations.

Between the eighteenth and early twentieth centuries, the SVK underwent a dramatic transformation that expanded the text from a short folk narrative to a several-hundred-folio/page Purāṇa compendium. In three stages, the often-anonymous scribes of the SVK wove into its Śākta narrative fabric a series of Śaiva and, to a lesser extent, Vaiṣṇava narratives culled from the major Sanskrit Purāṇas. This occurred in response to shifts in the religious, social, and political landscape in late medieval and early modern Nepal and the greater region that broadened Nepal's engagement with India and Brahminical Hinduism. Nepal's ruling elite sought to position Nepal as the "pure land of the Hindus" vis-à-vis Hindu India, which in their view had been defiled, first by the Mughals and again later by the British. With these developments, Svasthānī came to share the spotlight with—and was at times overshadowed by—Śiva and, to a lesser extent, Viṣṇu. That two great gods of the pan-Indic pantheon would displace a local goddess in her own devotional tradition suggests another way in which we may consider Svasthānī to have been "forgotten."

Throughout the SVK's history, scribes have asserted the text's origin in the *Skanda*, *Liṅga*, or *Padma Purāṇa*, though there is no evidence to support this. However, by the time the SVK crystallized into its current form in the twentieth century, the Purāṇic narrative additions alone constituted the first two-thirds of the SVK, relegating the foundational Gomā-Navarāj-Candravatī narrative to the last third of the text. In this way, the SVK had assumed the form, and also the function, of a Purāṇa as the primary source for religious, cultural, and social knowledge and practice for Nepali Hindus. The goddess Svasthānī and the *Svasthānī Kathā* serve as a reminder that Nepal, like different cultural and geographic regions of India, produced its own Hindu mythology, beliefs, and practices, which should be taken into consideration when investigating not just Hindu goddesses, but Hinduism as a whole.

Who is Svasthānī? Let us first consider her name. It is common for Hindu deities' names to reflect a key aspect of their nature, worship, mythology, or power. For example, Durgā, "the Impenetrable One," references her fierce, indomitable nature on the battlefield; Śītalā is "the Cool One," who requires cold leftover food in her worship and is believed to cool the heat of smallpox and other similar diseases; and Tvaritā, discussed in this volume, is called "the Swift One" on account of her ability to quickly heal the medical emergency of snakebites. Svasthānī's name translates literally to "the Goddess of One's Own Place." Which "place of one's own" this refers to, however, is not immediately clear. My deep reading of the *Svasthānī Kathā* narratives suggests that Svasthānī is the protector of one's own place, where "one's own place" is context sensitive and may hold a different meaning for devotees and audiences in different times and places.[33] Against the backdrop of Nepal's history of political and socioreligious positioning as a pure Hindu land, the place to be protected may simultaneously represent the individual, the home or family, and the larger local, regional, and state or even national community, as they negotiate the specificities of their daily lives and ways of life. The 1573 SVK, translated in this chapter, states: "This vow is indeed the path to the Supreme. Even as in this world the vow protects righteousness (*dharma*), so in the next world it preserves it. There is no other vow comparable in this world. There is no other protector!" Here the ritual vow and the goddess are collapsed into a singular protective role, which is further evidenced in Svasthānī's iconography.

Iconographic images of Svasthānī are historically rare, as she is customarily worshiped in the form of the SVK text itself. Yet the SVK provides an anthropomorphic description of Svasthānī:

> Her beauty is luminous like the color of gold. She has three eyes and her face is like a lotus. She sits on a throne that is a lion and is decorated with all kinds of ornaments. In her left hand she holds a blue lotus while making the fear-dispelling gesture. She holds her right hand in the boon-giving gesture. In her other right and left hands she holds a sword and shield upraised, respectively. Such is the image of the Supreme Goddess Svasthānī. Such is also the image of Śiva. The only different feature is his vehicle, which is a bull. One should meditate on me, whose symbol is the bull, in this four-armed form. Thus, meditate on Svasthānī and the Lord of the World.

Svasthānī is here described in terms associated with both benevolent and fierce forms of the Goddess. This ambiguity is, as we will see, further evidenced in her actions in the main narrative translated here.

Svasthānī is also here referred to as "the Supreme Goddess (Parameśvarī) Svasthānī." Taken together with the injunction in the text to meditate "on the image of Śivaśakti," this intimates that Svasthānī is closely associated with Śiva, who is commonly referred to as Parameśvara, the Supreme Lord, as his consort or *śakti*. As the narrative makes plain, however, Svasthānī operates independently of Śiva or any other male deity. Her strong association with Śiva as his consort eventually gives way in the nineteenth century to new iconography, if not an active storyline, in which Śiva is replaced by the Aṣṭamātrikā, the group of eight fierce Mother goddesses, who encircle Svasthānī in a protective embrace as she sits on a lotus flower (figure 9).[34] This image is included in most modern printed volumes of the SVK. It can be read as a Śākta response to the earlier influx of Śaiva and Vaiṣṇava Purāṇa stories, in order to reposition the Goddess more centrally and assertively, at least visually. More broadly, this development reflects the role of the *Svasthānī Kathā* as a prominent local warehouse and distribution center for an array of circulating narratives, beliefs, and worldviews within both local and more distant forms of Hindu belief and practice.

As our only source for the goddess and her tradition, the *Svasthānī Kathā* explains the origin and nature of Svasthānī's worship in the human realm; members of the divine realm of the gods are seen already worshiping Svasthānī. Following the pattern set by Tantric scriptures, the text opens with a conversation between Śiva and Pārvatī in which she asks him about the "secret," "supreme" vow that he has "kept secret" from devotees and is "difficult to obtain in the three worlds." Śiva lovingly assures her that "because of my great affection for you, I will tell you that which has not been told to anyone. . . .

On the fourteenth day of the bright half of the month of Māgh, women should perform the *vrata* of the Supreme Goddess Svasthānī, which is called the king of vows." Note that he specifically states that *women* should perform the vow. While men do perform the vow in Nepal today, Nepalis generally consider it to be a women's tradition.[35] Śiva then details the precepts for performing the ritual vow, after which Pārvatī further asks to hear "the story of who among humans first heard this story and of who first performed this vow." Śiva obligingly recounts the circumstances under which Gomā, Candravatī, and Navarāj encounter Svasthānī.

Svasthānī physically appears and briefly speaks in the narrative only once, but she nevertheless makes her presence known and demonstrates her power in no uncertain terms. Svasthānī first illustrates her benevolence when she grants the abandoned and desolate Gomā a boon (the return of her absent son) upon Gomā's successful completion of the Svasthānī vow, which Śiva indirectly brings to her attention at Pārvatī's behest. Navarāj's return is quickly followed by his coronation as king of a neighboring region. This reversal of fortune for Gomā, now Queen Mother, is underscored in later iterations of the SVK, which describe how the impoverished Gomā performed the vow with few resources, exemplified in her telling of the Svasthānī story (a critical element of any ritual vow performance) to her broom and stool because she had no one else to whom she could tell it. This highlights the accessible, lay nature of the vow and its local patron goddess, as well as the importance of piety and respect for divine beings.

Soon thereafter, Svasthānī also displays her temper and capacity for destruction when such devotion is absent. While returning from her natal home to reunite with her newly crowned husband and mother-in-law, Candravatī's palanquin bearers give her blessed food offerings (*prasād*) from a nearby performance of the Svasthānī vow by a group of celestial nymphs. An ignorant Candravatī promptly rejects the offerings and disparages the goddess. When traversing a river shortly thereafter, Svasthānī causes a storm to rise that washes away the bridge Candravatī and her palanquin bearers are crossing, causing the deaths of the bearers, who, as Svasthānī's devotees, go immediately to heaven. Candravatī is submerged into the raging waters, where she suffers from leprosy for the next twelve years, followed by another twelve years of misery on land. It is only after Candravatī is instructed to perform Svasthānī's vow *with devotion* and successfully does so that the goddess blesses her: "By the power of this vow Candravatī's appearance transformed and her body became divine—even more beautiful than before."

While not associated with disease in the way that, for example, Śītalā and Māriyammā are, the *Svasthānī Kathā* describes Svasthānī as both bringing disease to Candravatī and later removing the very disease she herself inflicted. In this way, Svasthānī aligns with many other local and regional goddesses who are the bearers of both a disease (as a punishment or warning for wayward or non-devotees) and its cure (as a reward for sincere devotion and proper worship). This emphasizes Svasthānī's local origins and reinforces her independent, more aggressive nature, which enables her to destroy and punish as readily as she can nurture and heal. Notably, modern devotees generally do not associate any malignancy with Svasthānī. At the same time, the positioning of Svasthānī as Śiva's consort at the opening of the text—and through various additional subtle means as the text expanded between the eighteenth and twentieth centuries—serves to "sweeten" and uplift her into the ranks of the pan-Indic pantheon, among the likes of Pārvatī and Durgā, thus leaning into to a wider and more "civilized"—that is, orthodox—Brahminical audience. It is this tension between the local and the translocal, the folk and the Brahminical, that gives the goddess Svasthānī and the *Svasthānī Kathā* much of their currency.

As the Goddess of One's Own Place, she is perpetually relevant for her devotees, no matter their circumstances. This relevance is evident in the SVK's expansion since its origin in the sixteenth century as a result of its scribes and audience reacting and adapting to shifting political, social, and religious contexts in Nepal and South Asia.[36] The *Svasthānī Kathā* textual tradition exemplifies the ways in which the relationships and tensions between Newar and Sanskritic, Brahminical forms of Hinduism, culture, and language promotion in Nepal and India, respectively, have been navigated and reflected within the folios of what is today one of the most widely read devotional texts in Nepal.

Fruit: The Svasthānī Tradition Today

Many Newar and Parbatiya Hindu families have handwritten SVK texts that have been passed down through the generations; a Newar friend showed me his family's SVK manuscript from 1764! Unfortunately, families with handwritten SVKs are increasingly unable to read them because knowledge of the classical Newar and Nepali languages and older scripts is rapidly disappearing among younger generations. Mass-produced, printed SVK books available in urban bazaars today are available only in the modern Nepali language and the ubiquitous Devanāgarī script. The demands and distractions of modernity continue to impinge upon the Svasthānī tradition in ways that endanger it (e.g., expanded work hours and commuting, and increasingly ubiquitous electronics that distract from or altogether preclude the nightly recitation) but also reaffirm its adaptability (e.g., new shorter retellings and a smartphone app).[37] Participation in the annual Svasthānī *vrata*, however, remains strong, if the public, communal observance of the vow in Sankhu, Nepal (on the northeastern outskirts of the Kathmandu Valley) is any indication. Participants have consistently numbered between two and four hundred women and one to two dozen men for at least the past two decades.[38]

The foundational story of the *Svasthānī Kathā* presented here, and the many other stories the *Svasthānī Kathā* has come to include, are inscribed upon the hearts and minds of Nepali Hindus from a young age. Envision Nepali girls and boys, together with their parents, cousins, aunts, uncles, and grandparents, gathered around a copy of the SVK, listening to the stories recited on the cold winter nights of Māgh as they wait patiently to enjoy the goddess's nightly blessed offerings of sweet treats. Many of these girls and boys will themselves later perform the ritual vow in the hopes of securing Svasthānī's favor. Just as Śiva and Pārvatī introduced Svasthānī's "secret" vow, already celebrated among the gods, to the realm of humans, this translation introduces Nepal's goddess Svasthānī and her vow, already celebrated among Nepal's Hindus, to the realm of English speakers.

SOURCE

The eight-folio SVK manuscript from 1573 CE translated here is the oldest extant SVK.[39] It is likely that an oral tradition preceded the emergence of written SVK manuscripts, though the lack of non-SVK documentation for the Svasthānī tradition makes this impossible to confirm. It is similarly difficult to definitively pinpoint the origin of the *Svasthānī Kathā* textual tradition to the 1573 manuscript. Available evidence culled from extant manuscripts, however, reveals no earlier SVK and a consistent increase in SVK manuscript production in the decades and centuries that followed.

Furthermore, it is on the basis of the 1573 SVK's "original," foundational Gomā-Navarāj-Candravatī narrative that the tradition later built and expanded itself with Purāṇic stories.

The 1573 version of the SVK is also noteworthy as the beginning of the written tradition because it is in Sanskrit. As noted previously, Sanskrit-language SVKs are rare in an otherwise prolific Newar-language and later Nepali-language manuscript tradition. The 1573 SVK's Sanskrit is grammatically corrupt in a manner that suggests significant Newar-language influence, a reflection of the linguistic skills and cultural orientation of its scribe. It also reflects the contemporary cultural currency gained by writing in Sanskrit, "the language of the gods," which linked the SVK to the older, authoritative Sanskrit literary tradition of the Veda, Purāṇas, and Tantras. Thirty years later, the second oldest extant (1603) SVK more explicitly asserted the Newar cultural origins of the tradition while simultaneously serving as a bridge between the cosmopolitan Sanskrit and vernacular Newar languages and worldviews. It did so by including in its opening ritual instructions (*pūjāvidhi*) and closing praises for the fruits to be reaped from the ritual performance (*phalaśruti*) nearly verbatim Sanskrit verses from the opening and close of the 1573 SVK. These verses were immediately followed by vernacular prose translations in Newar. The main narrative of the 1603 text is entirely in Newar.[40] It is still a common practice in modern, printed SVKs (and other Hindu religious texts in Nepal) to include the ritual instructions in Sanskrit, followed by a vernacular (Nepali-language) translation. These modern SVK books also present a 153-verse adaptation of the 1573 SVK before recounting the Svasthānī narrative in full in Nepali.

FURTHER READING

Birkenholtz, Jessica Vantine. 2018. *Reciting the Goddess: Narratives of Place and the Making of Hinduism in Nepal*. New York: Oxford University Press.

———. 2019. "On Becoming a Woman: *Shakti*, Storytelling, and Women's Roles and Rights in Nepal." *Signs: A Journal of Women in Culture and Society* 44, no. 2: 433–64.

McDaniel, June. 2003. *Making Virtuous Daughters and Wives: An Introduction to Women's Brata Rituals in Bengali Folk Religion*. Albany: State University of New York Press.

Pearson, Anne Mackenzie. 1996. *"Because It Gives Me Peace of Mind": Ritual Fasts in the Religious Lives of Hindu Women*. Albany: State University of New York Press.

NOTES

1. Svasthānī is pronounced "Swa-sthah-nee" or "Swo-sthah-nee."

2. The term *dharma* is used interchangeably with *vrata* (vow) throughout the text. In certain cases, *dharma* also indicates a broader notion of socioreligious responsibility.

3. The "holy hour" is approximately two hours before daybreak.

4. The guest offering (*argha*) typically consists of water, milk, *kusa* grass, yogurt, uncooked rice, sesame oil, clarified butter, and barley.

5. The word for "image," *pratimā*, often refers to a small gold or silver plate onto which the image of a deity is impressed.

6. The four ends of human life (*caturbhadra*) are traditionally understood to be *dharma* (duty/religion), *artha* (wealth and prosperity), *kāma* (sensual pleasure), and *mokṣa* (liberation from the cycle of rebirth). Some Nepalis distinguish a different scheme that substitutes *bal/śakti* (power) and *paramagati* (liberation) for *mokṣa*.

7. Indicating the older age of Śiva Bhaṭṭa, the six duties are teaching, studying, offering *yajña*, officiating at *yajña*, giving gifts, and accepting gifts.

8. "Devoted to her husband," or *pativratā*, literally means a vow (*vrata*) undertaken for the protection and well-being of a husband (*pati*). In addition to singular devotion to her husband, a wife's chastity is a crucial signifier—often the paramount signifier—of her identity as a *pativratā*, a woman who undertakes this vow.

9. A twice-born (*dvija*) is a man of any of the three highest-ranking Hindu classes: Brāhman (Brahmin), Kṣatriya, and Vaiśya. This term is used regularly throughout this text, though invariably it is in reference only to a Brahmin man. It is notable, however, that the term *vipra*, which refers specifically to a Brahmin, is also used, but far less frequently. This may reflect the Newar origins of the Svasthānī tradition, by employing a term more inclusive of several groups rather than the more exclusive label *vipra*.

10. The description of Gomā's growth here echoes Kālidāsa's description of Pārvatī's growth in his classic poem *Kumārasambhava* (1.25).

11. An ascetic of a particular Śaiva sect who uses a human cranium as a begging bowl.

12. In the original Sanskrit, the name given here and in the next sentence is that of Śiva Śarma, which, given the rest of the narrative, is clearly a mistake.

13. Namely, she immolated herself on the funeral pyre of her deceased husband.

14. *Puṃsavana* is the first of sixteen *saṃskāras*, or rites of passage.

15. *Sīmantonnayana*, literally, the parting of the hair: another of the sixteen *saṃskāras*, observed by women in the fourth, sixth, or eight month of their pregnancy.

16. It is not clear why the hair-parting ceremony is mentioned here, since it is typically performed prior to the birth of a child. After-birth rites include the childbirth ceremony (*jātakarman*), the naming ceremony (*nāmakaraṇa*), first outing (*niṣkramaṇa*), first solid food (*annaprāśana*), first haircut or tonsure (*cūḍākaraṇa*), and ear piercing (*karṇavedha*).

17. Although the name would be pronounced "Navarāja" in Sanskrit, we use the more familiar spelling Navarāj to convey its vernacular pronunciation in Nepal.

18. According to Hindu conceptions of time, each creation of the world has one Indra ruling it, and thus to live in the infernal underworlds for fourteen Indras indicates the time span of fourteen creations (and destructions) of the world, which is to say, a very, very long time.

19. *Airandi* refers to the castor oil plant, a small tree known to botanists as *Ricinus communis*.

20. "Made preparations" refers to assembling the eight pieces of bread as blessed food (*prasād*) for distribution to a husband or son.

21. The Sanskrit suddenly switches to the dual form to include two palanquin bearers.

22. According to Hindu mythology, mountains once upon a time had wings and flew about. One day, however, Indra became upset and cut off the wings of the mountains, whereupon they became stationary fixtures of the landscape.

23. The attribution of the *Svasthānī-vrata-kathā* to the *Liṅga* or other Purāṇas is spurious, though it is a common strategy for regional narratives seeking status.

24. Buddhists and Jains also perform *vratas*.

25. For a detailed examination of the Svasthānī *vrata*, see Iltis (1985).

26. Birkenholtz (2018, 32n24).

27. See in particular Bennett (1983), Birkenholtz (2018, 2n3), Iltis (1985, 1996), Tamot (1991), and Sharma (2001).

28. For a singular exception, see Birkenholtz (2018, 49, 50n25).

29. The Nepal-German Manuscript Preservation Project microfilmed and cataloged 689 SVK manuscripts, available at Nepal's National Archives. Āśā Archives, a smaller archive focused primarily on Newar manuscripts, has cataloged more than 80 SVK manuscripts.

30. Birkenholtz (2018).

31. Parbatiya Hindu beliefs and practices are rooted in the Sanskritic, Brahminical traditions of ancient India, while Newar Hinduism reflects considerable local influence specific to the Newar communities of medieval Nepal. See Gellner (1986) for an overview of Newar identity, language, culture, and practice.

32. Bennett (1983, 274–75).

33. Birkenholtz (2018, 46n30). See also Iltis (1996).

34. The "Eight Mothers" (*aṣṭamātrikā*) are an expansion of the group known as the Seven Mothers discussed in chapters 3, 4, and 8. For more on Svasthānī's iconography and connection with the Eight Mothers, see Birkenholtz (2013 and 2018, 59–72).

35. What constitutes a "women's tradition," however, is debatable. The *Svasthānī Kathā* was written by men and is suffused throughout with Brahminical patriarchal ideology that promotes asymmetrical social relations and valorizes male supremacy and gender discrimination (and, according to some Nepalis, violence) against women. See Birkenholtz (2019).

36. See Birkenholtz (2018).

37. Birkenholtz (2016, 85–106).

38. Birkenholtz (2018, 13n34).

39. The manuscript is currently held in the National Archives of Nepal in Kathmandu under the accession number NAK 3-191. It was microfilmed by the NGMPP under reel B13/42.

40. For a full transliteration and English translation of the 1603 CE Newar-language SVK, see appendices B and C in Birkenholtz (2018).

FIGURE 11. Kailā Devī and Cāmuṇḍā, by Laura Santi

CHAPTER 6

Kailā Devī

The Great Goddess as Local Avatar of Miracles

R. JEREMY SAUL

The next tale comes from Rajasthan (the Land of Kings), a large state in the northwestern part of India famous for its arid desert landscape, its energetic people, and the military culture of its historical rulers. Tourists come to Rajasthan to see its beautiful medieval palaces and forts, visit tiger reserves, ride camels, and enjoy colorful festivals. Pilgrims are drawn to the state's many important temples housing gods and goddesses, such as Kailā Devī, the subject of the present chapter.

This local goddess from eastern Rajasthan is widely revered for her miraculous interventions in the lives of devotees. The translation is based on a booklet titled *Śrī Kailādevī Itihās*, a contemporary and locally produced history of the goddess in Hindi written for pilgrims visiting the site. It is different than most of our prior sources insofar as it presents itself as a real account grounded in specific locations and referring to historical personages and dates. While the passage retells a story we have come to know from several chapters in the previous section—that of the goddess fighting and slaying the buffalo demon Mahiṣa and the "blood-seed" demon Raktabīja—it does so in passing, since it is much more concerned with narrating the goddess's relationship with sādhus and *babas*, holy men in the story who mediate between her and the larger community.

Readers should pay special attention to how the narrative deals with the issue of a goddess being the singular Great Goddess and simultaneously embodying many local divinities and pilgrimage sites. The persuasive function of miracle stories calls for analysis, as well as comparison to miracle stories in other religious traditions. The story and the essay describe the goddess possessing devotees and speaking through them. This too could be fruitfully compared with similar practices in other religious traditions. Are miracles and possession still relevant in this age of science and technology?

दानव का अत्याचार

जैसा कि ऊपर लिख चुके हैं कि सम्वत् १२०६ वि. में बाँसीखेडा नामक गाँव में राजा मुकुन्ददास खींची ने श्रीचामुण्डा मैया की आराधना के निर्मित एक मन्दिर चामुण्डा जी का बनवाया था । बाँसीखेडा के पास ही एक दूसरा प्राचीन गाँव उस समय था जिसे लोहर्रा नाम से जाना जाता था । ये गाँव भयानक घोर जंगल के मध्य थे । पास ही एक नदी बहती थी, जो आज भी कालीसिल के नाम से जानी जाती है । यहाँ के निवासी खेती तथा मवेशी पालन का काम करके अपनी गुजर-बसर करते थे । इस घोर बीहड जंगल में शेर-चीते जैसे हिंसक जानवर तो थे ही लेकिन उन दिनों वहाँ एक भयानक दानव भी पैदा हो गया था । हिंसक जानवरों का खतरा निरीह पशुओं तथा स्त्री बच्चों के लिए बना रहता था लेकिन अब तो बलवान पुरुष भी उस दानव के डर से थर-थर काँपने लगे थे । दुष्ट दानव का अत्याचार इतना बढ़ गया कि ग्रामवासियों का घरों से निकलना भी कठिन हो गया । आये दिन कोई न कोई मनुष्य उस दानव का ग्रास बनने लगा । ग्रामवासियों के आनंदमय जीवन में एकाएक यह भयंकर विपदा आ पड़ी-जिससे सब अकुला उठे और दानव से त्राण पाने की गुप्त मन्त्रणा करने लगे ।

ग्रामवासियों की बाबा केदारगिरि से विनती

लोहर्रा गाँव से कुछ दूरी पर वर्तमान मन्दिर से ३ किमी. दूर एक गुफा बनी हुई है जहाँ बाबा केदारगिरि रहकर माँ भगवती की उपासना में दिनरात तल्लीन रहते थे । ये बाबा सभी ग्रामवासियों के पूज्य थे जो समय-समय पर ग्रामवासियों को सद्मार्ग व दिग्दर्शन करार्त रहते थे । सहसा ग्रामवासियों को बाबा का ध्यान आया और वे यह विचार करके कि बाबा ही हमारी इस घोर विपदा का निवारण कर सकते हैं, ग्राम के वृध्द जन एकत्रित होकर बाबा के स्थान पर पहुँचे । बाबा जो इस समय शक्ति माँ की उपासना में समाधिष्ट बैठे हुए थे । ग्रामवासी आर्त होकार बाबा के चरणों में जा गिरे । उनकी करुणामई पुकार सुनकर बाबा का ध्यान टूट गया एवं ग्राम वासियों से दुखी होने का कारण पूच्छा । ग्रामवासियों ने अपनी सारी व्यथा अश्रुपूरित नेत्रों से आरतवाणी में बाबा केदारगिरि को कह सुनाई तथा कहा को हे महाराज हमें जैसे भी हो घोर विपदा से छुटकारा दिलवाइये । नहीं तो, यहाँ से दूसरे राज्य में जाने के अलावा हमें कोई भी अपने प्राणों की

FIGURE 12. *Śrī Kailādevī Itihās,* a Hindi work in the Devanagari script. Font "Shobhika" © IIT Bombay.

THE STORY OF KAILĀ DEVĪ

The Tyranny of the Demon

In the year 1149 CE, in a village named Bansikhera, a king named Mukund Das Khinchi had a temple built for the worship of the glorious mother Cāmuṇḍā. Near Bansikhera, there was another ancient village in the middle of a fearsome jungle. At that time it was known as Loharra. Nearby flowed a river today known as the Kalisil River. The inhabitants farmed and raised livestock for subsistence, but in this wild jungle predators such as tigers and cheetahs roamed about, and in those days a terrible demon appeared there. While the predators made the forest animals, women, and children afraid, the demon made even brave men shake in fear. This wicked demon caused such terror that the villagers could hardly leave their homes. In the following days, the demon started to eat one person after another, wrecking the once happy lives of these villagers. At this low point, they deliberated about how to find protection from the demon.

The Villagers' Plea to Baba Kedargiri

Some distance from Loharra, nowadays three kilometers from the Kailā Devī temple, there was a cave where Baba Kedargiri lived and worshiped the Goddess continuously every day and night. The villagers revered this *baba*, as he gave them advice from time to time. And so, suddenly the thought came to them that he could avert this terrible calamity. Hence, the village elders went to the *baba*'s place while he was in a deep meditation in worship of the Goddess Śakti Ma, the divine feminine Power. The distraught villagers fell at Baba Kedargiri's feet pleading for help, and hearing them, he broke his meditation and asked them the reason for their distress.

Their eyes welling up with tears, the villagers said to Baba Kedargiri, "O lord, deliver us from this terrible adversity! For otherwise, there is no one in any other kingdom who will be able to save us." Kedargiri reminded the villagers of how the goddesses Jagadambā and Cāmuṇḍā had once rescued the world from being consumed by such a demon. And upon considering the villagers' dire situation, Baba's heart melted with sympathy and he assured them that he, as a devotee of the Supreme Mother who created the world and is full of divine feminine power, fully trusted in her power.

Baba said, "O villagers, don't be worried. The Great Goddess and all the goddesses of the world will together remove our troubles. Even just hearing the story of the Goddess will lighten the burden in our hearts; so listen to a bit of her story now. The divine feminine power (*Śakti*)—in other words the Mother—will become an avatar. The sight of Mother Śakti will bring peace to this distressed world, for she has an invaluable gift in store for us that no one can take away. After all, she is Mother Nature, the underlying power of life itself. One who calls out 'Ma' or 'Mother' is filled with unequaled happiness. In times of personal hardship each of us is apt to utter, 'Hey Ma!' This is natural, for we know that a mother brings up a child with love. A mother keeps watch over her baby's eating and drinking, playing, and bathing. Mother has the sort of inner spirit that empathetically feels the hardships that her offspring experience, and she works to make them forget all their hardships, and averts their difficulties. This is how we should understand our loving Mother Śakti. Mother brings forth perfect, brave offspring. And our brave Mother, in the horrific time of war, puts a garland of victory and a sacred mark on the forehead of her son and sends him into battle. She gives him this blessing: 'You are the brave offspring of a brave Mother, so do not shame her womb!' Añjanī gave birth to brave Hanumān, Subhadrā to Abhimanyu, and Śakuntalā to Bhārat. In the same way, the great Maratha king Shivaji and many others are the offspring of the brave Mother. All of us beings in the world are the children of the Mother, and she will surely save us. Now, listen to the story of the buffalo demon Mahiṣāsura, and how the revered Mother came into this world to destroy him.

"In ancient times, a demonic king named Danu had two sons, named Rambha and Karambha. Both of these sons of Danu were full of might, but both were also childless. Therefore, to obtain children, both brothers began to perform austerities in honor of Agni, the fire god. When the god Indra learned of this news, he became afraid, thinking, 'Perhaps their sons will snatch my kingdom!' Rambha and Karambha were performing their austerities in the Land of the Five Rivers (Punjab). Rambha sat under a great tree and practiced ritual austerities, and Karambha immersed himself in cold water for the same reason. The king of the gods Indra disguised himself as a crocodile and arrived at this place and, going into the water, grabbed Karambha by the feet and put an end to him. But Rambha's meditative austerities were already complete, and so, pleased with his austerities, Agni offered him a boon. Rambha asked for a son who would be victorious over the three worlds.[1] Agni said, 'O Great Lord Rambha, whichever female attracts you will be impregnated with a son who is victorious over the three worlds!' Rambha came forward and bowed at the god Agni's feet, and then returned to his home.

"As it happened, this demon Rambha, feeling lusty, came across a buffalo cow. At that time, she was young and full of desire, and so Rambha impregnated her with his seed. But then a male buffalo came across Rambha shortly after he had mounted the buffalo cow, and as Rambha tried to escape, the male buffalo killed him. The other demons then killed the male buffalo, but let the cow go and started to put Rambha's body upon a funeral pyre. The buffalo cow entered the fire to sit in it as a *satī* and accompany her mate.[2] Then, with a terrible cry, a child was born from out of the fire. This child's name, Mahiṣāsura (buffalo-demon), is well known to all. And further, from the body of Rambha a second child emerged named Raktabīja (blood-seed).[3] Later, through the practice of severe austerities, both of these demons obtained boons from the god Brahmā that they could defeat all the gods. And so, they started to commit terrible deeds.

"These misdeeds sent the whole earth and the gods into a deep depression, whereupon one day they all came before Viṣṇu. Hearing of the gods' trouble, Lord Viṣṇu explained that the demons had received the boon that they could only be destroyed at the hands of a female: 'So from our own power let us create a powerful goddess (*mahāśakti*). That great goddess can kill the demons!' Thus, each of the gods contributed some of his inherent power (*śakti*) from his own body to collectively create a beautiful girl with eighteen arms. Each of the gods also endowed this great goddess with their weapons. They then praised her and informed her that there was a terrible demon, Mahiṣāsura, who was causing fear both on earth and in the realm of the gods: 'Therefore, help us destroy this wicked demon and his army of compatriots.' Following the gods' petition, the goddess proceeded to Mahiṣāsura, and killed him and all the prominent warriors in his army, including Ugravīrya, Bāṣkal, Durmukh, Biḍālākṣ, Tāmrākṣ, and others, thus enabling the gods to return once again to the kingdom of heaven.

"But then the two other demons, named Śumbha and Niśumbha, along with Raktabīja, had similarly obtained boons, and so they embarked on a path of transgression against the world. They troubled even the gods and established their own overlordship there in heaven. Feeling despondent, the gods started to worship the revered Mother Pārvatī, who produced a new goddess from her own body. This new goddess was supremely beautiful and powerful, and was given the name Kauśikī. Kauśikī's body became shriveled and black, and thereupon a second goddess appeared from out of it, whose name was Kālikā. Together, these two goddesses destroyed the demons Śumbha and Niśumbha and the rest, permitting the gods to happily return to heaven." Thus, Baba said, "She is the Universal Mother and Supreme Energy. Time and again she removes any distress from her devotees. We should all remember her always, for this is how our difficulties will be averted. Now, go to your village and always keep the revered Mother in your hearts. I will go to Hinglaj Mountain, where I too will worship Ma. There, I will please her and then bring her here to kill the demon." Having said this, Baba Kedargiri took leave of the villagers and worshiped in his cave, which he entrusted to a member of the royal house in that area who was regarded as a yogi (and who remains there even now). Then he went to Hinglaj.

Baba Kedargiri Goes to Hinglaj and Performs Austerities to Obtain a Boon

Baba arrived at Hinglaj and committed to sitting in one place as long as necessary. He thus began fearsome austerities in honor of Mother Mahiṣāsuramardinī (the destroyer of the buffalo demon), creator of the world. As the Supreme Feminine Energy, as the Mother Goddess who grants fearlessness to devotees, she was very pleased with this devotee's austerities. One day she appeared in front of him, breaking his meditative concentration. She appeared as a single beautiful woman, otherworldly and full of energy and loveliness. Her beauty was incomparable. She appeared as a young woman holding various weapons in her eighteen arms. Baba Kedargiri felt fear upon seeing this extremely brilliant vision. He shouted out, "Save me!" and fell at her feet. Suddenly, Mother reached out her boon-granting hand and took her devotee's arm. Making him sit, she laid her hand on his head, saying, "Devotee, your austerities are complete. What do you want? Ask me!"

Baba explained his purpose to the revered Mother, saying, "Ma, you pervade everything and know the entire being of your devotees. That is why I have come. Ma, fulfill my wish without delay: destroy that great evil and thereby grant peace to the people. This is my humble request." The goddess said, "I am very pleased with your selfless compassion and will quickly come to your area to end this suffering. And forever more, I will remain there and bring all your desires to fruition. Now, return to your land."

After obtaining the revered Mother's boon that he had come for, Baba returned to his cave. Hearing of his return, the villagers were overjoyed, and they came to meet him. Baba narrated the news, and told them: "There is no reason for worry; Ma is with us. Very soon our troubles will be over." In this way he consoled them, and bade them to go.[4]

The Devotee Bahora Sees the Goddess

In this part of the Aravali Mountains in eastern Rajasthan, near Kedargiri's cave, a devotee of the Gurjar caste named Bahora used to take his goats to graze in the jungle. He always remembered Ma and worshiped at her feet. This Gurjar named Bahora was born into the Karoliya clan in Bahoripur village. When Bahora Gurjar would take his goats to graze in the jungle, he would come to Baba Kedargiri and sit near him. He used to listen to him talk about Ma. From these meetings, faith in Ma began to take root in his heart, and so he would always think of her. Despite his unrefined way of speaking, he always sang devotional songs lauding Ma's glory, and kept singing with total absorption. He became so entranced with these songs that he even forgot about his own body. Mother saw her devotee's condition, and one day appeared before him.

Seeing Ma's beautiful form, Bahora was astonished. He could not understand the meaning of this sight. And he was transfixed by the invisible presence of Mother's power. Finally, seeing her devotee's situation, Ma felt compassion, saying, "O devotee! I am that power that you have been thinking of night and day! It is *my* glory that you continuously praise in song." Bahora remained silent, as he did not fully understand what she was saying or doing. Finally, he fell at her feet. Ma added, "I am pleased with your devotion. Today, I will give you a boon. Tell me what you desire!"

But what could Bahora say? Up until now he had not been able to understand, and in his broken, stuttering words, he could only say, "Are you truly that Mother—she who has given birth to the world? What I want is to always stand before you and thereby gaze on your image." Mother understood his words and said, "O devotee, I will appear to you from time to time. And later, when I am worshiped here in the form of an idol, you will see me up close by worshiping my image. And your image will be worshiped in addition to mine. You shall have the power to remove any troubles that people might suffer from ancestor spirits. Now go and herd your goats, but keep me in mind!" Having said this, Ma disappeared. This is the same Bahora whose image was later installed in front of Ma's present-day temple, where he remains facing her to this day.[5]

The Destruction of the Demon

For some time after the revered Mother had given Bahora his boon, she often came to Baba, where she liked to play dice. In this area, there had been a demon who was having difficulty finding any prey, causing him to wander here and there. And so, Ma went out in pursuit of that demon. After practicing her divine yoga, one day she finally came face to face with the demon. At that time, she took the form of a young girl.[6] Seeing her, the demon thought that he could at last satiate his hunger, so with delight he rushed forward to grab her. But Mother knew his intentions, and so immediately assumed the terrible form known as Caṇḍī. Seeing her intimidating appearance with all her weapons, the demon became afraid to challenge her, but finally mustered the courage. Mother struck the demon with her mace, and he, agitated, rose up to save his own life and ran off with Mother angrily pursuing him. After going some distance, the demon leapt from a hilltop into the Kalisil River below, and in hot pursuit, Mother did so too. The demon then jumped onto a mortar-shaped rock in the river, but Mother also jumped to that rock.[7] Catching hold of the demon by his hair, she then struck him on the forehead with her sword; he lay dead. The place where Mother killed that demon is now known as "Demon Pool." On the rock in that place, the demon's and Mother's footprints can still be discerned, and a small pavilion has been built there too. This "Demon Pool" is nowadays a half kilometer east of Mother's temple.

Ma Saves a Merchant Devotee's Boat and Becomes Absorbed in Thought

One day, Mother was playing dice with Kedargiri, as she was fond of doing, when suddenly the dice fell from her hand and she became very still. After some time, she returned to her normal state and started playing again. At first it seemed to Baba that nothing had happened and all was normal, but suddenly he noticed water dripping from Mother's hair. He asked in surprise, "Mother, what is happening?[8] There is water dripping from your hair!" Mother said, "It is nothing, Baba. Just play. What are you getting at with these words?" But the *baba* could not forget this matter, instead thinking to himself, "Mother will surely explain this to me." Mother then said, "Baba, I am telling you, you will not be able to see me in this form a second time." And she added, "Look Baba, you can see I have various devotees like you, and from time to time I come to help and protect them. Today, one devotee of mine had brought his goods by boat in the Yamuna River, but the boat got stuck in a whirlpool. In this time of trouble, that merchant devotee remembered me, so I went there to assist him. I saved him from the whirlpool, and that is why my hair is full of water from the Yamuna. Baba, don't be wondering how I could go so far from here and how I could rescue that boat. For me, this is all easy work. I am present in all places, and in accordance with what I said above, I will henceforth not be visible to you in this form." Having said this, the goddess disappeared! It is said that this happened in 1428 CE.[9]

Mother's Idol Is Brought from Nagarkot

In the days when heretics were ruling India, destroying idols and looting temples, Mother's image resided in a temple in the village of Nagarkot.[10] A sādhu named Yogiraj had great faith in Mother, and so worshiped her through that image. But when Yogiraj began to suspect that the heretics would destroy this image, he became very troubled and thought: "I must not let anyone break this statue of Mother." Yogiraj felt very distressed at this thought. Mother had stopped visiting Baba Kedargiri by that time, and so he likewise started to feel uncertainty about her, and he passed his time incessantly worrying. In the end, Mother came to Baba Kedargiri in a dream, saying, "O devotee, now I will come to you in the form of an idol. Put aside your worries. Soon enough, you will recognize me where I deign to stop, and there you are to build a temple for me."

At that same time, in Nagarkot, Mother came in a dream to Yogi Baba, saying, "O Yogi, my devotee! You shall take my idol from here to the east of Rajasthan, in the kingdom of King Mukund Das Khinchi.[11] Take it there and have him look after it. In this way, your worries will be over." In the morning, Yogi Baba remembered these words from his dream, and so he bundled up the image, loaded it on his ox, and quietly set off. Some days into his journey, he had arrived in the vicinity of Baba Kedargiri's cave. The fierce creatures of this terrible forest emitted fearsome sounds, and walking in the evening when the wind was blowing, it seemed all the more dreadful. But having faith in Mother while in this forest, he felt no fear. Thus enveloped in this jungle, after having passed over mountains and rivers, his destination came into view ahead.

He kept walking until evening arrived. The night was dark, and Yogiraj was afraid of predators. And then even his ox had grown tired and refused to move. So, on account of the darkness and the difficulties ahead, it became impossible to go any further. Baba hoped that he would somehow soon reach a protected place. Keeping faith in Mother, he lowered the idol from the ox in the jungle and started to rest. He had some consecrated food with him, and fed some straw to the ox. But the full night lay ahead. Then, however, Mother worked her magic.[12] Heavy-hearted, Baba shuddered at the thought of passing the night in this fearsome jungle with no village in sight. Baba sat with these thoughts in his mind, when suddenly a faint light appeared before him. He thought that perhaps it was a settlement. "Let's go there, so we can pass the night!" With this intention, he tried to put the statue back on the ox, but the statue would not budge. Even after several attempts, he was still unable to lift the statue. Baba brought his ox, but left the statue there while walking in the direction of the light. After some time he had come close to the light. It was no village at all, but a cave in which a holy man (Kedargiri) was sitting intently. Seeing the *baba* deep in meditation, Yogiraj uttered, "Praise to Almighty God!" Opening his eyes and seeing Yogiraj before him, Baba Kedargiri got up from his meditation and approached him. Baba then reverently bowed and brought Yogiraj into his hermitage. After treating Yogiraj with the utmost respect, Baba inquired about his situation. Yogiraj told him the entire story, and said, "Come with me, and I will bring my beloved Mother's idol here." Now Baba Kedargiri realized that this was the fulfillment of Mother's words in his dream, and he felt exceedingly delighted. His heart overflowed with the desire to see his revered Goddess. Baba gave a consecrated meal to his guest Yogiraj and let his ox graze, and then he explained to Yogiraj, "Look, at this time it is night, so it is not a good idea to go just yet. In the morning you can retrieve the statue and move on to your destination. Tonight you shall stay here." Baba then bade his guest to sleep on a mat. Yogiraj was very tired from the long road, so he quickly embraced the goddess of sleep, but Baba Kedargiri was thinking about Ma the whole night.

Mother's Immovability and Yogiraj's Return Home

That whole night, Kedargiri kept thinking about the goddess's idol. Reflecting on Yogiraj's words that he would entrust the idol to the care of King Mukund Das Khinchi, he felt that the statue should somehow or other stay right there. At first he was disappointed to think of this situation, but remembering Mother's power to work her will, he realized that "whatever place Ma accepts will be hers." Thinking this, his heart felt content. In the morning, when the birds had started fluttering and singing, he roused Yogiraj from sleep. From the east, the sun's glowing rays were starting to banish the night's darkness. Feeling invigorated by the power of the sun, Yogiraj and Baba Kedargiri performed their usual morning rituals. The shepherds were taking their animals to graze in the jungle, and soon a villager from nearby came to Baba's hut to pay reverence. Baba informed him about the statue and Yogiraj, and how the Khinchi king could help in taking the image across the Chambal River. The villager said, "Baba, the king has gotten word of your request, as someone from a nearby village came and told everyone about what has happened."

With his local followers, Baba Kedargiri escorted Yogiraj to Trikut hill, near the shore of a stream, where the statue had been left the night before.[13] All paid reverence to the image and, obeying the words of Yogiraj, tried to lift the statue onto the back of the ox. But they were unable to lift it. Two men with all their strength were not able to lift this rather small statue, so five men then tried. But the image refused to move from there. All were very surprised when even twenty or twenty-five men tried to lift the statue but met only defeat. They started to think about how else they might be able to get the image onto the ox. When they could think of no solution, Baba Kedargiri revealed what he had suspected all along: "Yogiraj, this is the revered Goddess whom I worship. She said to me in a dream, 'One day I will come from Hinglaj and Nagarkot, and in this way I will stop here.' In accordance with my dream, the statue has come to me, and now it will go no further. So please be at peace and return. Henceforth, I will assume responsibility in all ways for this idol." Having understood Baba's intent, all the villagers and Yogiraj agreed with these words. In the end, having accepted this outcome, Yogiraj stayed as Baba's guest for three more days before returning to Nagarkot. According to the elders, this happened around nine hundred years ago.

The Installment of Mother Kailā Devī's Image

After Yogiraj had departed, Baba called the villagers together. The Patels (of the Meena tribe) of Loharra-Pidhpur, the devotee of Bahoripura, Bahora Patel, and a Rajput chief named Bhomiya arrived. On this day, for the sake of celebrating the arrival of this idol, Baba took everyone's advice to have the Brahmins first perform an auspicious ceremony. It was the auspicious moment of Navratri, in the first fortnight of the lunar month of Chaitra (March–April).[14] So then what happened? News spread that the event would be around the first day of the first fortnight of Chaitra, and people from around the village started to assemble. By one o'clock quite a few, young and old, men and women, had come together for a great festival. Playing instruments of various kinds, such as drums, trumpets, conch shells, and cymbals, all started to cry out in praise of Mother and sang songs for her. Following ritual protocol, Mother's statue was first bathed in the Kalisil River and, following that, an altar was set up at the place where she had chosen to stop. All were so surprised to see that the same statue that twenty to twenty-five men had not been able to move some days earlier could now be lifted with ease by just two or three men and placed on the altar! At that time, Baba Kedargiri inaugurated Mother's ongoing service and worship.

Mother Kailā Devī Possesses Sukhdev Patel's Body

After the installation of Mother's image, villagers from the area started to regularly visit to worship her each week or month. Since Baba had to walk several kilometers to worship Mother, the devotees had a new hut built for him near her (where nowadays there is a police station). Currently all needs are accomplished with Mother's sacred ash.

In line with their local customs, all felt in their hearts that Mother could surely enter a person's body and thereby receive worship through that person. This would be her way to treat people's troubles and pains. All went to see Sukhchand Patel, who consistently worshiped Mother.[15] All together, they sat him down before Mother and then had him washed and bathed. They then sang devotional songs for Mother to the accompaniment of a shahanai oboe and started to call out, "O Mother, accept our prayer and possess the body of your devotee Sukhdev for the benefit of all who worship you." Baba Kedargiri likewise vigorously implored Mother. In the end, Mother's heart melted, and her spirit entered Sukhchand's body. Mother said, "Baba, I have accepted your prayer and come into the body of Sukhchand Patel. After all, divinity is always the basis of virtuous acts."[16] Having said this, Mother felt very pleased. Thus, Mother appeared in this miraculous form to all, and from her divine power at this shrine, pilgrimage started to grow. Nowadays, the goddess comes into the body of Sukhchand's descendant, Bharosee Lal Meena, whenever devotees arrange to honor her with religious songs and dance. And the goddess may even enter their bodies, too, so as to fulfill their wishes and provide resolutions for their troubles.

Devī Performs a Miracle for the Khinchi King

On the pretext of some mundane mistake on the part of Mukund Das (the Khinchi king of Gagraun), the emperor Dharmandha Badshah had captured and imprisoned [Mukund Das's] son.[17] Moreover, he had given the command that the son should die by hanging after a certain amount of time. Further, the Khinchi king himself was sentenced (in absentia) to death by being placed in front of a cannon that would be fired. Seeking relief from this terrible predicament, Khinchi proceeded to the image of the goddess Cāmuṇḍā in Bansikhera village, in the hope that Mother could release him from this death sentence. In Cāmuṇḍā Devī's temple, the king and queen started to implore her for help. The villagers thereupon told him all about Kailā Devī. With hope in his heart and devotion and great faith, the king then embarked on a pilgrimage to Kailā Devī. Following protocol, he prayed to her and arranged for a devotional song event in her honor. Mother was pleased, and so, entering the body of Sukhchand Patel, the medium of her temple, asked the Khinchi king why he had come. Facing the goddess [in the body of the medium], the king told his story, saying, "O Supreme Mother, please save my life and that of my son! I am in your protection." Hearing the Khinchi king's plea, the Supreme Mother answered, "O king, you will not have any misfortune! Your son will be acquitted from his sentence to die by hanging, and I myself will save you from death by cannon. Now go home and plant the sapling of a bullock heart tree.[18] Take the first blossoms that grow from it and place them in some copper pots, where they will grow into fruits. When the fruits have expanded to completely fill the pots, then go to a Brahmin and hire his son so that he can come with you on a pilgrimage to me. Then your work will be complete. Remember, divinity is ultimately the upholder of righteousness." Having said this, Mother's spirit left her medium's body. With faith in Mother Kailā, the king returned to his land, and following the Supreme Mother's words, planted the sapling of a bullock heart fruit tree. When the first blossoms came forth, he put them in very, very large copper pots. In the pots, the blossoms started to turn into fruits, which he realized was a miraculous sign from Ma.[19]

The emperor then rescinded the order for the execution by hanging of the king's son, but the Khinchi king himself would still need to be put to death. When [the king] had been arrested, he kept the Supreme Mother in his heart as he was brought before the emperor. In accordance with the emperor's decree, the king was placed in front of a cannon; the assistants tied him up and the artilleryman lit the fuse. But by the grace of the Supreme Mother, even after the executioners had made a fair amount of effort, the cannon would not fire. Having witnessed this, the emperor realized his own dishonor in this act, and pulled the king away and let him go. Embarrassed, the emperor declared that the king must be innocent, and, having returned his belongings, gave him permission to leave.[20]

The Brahmin's Son Is Sacrificed, and the Khinchi King Constructs a Shrine

Mukund Das Khinchi and his family proceeded to Mother's divine court in the temple. In gratitude to Ma Kailā for saving his life and that of his son, he announced that there would be a grand ceremony in Mother's presence to honor her. For this, the Brahmins and others of the surrounding villages were invited. A large number of people came to take consecrated food in Mother's temple and to witness her miracles. The devotional event thereupon took place, and the copper pots full of bullock heart fruit, along with the Brahmin's son, were duly presented to Mother. Mother came into her dedicated devotee's body (the Meena medium), and he touched a bundle of sacred peacock feathers on the head of the Brahmin boy, who thereupon started to shake.[21] Without speaking, the boy got up and pulled out the bullock heart fruit, one by one, from each copper pot and put them aside. Then from his mouth a very large bullock heart fruit started to emerge! Having seen this otherworldly sight, all were astonished and started to shout in praise of Mother. The Brahmin boy then took his place again.

While this Brahmin boy sat facing Mother (in the body of the medium), she picked up some sacred ash and put it on the boy's head. Immediately, the boy's body burst into flames and he turned into a pile of ash. Seeing this shocking scene, all stood up and started praying to Mother to bring the boy back to life. Mother responded, "For this purpose I had the king hire this boy. It was my secret plan; and why should that be?" All pleaded, "O Mother, this is not proper! If you are truly the Divine Mother, then bring this boy back to life!" Mother said, "I was merely showing you my power." Once she had said this, she splashed sacred water from the Ganges onto the boy's heap of ash, and he immediately emerged unscathed.[22] Having seen this, all became very happy, and started to shout praise for Mother. The king said to her, "O Mother, you do not need to show people such incredible acts, for this will only unsettle their hearts. We already know your power very well! For you have come before us as the Great Mother, the original divine feminine power (*śakti*). Hail to you!"

In the end, the king asked the goddess, "O Mother, what is your command for me?" The Supreme Mother said only, "Dedicate a proper shelter for me!"

Accordingly, the king immediately ordered that a beautiful shrine be set up for her, and this shrine was dedicated in 1432 CE.[23]

For Mother's inauguration, Brahmins led a ritual of Vedic mantras, and the king ordered a fire ceremony and a great feast for the Brahmins. Gowns were then bestowed upon the Supreme Mother Kailā Devī and Ma Cāmuṇḍā. Alms were given to beggars and funds allotted to perpetually attend to Mother's needs. Henceforth, every year at the time of Navratri (twice per year, around April and October), necessary things for the goddesses are brought here. The numerous ceremonies have grown in magnitude, and Ma Kailā Devī's devotees now even arrive from far away. Her glorious sacred flame brings peace to people in distress and makes devotees' wishes come true. On account of this, services for Ma and facilities for pilgrims, such as religious rest houses, roadside rest stops, and so forth, have been set up.

After the time of Mukund Das, the Khinchi king, the kings of Karauli took responsibility for this temple, and today it remains under their protection.[24] Kings Gopal Das, Dharm Pal, Gopal Singh, Pratap Pal, Madan Pal, Jai Singh Pal, Arjun Pal, Bhramar Pal, Bhim Pal, and Ganesh Pal and so forth, have provided much service in body and mind in terms of both time and funding, as needed. This brings the story of the preceding pages up to the present day. Devotional organizations have also contributed much time and energy to the development of the site, such as facilities for visitors, which has altogether transformed it. This is all Mother's doing (*līlā*). By Mother's grace, all has come to fruition. Having been so blessed by Mother, one accordingly asks of her: "What else shall I do, but offer everything to you?"

THE GODDESS IN CONTEXT: PILGRIMAGE, POSSESSION, AND THE ECONOMICS OF DEVOTION

The story of Kailā Devī exemplifies how local goddesses, with their own identities and histories, become drawn into the prestigious pan-Indian narratives of the Great Goddess. Devotees acclaim Kailā Devī as a local avatar of the Goddess who has come to earth, just as she presumably has at other goddess shrines, to save humanity from the pernicious effects of this era, known as the Kali Age in Hindu cosmology. According to classical Hindu scripture, the world is caught in an eternal cycle of progressive moral degeneracy, as witnessed in such current phenomena as global capitalism and the accompanying personal greed and societal corruption that threaten traditional

Indian values.[25] The inhabitants from the area of Kailā Devī's temple also have an economic interest in promoting her efficacy with the expectation of increasing pilgrimage to her temple and adjunct shrines. Linking Kailā Devī with classical Hindu mythology also serves to "upgrade" the site. This prompts some discussion about the historicity of the goddess: How much of what we read about her is ancestral "tradition," and how much reflects contemporary pragmatic aims?

Considering the way the story has come down to us, as a collection of folklore from anonymous local sources that was then propagated in printed handbooks targeting Hindi-speaking pilgrims, historicity is not easy to confirm. All we really know about Kailā Devī's history comes by way of her origin story, which was brought together in its current form in relatively recent times. Moreover, whatever local goddess she once was, she has now merged with the encompassing narrative of the pan-Indian Goddess. Granted, some local historical correlations, such as references to specific Rajput rulers and members of the local Meena and Gurjar communities, provide this goddess with a semblance of time and place. But these references have been embellished to substantiate the current administrative structure of the temple, so they may not necessarily be literally indicative of local antiquity. Or, interpreting Kailā Devī's story from a faith-based perspective, we could say that she is indeed very localized, but this local form is simply an emanation of the pan-Indian Great Goddess. Indeed, the story doctrinally largely follows this line of thinking. Either way, the following sections attempt to track Kailā Devī's trajectory and how her story upholds the conceptual unity of all Hindu goddesses.

Seed: Local Origins of the Goddess

Local histories highlight the Rajput kings of the Jadaun dynasty, who ruled the state of Karauli. Since around 1450, this domain has included the goddess's temple. Like many Indian kings, the Karauli Rajputs personally identified with a protective lineage goddess (*kuladevī*), in this case Kailā Devī, who they believed would lead their army to victory in times of warfare. As is the case with so many goddesses, the story of Kailā Devī that has taken shape in local lore emphasizes her superlative ability to destroy demons, who are always male, like an actual army in historical India. However, as is common among village goddesses throughout the subcontinent, Kailā Devī has a dual nature; she is both nurturing like a mother yet quick to become angry and cause harm if neglected. A traditional way to maintain Kailā Devī's goodwill and ensure her divine assistance in times of need was to offer animal sacrifices. Hence, following the pattern of many prior warrior kings, the Karauli Rajputs arranged for a goat to be sacrificed at Mother's temple on the eighth day of the waxing moon phase each month.[26] In accordance with the widespread rejection of animal sacrifice in contemporary India, at Kailā Devī's temple this tradition has been transmuted into a symbolic act: slicing off part of the goat's ear.

According to Kailā Devī's story translated here, she arrived at her present site around nine hundred years ago from a different locale. However, the dates presented in this story sometimes contradict each other; for example, the same king, Mukund Das Khinchi, is mentioned in connection with the founding of the goddess's temple in the twelfth century and also in the fifteenth century. This discrepancy may be due to the nature of the source itself, since it is a patchwork of episodes collected from multiple sources, and the compiler appears unconcerned about reconciling them. Further, the story implies that it is telling about these events from the perspective of the present day, as certain features of the current setting are described in the narrative: the existence of a police station near the temple and the inclusion of the personal name of the current medium in the goddess's temple. Notwithstanding the mixing of time references, it is clear that this region was formerly forested wilderness and scrub, inhabited only by wild predators, tribal groups mostly known for herding, and the occasional demon. Like so many goddesses, this one's demon-fighting fierceness made her perfectly suited for this region. Even nowadays, land adjacent to Kailā Devī is used as a tiger reserve. It is therefore all the more fitting that Kailā Devī should be regarded as a manifestation of the pan-Indian Goddess, who is commonly depicted riding a tiger.

Despite long-standing Rajput domination, an indigenous tribal presence persists and has even become integral to the present-day ritual regimen of Kailā Devī's temple. Nowadays, each night at 8:30 in the main temple, a particular man of the Meena tribe performs his exclusive hereditary right to channel the goddess as a service to pilgrims. Following a rousing evening prayer accompanied by cymbals and drums to summon the goddess (*āratī*), this medium crawls forward on the floor to meet the devotees who are sitting around the shrine. They blurt out questions of personal urgency, pleading for the goddess's assistance, although the medium's words in response are hardly audible in the tumult.[27] Kailā Devī's story tells how the goddess chose the Meena medium's ancestor to serve her, so his role is part of the official protocol here. But it is not clear if the Meenas truly had some ancient tradition of worshiping a local proto–Kailā Devī goddess, or if they simply took advantage of the arrival of pilgrims in more recent times. What the goddess's story nonetheless does make clear is that despite her convergence with the pan-Indian Goddess, local society now vigorously asserts its own special relationship with her.

Another local community, the Gurjars, have similarly claimed a role in Kailā Devī's devotional regime. Directly facing the goddess's temple is the temple of Bahora, or Bahora Bhagat (Bahora the Medium)—a Gurjar goatherd who had long ago led a life of notable faith in Kailā Devī and who was thus deified as her perpetual assistant. The goddess decreed that he would always have the power to intercede on her behalf, and so only his descendants are allowed the privilege of serving as her mediums. Unlike the Meena medium, though, the Gurjar medium is seemingly not restricted to working in the evening. Devotees are divided as to whether Bahora Gurjar or Kailā Devī should be visited first, but both shrines are nonetheless part of a standard pilgrimage, which also includes several sites nearby. It is apparent, then, that all the local groups—Rajputs, Meenas, and Gurjars—have upheld a role in the current devotional setup of the shrine. Their rationale for these privileges is explained in Kailā Devī's origin story. This arrangement has economic ramifications too. Most of the shopkeepers selling religious souvenirs to pilgrims are from the Rajput Jadaun clan, and devotees must purchase tickets to attend Kailā Devī's appearance through the medium. The Gurjar medium may operate only by direct donation, as is common at many Hindu shrines offering such services.

Kailā Devī's local nature can also be gleaned from comparison with surrounding sacred sites typically included as a circuit in a visit to her temple. For instance, it is considered auspicious for devotees to bathe in the nearby Kalisil River, a short stroll from Kailā Devī's temple, prior to entering the sacred sites, as this was where the goddess killed one of the demons that had been terrorizing the land. And around three kilometers from the main temple there is a popular cave shrine believed to be the site of Kailā Devī's first appearance in this region, when she answered the prayers of a holy man, as narrated in the story. The cave, which is now managed by local priests, offers opportunities to worship not only the goddess but also such deities as Bhairava (a fierce manifestation of Śiva) and Hanumān, who are nowadays often found alongside the Goddess in popular shrines (suggesting an instance of local and pan-Indian male deities converging).[28] All of these sites in the Kailā Devī complex, along with the goddess's local societal connections, are prominently featured in her origin story. The story thus serves as a kind of guidebook for pilgrims to understand the significance of the people and places that they will encounter here. Whatever the antiquity of Kailā Devī may be, the inclusion of these narrative elements makes it likely that the story has been shaped in modern times to justify the current ritual regime.

Flower: How Narratives Bid for Fame

From the mix of local and pan-Indian goddess elements in Kailā Devī's origin story, we can infer that a local form of Kailā Devī merged at some point in the past with the encompassing idea of the Great Goddess. But without historical documentation other than the origin story itself, it is difficult to track this convergence. What can be said is that in associating Kailā Devī with the pan-Indian Goddess, the origin story claims her to be as efficacious as, indeed one and the same as, the all-powerful Goddess who is already universally revered in the Hindu world for having vanquished various demons in the Purāṇic narratives such as the *Devī Māhātmya*.[29] This is essentially the same as what has happened to countless other goddesses in villages across India. In keeping with the multiplicity-within-unity theme (all goddesses being one), throughout Kailā Devī's origin story she is not only identified by her local name or some variant of it but also by a number of names or epithets, mostly corresponding to "Mother" in some form, such as Ma, *mātā*, and *maiyā*, and also in reference to her identity as Durgā, Mahāmāyā, and Śakti, all names that connote a universal feminine divinity not restricted to any one place.[30] Her profusion of names may seem confusing, but this also demonstrates the fluid identity of the goddess and the flexibility between local and universal forms.

Kailā Devī's story speaks of the goddess's capacity to relocate between several sites according to her own will or due to shifting conditions. This interchangeability between sites makes sense when we consider that most local goddesses are portrayed as representations of the Great Goddess. Hinglaj and Nagarkot are widely acknowledged in Hinduism as two out of dozens of real-life goddess shrines or *śakti pīṭhs* across South Asia.[31] Sanskrit scriptures tell us that the goddess Satī, bride of the god Śiva, fell in pieces to earth at these sites, which became sacred centers for goddess worship.[32] So linking Kailā Devī to this network of shrines clearly raises her profile. And yet, although Kailā Devī's present-day shrine is sometimes referred to as a *pīṭh*, including in her origin story, she is nowhere mentioned in classical Sanskritic scriptures. We can therefore suppose that Kailā Devī's linkage to the *śakti pīṭhs* marks an attempt to upgrade her by associating her with the prestigious goddesses of classical scriptures.

In Kailā Devī's story it is repeatedly made clear that she is equal to, or the same as, the pan-Indian Great Goddess. At the start of the story, Kedargiri Baba, a holy man, comforts villagers harassed by a demon with the knowledge that no obstacle in this world is too great for the Goddess provided that they demonstrate full faith in her abilities. At this point the goddess has not yet manifested as Kailā Devī, but it is also evident that her eventual arrival signals a localization of the Great Goddess. The goddess's universality is further reinforced when the holy man tells us that her readiness to save the world is like a nurturing mother's love for her children; thus the goddess is often called Mother. When the holy man then goes to the goddess shrine at distant Hinglaj, he engages in ritual austerities (fasting, meditating, reciting praises to the goddess, and so forth), a traditional method in Hinduism of entreating divine favors. Pleased with the holy man's demonstration of faith, she agrees to come to his area to kill the demon. This marks the beginning of the Goddess's local evolution as Kailā Devī.

Once the Goddess, or rather the goddess of Hinglaj, has killed the demon, she assures the holy man that she will always answer calls from her devotees to protect them. This message seems targeted at present-day devotees, who increasingly come from far away. In an additional episode she miraculously saves a merchant who is faced with drowning in the Yamuna, again reminding us that she will answer the call of the faithful in need of her assistance no matter where they may be. Thus, as much as we might think of the goddess as a local representation of the pan-Indian goddess, her local caretakers also aspire to extend the local goddess's realm of followers all across the Hindu world. In line with this expansion of locality, the reference to the merchant devotee may also mark an effort to appeal to that particular class of devotee, found in cities throughout India but often tracing their ancestry to Rajasthan's trade towns. Merchants are often instrumental in providing donations to maintain folk shrines in Rajasthan, if not elsewhere.

The second half of Kailā Devī's origin story reaches its culmination with the arrival of her idol. In the village of Nagarkot, the goddess of that shrine appears in a dream to a holy man named Yogiraj to command him to move her idol away because of the implied threat of Muslim iconoclasm.[33] The notorious Afghan Muslim warrior Mahmud of Ghazni is known to have sacked Nagarkot in 1009 CE, so the teller of this story might have been relying on readers' awareness of that incident. In fact, references to the Rajput king Mukund Das Khinchi's devotion to the goddess may similarly indicate an attempt to reconceptualize the goddess as a patron deity of valiant Hindu kings fighting to save India's traditional way of life when Muslim raiders were making more frequent appearances in India. In the story, the goddess of Nagarkot assures Yogiraj that in a new location, somewhere in the vicinity of eastern Rajasthan, she will receive the protection of the local king, who turns out to be a king of the Khinchi dynasty. The two holy men, one having worshiped the goddess of Hinglaj and the other that of Nagarkot, are then united and affirm that she will henceforth live at her present site. Inasmuch as this story repeatedly exalts the goddess in pan-Indian terms and highlights her interregional connections, it seems evident that the compiler of these episodes would like to reconfigure Kailā Devī as a local form of the Great Goddess. Thus, the local goddess is not simply forgotten as a result of some natural process of adoption into the pan-Indian pantheon; we can see local voices actively taking part in this reconfiguration.

Fruit: Kailā Devī's Significance Today

Kailā Devī, as a popular present-day avatar of miracles, continues to straddle regional and pan-Indian identities. For instance, although like many goddesses she is celebrated during the pan-Indian festival of fall Navratri, approximately in October, and again in the spring Navratri, around April, the latter of these celebrations has developed into a very personalized event linked to her origin story. The goddess's story tells us that after her image had arrived at its present-day site, the inauguration ceremony for her worship was performed at the beginning of Navratri in the month of Chaitra, so the festival each year effectively marks her birthday. A very intriguing episode toward the end of her story gives us another reason for the special resonance of the Chaitra festival. We learn that when the Khinchi king is in need of her assistance, the goddess directs him to place the blossoms of *rām-phal*, or bullock's heart—a local fruit related to the custard apple—in several copper pots. In conjunction with other supernatural events, the blossoms then miraculously ripen into full-blown fruits within the pots and subsequently emerge from the mouth of a Brahmin boy standing at the goddess's temple, while she possesses her Meena medium. Given that *rām-phal* trees fruit in April each year, this event seems aligned with the common perception that the goddess's power to provide miracles is at its height during the Chaitra festival.

In other ways too, despite her pan-Indian connections, Kailā Devī remains at the center of a rich local tradition. Among the many thousands of pilgrims arriving during the Chaitra festival, those coming on foot from the surrounding region often jointly carry long poles of bamboo stretching forty or fifty feet or more, which are decorated with colorful banners. These constructions are typically brought in recognition of miracles that the goddess has already granted, for which a vow was made to return the favor with this visit. While the practice of individuals bringing flags is known at other Hindu miracle shrines, the grand constructions brought to Kailā Devī are distinctive for their large scale and group effort. Especially unique to this shrine, many devotees from the surrounding region vigorously dance and sing in front of the goddess's temple in a style locally referred to as *lāṅguriyā*. This folk performance, offered in praise of the goddess and her divine assistants, traditionally included bawdy lyrics suggestive of wedding ribaldry.[34] With the increased prevalence of urbanized, "middle-class" devotees arriving by vehicle, many of whom prefer a "family-friendly" setting with chaste lyrics and no animal sacrifices, Kailā Devī's temple protocol is being pulled in the direction of a more generically orthodox Hindu piety.

Kailā Devī's dual aspect as both a nurturing mother and a fearsome opponent in battle is reflected in the fact that she is worshiped as not one but two "sister" goddesses, side by side, each with opposite personalities. One, properly Kailā Devī herself, is nowadays opposed to receiving blood and is more inclined to bestow wealth and well-being. Her sister, named Cāmuṇḍā, continues to prefer receiving blood and, at least according to some, is good at providing miracles for inflicting harm on enemies. In current ritual protocol, no sacrifice is allowed at the temple itself, so Cāmuṇḍā is forced to follow her sister's preference. References to past sacrifice do not specify Kailā Devī's current abhorrence of blood, so it is entirely possible that both goddesses once routinely accepted sacrifice, as required to protect Rajput kings and devotees seeking miracles. Indeed, devotees readily acknowledge that perhaps as recently as twenty years ago sacrifices were still taking place adjacent to the main temple itself.

Even in the presently modified ritual regime, Cāmuṇḍā actually does manage to turn the tables on her sister by receiving blood sacrifice, but only at several inconspicuous shrines dedicated for this purpose at the edge of Kailā

Devī's village. Families residing near these shrines keep goats on hand to sell to devotees and serve as executors of the sacrifice while the families watch. Whiskey is also commonly offered at these shrines, as was common at many goddess shrines in the past (but now often discouraged). Locals say that around 10 percent of pilgrims to Kailā Devī still offer such sacrifices. Since the two goddesses are always worshiped as a pair at these nearby shrines, as in the main temple, Kailā Devī is forced to attend sacrifices at the shrines even though she may not approve of this practice. Considering the two goddesses' indissoluble union, when devotees refer to the worship of "Kailā Devī," unless they are specifically differentiating between them, they generally mean them both as a composite divinity. The two goddesses' formal appearance is virtually identical in an aniconic folk style. But devotees are quick to identify a distinction due to their different habits: the idol of Kailā Devī, situated on the right side as one approaches, noticeably leans away from Cāmuṇḍā, supposedly to express her distaste for her sister's impure inclinations.[35]

SOURCE

The text offered here in translation, Moolsingh Jadaun Bhagirathwale's *Śrī Kailādevī Itihās* (The history of Kailā Devī), was obtained from several small Hindi-language booklets sold to visitors in the market adjacent to Kailā Devī's main temple. At least one booklet devotes special attention to the history of the local Jadaun Rajput ruling lineage. The several booklets that I purchased, from different authors and publishers, agree on the story's overall sequence of events, sometimes adding their own details. Authorship and especially dating are unreliable when it comes to devotional literature sold at shrines, as authors or compilers frequently present these writings as anonymous homages to the deity. In this case, judging by the authors' surnames, they are local Rajputs, undoubtedly proud of their dynastic connection to the goddess and therefore more open about acknowledging that devotional link. While we can suppose that these books were printed within the last few years, their antecedents are unknown. Some features of Kailā Devī's story, such as her connections to the pan-Indian Goddess, her miracles for faithful devotees, and the ritual importance of certain local communities, widely resemble a genre of devotional folk literature found at many shrines throughout Rajasthan, each reflecting local social hierarchies.

We could say that the story as it now appears represents a collection of local folk anecdotes brought together by several enterprising intellectuals; these are typically Brahmins, but in the case of Rajasthan's goddesses, Rajputs also identify with the locality of the goddess and feel motivated to promote her. This process probably first happened some decades ago, and now the booklets are endlessly reprinted without documenting how they were first assembled. Inhabitants of the area of Kailā Devī seem to concur with the current story, but in all likelihood their knowledge of particular details will vary significantly from person to person. The booklets as a repository of knowledge about the goddess have undoubtedly inculcated a standardized story among the local public and visitors, no matter what their original understanding of the goddess may have been. So what devotees nowadays say about Kailā Devī dovetails with the devotional booklets. If one were to conduct extensive research in surrounding villages, one might uncover some less-standardized narratives, too. In fact, only a small number of pilgrims buy the booklets, but enough of these booklets have entered circulation within the devotional population, in conjunction with locals' affirmations of their authority, that the story we have here is now accepted as the goddess's true history.

FURTHER READING

Entwistle, A. W. 1983. "Kailā Devī and Lamguriya." *Indo-Iranian Journal* 25, no.2 (March): 85–101.

Erndl, Kathleen. 1993. *Victory to the Mother: The Hindu Goddess of Northwest India in Myth, Ritual, and Symbol.* New York: Oxford University Press.

Grodzins Gold, Ann. 2008. "Deep Beauty: Rajasthani Goddess Shrines above and below the Surface." *International Journal of Hindu Studies* 12, no. 2: 153–79.

NOTES

1. The "three worlds" refers to the heavens, the earth, and the underworlds.

2. The word *satī*, which literally means "good woman," has come to be associated with the rare and controversial, yet culturally honored, practice of a woman burning herself on the funeral pyre of her deceased husband.

3. Raktabīja's name refers to his supernatural ability to generate a copy of himself from every drop of his blood that touches the earth.

4. This paragraph is added from a section called "The Goddess's Appearance in Baba's Cave," which has otherwise been abridged.

5. The Bahora image at the Kailā Devī temple attracts devotees seeking relief from spirit possession, which Bahora is reputed to be able to cure.

6. On the goddess appearing in the form of a young girl, see also, in the present volume, chapters 3 and 7, and note 84 in chapter 4.

7. The Hindi term used for the rock in this story is *silā kī patthar*, which generally means a mortar (flattened or hollowed out rock).

8. The query in the Hindi text is *mātā, yah kyā aur kaisī līlā hai?*, which more literally means "Mother, what kind of 'play' is this?" The term *līlā* is commonly used in reference to divine actions for which no logical explanation is forthcoming.

9. The dates cited in this story do not really line up. There are two main sets of dates, from the eleventh or twelfth centuries, and from the fifteenth century.

10. The village here called Nagarkot is presently the town of Kangra in the mountains of Himachal Pradesh, where several important goddess sites (*śakti pīṭh*) are found. The reference to heretics (*vidharmī*) seems to be an allusion to iconoclastic Muslim rulers, who were expanding their power in northern India in the eleventh century, when this part of the origin story takes place.

11. Since the beginning of this narrative states that Mukund Das founded the temple for Cāmuṇḍā in 1149 CE, it appears that this episode also took place around the same time. This is not entirely consistent with the statement in the story that Kailā Devī came to Mukund Das's attention "nine hundred years ago." In any case, Cāmuṇḍā's image was only later brought to Kailā Devī's temple.

12. The Hindi term used here is *vicitra līlā*, or "magic play." As elsewhere in the narrative, Mother has the capacity to favorably change the outcome of devotees' predicaments according to her whim, which is described as a kind of magic.

13. This is the present location of Kailā Devī's temple.

14. Since the month of Chaitra is also the occasion for Kailā Devī's biggest annual festival, the fact that she first arrived at her present site during that month makes the annual celebration like a birthday for her. However, it is the time for major goddess celebrations elsewhere in India as well, so the date of Kailā Devī's foundation seems to be an example of how the local deity is made to conform to the ritual calendar of the pan-Indian Great Goddess.

15. Sukhchand is used here as an alternate name for Sukhdev.

16. At this point, the goddess seems to be suggesting that such capabilities as performing possession are evidence of the ultimate power of the divine.

17. Gagraun is in the region to the south of Kailā Devī's temple.

18. The bullock heart tree, also known as custard apple, is called *rām-phal* in Hindi.

19. It is noteworthy that this fruit normally ripens in the month of Chaitra, the hot season and the time of Kailā Devī's grand annual festival. The timing of this miraculous outcome thus dovetails with the time of year when the goddess's powers are believed to be at their strongest.

20. The last three sentences of this section have been abridged.

21. In Hindu folk practice, it is common at times of worship for those, such as priests, who are regarded as being endowed with divine power to bless devotees with a peacock feather, which in this setting is regarded as having divine qualities. This act causes a

transference of supernatural power to the devotee, which in some instances could result in divine possession.

22. Lightly splashing water brought from the sacred Ganges on the gathered devotees is still a normal part of the nightly ritual led by the Meena medium. This mode of blessing is standard at many Hindu shrines.

23. The date for the completion of this temple is unexpected, given that the initial events and Khinchi's dedication were dated to 1149 CE (1207 in the Vikram calendar, a traditional system for counting years that remains in use in northern India). One might suppose that these two dates reference two separate Khinchi kings, but in fact they are specified by the same personal name, Mukund Das.

24. Three sentences have been abridged here.

25. On the Kali Yuga, see J. F. Fleet's technical discussion (1992).

26. Brajendrapal (1990, 25), discusses the significance of the eighth (*ashtami*) day at the Kailā Devī temple.

27. Locals say that the current medium's grandfather and great-uncle had contested which of them was truly the goddess's chosen medium and thus entitled to receive funds on her behalf. So the king tested each one's ability to channel the goddess and decided on the grandfather of the current medium.

28. Devotees say that in current practice, in addition to prayers of various sorts to the goddess and adjunct deities, visitors particularly wish for favorable outcomes pertaining to home life or home construction. Scattered around the cave are hundreds of miniature makeshift homes that pilgrims have assembled from stones found on the rocky ground.

29. For an introduction to the cultural significance of the myths recounted in the *Devī Māhātmya*, see Kinsley (1988, 95–105).

30. Devotees do not entirely agree about the meaning of the name Kailā Devī itself. The devotional handbooks sold near the goddess's temple suggest that the name could refer to her efficacy or skill (*kalā*) in performing miracles; hence her name could be rendered "the miracle goddess" based on this derivation. Additionally, the handbooks impute a linkage to the Kali Yuga, when humanity is in great moral peril and needs divine saviors like this goddess. However, neither of these derivations is likely, linguistically speaking.

31. For a recent study of the goddess at Hinglaj, see Schaflechner (2018).

32. For a basic introduction to *śakti pīṭhs*, see Kinsley (1988, 184–87).

33. Numerous Hindi booklets on the *śakti pīṭhs* in this region are available at these shrines. Kathleen Erndl's (1993) study of pilgrimage to these shrines is a comprehensive English-language work on the subject.

34. Decades ago, A. W. Entwistle (1983) wrote what may be the only previous English-language article pertaining to Kailā Devī, in which he focuses on *lāṅguriyā* songs. More generally, Hindu goddesses who have a fierce demeanor are often considered to be partial to rough or vulgar singing. In recent years, with the general trend to domesticate them in line with "upwardly mobile" sensibilities and higher-caste values, there has been a movement to "clean up" such songs to Kailā Devī and goddesses

elsewhere in India. For an example of this process in a different geographical locale, see M. J. Gentes's work (1992, esp. 305) on the high-caste appropriation of the Bhagavatī goddess of Kodungallur, Kerala, and the consequent discouragement of vulgar singing.

35. Jadaun Bhagirathwale (n.d., 43) notes several possible reasons for Kailā Devī's bent posture, including the one cited in this chapter. Devotees interviewed at the temple cite Kailā Devī's distaste for her sister's habits more often than other possible reasons for her posture.

FIGURE 13. Bahucarā Mātā, by Laura Santi

CHAPTER 7

Bahucarā Mātā

She Who Roams Widely

DARRY DINNELL

To the southwest of Rajasthan lies Gujarat, the state in India where our next tale originates. As a largely peninsular state on the Arabian sea, it has a rich history of seafaring. Its ancient trading networks linked merchants in Gujarat with Africa, the Arab peninsula, Persia, and other Indian ocean ports. The state is home to an array of religious communities including Hindus, Muslims, Jains, Christians, Sikhs, Buddhists, Jews, and Zoroastrians. It thus features many impressive temples and other pilgrimage sites, including the ashram of Mohandas K. Gandhi, who championed Indian independence from British rule. The landscape varies from the desolate Rann of Kutch in the north, one of the world's largest salt marshes, to fertile farmland in the south. It is home to many tribal villages and a national park with the last wild population of Asiatic lions in the world.

The translated story tells of the popular goddess from Gujarat named Bahucarā Mātā. As in the previous chapter, the source is a contemporary booklet in the local language (Gujarati) marketed to pilgrims and local devotees. The focus of the passage is the tale of a demon named Daṇḍhāsur, who torments the world, and how the goddess interacts with him. However, the story takes an unexpected turn, making it different than many of the other demon-versus-goddess battle stories we have encountered thus far. The passage ends with references to gender-bending miracles at sacred sites near the goddess's temple.

In the past, Bahucarā Mātā was mainly associated with non-Brahmin groups such as Rajputs, farmers, local tribal groups, Muslims, and third gender Pāvaiyās. As the essay discusses in detail, she has recently risen to fame among a more orthodox public. Readers should compare her origin story here with the competing stories summarized in the essay. Attend to how the translated narrative works to "Brahminize" Bahucarā and downplay unorthodox elements associated with her, such as animal sacrifice and nonheteronormative genders.

બહુચર્માની ઉત્પત્તિકથા

ચુંવાળમાં બિરાજતાં શક્તિ બહુ બહુચરાજી આધશક્તિનું સ્વરૂપ છે. મા બાળા-સ્વરૂપે વરખડીના ઝાડ નીચે સ્વયં પ્રગટ થયાં, જેની કથા આ પ્રમાણે છે. ધર્મારણ્ય ક્ષેત્રમાં દંઢાસુર નામનો એક અસુર પ્રજા, બ્રાહ્મણો તેમજ ઋષિઓને ખૂબ જ હેરાન કરતો. એ દંઢાસુર પરથી ચુંવાળ પ્રદેશ 'દંઢાવ્ય' તરીકે પણ ઓળખાય છે. આ દંઢાસુરને એવું વરદાન મળેલું હતું કે જે તેની સામે લડવા આવે તેની અડધી શક્તિ દંઢાસુરમાં આવી જાય. લડાઈમાં દંઢાસુરની શક્તિ દોઢી થઈ જતી હતી. આથી તે દોઢારાક્ષસ તરીકે પણ ઓળખાતો. દંઢાસુર અતિ ખળવાન અને ક્રૂર હતો. ઉપરાંત એનો જેવા જ બળિયા બીજા અસુરોની તેની પાસે વિશાળ સેના હતી. તેણે એક પછી એક પૃથ્વી પરના બધા રાજાઓને હરાવી, તેમને પદભ્રષ્ટ કર્યા અને પોતે આખી પૃથ્વીનો માલિક બની ગયો. અસુરસેના આખી પૃથ્વી પર ત્રાસ વરસાવવા લાગી. ઋષિઓના યજ્ઞોમાં અસુરો વિઘ્ન નાખવા લાગ્યા. એ સમયે સરસ્વતી ક્ષેત્રના સિદ્ધપટન (હાલનું સિદ્ધપુર)માં નિવાસ કરતા સત્યવ્રત મુનિથી આ સહન ન થઈ શક્યું, અને તે દંઢાસુર સમક્ષ જઈ તેને કહેવા લાગ્યા : "હે મદોન્મત અસુરરાજ! દુર્જળ પ્રજા પર અત્યાચાર કરી અને ઋષિઓના યજ્ઞો બંધ કરાવી તું તારી શક્તિ બતાવવા માગતો હઈશ ; પણ એ તારી કાયરતા છે. શક્તિ બતાવવી જ હોય તો જા એની પાસે, જેણે તારા વડવા ધૂમ્રલોચનને અંબા બની રણમાં રોળ્યો હતો. તારા સગા રક્તાસુરના લોહીના એક એક ટીપામાંથી તેના જેવા બળવાન અસુરો પેદા થતા હતા ત્યારે કાળિકા બની એ રક્તાસુરનું લોહી જેણે પીધું હતું. અસુર અરુણને મારવા જે ભ્રામરી દેવી ભમરી બની હતી. અસુર રાજ મહિષાસુર જેના કોપથી બચવા માટે પાડાનું રૂપ લઈ ભાગ્યો હતો, એ અંબાજી જેણે ત્રિશૂળના એક જ ઘાથી મહિષાસુરને યમ સદન પહોંચાડયો હતો. ચામુંડા બની ચંડ-મુંડ જેવા મહાબળવાન અસુરોને હણ્યા હતા. જે શક્તિએ શુંભ-નિશુંભને ધૂળ ચાટતા કર્યા હતા. વિશ્વના સૌ પ્રથમ અસુરો મધુ-કૈટભને મારનારી મહામાયા યોગમાયા-આધશક્તિ ભગવતી પાસે જઈ તારી શક્તિ બતાવ અને તારા પૂર્વજોનું વેર લે, ત્યારે તું ખરો શક્તિશાળી ગણાય." મુનિ સત્યવ્રતનું આ વચન સાંભળી દંઢાસુરને મા યોગમાયા શ્રી ભવાનીને જોવાનો અભરખો જાગ્યો. તેની સાથે લડવાના કોડ જાગ્યા. તેણે પાંચ નદીઓ જ્યાં વહે છે, તેવા પંજાબ પ્રદેશમાં જઈ ભગવાન શંકરનું ઘોર તપ આદર્યું. પોતાની તમામ શક્તિ શિવજીની ભક્તિમાં ફેરવી નાખી. ભગવાન આશુતોષ અસુરરાયની ભક્તિ જોઈ પ્રસન્ન થયા, અને દંઢાસુરને કહ્યું: "હું તારી ભ

FIGURE 14. *Śrī Bahucarā Ārādhanā,* in the Gujarati language and script. Font "Noto Serif Gujarati" © The Noto Project Authors.

THE ORIGIN STORY OF BAHUCARĀ

In the Chunval region of Gujarat, the Supreme Feminine Power manifests as the esteemed goddess Bahucarā. Mā's incarnation in the form of a girl took place under a Varakhaḍī tree, as described in the following true account.[1]

In a sacred grove, a demon by the name of Daṇḍhāsur was harassing numerous Brahmins, *ṛṣis*, and other people. Because of this demon Daṇḍhāsur, the Chunval area is also referred to as "the place where Daṇḍha came" (Daṇḍhāvya). Daṇḍhāsur had obtained a blessing whereby anyone who fought with him gave half of their power to him. In battle, the power of Daṇḍhāsur became 1.5 times as strong.[2] For that reason, he was also referred to as "Demon-and-a-half." Daṇḍhāsur was exceedingly violent and cruel. Moreover, his massive army of demons was just as mighty. One by one, he overpowered all the kings of earth, in this way deposing them and making the earth all his own.

With the arrival of the demon army, terror rained down abundantly on earth. The demons even shut down the Vedic fire sacrifices of the *ṛṣi* sages. At this time, making his home in Siddhapatan of the Sarasvati River area (present-day Siddhapur) was the sage named Satyavrat, who, unable to bear this suffering, came into the presence of Daṇḍhāsur and said: "You wanted to show your power by committing atrocities against powerless people and by extinguishing the fire sacrifices of the *ṛṣi* sages; but that was actually a sign of your cowardly nature. Your ancestor Dhūmralocana showed off his power in much the same way and was crushed in battle by Durgā. Similarly, your blood relatives, the mighty *asura* demons, were created one by one from drops of Raktāsura's blood, and then Kālikā drank this blood of Raktāsura.[3] Bhrāmarī Devī became a female wasp to beat the *asura* Aruṇ.[4] The demon king Mahiṣāsura, taking the form of a buffalo, ran away to be freed from her rage, and from only one blow from her trident, the revered Mother sent him to the abode of Yama, lord of the dead. The goddess Cāmuṇḍā slaughtered vastly powerful demons like Caṇḍa and Muṇḍa. That Śakti made Śumbha and Niśumbha bite the dust. Only when you display your powers before the supreme Goddess Ādyaśakti Mahāmāyā Yogamāyā—who is the destroyer of the greatest among all demons, such as Madhu and Kaitabh—will you be counted among the truly powerful."

Hearing this speech of the sage Satyavrat, the aspiration to behold Mā Yogamāyā Śrī Bhavānī was awakened in Daṇḍhāsur. An intense desire to quarrel awoke as well. Now he moved into the land of Punjab where the five rivers flow, for it was here that Lord Śiva began his austere penances. The entirety of Daṇḍhāsur's personal power stirred with devotion to Śiva. Lord Śiva, who instantly satisfies devotees, saw the devotion of the demon king and became pleased. He said to Daṇḍhāsur, "I am delighted with your devotion. Therefore, choose a boon in return."

Daṇḍhāsur said, "Lord! Your compassion is very apparent to me. But it was not quite sufficient for many of my kind, and the supreme Goddess Ādyaśakti, the destroyer of my ancestor Dhūmralocana, has awoken in me an intense desire to battle. That way, the prowess of my power can be demonstrated to Śakti, slayer of other demons like Madhu-Kaitabh, Aruṇ, Raktabīj, Śumbha and Niśumbha, and Mahiṣāsura."

Śiva came to understand that Daṇḍhāsur was demanding to die at the hands of the Goddess. Saying "So be it!," Śiva disappeared.

Daṇḍhāsur, with his power henceforth multiplied, spread terror in the three worlds. After he conquered earth, he invaded the subterranean world. Vāsuki, serpent king of the subterranean world, lost courage in battle against Daṇḍhāsur. The demons became snake charmers and enslaved this serpent world. A number of the serpents slipped away and roamed the earth. Even though he had conquered the earthly world and underworld, Daṇḍhāsur was still not content. He embarked upon an invasion of the heavenly world. Stirring up boundless aggression and rage from drinking liquor, the demons attacked heaven. The gods understood that in battle their defeat was certain, and for that reason they retreated. With their families in tow, the gods began to run. Indra's army scrambled away in confusion. Seeing this, Indra also fled. In an instant, heaven was emptied of gods. The denizens of heaven—horse-headed *kinnar* musicians, *yakṣa* nature spirits, *gandharva* musicians, *apsarā* performers, and even individual souls (*jīva*)—ran to escape. The gods gathered near Viṣṇu in the milk ocean and called on the Supreme Feminine Power.

Hearing refrains of the gods' persecution at the hands of Daṇḍhāsur, the Goddess spoke: "With the flock of gods dislodged, I will inhabit the place of my sacred throne (*śaktipīṭha*). This site will become famous from the name of the mother goddess Bahucarā."[5] The non-dual Supreme Mother issued forth from the syllable AUṂ. She came to be known as the tripartite goddess because her form extended from the three syllables "A," "U," and "MA." The goddess, who wanders widely (*bahu vicarī*) even as she resides in the three worlds of the heavens, the earth, and the nether regions, came to be known as Bahucarā, or "the beautiful young woman of the three cities" Tripurā Bālāsundarī, and so forth. Just as the *Bhāgavata Purāṇa* says, "She has many names in many houses, therefore she became known as Bahunāmā."[6]

Fearing the demons, Indra and the other gods of heaven went running. As a result of that, Daṇḍhāsur became excessively powerful. "Now, I will also have a vision of this Supreme Feminine Power," Daṇḍhāsur said, and with this kind of pride, he moved into the abandoned streets of heaven. On the twelfth day of the lunar fortnight, the girl-aspect of Mother Bahucarī, a tiny, handsome, and charming girl-form, became self-manifest under a Varakhaḍī tree. The entirety of heaven performed a poem of praise to Mā. With Śiva having fulfilled the boon given to Daṇḍhāsur, the Great Goddess of Illusion took the form of her avatar, the beautiful young girl Bālātripurāsundarī. The *ṛṣi* sages of the *Mahābhārata* epic were pleased by this appearance of Mā and started singing her praises. Thus, the first manifestation of Mā began.

Daṇḍhāsur searched around and around and eventually came into the vicinity of the Varakhaḍī tree, which he approached. Under the tree he saw a girl seated alone. At that point, a number of contrasting feelings including compassion came over that girl. Seeing the girl, compassion came to Daṇḍhāsur. Approaching the girl, he inquired: "Daughter! Why are you sitting here alone?"

The girl, in her own playful, childish way of speaking, said, "From your actions, the gods went running away, so I am here alone. My name is Bālātripurāsundarī."

What will this girl do here alone? Here now, I'm going to take her with me to the earth. Having reflected to this effect, Daṇḍhāsur submitted the following for the girl's approval: "You are not any of my progeny and so you are an orphan here. For that reason you are my daughter, as per the custom of earth people."

Hearing this speech from Daṇḍhāsur, Tripurāsundarī came over to the earth for his sake to stay in the forest of Boru in the Chunval region, in the sacred grove. Because of the tyranny of Daṇḍhāsur over the earth, *ṛṣis* stopped performing Vedic sacrifices such as *yajña, homa,* and *havan*; thus, the god Varuṇa became displeased and stopped rain from falling to the earth. Rivers, streams, lakes, small ponds, and water wells all dried up. Even Daṇḍhāsur became perplexed and asked the demons, "What are we to do now without water and cooked food?"

The demons gave the following counsel: "There is no need for alarm. Whatever you find, whether a cow, a buffalo, a bullock, a goat, a deer, chickens or ducks, cut them to pieces, and start drinking their blood." The demons gave this advice following the level of their intelligence. But the Śiva devotee Daṇḍhāsur remained disheartened.

The vehicle of Śiva is the bull Nandi. What kind of misfortune, then, comes from this task of slaughtering a cow? In the Perfect Age (Satya Yuga), even demons did not slaughter cattle. In due time, Daṇḍhāsur became very thirsty. Nowhere in any direction was there a body of water. He began to struggle hopelessly toward the goal of finding water. His throat was parched. Presently, it seemed like he would die of thirst; nonetheless, Daṇḍhāsur did not slaughter a cow. From their blood, Daṇḍhāsur could not slake his own thirst. Seeing this, Bālātripurāsundarī became very pleased with Daṇḍhāsur, and thus she thrust her trident into the ground. A torrent of water streamed up from the soil. Mā was bringing water from the underworld to the earth-realm. This water is today called the "Mansarovar." Drinking the water, Daṇḍhāsur became satiated.

This girl who had brought herself from heaven to earth was beginning to enter adolescence. Seeing the beautiful and varied forms of the girl, warped thoughts came into the demon's mind. Daṇḍhāsur wondered: *What purpose is there in viewing the daughter of my enemy as my daughter? I reckon that she is like wealth that I gained by conquering heaven. In this way, I staked my claim on her. In two to four years, this girl will be eligible to wed. Her youthful form will awaken, blossoming in the way that a lotus blooms atop a pond. So, why shouldn't I just make her my wife and enjoy her?* Sensing the intentions of Daṇḍhāsur, Bālātripurāsundarī tried her best to reason with that king among demons, but the lust-blinded Daṇḍhāsur did not falter and said with pride, "Supreme Goddess, I recognized you immediately when I saw you sitting alone in heaven. So too on a second occasion when the trident struck the ground, bringing water from the underworld up to the earth realm. Consider, then, that I am able to enjoy beautiful women of the earth-realm, serpent women of the underworld, and the divine performers (*apsarā*) of the heaven realm. You should also know why I came up with such a thought. For a long time, you were like a daughter to me. So, to avoid the awakening of any feelings of parental love toward you on the battlefield, and also to avoid the possibility of you showing compassion toward me by thinking of me as your foster-father, I came up with these crooked thoughts. Great Goddess of Illusion, slayer of Dhūmralocana, Śumbha and Niśumbha, Aruṇ, Raktāsura, Mahiṣāsura, and Madhu and Kaitabh! Today you shall behold my devilish power!"

Hearing this sort of demonic speech, the limbs of the goddess began to shiver with anger. From this shivering, the three worlds also trembled. Mā's eyes reddened. On account of this, the moon and sun began to take on a red luster. From this anger, the face of Mā seemed to become like red copper. The flames of the fire god Agni manifested on earth. The oceans were pushed to their limits. The mountains began to rock. The earth came free from the hands of the eight guardians of the directions. The wind god, Pavandeva, erring in his direction, ran from the atrocious sound accompanying that. The sky was covered over by a cloud of dust and terrible tornadoes. The *ṛṣis*, Brahmins, and virtuous persons performed praise poems to the blessed Mother. The Goddess Bālātripurāsundarī appeared in her fierce form.[7]

The blessed Mother let her hair loose. From her hair, many powerful goddesses, much like the Blessed Bahucarā, appeared and set out to totally annihilate the demon armies.

Daṇḍhāsur and his demon army approached the full power of Mā and waged war spiritedly. Daṇḍhāsur's saber clashed with Mā's broadsword. The ten directions began to tremble.[8] The divine serpent Śeṣa spread its hood and began hissing. Because of this, the earth became unsteady. Water of the ocean spread streamlike on the ground and revealed the vacant ocean bed. From the scintillation of Mā's sword that shivered from having been run into, the Himalayas started to melt. The resulting glacial meltwater spread over the earth. The fearsome *yoginī*s of the battlefield, catching hold of the demons, mercilessly started chopping them to bits and began to fill skull-cups with their blood. Mā's rooster, from the spike of his own claws and, in the very same way, with his beak, killed a thousand demons. A commotion moved through the demon army. Managing to escape from the battlefield, the demons began to run away.

Mā struck Daṇḍhāsur with a left-legged kick, and he began to vomit blood and also to crow; because he was issuing that kind of sound, the demon king started to weep. The wickedness of the demons began to be remedied. Seeing Daṇḍhāsur crowing, all the other demons followed suit. The spot where that took place is called Kukvāī. Challenging the Supreme Feminine Power, Daṇḍhāsur was struck down. His ego was decimated. His subtle life force ran away to escape. Bahucarā pursued Daṇḍhāsur. For the purpose of getting away, Daṇḍhāsur took the form of a white rooster. With the speed of the wind in her favor, Bahucarā grasped Daṇḍhāsur. The rooster mount of Mā made Daṇḍhāsur, the one-time fanatical zealot who had turned into a white rooster, bleed by using his beak, nails, and claws. Daṇḍhāsur fell, and the goddess lifted her trident, which had fallen on the ground. Daṇḍhāsur performed a praise poem to the goddess and requested of her, "O Mother! Make all of us demons into your roosters and take us to your lotus-feet."

Because of this trident, the wounds of every one among the evil—past, present, and future, and in heaven, the underworld, and the realm of the dead—were spilling out torrents of blood. Daṇḍhāsur died. The gods showered flowers over Bahucarājī and performed reverent praises to her. The *ṛṣi* and the *muni* sages directed a prayer to Mā to pacify her fearful form. The goddess once more assumed her pleasant form—that is to say, her young girl incarnation. To all involved, she gave a benediction and followed with a speech. "This Chunval country is counted as a perfect seat for the goddess due to the falling of the arm of the goddess Umā.[9] This place here will become my goddess throne. Taking the form of Bahucarā, I will make the suffering of my devotees go away."

The place where Ma extracted the water from the underworld with her bewitching trident is called Mansarovar. Located here is a watch-gate of a nature spirit by the name of Jṛmbhak.[10] If a man who is naturally born without manliness bathes here with faith, then he attains manliness, and all his wishes are fulfilled.

After the killing of Daṇḍhāsur was done, the goddess Ambā unburdened herself of the exhaustion of war in the forest of Bhoru of Shankalpur. At present, this resting place is identified as an outskirt of the town of Shankalpur. Containing her own fierce form, and taking on her opposite pleasant girl form, the Supreme Feminine Power came under the Varakhaḍī tree and disappeared. The *ṛṣi* sages performed a hymn of praise to the goddess. Thus, the first manifestation of goddess Bahucarājī was completed.

After this, the *ṛṣi* and *muni* sages of the Sarasvati-Sabarmati area—Kandarm Ṛṣi, Bhagavān Kapiladeva, and the highest *ṛṣi-muni* Satyavrat—came to the sacred grove and began performing hymns of praise: "Mā, you've made us liberated from the demons' tyranny over the three worlds, bringing your benevolence over these realms. We will keep making praise poems and prayers in future births." Saying this, the *ṛṣi-munis* and *siddhas* performed the eight-point bow (fully stretched out on the ground) to the revered Mother. Seeing this, Mā appeared at once, and having purified everyone by granting a vision to them all, said: "O *munis*, for the purposes of establishing righteousness, I took possession of my Bālātripurā avatar on earth, killed the demon Daṇḍhāsur, and liberated the three worlds from the tyranny of the demons. Please perform a ritual of worship marking my deed of founding this place. Making my abode in this place for all time, I will fulfill the wishes of all my devotees." Having said this, Mā disappeared. This was the second manifestation of Bahucarā. To honor Mā's request to solidify the true knowledge of her founding, all the *munis* came together on the Sabarmati-Sarasvati banks and performed a ritual fire sacrifice to the Goddess as well as a ritual at the hands of Bhagavān Kapiladeva, with the sweet jaggery of Bahucarājī to establish the perfect diagram (*siddhayantra*) for the worship of Bālātripurāsundarī. At present, this crystal diagram is housed in a chamber that is covered with gold. It is being worshiped even today. The Mother's devotees keep religious vows out of faith, and in that way doing ritual offerings to Mātājī sets in motion the completion of all their desires; many also leave roosters to play in the temple. Children who are born of a pledge made to the mother are named "Becar," and their hair-cutting ceremony is performed here.

The very place upon which the ritual fire sacrifice was done—a pit, following the custom of the scriptures—having been filled with water from the underworld, is the "Mansarovar" of today. From bathing here, one can destroy inclinations against the laws of nature, and in that way they are put at ease. Nearby is a lake of life-giving water. It is here that Mātājī brought forth onto the earth the spring of water from the underworld, after slaying the sly demon Daṇḍhāsur with her trident. Bathing in this water manifests manliness in a man devoid thereof. From taking a bath here, many a male lacking manliness is made into a complete man. Here is located the watch-gate of nature spirit Jṛmbhak. In this manner, renowned miracles in the *Mahābhārata* took place: Śikhaṇḍī, born as a daughter of Drupad, became male and fought against his paternal grandfather Bhīṣma in battle; the powerful warrior Arjuna performed a loss of masculinity because of a curse from a divine damsel of the heavenly world; the celestial musician Akṣasena became cursed in heaven; the young Brahmin Yaśodhar came to protect the hero Vikram; and Rājkumar was born from the famous Rājkumar Solanki lineage—these are all examples that have risen in the popular imagination. A much more recent example comes from Dhandhuka Taluk's Aniyali village, where a young woman was transformed into a man. Mā frequently grants a vision to her devotees, freeing them from suffering.

THE GODDESS IN CONTEXT: HEART OF DIVERSE COMMUNITIES

In contemporary Gujarat, Bahucarā Mātā is, in a word, ubiquitous. Her distinctive image—a young woman seated upon a disproportionately large rooster—is pervasive throughout the state, appearing on billboards, businesses, and motor vehicles, among other public spaces. Framed posters, DVDs, and devotional songs dedicated to the goddess are on sale in virtually any town, and music videos featuring Bahucarā-themed devotional songs and narratives are easily accessible on social media sites like YouTube and WhatsApp. This sort of prevalence and versatility is conveyed by Bahucarā's name itself, which can be parsed as *bahu* (many, much) and *cara* (moving, walking, wandering), rendering the goddess "she who roams widely."[11] At the same time, however, the title "Mātā" (an honorific form of "mother") links Bahucarā to a network of goddesses who traditionally flourished in highly localized village settings, having only recently gained a larger following. These goddesses were generally worshiped by lower castes, Dalits, and other non-elite groups, often by way of rituals not normally approved of by orthodox high-caste Hindus, including animal sacrifice, liquor offerings, and possession-like trance states. While Bahucarā has gained a mainstream, cross-caste following today, especially at her famed temple in the Chunval district of northeast Gujarat, known as Becharaji (a variant spelling of the goddess's name), her principal supporters have throughout history typically come from non-Brahmin castes such as the princely Rajputs, pastoral Charans, and tribal Kolis, as well as decidedly non-elite groups such as the transgender Hijras/Pāvaiyās and the Muslim Kamalias. The recent intensification of these efforts toward "Brahminizing," or mainstreaming, Bahucarā have heralded her gender-switching capabilities only insofar as they uphold procreative, hetero-normative sexuality, an attitude that has done little to curb the marginalization of the Hijras at Becharaji and beyond.

Seed: Origins of Bahucarā Mātā

Bahucarā Mātā has multiple origin narratives that reflect the various groups that have shaped her history. In one of the most prominent accounts in the folklore, Bahucarā is presented as a girl from the pastoral, bardic Charan caste who undertook a journey between two villages along with her sisters and other members of her community.[12] On their way, the party was intercepted by brigands from the Koli tribe. With her chastity at risk, Bahucarā promptly grabbed a sword from a boy in her group and cut off her own breasts, perishing on the spot.[13] Her sisters also killed themselves, and as a result all three young women became goddesses. The spot where they died was marked by memorial stone slabs, and later these developed into small temples that are said to have expanded into the present-day Becharaji site. In another version of this tale, Bahucarā fends off analogous male attackers by threatening to compromise their masculinity and follows through on the threat.[14]

The notion of gender transformation recurs frequently in Bahucarā's origin stories. One such narrative involves the Solanki Rajput ruler Vajeshih from Chanasma, an area in close proximity to the Becharaji temple. Vajeshih and his wife were for a long period of time unable to have children and remained without the all-important son who would be his successor. When they did manage to have a child, it was a girl.[15] In their desperation for a baby boy, the parents gave their daughter the masculine name Tejpāl and thereafter raised the child as a male. Once he was grown, it was arranged for the supposed son to be married to the daughter of the king of nearby Patan. A short while after the wedding, Tejpāl's virility came into question, and he fled Patan on the back of a mare. In all the commotion, he paid little if any heed to a female dog that followed close behind him as he escaped. After some time on the run, Tejpāl stopped for some much-needed rest at a pond under a Varakhaḍī tree, which can grow in all terrains and bears leaves year-round over a life span of several centuries.[16] The dog, also seeking relief, took a dip in the pond and miraculously emerged from the water as a male.[17] Witnessing this, Tejpāl decided to experiment, coaxing his mare to bathe in the water, and sure enough, it came out as a stallion. Tejpāl wasted little time diving into the pond himself and in similar fashion transformed into a male. Tejpāl rode back happily to Patan, eager to renew his acquaintance with his bride. As an expression of his thankfulness, he made the pond into a sacred site known as the Mansarovar, or "lake of desire," which is also mentioned in the story translated in this chapter. Mansarovar is a wish-fulfilling pond paralleling a body of water of the very same name found in the *Mahābhārata* and other Sanskrit texts.[18]

These themes of gender switching and emasculation in Bahucarā's folklore ultimately connect back to her association with the Hijras (or *Hījaḍās*), a broad term used mostly in northwest India to refer to transgender persons. Yet another Bahucarā origin narrative once again tells of a prince whose parents wanted him to wed, regardless of his lack of interest in the prospect of married life.[19] Despite his indifference, his parents persisted, soon enough selecting Bahucarā to be his bride. The marriage took place but was never consummated. On the wedding night, the prince rode away into the forest, leaving Bahucarā lying on their marital bed. Over the course of months, this routine continued night after night, and Bahucarā grew more and more agitated. Seeking answers, she followed her husband as he went off on one of his evening sojourns. She eventually found him in a forest clearing, carrying on "like the Hijras."[20] Bewildered by the sight, Bahucarā made her way home. When her husband arrived back home, she confronted him with the details of what she had observed. He then professed his urge to eschew the life of marriage and children, claiming he was "neither man nor woman."[21] Bahucarā flew into a rage and accused her husband of ruining her life by hiding the truth about his gender identity. She then cut off his genitals as punishment, referring to this process of emasculation as "liberation" (*nirvāṇa*). From that point on, the prince lived as a woman.[22]

The historical origins of Bahucarā's primary site at Becharaji can be traced back to around the twelfth century CE, when the original shrine was built by a sovereign named Sankhal Raj.[23] By the thirteenth century, the Bahucarā temple was gaining in prominence, and it was during the Sultanate period (1407–1584 CE) that this site came to be recognized as a sacred goddess site (*śaktipīṭha*).[24] *Śakti pīṭhas*, literally "seats of Śakti," refer to a loosely connected network of scores of sites located throughout India and other parts of the subcontinent that are dedicated to goddesses. These heavily visited sites command respect due to their foundations in the *Devī Bhāgavata Purāṇa* and other Śākta Sanskrit works. In these texts, the *śakti pīṭhas* are conceived as the locations where parts of the primordial goddess Satī fell after her corpse was dissected by Viṣṇu's discus; Becharaji, for instance, is identified as the place where her arm landed. The Becharaji shrine owes much of its grandeur to major expansions and fortifications that were made in the eighteenth century under the supervision of the Gaekwars, a martial clan that enjoyed power under the Maratha Empire (1674–1818 CE).[25] In the mid-eighteenth century, Damajirao Gaekwar (1732–1768 CE) granted three villages for the temple's maintenance.[26] In 1779 Manaji Rav Gaekwar built the largest of the temples on the grounds, which remains a major place of worship.[27]

The main object of worship at Becharaji is a *yantra*, or sacred geometrical diagram, embodying Bālātripurā. This epithet refers to the girl (or *bālā*) form of Tripurāsundarī, paramount goddess of the pan-Indian Tantric Śrīvidyā tradition.[28] The Bālātripurā *yantra* was likely placed in Becharaji's intermediate temple in the eighteenth century around the time of its construction by a Maratha named Fadnavis, and it remains there to the present day.[29] This affirms Bahucarā's long-standing Tantric aspect, *yantras* having been present at Becharaji from as early as the Mughal period (sixteenth century CE).[30]

Flower: Becharaji's Boom

By the 1880s, the Bahucarā temple at Becharaji had amassed substantial wealth, readily apparent from the wells, tanks, public gardens, and pilgrim lodgings (*dharmaśālā*) that had been built on its grounds, not to mention its reputation for generous charitable contributions.[31] Evidently Becharaji was supported by a steady stream of pilgrims by this point in the nineteenth century. Bahucarā was most often sought out for remedying speech impediments and abnormalities of the spine, as well as to ensure the birth of children, particularly sons.[32] In addition to providing cures for health issues, Bahucarā could also fulfill practically any desire. The pond on the temple grounds known as Mansarovar was famous for granting devotees' requests. For that reason, visitors would remain seated by the wish-fulfilling waters of the Mansarovar, fasting until they heard the Mātā's voice promising to grant them their desires.[33]

By this point in its history, Bahucarā's Becharaji temple had become predominantly associated with several non-Brahmin groups, each of which undertook ritual duties and shared in a portion of the funds generated by the site.[34] The most politically powerful among these groups were the Solanki Rajputs, a landholding martial clan who trace their roots back to the Chaulukya princely state (940–1244 CE). These Rajputs acknowledged Bahucarā as their *kuldevī*, or family goddess, and afforded her the highest praise in early Gujarati-language print materials, where she is described as no less than the "proprietress" of the Solankis and is all the while homologized with Tripurāsundarī.[35] Another group historically prominent at Becharaji were the Kamalias. Kamalias may originally have been sweepers, forming a subgroup of the Dalit community known as Valmikis.[36] After the sultanate ruler Alauddin Khalji captured the temple around the turn of the fourteenth century, the Kamalias reportedly were forcibly converted to Islam.[37] According to one folk narrative, a soldier from Alauddin's army stole a rooster that had been gifted to Bahucarā and cooked it, serving the meat to his platoon. After the soldiers had consumed the chicken, the rooster began to scream the name of the goddess from within the soldiers' stomachs. They promptly begged the goddess for forgiveness, and in the spirit of contrition, a man named Kamal promised to stay at this site with his Muslim wife and serve the goddess thereafter.[38] The present-day Kamalias are descended from him, and they function as musicians and servants to the goddess at Becharaji.[39] Kamalias and Solankis mutually ran the Becharaji site and also shared temple offerings. This arrangement occasionally led to violent conflict, as both groups vied to claim the entirety of the proceeds for themselves.[40]

The third major stakeholding group at Becharaji were the Pāvaiyās, a Gujarati term roughly equivalent to the designation "Hijra." The Pāvaiyā community at Becharaji and in Gujarat at large, like other Hijra groups, consists mainly of nonheteronormative or nonprocreative men who wear women's clothing and ornamentation. Generally, they behave in an effeminate manner, often exaggeratedly so. New initiates to the group are usually men suffering from what is frequently glossed as "impotence," referring to any number of physical or psychological factors that keep them from pursuing conjugal relationships with women, including but not limited to homosexuality, erectile dysfunction, and self-identification as a woman. These new initiates are taken on as "daughters" of older members.[41] Many undergo a ritual castration of both penis and testicles in order to consolidate their identity in the group. In the past this initiation typically took place at the Becharaji site itself and was supervised by the chief Pāvaiyā priest of Bahucarā. Before the operation, the initiate was dressed in women's attire. After the operation, betel nut was spit onto the wound, which was then dressed with ashes.[42] Pāvaiyās at Becharaji have customarily collected alms and bestowed blessings upon young children. In bigger centers like Ahmedabad, Pāvaiyās often performed in plays and at private weddings and birth-related functions, as has been their role in other places outside of Gujarat, where they have been sought after to grant fertility, prosperity, and long life to married couples and their children.[43] Hijras in other parts of India also undergo similar initiation rituals with Bahucarā overseeing them. In fact, throughout north India, it is Bahucarā herself who summons forth would-be Hijras, materializing in the dreams of impotent men and ordering them to go through with the emasculation operation.[44] During the operation itself, which still occurs despite being illegal, the person undergoing the procedure looks at a picture of Bahucarā and constantly repeats the goddess's name.[45] After the initiation, Hijras are considered intermediaries of the Mātā, as the operation invests them with Bahucarā's power.[46] However, since the nineteenth century in both Gujarat and beyond, Hijras have also become associated in the public imagination with prostitution, which has become increasingly prevalent as demand for their traditional services declines.[47]

In spite of their diverse identities, the Solankis, Kamalias, and Pāvaiyās are all markedly non-Brahmin, and in the case of the latter two groups, non-elite. Consequently, non-Brahmin priests handled the rituals at Becharaji for a significant portion of the site's history, the temple staff operating without a Brahmin until 1859.[48] This non-Brahmin influence was reflected in the non-vegetarian rituals that were often conducted at the site. Animal sacrifices to Bahucarā were commonplace throughout much of the temple's history, taking place in the open air on a pyramidal altar.[49] Navratri and other festival days were apparently high time for sacrifices of goats or buffalo calves. At other non-festival junctures, such as when people came to fear that the lives of family or friends were in danger, liquor was included with the animal flesh, as these kinds of offerings have been (and still are) thought to satisfy the capricious whims of non-vegetarian Mātās.[50] The groups providing these blood and alcohol offerings to Bahucarā were most typically Rajputs, Kolis, and Bhils, though rumors circulated in the late nineteenth century that even elite groups like Brahmins and Vaiṣṇava Baniyas would put aside their stringent standards of purity to do the same sorts of rites, albeit in secret and under the cover of night.[51]

Given the prominence of non-Brahmin groups and practices, Gujarati elites periodically sought to "cleanse" the Becharaji temple grounds and the goddess herself by discouraging non-Brahminical practices. The seventeenth-century Jain poet Gunavijaya documented grievances aired to local governors, which supposedly led to a temporary decree that violence had to be stopped at the Bahucarā shrine, with protection even for the fish in the pond.[52] The famous Gujarati devotional poet Vallabha (ca. seventeenth century CE), a Brahmin by birth, is widely credited with making Bahucarā and Becharaji famous. In the process, he also effectively distanced her in some measure from her non-Brahmin faithful by tailoring her toward Vaiṣṇava devotional tastes that were gaining momentum in late-Mughal Gujarat, thereby allowing abstemious, vegetarian Viṣṇu-worshipers to visit the goddess and integrate her site into their pilgrimage networks.[53] More recently, a bookseller by the name of Bhudralal Gangaji accentuated Bahucarā's Sanskritic, Vaiṣṇava roots, publishing a text in 1919 that linked the goddess to the *Bhāgavata Purāṇa*, the *Devī Bhāgavatam*, and even the Veda.[54] Another author, Rammohanray Desai, also hearkened back to Bahucarā's Sanskritic past by emphasizing her equivalency to the Tantric Bālātripurāsundarī in order to underscore her purity.[55] In a similar spirit, the Pāvaiyās were also subject to regulation. For instance, the emasculation rite was outlawed by local royals in 1880, even in the face of intensive protests by the Pāvaiyā community, which was forced to carry out the initiation surreptitiously from that point on.[56]

Fruit: Toward Pan-Indian Popularity

Bahucarā can hardly be characterized as a minor goddess when we consider her prevalence in Gujarati public spaces and the ever-growing reputation of her *śakti pīṭha* at Becharaji. If anything, visual culture, television, and social media have made her more popular than ever. Apart from Bahucarā's traditional supporting castes, Becharaji attracts an increasing number of middle-class and upper-caste devotees from within and outside of Gujarat, including celebrities and politicians, perhaps none more distinguished than Indian prime minister Narendra Modi.[57] Expensive saris are in no short supply among women who travel from nearby cities with their families to undertake their children's first hair-cutting—a ritual customarily performed at the site—and to receive blessings from the Pāvaiyās, who still circulate on the temple grounds. At present, the temple buildings bear an unprecedented polish, having been reconstructed in sparkling white marble starting around 2009. This massive refurbishment was overseen by a government-installed temple trust, which is also responsible for funding Becharaji's cadre of Brahmin priests.[58] These Brahmins handle the *pūjās*, *yajñas*, and all other ritual components at the site, as non-Brahmin priests are no longer employed at Becharaji.[59] Predictably, animal sacrifices and liquor offerings have also disappeared, and in consonance with the Sanskritic, pan-Indian goddesses to whom she is held to be equivalent, Bahucarā is now identified as vegetarian. It is the non-Brahmin, non-elite, and village-styled Bahucarā, then, that seems to have become marginalized and largely forgotten.

Nonetheless, Bahucarā remains a patron deity for Gujarati Pāvaiyās, as well as for a variety of transgender communities throughout India. Virtually every Hijra household has a small shrine dedicated to the goddess, particularly in the north, and all Hijras seek to visit Becharaji at least once in their lives.[60] In Mumbai, Bahucarā still plays a crucial role in the initiation ceremony into the Hijra community.[61] In south India, the transgender Tirunaṅkais worship Bahucarā at a number of important functions.[62] Bahucarā has even spread outside of India's borders to Southeast Asia, as is evident at the temple in

Klang, Malaysia, where she represents the patron deity. In this context, she has taken on the flavor of locally popular south Indian village goddesses like Māriyammaṉ, adopting a distinctly regional iconography and color scheme, as well as a vernacular name, Powtirachi. Tirunaṅkais participate at the forefront of rituals at the Klang temple as well.[63]

Despite Bahucarā's expanding geographical reach and the changes in her audience and ritual repertoire, her Tantric connections with Bālātripurāsundarī remain. These Tantric correspondences certainly have not alienated patrons; in fact, they may actually attract them, as for many middle-class pilgrims contemporary Tantra is associated with fast gratification regarding solutions to this-worldly problems and wishes for material gain. It is Bahucarā's Tantric aspects that often figure prominently in the numerous devotional pamphlets for sale at the Becharaji marketplace and elsewhere, which elaborate on *yantras*, mantras, and other Tantric apparatuses of the goddess. All the while, these texts follow in the footsteps of Vallabha and other commentators of the past, expounding Bahucarā's Purāṇic and Vedic resonances in an effort to sturdily situate her in a pure, Sanskritic past.

SOURCE

The narrative translated in this chapter comes from the *Śrī Bahucarā Ārādhanā* (Adoration of Bahucarā), just one among the many economically printed, Gujarati-language pamphlets about gods and goddesses that are widely available at book stalls in Becharaji and beyond. For just 50 rupees (approximately a dollar) or less, these publications provide texts of prayers, praise poems (*stuti*), and devotional songs, as well as accounts of miracles a deity has performed. They may also provide instructions for carrying out particular domestic rituals and votive rites. Owing to their status as spiritually charged objects, the pamphlets themselves are commonly included among devotional items in household shrines as articles of worship. In addition to their ritual uses, these publications spur the imagination of devotees, providing stories, testimonials, and folk etymologies that root familiar gods and goddesses in contexts that are at once Sanskritic and vernacular, pan-Indian and localized, timeless and contemporary.

The *Śrī Bahucarā Ārādhanā* is no different, and the main narrative translated here, the "Bahucarmānī Utpatti Kathā" (The origin story of Bahucarā), strives to establish Bahucarā in all these contexts. In pitting her against a demon threatening the entirety of the cosmos, the narrative evokes tropes of the Purāṇic, Sanskritic past, when goddesses like Durgā and Kālī vanquished similar threats to the cosmos. To the same effect, the story regularly refers to Bahucarā as the Supreme Feminine Power (Ādyaparāśakti) or variations thereof, lofty epithets with which Durgā and Kālī are synonymous, calling to mind the universal, monotheistic overlay often propounded in mainstream, Brahminical Hinduism. As could be expected of a Sanskritic goddess, Bahucarā as she is depicted in this narrative decries the killing of animals and endorses a Brahminical ritual repertoire. Even more remarkably, the demon himself claims an aversion to consuming animal products, further underscoring the Brahminic sensibilities (in this case vegetarianism) that inform this telling. The tale also emphasizes Bahucarā's long-standing homology with the Tantric goddess Tripurāsundarī of the Śrīvidyā tradition. At the same time, the story incorporates familiar landmarks of Bahucarā's *śakti pīṭha*, such as the Varakhaḍī tree and the Mansarovar. The wish-fulfilling stream is, as could be expected, referenced vis-à-vis gender, but in this case, curiously enough, it is the water's ability to *restore* full masculinity that is highlighted. Rather than validating or even acknowledging the transgender identity of the Pāvaiyās or Hijras, the story keeps Becharaji's purview within mainstream Indian procreative or heteronormative mores of sexuality. Beyond all the localized associations, in the story translated here Bahucarā seems by no means limited to the site of her *pīṭha* or her region; rather, she is truly a divinity who can move many places—heaven, earth, and the underworld, among others—and is in that way suggestive of a Great Goddess in the pan-Indian idiom.

FURTHER READING

Fischer, E., J. Jain, and H. Shah. 2013. *Temple Tents for Goddesses in Gujarat*. New Delhi: Niyogi.

Nanda, Serena. 1990. *Neither Man nor Woman: The Hijras of India*. Belmont, CA: Wadsworth.

Reddy, Gayatri. 2005. *With Respect to Sex: Negotiating Hijra Identity in South India*. Chicago: University of Chicago Press.

Sheikh, Samira. 2010. "The Lives of Bahuchara Mata." In *The Idea of Gujarat: History, Ethnography and Text*, edited by Edward Simpson and Aparna Kapadia, 84–99. Hyderabad: Orient Blackswan.

NOTES

1. The Varakhaḍī tree may correspond to the tree botanists identify as *Salvadora persica*; however, its identification remains doubtful.

2. The text suggests here that Daṇḍhāsur wielded his own strength plus half of his opponent's power, which seems to follow after Vālī in the *Rāmāyaṇa*. Like Vālī, the 50 percent Daṇḍhāsur gained from his opponent would presumably vary depending on the strength of his opponent. Daṇḍhāsur, as well as his boon, closely parallels the demon Bhaṇḍāsura of the *Brahmāṇḍa Purāṇa*. Bhaṇḍāsura has very similar powers and is defeated by Lalitā, a goddess tied to Bālātripurāsundarī.

3. Raktāsura is the same as the demon Raktabīja, who was slain by Kālī, as recounted in the classical Sanskrit *Devī Māhātmya*.

4. Bhrāmarī Devī is a goddess of black bees who appears in chapter 13 of book 10 of the *Devī Bhāgavatam*. The chapter recounts how a demon Aruṇa, after performing increasingly difficult penances, gains unprecedented *tapas* (spiritual heat). With this *tapas*, he secures a boon from Brahmā that he cannot be killed by any man or woman, biped or quadruped, or any combination thereof. With this power, Aruṇa conquers the entire universe, including the gods, in short order with help from his demon army. The Devī intervenes, making an appearance surrounded by bees. She then sends out a variety of black bees, hornets, wasps, and so forth in a swarm that covers the earth. These flying insects rip apart the demons, including Aruṇa, liberating the universe.

5. This line is difficult to interpret. I have omitted the name "Gāyatrī," which is put in parentheses in the original between "mother goddess" and "Bahucarā." Gāyatrī is a goddess who personifies the Gāyatrī mantra, a Vedic hymn with everyday usage in many strands of contemporary mainstream Hinduism. As the text goes on to explain, Bahucarā is, like Gāyatrī, also synonymous with a Sanskrit mantra. The parallel with Gāyatrī as goddess/mantra also further underscores Bahucarā's Brahminical, Sanskritic associations here.

6. The original text paraphrases, but does not cite by name, the *Bhāgavata Purāṇa*. The passage referred to is *Bhāgavata Purāṇa* 10.4.13, which is part of the story of the goddess Yogamāyā appearing to the demonic king Kaṃsa, who is about to kill Devakī and Vasudeva's girl child, who is really the goddess in disguise. The goddess then rises up and shows her true form as Yogamāyā as she chastises Kaṃsa.

7. The fact that the Goddess is here referred to as Bālātripurāsundarī is significant. *Bālā* means young girl, and the whole name means "Beauty of the Triple Cities in the Form of a Young Girl," so this epithet is calling attention to the fact that the goddess prefers a more mild, peaceful demeanor but has assumed a fierce form to annihilate the demons. See also chapter 3 on the theme of the Goddess's girlhood.

8. The ten directions are the four cardinal directions, the four intermediate directions, plus the zenith and nadir (up and down).

9. This refers to the myth of various body parts of the goddess Satī falling all over the Indian subcontinent and thereby sanctifying particular sites.

10. The word translated as "nature-spirit" is *yakṣa*. Jṛmbhak is used as a proper name here, but in classical Indian literature *jṛmbhaka* refers to a type of spirit that inhabits weapons. The name literally means "gaper" or "yawner."

11. Alternatively, but with a similar meaning, Fischer, Jain, and Shah rendered her name as "she who can move anywhere" (2013, 162).

12. See Forbes (1973, 426).

13. Fischer, Jain, and Shah (2013, 166).

14. Fischer, Jain, and Shah (2013, 166).

15. Fischer, Jain, and Shah (2013, 166).

16. Fischer, Jain, and Shah (2013, 166–68).

17. Fischer, Jain, and Shah (2013, 168).

18. The Mansarovar has been identified with a number of locations throughout the subcontinent, though the most prominent is in modern-day Tibet. This particular site has pan-Indian significance and remains a popular pilgrimage spot for Hindus, Buddhists, and Jains.

19. See Nanda (1990, 25).

20. Nanda (1990, 25).

21. Nanda (1990, 25–26).

22. Nanda (1990, 26).

23. Sheikh (2010, 86).

24. Padmaja (1982, 38).

25. Sheikh (2010, 86).

26. Sheikh (2010, 85).

27. Campbell (1883, 609).

28. Śrīvidyā (literally "auspicious wisdom") is a Śākta religious system that spans the Indian subcontinent, the roots of which can be traced back to the late classical period. For more on Śrīvidyā, see Brooks (1992). The spelling "Tripurāsundarī" follows the Gujarati convention; in Sanskrit, it is more properly spelled "Tripurasundarī."

29. Sheikh (2010, 87).

30. Padmaja (1986, 243).

31. Sheikh (2010, 86).

32. Sheikh (2010, 85).

33. Forbes (1973, 428).

34. Sheikh (2010, 87–88).

35. These sentiments can be found, for instance, in the *Solanki-no Garba*, a tiny handwritten Gujarati-language pamphlet of devotional poems from 1870 that centers on Bahucarā Mātā from the outset.

36. Fischer, Jain, and Shah (2013, 169).

37. Padmaja (1986, 246).

38. Fischer, Jain, and Shah (2013, 169).

39. Sheikh (2010, 93).

40. Sheikh (2010, 93).

41. Campbell (1890, 21).

42. Campbell (1890, 21).
43. Nanda (1990, 2).
44. Nanda (1990, 25).
45. Nanda (1990, 27).
46. See Shah (1961, 1327). See also Nanda (1990, 67).
47. Forbes (1973, 428) and Nanda (1990, 53).
48. Sheikh (2010, 88).
49. Forbes (1973, 427).
50. Forbes (1973, 427–28).
51. Forbes (1973, 427–28).
52. Sheikh (2010, 91–92).
53. Sheikh (2010, 95).
54. Sheikh (2010, 91).
55. Sheikh (2010, 90).
56. Campbell (1901, 507).
57. Sheikh (2010, 87).
58. Fischer, Jain, and Shah (2013, 169).
59. Padmaja (1986, 245).
60. Nanda (1990, 24).
61. See Roy (2017, 389–418).
62. Craddock (2012).
63. I am indebted to Praveen Vijayakumar of the University of Pennsylvania for drawing my attention to the Malaysian Bahucarā tradition in an email communication on March 5, 2018.

FIGURE 15. Rāṣṭrasenā, by Laura Santi

CHAPTER 8

Rāṣṭrasenā

Hawk Goddess of the Mewar Mountains

ADAM NEWMAN

The following tale concerns a goddess from the mountains of the Mewar region of southern Rajasthan, not far from the so-called City of Lakes, Udaipur. The goddess is variously named Rāṣṭrasenā, "Army of the Kingdom," or Rāṣṭraśyenā, "Hawk of the Kingdom," and she is visualized either in the form of a hawk or as a four-armed woman holding weapons to protect the kingdom from invasions. Her story is told in two chapters of a fifteenth-century Sanskrit work titled *The Glorification of Ekaliṅga* (*Ekaliṅga Māhātmya*). It takes its name from the shrine of Śiva, here called Ekaliṅga, located near Rāṣṭrasenā's high hilltop shrine.

Like so many others in its genre, this locally produced text claims to be part of a famous Purāṇa; in this case, the ancient *Vāyu Purāṇa*. Therefore, the passages here are framed as a conversation between the god of the wind Vāyu and Nārada, a messenger of the gods. Nested within this broader conversation are two other narrative frames: sub-conversations between a Purāṇic bard ("the bard") and Śaunaka, a famous sage on the one hand, and a king named Suṣumāṇa and his royal priest Vedagarbha on the other.

The first chapter selected for translation is a general account of the goddess's origin as an emanation of the goddess Vindhyavāsā (She Who Dwells in the Vindhya Mountains; a common epithet for Durgā). It describes Rāṣṭrasenā's blessings and the benefits that she bestows on the inhabitants of her lands. The second chapter is rather different, and more technical; it is an account of how a specialist should worship her. While the source as a whole is not a Tantra, this chapter shows heavy influence from Tantric rituals: the type of mantra used to worship the goddess and the coded way of revealing it, the visualization of the syllables of the mantra in the body of the specialist (*nyāsa*), and the prescription to worship her in a typical Tantric-style maṇḍala.

As you read, consider the significance of the narrative setting up an equivalence between local sacred geography and sacred sites farther afield. Think of ways your own culture may do the same. Consider, too, how religious texts like this one can show the influence of political interests. Several other fascinating dimensions to this goddess are discussed in the essay that follows.

॥ एकलिङ्गमाहात्म्यम् ११ ॥

अथैकादशो ऽध्यायः ॥ नारद उवाच ॥ एकलिङ्गस्य माहात्म्यं त्वयोक्तं च श्रुतं मया । समीपे यानि लिङ्गानि यानि तीर्थानि शंस मे । राष्ट्रसेनेति या देवी तन्ममाचक्ष्व सर्वाङ्ग ॥ वायुरुवाच ॥ एकलिङ्गे गते तत्र कैलाशः पर्वतोत्तमः । स त्रिकूटो ऽभवच्छृङ्गी सर्ववृक्षसमन्वितः ॥ मानसं तत्सरो जातं जाह्नवी कुटिला ऽभवत् । अथैकलिङ्गस्याग्नेय्यां दिशि कुण्डं महत्तरम् ॥ भवान्या कामधेनूत्थं पञ्चगव्यं निवेशितम् । स्वकरेणैव कुण्डे ऽस्मिन् तत्करज इति कथ्यते ॥ लोकानां पावनार्थाय सर्वतीर्थमयं पुनः । तस्मिन् कुण्डस्थतोयेन उद्धृतेन समाहितः ॥ स्नात्वा तत्रैकलिङ्गस्य प्रीतये शुभमाचरेत् । सर्वान् कामानवाप्यान्ते शिवलोकमवाप्नुयात् ॥ दर्शने करकुण्डस्य यत्फलं समवाप्नुयात् । तत्फलं समवाप्नोति स्मरणादेव नित्यशः ॥ शिवपार्श्वेन्द्रसरसि यज्जलं दृश्यते सर्वकामदम् । अग्नीषोमस्वरूपं तज्जानीहि सर्वकामदम् ॥ तत्राभिषेकं यः कुर्यात्सर्वतीर्थफलं लभेत् । तस्मिन्सरसि यः स्नात्वा करोति पितृतर्पणम् ॥ श्राद्धं कृत्वा नमस्कृत्य विन्ध्यवासां ततो हरम् । सर्वान्कामानवाप्नोति रुद्रलोकं स गच्छति ॥ एकलिङ्गादुदीच्यां वै जातं तीर्थद्वयं परम् । केदारकुण्डे यः स्नात्वा स्नात्वा कुण्डे ऽमृताख्यके ॥ केदारेश्वरमभ्यर्च्य अमृतेशं तथा मुने । सर्वान्कामानवाप्यान्ते ह्यमरत्वमवाप्नुयात् ॥ अथ सा विन्ध्यवासा तु पूर्वस्यां दिशि नारद । पर्वताग्रे ह्यथारामे सर्वर्त्तुकुसुमोद्भवे ॥ प्राकारान्तर्गते हर्म्ये स्वर्णसिंहासने शुभे । स्थित्वा तत्र मतिं चक्रे राष्ट्ररक्षणहेतवे ॥ स्वदेहाद्राष्ट्रसेनां तां सृष्ट्वा स्थाप्याथ तत्र सा । तस्याः स्वरूपे दृष्ट्वा वै हृष्टा वाक्यमुवाच ह ॥ श्येनारूपं सम्यगास्थाय देवि राष्ट्रं त्राहि त्राह्यतो वज्रहस्ता । दुष्टान्दैत्यान्राक्षसान्वै पिशाचान्भूतान्प्रेतान्योगिनीजृम्भकेभ्यः ॥ दुष्टग्रहेभ्यो ऽन्यतमेभ्य एवं श्येने त्राणं मेदपाटस्य कार्यम् । ये ऽस्मिन्देशे प्रातियोत्स्यन्ति केचित्ते हन्तव्या मायया दुष्टरूपाः ॥ जयः कार्यः स्वदेशीये भूपाले च तथा जने । अस्य लोकस्य भूपस्य नित्यं पूजा भविष्यति ॥ अष्टम्यां च चतुर्दश्यां संक्रान्त्यादिषु पर्वसु । पूजयेत्तां राष्ट्रसेनां तद्रूपां च स्त्रियं तथा ॥ ब्राह्मणानपि सम्पूज्य देवी प्रीत्यै विशेषतः । तेन तुष्टा राष्ट्रसेना पूजकानां वरप्रदा ॥ तस्मात्सम्पूजयेद्भक्त्या राष्ट्रसेनां विधानतः । चैत्रमास्यसिते पक्षे भक्त्या नित्यं प्रपूजयेत् ॥ राष्ट्रसेनेति नाम्नीयं मेदपाटस्य रक्षणम् । करोति न च भङ्गो ऽस्य यवनेभ्यो ऽपरागदपि ॥ इति श्रीवायुपुराणे मेदपाटीये श्रीमदे-

FIGURE 16. *Ekaliṅga Māhātmya*, a Sanskrit work in the Devanagari script. Font "Free Serif" © gnu.org.

THE MANIFESTATION OF RĀṢṬRASENĀ

Nārada said to the wind god Vāyu: "You taught me the glory of Lord Ekaliṅga and I have learned it. Now please extol for me the virtues of the pilgrimage places and *liṅgas* in the vicinity, and, O omnipresent Vāyu, introduce me to the goddess named Rāṣṭrasenā."

Vāyu replied: "If one goes to Ekaliṅga, the mountain there is equivalent to Mt. Kailash; it became the jagged Trikūṭa Mountain, covered in thickets of all kinds of trees.[1] Just as the Mansarovar Lake becomes the Ganga River, so the great bathing tank to the southeast of Ekaliṅga becomes Mewar's winding Kutila River. Pārvatī deposited into that bathing tank with her own hands the five substances that come from the wish-granting cow.[2] For that reason, the bathing tank is called 'Karaja,' meaning 'born from her hands.'[3] And the goddess constructed that bathing tank, the embodiment of all pilgrimage places, in order to purify the people of this world. A person whose mind is devout should bathe with water taken from that tank and perform there the virtuous acts that please Ekaliṅga. In this life he will obtain all his desires, and in the end he will reach Śiva's world. Whatever good results a person might obtain upon seeing the Karaja pond will always be availed to him merely by remembering it. Dear sage! Know that the water that is seen in Indra Lake near Ekaliṅga is the true form of the gods Agni and Soma and bestows all desires.[4] Whoever does ablutions there will obtain the benefits of visiting every pilgrimage place in the world. Whosoever bathes in that lake and performs the rite of pleasing the ancestors, and then performs the ancestor rituals (*śrāddha*) and honors Vindhyavāsā and Śiva, that person obtains all of their desires and enters Śiva's heaven.[5] Present to the north of Ekaliṅga were two supreme pilgrimage places—Kedāra bathing tank and Amṛta bathing tank. O sage, whoever bathes in the Kedāra and Amṛta tanks and worships the lords Kedāreśvara in one and Amṛteśa in the other, obtains all desires, and at the end of life reaches immortality.[6]

"Then, O Nārada, Vindhyavāsā seated herself on a glorious golden lion throne, in a walled palace set on the summit a mountain to the East surrounded by a lovely garden where flowers bloom in all seasons. Then, she set her mind on protecting the empire. Vindhyavāsā then emitted the goddess Rāṣṭrasenā from her own body, after which she installed her there, on the mountain. Delighted at seeing herself in the form of Rāṣṭrasenā, Vindhyavāsinī said these words to her: "O goddess, take fully the form of a hawk and protect the kingdom! Destroy the evil demons—*daityas, rākṣasas, piśācas, bhūtas,* and *pretas*—with the thunderbolt (*vajra*) you hold.[7] While in the form of a hawk it is your duty to protect Medapāṭa (Mewar) from *yoginīs* and *jṛmbhakas*, evil Seizer demons, and others.[8] If some evil people come to this country desiring war, you should destroy them with your spells and powers."[9]

"If the local king and people in Medapāṭa are to be victorious, then the ruler of these people should worship Rāṣṭrasenā daily. On the eight and fourteenth days of the waxing and waning moons, when the sun passes from one zodiacal sign to another, and on other such transition days, one should worship Rāṣṭrasenā and also women who look like her.[10] One should properly worship all Brahmins in order to please the goddess completely. By doing so Rāṣṭrasenā, delighted, grants wishes to those who worship her. Therefore, one should worship Rāṣṭrasenā with complete devotion in the proper way. One should worship her daily with devotion during the bright half of the second lunar month in Spring. The goddess named Rāṣṭrasenā is the protector of Medapāṭa. Because of her, the empire will not be destroyed by foreigners or by any other invader."[11]

Thus ends the chapter called "The Manifestation of Rāṣṭraśyenā," the eleventh in the *Ekaliṅga Māhātmya* of Mewar, in the glorious *Vāyu Purāṇa*.

Rules for the Worship of Rāṣṭraśyenā

Nārada said to Vāyu: "Earlier you spoke about Rāṣṭraśyenā, the goddess who destroys her enemies. Please explain the rules for her worship, she who is the family deity of the venerable Bāṣpa.[12] Please describe how the sage Śivaśarman properly performed the worship of Rāṣṭraśyenā.[13] O Vāyu, please succinctly cut through all of my doubts."

Vāyu replied: "O Nārada, listen attentively to the auspicious words I am about to speak. From the mere act of hearing these words, a person is released immediately from their faults.

"Now, having bathed in the eight pilgrimage places beginning with the Kutila River and ending at Indra Lake, Śivaśarman came to Rāṣṭrasenā together with his sons and grandsons in order to worship her. First, they worshiped a local Bhairava, and then they worshiped the host of other attendant deities there, O eminent sage.

"The great sage Śivaśarman saw her seated upon a throne made of jewels, inlaid with beryl, crystals, and adorned with gold.[14] That pale-limbed goddess appears dressed in resplendent red and adorned in golden ornaments. She resembles the glory of the sun and the splendor of the moon. Her eyes are like glorious lotus leaves, her nose beautiful, her voice like a nightingale. She wears an opulent pearl and coral necklace, with large and rising breasts. She is heroic, holding a sword and shield, and equipped with bow and arrows. Her face is always pleased; she is like a living autumnal moon. The great goddess has four arms and is endowed with external signs of youth and other qualities. She is served by the *kiṃnaras* and the *gandharvas*, O eminent sage.[15] Śivaśarman himself honored her with devotion. One should offer incense, sandalwood paste, various types of fruit, eatables, and betel nut mixed with thickened milk, candied sugar, and clarified butter, according to the rules given in the scriptures, and then perform a lamp offering ritual.[16] O eminent sage, one should recite the root mantra of Rāṣṭrasenā according to his ability after sanctifying the body with mantras.[17] Śivaśarman, having offered prayers, said: 'O sinless Mother! Please give me your command to stay right here in your presence,' and then he praised her saying, 'by your grace let there be no obstacle.'"

Vāyu then said, "From that time on, the great sage Śivaśarman lived at that pilgrimage place together with those Brahmins who know the *Atharva Veda*, and the students, and the students' students, all the while concentrating on Ekaliṅga in his heart."

Nārada said, "O Vāyu, please relate to me precisely the rules for the worship of Rāṣṭraśyenā with all of its constituent parts. Please also tell me her mantra sanctification rite that is used to avert great dangers."

Vāyu replied, "The supreme power known as Rāṣṭraśyenā was honored by sages beginning with Hārīta, Takṣaka, Indra, and many others. I will tell you her mantra, which bestows all accomplishments. The knower of mantras should raise her as '*rama* followed by *la*, *vara*, and the sound *yū* with a dot, followed by Rāṣṭraśyenā.' With '*namaḥ*' at the end, the mantra has eight syllables[: RMLVRYŪṂ RĀṢṬRAŚYENĀYAI NAMAḤ].[18] To please the goddess, he should recite the mantra one hundred thousand times and make offerings of rice pudding into the sacred fire every tenth recitation.

"The *ṛṣi* of the mantra is Brahman, and the meter is Gāyatrī. The goddess of the mantra is Rāṣṭraśyenā, the seed syllable is RAṂ, and the feminine power is YŪṂ. The spike is said to be a fan. The purpose of this mantra is to perfect the four social classes, and one forms her body within oneself by installing her mantra-limbs, beginning with RA. First install the Sanskrit letters, and then consecrate the body with the six mantra-limbs, purify the elements, and then perform the rite to establish her vital energy within.[19] Then the mantra practitioner, his body purified, his mind free from greed, should worship the goddess with the five offerings in due order.[20] When he has offered the eatables and so forth, he should next perform the immortalizing rite with the root mantra, the enclosing rite with the armor mantra, and the protection rite with the weapon mantra, which should never be overlooked.[21] After this, one should offer water respectfully to the goddess while reciting the root mantra. The mantra practitioner should pronounce the mantra for the goddess with the word 'hail' (SVĀHĀ), but he should not say 'homage' (NAMAḤ) at the end.[22] The worshiper should offer water for Rāṣṭrasenā to sip, and should offer her betel nut. Next, one should give her lotions and adorn her with various kinds of garlands. After giving these pleasing objects to the goddess, the worshiper should present flowers to her with open hands.

"Next, the worshiper should fully worship the retinue of mantras, beginning with the mantra-limbs of Rāṣṭrasenā. He should draw a lotus with eight petals inside of which is a hexagonal diagram, and all of this in a square furnished with four doors. The worshiper performs the worship of the Mother's feminine powers of the throne, then worships the six principal parts of the body in the six corners of the hexagram.[23] On the eight petals of the lotus, worship the eight Mothers beginning with Brāhmī, and in the square one should worship Indra and the others with their weapons and vehicles. One worships Rāṣṭrasenā sequentially within the five groups of divinities.[24] That lord of sages, having worshiped Rāṣṭrasenā one last time, should dismiss the goddess according to the ritual guidelines.

"O Brahmin, these most supreme procedures for worshiping Rāṣṭrasenā have thus been narrated. Whoever worships her with devotion in this way goes to the highest state. The person who worships Rāṣṭrasenā will not be conquered by fear—whether they are in war, in disputation, or in a distant land. If a person who is mentally focused listens to these rules every day, or if that person should cause others to listen to them, they both will receive a reward from the goddess immediately. Of this there is no doubt. Local people, who worship Rāṣṭrasenā with the repetition of prayers, oblations, and praise, whether they are with faith or without faith—all of these lead to union with her. The sage who is entirely engaged in meditation and who is abstemious in his appetite during the festival of nine nights [. . .]."[25]

The bard said, "Vāyu taught this Purāṇa which bestows the highest truth. After hearing the Purāṇa thus, and having performed the worship of

Rāṣṭrasenā, Nārada, the son of a Brahmin, went to heaven. For one who would worship Rāṣṭrasenā in the morning, at noon, and in the evening with devotion, there is nothing that cannot be accomplished. To those lofty men who worship virgin girls in that way, that most supreme goddess Rāṣṭrasenā gives anything they want.[26] Those kings who make a burnt offering at Rāṣṭrasenā's temple according to the rules will never fear their enemies during times of great danger and great portents.[27] During times of war and violence one should concentrate on calling to mind Rāṣṭrasenā in the form of a female bird holding a thunderbolt weapon. Likewise, during times of peace, one should remember her gentle and auspicious form. Even the goddess of learning, Śāradā, with her hundreds of thousands of births and with her innumerable mouths, is not able to describe to us all of Rāṣṭrasenā's ocean of qualities.[28] I spoke about this briefly, and having made this known to you, O son of a Brahmin, even I am not able to speak further about her other magnificent qualities. You have wealth, you have accomplished your goals, and above all you possess omniscient knowledge. As if ignorant, you asked about the glory of Ekaliṅga. Wanting to benefit the community, a knowledgeable person helps them to remember what they have forgotten. By remembering, they will all reap the fruits of a successful life, just as I did, O eminent sage."[29]

Vedagarbha said, "O very wise Suṣumāṇa, please attend to these words of mine. One should first worship Gaṇeśa, then install the sage mantra with the mantra-limbs, and should finally worship the god who is the protector of gods, who is the giver of rewards. If you worship in this way, you will face no obstacles anywhere."[30]

Thus ends the chapter called "The Rules for the Worship of Rāṣṭraśyenā," the twenty-ninth in the *Ekaliṅga Māhātmya* of Mewar, in the glorious *Vāyu Purāṇa*.

THE GODDESS IN CONTEXT: A FORGOTTEN GODDESS OF WAR FROM RAJASTHAN

The narrative of the goddess Rāṣṭrasenā comes from two chapters of a fifteenth-century Sanskrit text known as the *The Glorification of Ekaliṅga* (*Ekaliṅga Māhātmya*; hereafter ELM). It is a mythical and historical narrative about the founding of a temple for a local form of Śiva known as Ekaliṅga. The name Ekaliṅga literally means "solitary *liṅga*," referring to the popular iconic form that represents Śiva. Today the site, in the Mewar region of southern Rajasthan, is called Ekliṅgjī. The narrative of Rāṣṭrasenā in the ELM depicts her emanation from the goddess Vindhyavāsinī (also spelled Vindhyavāsā), her placement in a physical temple high on a hill near to that of Ekaliṅga, and the rules for her proper worship. Also known as Rāṣṭraśyenā, she is described as emerging from the body of Vindhyavāsinī in the physical form of a hawk or in the form of a four-armed woman holding weapons to protect the kingdom from military invasions. Importantly, Rāṣṭrasenā does not appear in any other historical record in India before her appearance in the ELM. Her emanation from Vindhyavāsinī, together with her hawk appearance, makes her an especially interesting and unique local goddess from a little-studied kingdom.

Seed: Bird-Headed and Mountain Goddesses

The feminine divine has a long history in southern Rajasthan, as it does in South Asia more generally. We can trace the possible origins of Rāṣṭrasenā back in two directions: one, to early goddess cults in the Mewar region described in inscriptions; and two, to groups of pan-Indian goddesses who are often depicted as theriocephalic—having the heads of birds and other animals.

The earliest records of goddesses in Mewar are inscriptional records that date from the seventh century onward. They mention goddesses such as Durgā, Vindhyavāsinī (the Goddess Who Dwells in the Vindhya Mountains), Araṇyavāsinī (the Goddess who Dwells in the Forest), and Vaṭayakṣinīdevī (the Goddess Spirit of the Banyan Tree). These goddesses are all in some way connected with forests, trees, mountains, and wild areas outside of human habitation. Locations such as these are often associated with dangerous spirits, gods, and goddesses, who can either be beneficial or harmful to those who wander into those spaces. Of these mountain- and forest-dwelling goddesses, it is Vindhyavāsinī who is the most important for understanding the origins of Rāṣṭrasenā. However, before discussing the narrative of Vindhyavāsinī we must first look briefly at the history of bird-headed goddesses in ancient India.

In India, bird-headed goddesses are most closely associated with the divine grouping of female figures known as the "Mothers" (*mātṛs*, *mātṛkās*), but they have other connections with beautiful and sometimes malevolent female tree spirits called *yakṣiṇī*s and with female spirits who "seize" and possess human beings, the *grahaṇī*s. The earliest material and literary evidence for independent mother goddesses is found in the Kushan period sculptural and literary record (first to third centuries CE), although it is almost certain that these records represent a long process wherein a diverse range of local goddesses, spirits, and other forms of the feminine divine were codified and brought into the Sanskrit tradition.[31] The mother goddesses found in these early inscriptional records are depicted as feral dogs, cows, or more commonly, birds.[32] The most well known of the Kushan-era goddesses include Kākī, Ṣaṣṭhī, Vinatā, Revatī, and Pūtanā, and they are commonly depicted in the literary and iconographic records as being either bird-headed or entirely avian: Kākī means "female crow;" Ṣaṣṭhī is also known as Winged Ṣaṣṭhī (*pakṣaṣaṣṭhī*); Revatī is described as a bird and a female spirit that possesses people; and in the *Harivaṃśa*, Pūtanā is described as having avian features and is alternatively named Pūtanā Śakunī, which David White translates as "Stinky Female Bird."[33] Similarly, in the ninth-century *Gaüḍavaho*, Revatī is said to be a bird-headed attendant of the pan-Hindu goddess Vindhyavāsinī.[34] These goddesses are also often connected to war; disease; death; childbirth and children; and inauspicious locations such as forests, trees, crossroads, or mountains. While these goddesses are independent deities, they are also important because of their connection to the pan-Indian goddess Vindhyavāsinī as described in her early narratives.

Rāṣṭrasenā's sudden appearance in the ELM calls for a brief speculative excursus on the possible origins of this goddess. As previously mentioned, Rāṣṭrasenā does not appear in any other record before the fifteenth century *Ekaliṅga Māhātmya*. It is possible that Rāṣṭrasenā was an original creation of the author(s) of the ELM, but it is more plausible that a preexisting Bhil tribal goddess from the region was adapted into the Sanskritic pantheon. Support for this hypothesis is found in the literary and epigraphic records dating to the thirteenth to fifteenth centuries, the very period in which the ELM was written and Rāṣṭrasenā introduced as an important martial goddess.

The Bhil have had a long, and not always peaceful, relationship with the Guhila rulers of Mewar. The narratives related to the formation of the Guhila kingdom in Mewar at its earliest stage all have a connection in some way to the Bhil tribe, and their political integration into the larger state structure is evident in these stories. For the period in question—the thirteenth to fifteenth centuries—we see both an attempt to integrate Bhil groups into the Guhila state structure and efforts to defend the state against Bhil insurgents. Local traditions and modern memorial sites in Mewar, such as City Palace Museum and Moti Magri in Udaipur, preserve narratives relating to Bhil participation in the battles fought by Rāṇa Hammīra and especially the battle of Haldīghāṭī under Mahārāṇa Pratāp. At the same time, particularly in the fifteenth century, several steps were taken to fend off Bhil attacks on the kingdom. Due to recurrent revolts by the Bhils in the fifteenth century, the ruler of Mewar, Mahārāṇā Kumbha, engaged in the largest fort-building project to date, including the repairing of walls and outdated forts, especially at mountain passes where Bhils typically were the most difficult to control. Bhils were known to control and protect the forest, hill, and cave passes that were essential in the larger trade networks of Mewar inside and outside of the region, and so control of the Bhil by the Guhila rulers was essential to economic and political state expansion.

Protection of Mewar's political and economic structure was in many ways dependent on the control of these potentially aggressive Bhil forces, and this control was in part centered on assimilation and pacification through the adoption of local religious elements. In fact, the pacification of the Bhils through religious devotion is recorded in the literary record. Chapter 28 of the ELM states that over time the Bhil people were made to abandon their violent behavior through their devotion to Śiva.[35] It remains possible that Rāṣṭrasenā was given space in the literary landscape of the ELM as a theriomorphic regional goddess who protected the state from invading armies, while at the same time she was given a physical site in the geographic landscape—on top of a militarily strategic hill. This may have been done in an attempt to pacify Bhil tribal aggression toward the Guhila state and their control of key trade passes.

No direct evidence links Rāṣṭrasenā to the Bhil tribe. However, her theriomorphism and the political and military context in which she suddenly emerged suggest a possible connection with a preexisting local goddess. The patronage of local goddesses mentioned previously—such as Ghaṭṭavāsinī, Vaṭayakṣinīdevī, and Araṇyavāsinī—indicates a concerted effort on the part of the Guhilas to incorporate local, and perhaps tribal, goddesses into the expanding state structure dependent on the legitimizing power of these goddesses. I now return to the relationship between Rāṣṭrasenā and Vindhyavāsinī in the early literary record.

The sixth-century *Skanda Purāṇa* depicts a battle between the goddess Vindhyavāsinī and a formidable army headed by two demons, named Śumbha and Niśumbha. At the start of the battle Vindhyavāsinī emits from her body (specifically from her limbs) a retinue of terrifying female figures that lead their own individual troops of animal-headed goddesses in the battle. Included in the long list of names are Revatī, Pūtanā, and Ṣaṣṭhī—the same goddesses found in the Kushan-era sculptural and literary records previously mentioned. These goddesses are armed with weapons and armor and are clearly meant to evoke a sense of dread not only in the demon army whom they are about to attack, but in the reader or listener of the narrative as well. Yuko Yokochi summarizes the scene thus: "Then, beating drums and shouting battle-cries, the well-armed goddesses go before Devī. Their battle-cries disconcert the demons and terrify the elephants and horses in their army into discharging excreta. They seem to make the earth quake, the oceans tremble and mountains shudder, and to split the roof of the sky. Looking like a mass of clouds in the rainy season, adorned with banners and standards, the army of the goddesses rapidly approaches the demons. The demons see the menacing army approaching them."[36] The frightening appearance of these goddesses serves the purpose of instilling in the reader or listener an image of the dreadful nature of these emanations of Vindhyavāsinī, emphasizing their nature as warrior goddesses capable of destroying any foe, demon or otherwise. However, it is not a mere narrative flourish to describe these goddesses as being terrifying on the battlefield. Instead, it serves a deeper didactic purpose, which is to describe to the audience in no uncertain terms that even these "smaller" goddesses—"portions" (*aṃśa*) of the greatness of Vindhyavāsinī—are nonetheless powerful warriors in their own right.

After the victory in battle, Vindhyavāsinī places all of her emanated theriocephalic goddesses in particular cities and countries throughout the Indian subcontinent. Some of them go on to inhabit specific named locations, while others are placed vaguely in "various other villages, cities and towns, or on mountains."[37] The parallels between the ELM narrative translated in this chapter and that of the sixth-century *Skanda Purāṇa* just outlined call for analysis and comparison with other chapters in this volume, such as the story of Kauśikī in chapter 3.

Flower: Rāṣṭrasenā in the Ekaliṅga Māhātmya

Our goddess goes by two related names in the ELM. As Rāṣṭrasenā she is the goddess who serves as the "Army of the Kingdom." She is also known as Rāṣṭraśyenā, the "Ladyhawk of the Kingdom."[38] As indicated by her name, Rāṣṭrasenā/Rāṣṭraśyenā is therefore a warrior goddess who has taken the form of a hawk in order to protect the kingdom of Mewar. These two aspects, her hawk form and her role as the protector of the kingdom of Mewar, symbolized by the weapons she holds, are perhaps the most important elements in her iconography. Both are central to understanding her role in the ELM and in the history of the region. To understand Rāṣṭrasenā one must first begin with her physical temple and its place in the geographical landscape.

The temple to Rāṣṭrasenā sits high upon a hill about a mile east of Ekliṅgjī temple, as the crow flies. While the current path up the hill is mostly paved, it is a steep and difficult climb. From behind the main boundary wall of Ekliṅgjī, overlooking Indra Lake, one can see Rāṣṭrasenā's temple distinctly, dominating the immediate landscape. The physical proximity of the temple to Rāṣṭrasenā is important, mainly because she forms a third "point" in a visual triangle in the landscape, comprised of her temple and those of Ekliṅgjī and Vindhyavāsinī. Situated as it is on the top of a steep hill, Rāṣṭrasenā's temple has a 360-degree view of the valley below overlooking—and protecting—the royal temple of Ekliṅgjī and the temple of Vindhyavāsinī. Rāṣṭrasenā therefore sits atop perhaps the most militarily strategic location in the surrounding area, having a bird's-eye view of the entire landscape below. I now return to the ELM and the argument already laid out concerning the historical context of theriocephalic goddesses in early Indian religious thought in order to connect the temple of Rāṣṭrasenā to the physical and textual landscape.

One of the most important passages concerning Rāṣṭrasenā in the ELM occurs at 11.15–16. It reads as follows:

> Vindhyavāsā then emitted the goddess Rāṣṭrasenā from her own body, after which she installed her there, on the mountain. Delighted at seeing herself in the form of Rāṣṭrasenā, Vindhyavāsinī said these words to her: "O goddess, take fully the form of a hawk and protect the kingdom! Destroy the evil demons—*daityas*, *rākṣasas*, *piśācas*, *bhūtas*, and *pretas*—with the thunderbolt (*vajra*) you hold. While in the form of a hawk it is your duty to protect Medapāṭa (Mewar) from *yoginīs* and *jṛmbhakas*, evil Seizer demons, and others. If some evil people come to this country desiring war, you should destroy them with your spells and powers."

It is at this moment in the ELM narrative that Rāṣṭrasenā appears, having emerged from the body of Vindhyavāsinī and taking the form of a hawk on the very hilltop where she currently resides. In this verse Rāṣṭrasenā is depicted as holding a thunderbolt weapon, and further on in the narrative she is described as carrying a sword, shield, and bow and arrows. Rāṣṭrasenā has two physical forms as described in the ELM: a gentle (*saumyā*) form and the form she takes when she is prepared for battle. In the former she is described as a young woman adorned with beautiful ornaments and seated upon a throne, while in the latter she takes the form of a hawk.

What reason might the author(s) have had for including Rāṣṭrasenā in the ELM? Some historical context will be helpful here in understanding her role as the protector of the Mewar kingdom. It is certain that between the eleventh and fifteenth centuries, the Ekliṅgjī temple site had been threatened or attacked by Muslim-led forces on multiple occasions. Incursions by the Delhi sultan Altamsh, Sultan Alā-ud-dīn Khaljī, Aḥmad Shāh of Gujarat, Ghīyāth-ud-dīn of Malwa, and others paint a clear picture of constant threat to, and even partial destruction of, the Ekliṅgjī temple site. Inscriptional evidence shows that just before the composition of the ELM, the ruler of Mewar, Mahārāṇā Mokal, had large walls constructed around the temple complex, an indication that the temple was at some time directly threatened by military invaders.[39] As the royal temple, Ekliṅgjī was the most important religious site in Mewar. From at least the tenth century, the Ekliṅgjī temple complex was the center of religious power and political authority for the kingdom, and it was also the source of royal legitimacy for the rulers of Mewar. Therefore, as a potentially malevolent warrior goddess situated high upon a hill near Ekliṅgjī, Rāṣṭrasenā was no mere afterthought to the textual landscape of the ELM or to the physical landscape of Mewar. Despite the relatively small number of verses dedicated to her in the ELM, Rāṣṭrasenā was one of the most important goddesses in fifteenth-century Mewar.

Fruit: Rāṣṭrasenā after the ELM

Rāṣṭrasenā appears two more times in the narrative literature after the ELM. She is mentioned in the seventeenth-century *Amarakāvyam*, a text written by a local Mewari named Raṇachoḍa Bhaṭṭa. Bhaṭṭa's work recast the older thirteenth-century story of the establishment of the kingdom of Mewar, including the narrative of the two most important kings in the region, Guhila and Bappā Rāval, as well as the creation of Ekaliṅga temple, into a more popular context. In the *Amarakāvyam*, Rāṣṭrasenā still appears to be central to the pantheon of deities associated with Ekaliṅga. Bhaṭṭa writes that Rāṣṭrasena's temple image, along with Vindhyavāsinī's image, was turned into gold by Guhila, one of the progenitors of the royal lineage of Mewar, through his kingly power.[40] The current temple images are not made of gold; therefore we can either understand the story as a mythical claim to Guhila's spiritual power—derived from his divine right to rule—or interpret it literally and speculate that the golden images were looted at some point.

Rāṣṭrasenā's final appearance in historical literature is in Muhaṇot Nainsī's seventeenth-century Marwari account of the history of Mewar, entitled *Nainsī rī Khyāt*. Similar to the narrative found in the *Amarakāvyam*, the *Nainsī rī Khyāt* relates the story of the founding of the Ekaliṅga temple by the early king Bappā Rāval. According to this narrative, Bappā Rāval served the sage Hārītarāśi for a number of years, and Hārītarāśi, for his part, worshiped both Ekaliṅga and Rāṭhāsenā (Rāṣṭrasenā). After many years Bappā Rāval still was not able to procure a kingdom, and after petitioning Rāṭhāsenā, Hārītarāśi was told to worship Mahādeva in order to acquire a kingdom for Bappā. After some time Mahādeva and Rāṭhāsenā were pleased by the devotion of Hārītarāśi, so they gave the kingdom of Mewar to Bappā.[41] This narrative is important because in it we see a significant shift in the role of the goddess Rāṣṭrasenā regarding the legitimation of royal power: it was through her grace, as much as that of Ekaliṅga, that the kingdom of Mewar was bestowed on Bappā Rāval. This narrative is a major change in what appears in inscriptional records dating to the tenth and fifteenth centuries, and it is a critical change from the narrative found in the ELM. In earlier records it is through the grace of Ekaliṅga and Vindhyavāsinī—and not Rāṣṭrasenā—that the kingdom of Mewar was given to Bappā Rāval. That the emphasis shifts from Vindhyavāsinī to Rāṣṭrasenā in the *Nainsī rī Khyāt* says something quite important about the increasingly central role of this militaristic goddess in the legitimation of political power in seventeenth-century Mewar.

Rāṣṭrasenā is not mentioned in James Tod's well-known nineteenth-century history of Mewar, *Annals and Antiquities of Rajasthan*, despite his references to many local goddesses such as Ambamātā and Vyanmātā (Bāṇmātā).[42] Tod repeats the thirteenth-century narrative that has Ekaliṅga and Vindhyavāsinī bestow the kingdom of Mewar on Bappā Rāval, but there is no indication of the seventeenth-century narrative shift to Rāṣṭrasenā's role in political legitimation that we find in the *Nainsī rī Khyāt*. Rāṣṭrasenā's omission from Tod's history of Mewar is not definitive evidence that she was no longer central to the lives of those living in the region at that time, but it is perhaps indicative of a decline in her role as the primary protector of the kingdom. Over time that duty had shifted in favor of the militant tutelary goddess (*kuladevatā/kuladevī*) and protector of the royal family known as Bāṇmātā (Arrow Mother), who still serves in that function today.

Today Rāṣṭrasenā (now known as Rāṭhāsaṇ Mātājī) still occupies the same mountaintop temple described in the ELM. However, based on my observations, pilgrims seldom make a climb up the steep path to visit and worship her, except during the festival of Navarātri and a few other holidays throughout the year. A modern description of the temple is given in a ten-rupee tourist pamphlet sold outside the temple gates of Ekliṅgjī, and it recounts a brief episode that took place at Rāṣṭrasenā's temple at an unknown date. In the episode described in the pamphlet, a local king from Delwara wanted to sacrifice an elephant to Rāṣṭrasenā in order to gain her favor, but when he had it brought to the mountain, the elephant driver refused to let the sacrifice be carried out and instead offered himself as a substitute. The author of the pamphlet concludes rather abruptly that in the end both the elephant and the elephant driver were sacrificed to Rāṣṭrasenā. The author does not give a date for the story, nor is there any indication of whether the elephant driver was intentionally sacrificed or if it was an accident (the elephant seems to have been pushed off the side of the mountain). It is nonetheless interesting to note that at some point in the recent past animal sacrifice was still being performed at the temple, a custom that to my knowledge is not performed today.

The current temple to Rāṣṭrasenā is rather small, and her image (*mūrti*) installed there offers no indications that she is a bird or in any way birdlike. She is dressed in yellow cloth, draped in garlands, and her face is entirely black except for two bright yellow swirls painted on her cheeks just below her eyes. She is flanked by Kāla and Gorā Bherujī, local forms of Bhairava, himself a terrific form of Śiva. The presence of these two fierce guardian deities bolsters the theory that animal sacrifice took place at Rāṣṭrasenā's temple in the past. Despite her description as a hawk goddess prepared for war in chapter 11 of the ELM, her image today is pacified and is perhaps more representative of her auspicious nature, as described in the translation of chapter 29.

SOURCE

The source of the narrative is the fifteenth-century *Ekaliṅga Māhātmya* (ELM). The Sanskrit ELM has been published twice, first by Premlata Sharma in 1976 and again in 2016 by Shri Krishnan Juganū and Bhanwar Sharma, who also translated the text into Hindi in their edition. Both published editions rely on a manuscript from 1857 currently housed in the Udaipur City Palace

Library. According to Dr. Shri Krishnan, there are a translation of, and commentary on, the ELM written in Mewari and a Sanskrit illustrated manuscript, neither of which could be located during my research.

Based on the chronology of the kings of Mewar given in the twenty-sixth chapter of the ELM, it is fairly certain that it was written shortly after the end of the reign of the Mewar ruler Rana Kumbha (1433–1468) and perhaps during the time of his son Rana Raimal. The ELM is part of a large genre of religious narratives in India called *māhātmyas* or *sthalapurāṇas*, texts primarily concerned with glorifying local gods and goddesses, temples, and geographical regions. The authors of *māhātmyas* and *sthalapurāṇas* often associate these local narratives with one or another of the more well-known, and generally older, Purāṇas as a method of establishing the legitimacy and authority of their local narratives. The ELM states that it is a part of the *Vāyu Purāṇa*, although the connection between the *Vāyu Purāṇa* and the ELM is rather indirect. As a member of the *māhātmya/sthalapurāṇa* genre, the ELM is very closely connected to southern Rajasthan in the fifteenth century. The narrative therefore can tell us a lot about the concerns of local rulers and priests and provides a window into how they imagined their place in the wider Hindu world. Through an intriguing blend of historical actors, places, and landscapes, together with translocal Hindu landscapes and cosmologies, the ELM presents to the reader a vision that is both outside local time and space yet intimately connected to the local region of Mewar.

The translation comprises chapters 11 and 29 of the ELM. Outside of these two chapters Rāṣṭrasenā is only mentioned three other times, and so out of the two thousand or so verses that make up the thirty-two chapters of the ELM, only two chapters are dedicated to her. Nevertheless, because of the role she plays in protecting the kingdom, Rāṣṭrasenā remains one of the most important deities in the entire narrative.

FURTHER READING

Humes, Cynthia Ann. 1996. "Vindhyavāsinī: Local Goddess Yet Great Goddess." In *Devi: Goddesses of India*, edited by John Stratton Hawley and Donna M. Wulff, 49–77. Berkeley: University of California Press.

Kapur, Nandini Sinha. 2002. *State Formation in Rajasthan: Mewar during the Seventh-Fifteenth Centuries*. Manohar: New Delhi.

Lyons, Tryna. 1999. "The Changing Faces of Ekliṅgjī: A Dynastic Shrine and Its Artists." *Asiae* 58, nos. 3/4: 253–71.

Yokochi, Yuko. 2004. "The Rise of the Warrior Goddess in Ancient India: A Study of the Myth Cycle of Kauśikī-Vindhyavāsinī in the Skandapurāṇa." PhD thesis, Rijksuniversiteit Groningen.

NOTES

1. Mt. Kailash refers to the Himalayan peak in Tibet that Hindus regard as the home of Śiva. The Trikūṭa Mountain is another sacred peak in the Himalayas, and the text here is asserting the local Rajasthani Mountains' spiritual equivalence to the Himalaya.

2. The five substances (*pañcagavya*) that are produced by a cow are milk, curds, ghee, urine, and dung. The wish-granting cow (*kāmadhenu*) is considered to be the divine mother of all cows, who provides her owner with anything he or she may desire.

3. The author is playing with the words *svakareṇa*, meaning "by her own hand," and *karaja*, meaning "born from the hand."

4. This is referring to Indra Sarovar, a lake directly behind the Ekliṅgjī temple and an important place of pilgrimage.

5. The *śrāddha* rite is a ritual for deceased ancestors, specifically for one's paternal and maternal parents, grandparents, and great-grandparents. During this ritual, a son offers balls of rice (*piṇḍa*) that nourish the deceased ancestors in the afterlife and provide for them a body so that they can move on from the world of the hungry ghosts (*preta*) to the world of the ancestors (*pitṛloka*). In this verse, Śiva is referred to by his alternative names, Hara and Rudra.

6. The Sanskrit original inserts the phrase "The bard said" here, which appears to be a mistake, as the narration of Vāyu to Nārada continues; we omitted it in the translation.

7. The *daitya*s are demons or anti-gods (*asura*) born of Diti and the sage Kaśyapa. *Rākṣasa*s are generally demonic beings described as being ugly in appearance, having fangs and long claws, and being large in size and desirous of human blood. *Piśāca*s are impish, demonic creatures that eat human flesh and often lurk in the darkness and haunt cremation grounds and other inauspicious places. *Bhūta*s are malevolent ghosts. *Preta*s are ghosts who haunt the living and are sometimes described as having large, distended stomachs and very thin necks so that they are in a constant state of hunger and dissatisfaction.

8. Medapāṭa is the Sanskrit name for the region of Mewar. It means "an expanse of fat." This unusual name is explained at the beginning of the *Ekaliṅga Māhātmya*. It describes the earth itself, and specifically Mewar, being constructed by leveling or flattening out the bones and fat of two mythic demons after they were killed in a battle with Viṣṇu. *Yoginī*s have a long history in India, and the bird-headed goddesses described above, interestingly, share many of their features. There are sometimes said to be sixty-four *yoginī*s, many of whom are bird faced, who derive from the eight Mothers (*aṣṭamātṛkā*). They can be either benevolent or dangerous. See White (2003) for a

detailed study of the *yoginīs*. *Jṛmbhakas* are a type of fearsome spirit that inhabits weapons. The word itself comes from *jṛmbh*, meaning "to open the jaws wide, yawn, or gape," probably indicating the imagined frightening appearance of a mouth opening wide to consume a person.

9. The term *māyā* can be translated variously as illusion, fraud, trick, or ignorance. Here, I have chosen to highlight the negative and destructive nature of *māyā* as magical powers and spells.

10. The phrase "and also women who look like her" (*tadrūpāṃ ca striyaṃ tathā*) is ambiguous. It may be suggesting that all women share in the form of Rāṣṭrasenā and deserve worship, or it may suggest that particular features qualified certain women as being similar to Rāṣṭrasenā and thus objects of worship.

11. The author of the *Ekaliṅga Māhātmya* uses the active verb in a passive construction here.

12. In the *Ekaliṅga Māhātmya*, Bāṣpa is the name used for Bappā Rāwal, the mythico-historical progenitor of the Mewar royal lineage and, according to the narrative, the king who had the Ekaliṅga temple built.

13. Śivaśarman is the father of Bappā Rāwal, according to the *Ekaliṅga Māhātmya*.

14. *Vaiḍūrya* is a generic name for beryl, despite the claim of Sanskrit dictionaries that it is specifically cat's-eye beryl. See Biswas (1994).

15. *Kiṃnaras* and *gandharvas* are classes of celestial beings associated with music and song.

16. *Ārātrika* is the lamp-offering ritual today known as *ārtī* or *āratī*.

17. The *aṅganyāsa* rite is part of a larger ritual wherein the body is purified and made fit to worship a deity. The rite of *aṅganyāsa* entails touching certain parts of the body with one's hand while reciting mantras in order to make those body parts, and the entire body, pure.

18. This interpretation of the mantra is hypothetical and follows the suggestion of Michael Slouber, who identifies it as coming from the ancient Tantric category of "heap" (*kūṭa*) mantras, formed by piling particular consonants upon each other with a single vowel at the end. This practice is seen as early as the tenth century CE in sources like the Jain *Jvālāmālinīkalpa* and the *Bhairavapadmāvatīkalpa*, both of which rely on older Śaiva Tantric sources. The sequence MALAVARAYŪṂ is prefixed with varying initial consonants in these Tantras. According to Dory Heilijgers-Seelen's *The System of Five Cakras in Kubjikāmatatantra 14–16* (1994), the sequence RMLVRYŪṂ is one of five such "heap mantras" in the Kubjikā system of the *Śrīmatottara* that are linked to the five elements via their initial consonant (22). In this case, the initial consonant R represents the Fire element and also corresponds to the initial letter of Rāṣṭraśyenā's name. An alternative interpretation has the mantra reciter pronounce each consonant of the heap mantra with a short *a* vowel and not count the goddess's name toward the total number of mantra syllables. The translation of these verses follows Shaman Hatley's emendation of the hypometrical 29.19b from *rāṣṭraśyenāṃ tāṃ* to *rāṣṭraśyenāntāṃ tāṃ*.

19. In the *mātṛkānyāsa* Tantric rite the practitioner calls down and installs the letters of the Sanskrit alphabet onto the body in order to make it pure. *Bhūtaśuddhi* (Skt.,

"purification of the elements") is a ritual that involves washing the body in order to remove physical impurities so that the physical body is fit for initiation and worship. See White (1996, 270–72). Establishing the goddess's vital energy refers to the ritual known as *prāṇapratiṣṭhā*, the infusing of life breaths into an icon (*mūrti*) before it can be worshiped. The rite of *prāṇapratiṣṭhā* brings the deity into the icon, transforming it from an inanimate object into the deity herself. In this case, the body of the worshiper substitutes for the icon.

20. Typically these five are sandalwood paste (*gandha*), flowers (*puṣpa*), incense (*dhūpa*), a lamp (*dīpa*), and food (*naivedya*).

21. On these various rites, refer to the modern dictionary of Tantric technical terms *Tāntrikābhidhānakośa*, volumes 1–4 (see Brunner-Lachaux, Oberhammer, and Padoux 2000), s.v. *amṛtīkaraṇa*, *avaguṇṭhana*, and *rakṣā*.

22. The translation is based on an emendation suggested by Michael Slouber: instead of the edition's *na mametyantato vadet* at 29.26d, we should rather read *na nametyantato vadet*, understanding *namety* as an irregular phonic combination of *namaḥ* and *iti*.

23. These six are the two arms, two legs, head, and torso.

24. The term *pañcāvaraṇa* refers to "five circuits of divinities" in a maṇḍala. The occupants of the five circuits are not specified here but may be the following five groups of divinities: (1) the *brahmamantras* and the *aṅgamantras*, (2) the Vidyeśvaras, (3) the Gaṇeśvaras, (4) the World-guardians, and (5) the Weapons of the World Guardians.

25. The festival of nine nights (Navarātri) commemorates Durgā's battle to slay the buffalo demon. The last half of this verse is missing in the only available manuscript of the *Ekaliṅga Māhātmya*. The gap in the original text may continue, since here the Vāyu-Nārada conversation ends abruptly. The next paragraph begins the bard-Śaunaka conversation without any transition.

26. *Kumārīpūjā* is a ritual in which one or more young girls (*kumārī*) represents the feminine divine and is worshiped during particular ritual and festival occasions.

27. "Great portents" refers to major, unexpected events such as earthquakes, eclipses, and the like.

28. Śāradā is an epithet of Sarasvatī.

29. This point marks another rough transition in the original text. The final paragraph switches abruptly to the Suṣumāṇa-Vedagarbha conversation.

30. "Gaṇeśa" is a conjecture; the edition reads *gaṇarpa*.

31. For a survey of animal-headed, and specifically bird-headed, goddesses in Kuṣāṇa period sculpture, see Joshi (1986, 105–9). On the same subject in Kuṣāṇa-era literature, see 64–79.

32. Joshi (1986, 4). Among the thirteen types of *mātṛkās* in Kuṣāṇa art categorized by Joshi, bird- and animal-headed *mātṛkās* constitute the second largest category.

33. White (2003, 49–53).

34. Joshi (1986, 6). See also the *Gaüḍavaho* of Vākpati, edited by Pandurang Pandit (1887, vv. 327–30).

35. ELM 28.45cd–46ab: *bhillaś ca vividhākārair vṛtaṃ paramadhārmikaiḥ. śivabhaktiratair vīrair bhūtahiṃsādivarjitaiḥ.*

36. Yokochi (2013a, 126–27).

37. Yokochi (2013a, 135).

38. *Śyena* can refer to a hawk, eagle, or falcon in Sanskrit. See Dave (1985, 199).

39. Śṛṅgī-ṛṣi Inscription of Prince Mokala (1428), *Epigraphia Indica* 23 (1935–1936): 230–41.

40. Kapur (2002, 255).

41. Jinavijaya Muni (1960, 11).

42. See Tod (1914, 225); for a brief account of Ambamātā and animal sacrifice at her temple see 551.

PART THREE

Tantras and Magic

FIGURE 17. Rangda, by Laura Santi

CHAPTER 9

Rangda in the *Calon Arang*

A Tale of Magic

THOMAS M. HUNTER AND NI WAYAN PASEK ARIATI

This chapter commences our third and final set in the book, focusing on tales of the Tantras and magic. We have already become acquainted with Tantric traditions in the introduction and the chapters on Kauśikī, the Seven Mothers, and Rāṣṭrasenā. This last set features the Tantras more prominently. The other three in this final group are translated from primary Tantras directly, whereas the current one, the sixteenth-century *Calon Arang*, is a Middle Javanese literary work from Bali with prominent Tantric themes.

Bali is a Hindu-majority island in Indonesia, a large tropical archipelago nation whose population is now predominantly Muslim. Previously known as the "East Indies," Indonesia literally means "Indian islands" owing to the prominent influence of India on the local culture. The events of the story are set in eastern Java during the reign of the eleventh-century emperor Erlangga. It is a tale that remains popular in Bali, particularly in the enchanting performances of the Barong-Rangda dramas.

The *Calon Arang* focuses on the story of a widow and sorceress, who is variously called Rangda (the widow) of Girah or Calon Arang (the candidate in sorcery). Both of these terms are alternatively used as titles and as the proper names for Rangda. Although she is here portrayed as a human being with supernatural powers, the tradition comes to understand her as a form of the great Hindu goddess Durgā. As discussed in the essay, this is partly due to her similarity to an even older figure from Javanese mythology named Ra Nini, who is unambiguously linked with Durgā. But the makings of such a shift in identity between mortal and divine are present in the story itself, and readers should try to identify elements that support it. Rangda's persona here also calls for analysis of the ideas of gender, sexuality, and spiritual power promoted in the story. Rangda plays a role similar, in some respects, to various "witch" characters in European folklore, yet the striking cultural differences should give us pause when assessing the meaning of her character.

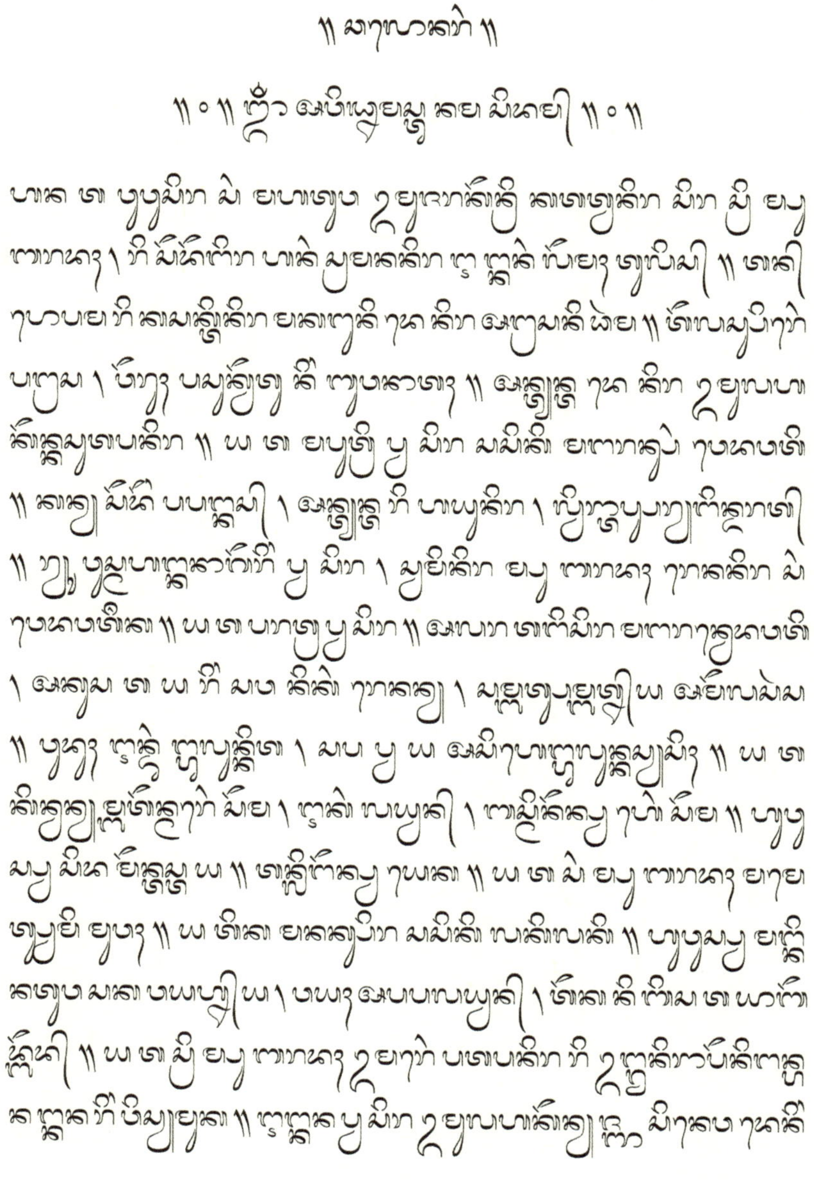

FIGURE 18. *Calon Arang*, a Middle Javanese work in the Balinese script. Font "Aksara Bali" © Khoi Nguyen Viet.

CALON ARANG: A TALE OF MAGIC

After the death of her mother, the daughter of the sage Baradah, named Wedawatī, was mistreated by her stepmother and twice fled to the Lĕmah Tulis cremation ground. On the first occasion, the sage Baradah was able to coax Wedawatī away from the place where her mother was cremated, but on the second occasion he was unsuccessful, so with his disciples he moved his hermitage to the Lĕmah Tulis cremation ground.[1]

We will speak no more about the tranquil sage Baradah. Our discourse now is on the Supreme Lord in Daha, whose rule was untroubled as he achieved world dominion. Under his rule the land was prosperous and tranquil. His consecration name was Mahārāja Erlangga. His inclination to the life of a sage was awe inspiring. There were no others in the lands and seas of the archipelago who could be considered his equal. Now at that time, the widow of a nobleman lived in Girah, named Calon Arang.[2] She had one child, a daughter named Ratna Manggalī, meaning Auspicious Jewel, who was very lovely in form—a true "jewel of the palace." But a long time had passed, and no one had come to seek the hand of Ratna Manggalī—none from Girah, let alone from Daha or the neighboring countries. There was no one anywhere brave enough to seek the hand of Ratna Manggalī, the child of Rangda of Girah, for it was widely known in the world that the Lady of Girah practiced the evil arts. All kept a distance from seeking the hand of Ratna Manggalī. Rangda then said to herself, "Ah, what is it that is making it so no one seeks the hand of my daughter? Even though she is beautiful, there are none who ask after her. It pains my heart. And so, I will make use of my sacred book of spells. I will take up my precious Tantric book and will approach the feet of the great goddess Śrī Bhagawatī (Durgā), asking for her favor, that all the men of this country be annihilated."[3] Taking up her book, Rangda went to the cremation ground with all her pupils to beg for assistance at the feet of the Supreme Deity, the Goddess Bhagawatī.

The names of each of her students were Wĕkśirṣa, Mahiṣawadana, Si Lĕndya, Si Lĕndĕ, Si Lĕndi, Si Guyang, Si Larung, and Si Gaṇḍi. Those were the ones who accompanied Rangda of Girah, and who danced with her in the cremation ground. Without fail the goddess Durgā appeared with her troops, who all joined in the dancing. Rangda, the candidate in witchcraft (*calon arang*), intoned a hymn of praise to the goddess Bhagawatī. The goddess spoke,

"My, my, my. My dear child, Calon Arang, what is your purpose for coming here with all your students, all offering respect, bowing with folded hands?" Rangda asked reverently, "This humble person, your child, asks that all the people of this country be annihilated. This is what your child asks." The goddess said, "My, my, my. My dear child. I allow it, but not as far as the center of the kingdom. Do not kill indiscriminately, simply from the height of your rage." Rangda agreed and took leave of the goddess, saying to her, "With your permission, I will take my leave."

Calon Arang departed quickly with her students, who now danced in the graveyard. In the middle of the night they danced, while sounding *kemanak* and *kangsi* gongs. When they had finished dancing, they returned to Girah and went in high spirits to their homes. It was not long before the people of the surrounding villages began to fall ill and die, their bodies piling up one atop the other. We will speak no more of Calon Arang here, but of the lords who ruled the country who had come for audience in the outer courtyard of the king, Śrī Mahārāja Erlangga. The prime minister now spoke: "Your humble servant offers his words at the dust of your feet.[4] Many are the people of the Supreme Lord who have died, struck down by chills and burning fever, passing into the beyond within one or two days. It is said that the one who is causing this is the widow of Girah, Calon Arang. She and her students have been dancing in the graveyard. There are many who have now taken her as their guru." Thus were the words of the prime minister.

All of those who had come to the audience hall agreed that what the prime minister had said was true. The king appeared saddened and then furious, saying "Where are my special agents?" In a short while, his "hands of darkness" had arrived. He said, "Go now and slay Calon Arang. Do not go alone. Gather all your men and go in force. Do not be careless." All of the king's men took their leave after saying respectfully to the king, "Your humble servants accept your order and will carry out to the fullest your order to kill the widow of Girah."

All of his men now set out. We will not speak of them along the way. They moved quickly and arrived at the home of Calon Arang when she was still sleeping. There was no sign of anyone awake anywhere. Without delay, they tied up the hair of Rangda and unsheathed their swords. As they were about to stab Rangda, their hands shook violently. Calon Arang woke up with a start. A blinding flash of light issued from her eyes, nose, and mouth, blazing brightly, flaring up, burning hotly, and enveloping the king's men in flames.

Two of the king's men immediately crossed over to the shore of death. The others retreated, their strength quickly draining from them.

We will not speak of what happened along the way. They had arrived now in the king's hall. Those who had survived spoke humbly to the king, "We humble servants of the lord king are worthless. Two of our own have been slain through the black magic of the widow from Girah. Fire emerged from her body, flowing out of her and incinerating two of the king's men." The king fell silent, rendered speechless by what his men had told him. The king then said, "O first minister, this news relayed by our secret forces perplexes me. What will you decide when you discuss this with my council of ministers?" With that the king left the hall of audience, his heart heavy from the loss of two of his secret forces. We will speak no more of the king, but will tell now of Rangda of Girah.

Her anger grew greater from having been attacked, let alone that it was by the king's men. Now Calon Arang spoke to her students, telling them they should come along to the cremation ground. She again took out her book of sacred spells and set out with her students. They arrived at the edge of the cremation ground, shaded by a massive kapok tree. Runners thick with leaves spread as far as the ground. Beauty was everywhere. Beneath the shading kapok the ground was level, and as clean as if it had been swept every morning and evening. That was where Rangda sat, surrounded by her students. Si Lĕndya asked Rangda, "Why are you reacting like this to the king's anger? It would be better to seek salvation by showing respect to the holy sage, who can point out the way to deathless salvation." Then Si Larung said, "Why are you afraid of the king? On the contrary, I say that we should strengthen our attack, taking it to the very center of the country." All the others agreed to what Larung said, for it was in accord with Calon Arang's intentions. She said, "I agree completely with what you have said, Larung. Come then, and sound out the *kangsi* and *kemanak* gongs and we will dance. Everyone should dance one by one, and I will determine which task you will be suited for."

Without delay Si Guyang danced in a crouching position while clapping her hands and breathlessly turning her overskirt upside down.[5] She directed her fierce gaze to the right and left with staring eyes. Now Si Larung danced like a tiger about to rip apart its prey, naked, and with her hair loosened and spread wide. Then, Si Gaṇḍi danced with hopping movements, spreading wide her hair following the movements of her eyes as red as *gaṇitri* seeds. Si Lĕndi danced with quick, bouncing steps while flicking her sash. Her eyes flashed like fire about to flame up as far as her hair. Now Wěkśirṣa danced in a bowing stance. Naked, she spread her hair to follow the unblinking stare of her shifting eyes. Si Mahiṣawadana danced on one foot. Then she turned upside down with her tongue protruding and her hands held out like sharp claws.

Calon Arang was pleased in her heart. After they had danced she gave each one a share in what they were about to do. "Divide up the work of the five quarters of the world," she said. "Si Lěndě go to the south, Si Larung to the north, Si Guyang to the east, Si Gaṇḍi to the west. I, Calon Arang, will stay at the center, along with Si Wěkśirṣa and Mahiṣawadana." After that, they broke up and spread out to the five quarters of the realm, while Calon Arang and her companions went to the center of the cremation ground.

There, they found the corpse of a man who had died on a *tumpěk* day.[6] They set him up and tied him to a *kěpuh* tree. By blowing the breath of life into him, they brought him back to life. Si Wěkśirṣa opened his eyes, and Mahiṣawadana brought his wilting corpse back to living form. The corpse now spoke, asking, "Who is it that has brought me back to life? I am deeply in your debt and don't know how I can repay you. I want to serve you. Untie me from the trunk of this *kěpuh* tree, and I will serve you faithfully. I will attend upon you and worship you alone, licking the dust from under your feet." Without a moment's hesitation Si Wěkśirṣa said, "So you think you are going to live on forever! Not so! At this very moment I'm going to cut your throat with my machete." In a flash she had decapitated the corpse, whose head flew off as blood gushed from his neck, and his blood pooled around his corpse. Calon Arang then washed her hair with his blood so that it became thick and matted.

She took up his intestines as her sacred cord and draped them as a garland around her neck. The corpse was disemboweled and his innards cooked as an offering for the lowly spirits, all of whom had gathered there since the earlier appearance of the goddess Bhagawatī and her troops. In a flash, the goddess appeared from her heavenly abode, saying to Calon Arang, "My, my, my. My dear child, Calon Arang. Why have you come singing my praises and making me a sacrificial meal? I accept your praises." Rangda of Girah now said, "The ruler of the realm is angry with me, your humble servant. My request is that the people of the realm be annihilated, even up to the center of the kingdom." The goddess replied, "Alright then, I find favor with you, Calon Arang. But be mindful. Do not be careless!" Calon Arang now took her leave, while intoning a hymn of praise to the goddess. Quickly setting out, she and her students danced now in the crossroads.

The entire country was struck hard by disease. The sickness went on for one night or two, always marked by fever and chills. People died and were buried one by one. Among two friends one would bury the other in the morning and in the evening be buried himself. Corpses were piled up in heaps on the cremation ground; there were so many that they stopped up the drainage channel of the graveyard. There were corpses in the fields for dry crops and in the open spaces of the towns, while some rotted in homes. Dogs howled as they fed on corpses. Crows swarmed in the skies and pecked at the corpses together. Flies buzzed and hummed as they swarmed into homes. Many homes now lay empty and deserted. There were those, too, who fled to places far from the contagion, carrying on their backs those who had already been stricken. Some carried their children in slings or led them by the hand. One who was carrying another saw a howling demon (*bhuta*) who shouted out, "Don't run away. Your village is safe, free of disease and the plague. Come back here; you will live!" After the "thieving demon" said this, many died along the way. Those who fled carried others on their backs. The demons in empty houses leapt about merrily, laughing and joking. There were others in the town square and the great highway. Si Mahiṣawadana entered a house by way of a gap in the wall of the compound, and all the people there fell ill. Si Wĕkśirṣa slipped through the bamboo slats of the sleeping quarters of one house and cut the throats of the sleepers, seeking a *caru* offering of blood and raw flesh.[7] "That's what I want," said Wĕkśirṣa, "don't make me wait." We will speak no further of those who died in the plague or of the demons who seized them and carried them away. We will speak now of the Lord King in his royal city, as he held audience in the outer courtyard.

The audience was subdued, as the king's mood was pained and dark, uncertain about what he should do about the deaths of so many of his subjects and the illness of others. It was as if the light of the kingdom had gone out. Without further delay, the king ordered his prime minister and his council of ministers to send out invitations to all of the Brahmins, Rĕsis, Bhujangas, and gurus of the realm. He ordered them each to seek a solution and to perform the Vedic fire ritual (*homa*), for there were many who were dying in the epidemic. The gurus and Brahmins performed a *homa*, propitiating Sang Hyang Agni, god of fire. About the middle of the night, the four-armed god emerged from the sacred fire and said, "Oṃ, Oṃ. There is one who is an accomplished Lord of Yogis, Śrī Baradah whose hermitage is in the Lĕmah Tulis cremation ground. It is he who can exorcize your realm, ridding the earth of its impurity and bringing it back to an auspicious and bountiful state." After saying this, he vanished into thin air, entering the state of spiritual liberation and disappearing. All the great sages who heard this were pleased at heart. All who had performed the *homa* had heard the words of the four-armed god.

The gathered sages reported to king Erlangga on the appearance of the four-armed god from the ritual fire. The king ordered a young nobleman named Ken Kanuruhan to go to Lĕmah Tulis and ask for the sage's help. Mpu Baradah greeted the nobleman with great courtesy, and for his part Ken Kanuruhan informed the sage that the king had asked him to summon him to court. He informed him how at court, the king and his assembled nobles would beg him to rescue the realm from the attack of Calon Arang and her pupils.[8]

Ken Kanuruhan said to Mpu Baradah, "The reason for the epidemic is that the widow from Girah has a daughter named Manggalī, but all the men of the realm are averse to marrying her. Seeing that there are none who will ask for her daughter's hand in marriage, Calon Arang is in a rage, grieving and angry over the fate of her child." [Mpu Baradah said,] "Yes, it is just as you say. I am not averse to offering my help. There is a student of mine who will accompany you, Kanuruhan, to the royal city. He is my son named Mpu Kebo Bahula. Kanuruhan should escort him into the presence of the one who rules the realm and tell him that Bahula will ask for the hand of Manggalī in marriage. Thus are my instructions. The king should provide the dowry, no matter how much is requested. I will advise Bahula that he should be happy with Manggalī and enjoy the pleasures of the bedchamber with her." Ken Kanuruhan agreed.

Mpu Baradah ordered his followers to prepare a feast for Ken Kanuruhan. There was feasting, drinking of rice wine and sugar cane liquor, and entertainment, including the singing of *kidung* lyrics. The following day Ken Kanuruhan and his companions returned to the capital and the court of Erlangga.[9]

Ken Kanuruhan bowed low at the feet of the Lord of Men, then said, "I was not able to bring the great sage here, but have brought his son and pupil Bahula, who has come here to pay respects at the feet of the king. He has been ordered to ask for the hand of Manggalī in marriage." Now the command of the sage who resides in Buh Citra was as follows, "Whatever bride price Calon Arang asks, you, the servant of the god-king, should fulfill her wish. When Bahula and Ratna Manggalī are happy together, then the great sage Baradah will come to visit Mpu Bahula." His royal highness then said, "I agree with what you propose. Go then along with your men and accompany Mpu Bahula to Girah." We will not relate the tale of their time along the way.

They arrived quickly in Girah and found their way to the outer courtyard of Calon Arang's house. Mpu Bahula took his seat on the bench set aside for guests. In a few moments Calon Arang emerged. Without hesitating, she greeted the honored guest, saying, "Oṃ, Oṃ. We are fortunate indeed, good sir. Where do you, my guest, hail from? And where is your home, honored sir? You have the appearance of someone of high birth, but I do not know how I should address you." Mpu Bahula got down from his seat and adjusted the tip of his lower wrap. Then he spoke slowly, saying, "Truly you are well versed in the scriptures. It is as if sweet syrup is dripping from your tongue as you speak. I hope that I will accept properly whatever you may bestow upon me. The purpose in my coming here is to ask leave to serve you faithfully." The widow of Girah replied, "Well then, my boy, let us sit together inside for awhile." Mpu Bahula and Calon Arang then sat together.

Mpu Bahula said, "I would like to humbly ask for your favor: that you take pity on me who have come with the desire to propose marriage with your daughter Ratna Manggalī. But perhaps I do not know yet what is in your heart. In regard to my origins, I am a young Brahmin student from Gangga Citra, the son of the great sage who is the lord of the Lĕmah Tulis hermitage. My name is Bahula. It was the great sage who ordered me to come here and ask for the hand of Ratna Manggalī in marriage." Calon Arang remained silent for a moment. Looking within her heart, she was overjoyed that she would have Mpu Bahula as her son-in-law and would moreover join with the family of the great sage as an in-law (*warang*). Her heart was happy indeed.

She then said, "How could I not be happy that you have asked for my daughter's hand, Mpu Bahula? And moreover that it is at the command of the great sage? But do not be unfaithful to Ratna Manggalī." Mpu Bahula replied, "How could it ever be that I would be unfaithful to Ratna Manggalī? There is also this letter of agreement. My royal master has said that whatever you may ask as the bride price he will have it brought to you." Calon Arang said, "Eh, my boy. The size of the bride price is not at all important to me. If you will just be true to your promise whatever payment you offer will be enough." This is what the young Mpu offered: betel quid as a sign of the betrothal, silver for the new household, a precious shawl, and shining jewels of the nine types. Calon Arang then accepted the gifts of Mpu Bahula. It would take quite some time to describe everything. We will not speak of what happened in the evening and night. Ratna Manggalī and Mpu Bahula were sent off together to experience the pleasures of mutual affection, of becoming the deities of the evening and night. We will speak no further of Mpu Bahula.

We will speak now of Calon Arang. When evening was approaching, she would take her book of sacred formulas in hand and depart immediately for the cremation grounds, returning only in the middle of the night. And she did this every night. Mpu Bahula then said to Ratna Manggalī, "My beloved younger sister, what is it that makes your mother go out in the middle of the night?[10] It concerns me, sister. Live or die, I want to follow her and find out what she does. Tell me truly, dear sister, what it is that she does, for I am truly concerned." Ratna Manggalī then said, "My dear older brother, I will tell you the entire truth, but you must not follow her ways, brother, for mother goes to the cremation grounds to practice black magic (*tĕluh*), and it will bring about the destruction of the realm. That is why so many people have died, and there are corpses piling up in the fields and the cemetery. That is what mother intends." Mpu Bahula said to his wife, "My precious beloved, the very life within my heart, most precious jewel of the realm, I would like to be entrusted to know what is written in your mother's book. I would like to take the book she carries into my own hand." Then, when Calon Arang had gone out again, Ratna Manggalī gave the book Rangda takes with her to the cremation grounds to Mpu Bahula. Mpu Bahula read the book, then asked leave of Ratna Manggalī to show the book to the great sage. Ratna Manggalī agreed, and Mpu Bahula then went quickly to Buh Citra. We will not describe his passage along the way.

Quickly he arrived in the hermitage in the cremation grounds there. He went straightaway to the pavilion, where he found the great sage being attended upon by his students. Suddenly Mpu Bahula burst in, carrying the sacred book. Mpu Bahula made a bow of reverence at the feet of the gentle sage, then took dust from the feet of that Lord of Yogis and placed it on the crown of his head. The heart of the sage was gladdened at the arrival of his student. He said, "Oṃ. Oṃ. My child Bahula has arrived carrying a book for me. Is that possibly the book belonging to Calon Arang?" Mpu Bahula replied that it was indeed the book of Calon Arang. Immediately the sage took the book in his hand. The aim of the book was the achievement of the highest good, the way that is most suitable and proper to achieve spiritual power, the epitome of religious teachings. Such were the contents of the book. But this is not how it was put to use by Calon Arang, who used it for the left-hand path of black magic, to bring harm to the world. The great sage said to Mpu Bahula, "Go back to Girah as fast as you can. Take the sacred book with you and have Ratna Manggalī store it safely away. I will follow you there after some time. I will come by way of the villages that have been struck by the plague and the cremation ground at the edge of the great field. You go ahead first." Without hesitation Mpu Bahula took his leave, making the *añjali* gesture with his hands and taking the blessing of the dust of the sage's feet.[11] Then he set out.

We will not speak of what happened along the way. He arrived quickly in Girah and told Ratna Manggalī to put her mother's book back in its place. We will not describe what Mpu Bahula and Ratna Manggalī did as they passed the night in mutual affection. Calon Arang was pleased at heart, her love growing ever greater for her son-in-law. She brought them gifts all the following day and never failed to ask after their well-being.

We will speak now of the sage in Lĕmah Tulis. On the following day, the excellent sage Baradah set out from his hermitage, accompanied by three of his students. They moved along swiftly, but we will not describe their journey. Quickly they arrived at a village that had been decimated by the plague, the road deserted and overgrown with thick grass. They came upon a man about to put the torch to a corpse. The Lord of Yogis felt pity for the widow, who had thrown herself upon the corpse, wailing from grief. The corpse had been wrapped in a white cloth. The sage said, "I feel great pity for you, as you cry out in grief and cradle the corpse of your husband. Please open the shroud so that I can see your husband." When it had been opened once, the husband's heart beat. When opened twice, he began to breathe. In roughly the time it takes to twice take betel quid, the man who had died sat up, thanks to the hand of the sage of great peace.[12] The one who had died now addressed the sage, saying, "I am forever in your debt. There is no way I will ever be able to offer repayment at your feet." The sage replied, "There is no need for words like that. Let it be. Either stay here or return to your own home. I will continue on my way."

The sage continued on his way. Now he came upon three corpses in a row. Two of them were still intact, while the third had already started to decompose. He sprinkled them with holy water, the most pure Ganges water (*gangga tirta*).[13] Even the one whose corpse had rotted came back to the life he had had in the past.

The sage went on quickly, arriving now at the empty yard of a house, its front courtyard empty and overgrown with thick grass. He went inside the house and found the inhabitants all sick, with one already dead. The neighbors on all sides were also sick. One of them was continuously moaning in pain, while nothing was left of another but her breathing. The Lord of Yogis sprinkled them both with holy water. When they both came to life, they praised the sage with sacred hymns and words of homage, then kissed the dust at his feet. Baradah ordered his two students to return to Lĕmah Tulis, which had been left empty. They did so, but we will not describe what happened along the way.[14]

The sage now set out in the southwest direction, the way taking him past the cremation ground at the edge of the great field—its grasses tall, mixed with trees, great ferns, and giant purple milkweed. Jackals howled as they feasted on corpses they found among the clumps of giant ferns. Crows kept up a din from the trees. When the great sage arrived there, the jackals stopped howling and the crows fell silent. Wherever the sage turned, those who were sick were healed and those who had died came back to life as soon as they saw the sage standing there in the cremation grounds. There was a woman who was crying as she ran hither and yon without any idea of what she was doing. When the sage appeared before her eyes, she approached him and offered praises at his feet. The gentle one then said, "I humbly ask for pity at the feet of the great sage. I wish to follow after my husband.[15] My heart grieves for him. I beg for mercy at your feet. Please grant me the power I need to follow after my husband. I beg this at the dust of your feet." The Lord of Yogis replied, "I am not able to do that at this point. If your husband's remains had not yet decomposed it might be that you could meet with him again. But once his remains decayed it would no longer be possible to meet him in this life. Rather, you will meet him again in death. I will point out the way to heaven that is open to you, and that has opened to your husband. Here is the instrument you will need. Do not refuse; go ahead and take it. And here is my word to you, remember it well: you will find your husband." The woman bowed low as she heard the words of the great sage.

We will speak no more of the woman, who was now free to depart. We will speak instead of the great sage, who now arrived quickly in the center of the cremation grounds. There he came upon Si Wĕkśirṣa along with Mahiṣawadana, the students learning magic from Calon Arang. When they saw the Lord of Life arrive, Si Wĕkśirṣa and Mahiṣawadana approached him reverently, offering praise at his feet.

The great sage Baradah now said, "Hey, where are you two going, having offered a bow of reverence in the middle of this cremation ground? Where do you come from, and what are your names? Since I know not, please enlighten me." Si Wĕkśirṣa and Mahiṣawadana replied, "We are Si Wĕkśirṣa and Mahiṣawadana who have come to make a bow of homage at your feet. We are students who bow at the feet of our mistress, the reverend widow of Girah. We have come to beg you to purify us, releasing us from the stain of our sins." The Lord of Yogis immediately replied, "I will not be able to release you until I have done so for Calon Arang. Go now to Calon Arang and inform her that I have arrived here. I wish to meet and speak with the one who is my in-law." Si Wĕkśirṣa and Mahiṣawadana now took their leave, and the two of them then set out.

We will speak now of Calon Arang, who was just then completing her prayers and offerings in the shrine of the cremation ground. She had just completed attending on the goddess Bhagawatī (Durgā). In her communication with the widow from Girah, the goddess had instructed her, saying, "Do not be careless, for I sense death approaching." Thus spoke the goddess, and this disturbed Calon Arang. She fell silent, dumbfounded as she thought about what the goddess had said. In a moment, Si Wĕkśirṣa and Mahiṣawadana arrived together. The first thing they did was to tell Calon Arang that Baradah, Lord of Yogis, had arrived. Calon Arang said, "Aha, so you are saying that my in-law Baradah has come here. Let me prepare then to receive him with honor." Calon Arang set out in a flash. When she arrived before the great ascetic, the widow Rangda of Girah greeted him, the Lord of Life.

She said, "I am your humble servant, and I feel fortunate that you, a great sage who is my honored in-law, has come here. It is my great pleasure that you, a sage without attachments to things of this world, have come. I wish to be instructed in the true spiritual way." The lord of sages replied, "Ah, sister-in-law, your words and what you desire are most fitting. So then, I will instruct you in proper conduct. But do not become angry, sister-in-law. I will instruct you first. Because you have killed many people using black magic, you have brought pollution upon the world, causing pain and suffering and killing people everywhere. How great is the calamity you have brought upon the world, with so many people falling ill! The misfortune you have caused is excessive, bringing death to the entire land. There is no way you can be purified except by way of death. And even then, since you know nothing of the coming in and going out of the way of release, how could you ever be purified?" Calon Arang said, "What you mean is that the punishment for my sins in this world will be great. If that is the case, then please purify me, O sage of noble nature;

show me the affection due a sister-in-law." The lord of sages replied, "I cannot now release you from sin." Calon Arang now replied, her face flushed red with fury at being refused by the great sage. "That was my intention in becoming your in-law, that you would release me from the stain of my sins. But you are averse to purifying me. So be it. I am willing to pay the final price for my sins and to face any obstacle. That is why I will cast a spell on you." Calon Arang then danced, tossing her matted locks, her eyes whirling as she cast piercing glances in all directions, like a tiger intent upon pouncing on her human prey. She pointed with sharply extended fingers at the sage. "You will now die at my hands, Baradah, Lord of Yogis. It appears that you do not know the meaning of being a true in-law. Watch as I cast a spell on this great banyan tree. Watch closely, Baradah."

In a flash, that great banyan tree was utterly destroyed down to its roots by the evil eye of Calon Arang. The great sage replied without hesitating, "Go ahead then, sister-in-law, bring on your most powerful magic, how could it be that it would surprise me?" Now Calon Arang redoubled her efforts. Now fire emerged from her that flared up, blazing and spreading in all directions, like a great thunderclap that engulfs a forest and incinerates all the trees. Fire emerged from her eyes, nose, ears, and tongue, flaring out and licking at the body of the holy sage. But the sage was unperturbed, and continued to hold fast to the life of this world. The holy man now said, "Your witchcraft has failed to kill me, oh sister-in-law. Now I will sweep away your life. May it be that you die now, there where you stand." After saying this he made a quick movement with his hands, and in a moment, Calon Arang had passed into the beyond, right where she stood.

Now the sage Baradah thought in his heart, "Oh dear, I have not yet given instruction to my sister-in-law on the way of liberation. May it be that you return to life, O sister-in-law." At that very moment Calon Arang came back to life. Then, angry and offended, she reviled the sage. "I was already on the other shore. How could it be that you would bring me back to life?" The king of sages remained calm and said, "Eh, dear sister-in-law, the reason that I brought you back to life is that I failed earlier to inform you of the way to liberation, to point out the path to heaven, and to ensure that you are released from the obstruction of your sins. And I failed to teach you the pinnacle of religious instruction." Calon Arang said, "My, my, my! So that's how it is. How fortunate I am that you have shown compassion for me, that you, Lord of Yogis, will release me from my sins. I bow low now to the dust of your feet, you who have slowly come round to granting me purification." Calon Arang then immediately made a gesture of supplication at the feet of the sage. It was then that she was instructed in the path of liberation, shown the way that leads to heaven, and especially given instruction in the in-breath and out-breath of the world.[16]

After she had been instructed in the process of dying by the Lord of Yogis, Calon Arang became happy and free from care, tranquil and established in transcendent knowledge. No longer inclined toward her past evil ways, she focused all her attention on the teaching of the great sage. It was then that Calon Arang took her leave, first offering praises at the feet of the eminent soul. The great sage then said, "Go then, sister-in-law, may you be released and return to your own true form." With that, Calon Arang disappeared into the beyond. Her purification truly complete, she merged now with the unseen. The Lord of Life now cremated the body of Rangda. Now it had dissolved, turned completely to ash. We will speak no more of it.

Now Wĕkśirṣa and Mahiṣawadana begged to be accepted as students of the sage. What was the reason for their request? It was because they were not empowered to join in being purified along with Rangda of Girah. The two of them were accepted as ascetics by the great sage. We will speak no more of them, nor of Calon Arang. The Lord of Life set out now, aiming to reach Girah, to look in on Mpu Bahula and to tell him that Calon Arang had crossed to the other shore. The sage quickly arrived in Girah and went to the sanctuary of the ancestors. So it happened that someone went to Mpu Bahula to inform him that the lord of sages had arrived. Without hesitating Mpu Bahula went to offer his respects and service to the great sage, bowing low and requesting favor at his feet. He took the dust from the feet of the sage, putting some on his tongue as the source of life itself and placing some on the crown of his head. The Lord of Yogis said, "Eh, Mpu Bahula I have come to inform you that my sister-in-law Calon Arang has died, merging with the beyond after I completed her purification. This is what I ask of you now: go to the royal city and inform the lord king that Calon Arang has died.

"Si Wĕkśirṣa and Mahiṣawadana have begged to be accepted as my disciples and have both become my followers. Please inform the king that I am here." Mpu Bahula immediately offered homage and praise to the great sage, then set out for the royal city. We will not describe what happened along the way. He quickly arrived at the palace and came upon the king sitting in audience in his court, sitting calmly as he was attended upon by all his foremost ministers of state, the prime minister, Amangkubumi, and all the holy men of the Rĕsi, Siwa, and Brāhmana orders.

THE GODDESS IN CONTEXT: DURGĀ IN THE CULTURAL IMAGINATION OF BALI

The Calon Arang tale translated here dates to the sixteenth-century Balinese court in Gelgel, which liberally supported the literary, performing, and visual arts that live on in the traditional performing arts of Bali. While in this tale Rangda is portrayed as a human actor who derives her strength from her study of black magic and her devotion to the goddess Durgā, in later developments of the story she comes to be understood as divine. In a confrontation that many scholars see as basic to the Balinese understanding of the doctrine of *rwa bhineda*, "unity in duality," the mask of Rangda is paired with the mask and costume of a colorful "Chinese lion" called Barong. Since this confrontation can never lead to victory for either Rangda or Barong—both representing equally powerful spiritual forces—Rangda has come to be considered sacred and immortal and, in many eyes, identical with the goddess Durgā herself. This association is strengthened by the commonly held idea that Barong represents the god Śiva, the peaceful side of the divine order, ever in contrast and struggle with the wrathful and destructive Rangda, who can be periodically purified but never fully overcome. The following sections track the development of this tradition from its roots in the *Sudamala* and *Calon Arang* narratives to its contemporary performative traditions.

Seed: Ra Nini, the "Divine Grandmother" of the Kidung Sudamala

In order to understand the evolution of the figure of Rangda, we need to look first to an earlier literary work from the *kidung* genre, called the *Sudamala*.[17] The word *sudamala* ultimately goes back to Sanskrit *śuddha-mala*, "purified stain." This story played a unique role in fourteenth-century Java and continues to live on in the shadow plays (*wayang*) of Java and Bali, where the *Sudamala* story is central to the exorcistic plays performed to release a family from impurity arising from the birth of twins. In this tale, the god Śiva learns that his wife Umā has committed adultery with the creator god, Brahma, "sharing with him her betel quid." Śiva then curses Umā to take on a demonic form as Durgā and reside in an earthly cremation ground for a period of twelve years, until a twin will arrive who is entitled to perform an exorcism, returning her to her auspicious state. While the *kidung* version of this tale is no longer popular in Bali, it lives on in the popular imagination of Java and Bali in the form of shadow plays based on the story. These *Sudamala* shadow plays are still performed as part of exorcistic rituals of purification (Jav.: *ruwat*; Bal.: *lukat*).

This tale had a special meaning for the two royal court centers of East Java. In the *Calon Arang* story translated here, its influence is apparent in the location of the hermitage of the sage Mpu Baradah at *Lĕmah Tulis*, a name that means "the field of writing." This refers to the legend that Mpu Baradah magically divided the East Javanese realm into two parts at the order of Erlangga, who is known to have abdicated in favor of his two sons upon retiring to the life of a forest mendicant. Erlangga's noble act had the unintended consequence of continuing tensions between the "eastern" and "western" courts of Janggala/Kahuripan and Daha/Kaḍiri. The two polities were reunited in the mid-thirteenth century by Wishnuwarddhana, but intense rivalries reappeared in the later fourteenth century, leading to the Parĕgrĕg war of 1304–1306. The fact that the *Sudamala* tale is copiously illustrated in temple reliefs of Candi Tigawangi, located not far from the royal center of the "western court" of Kaḍiri, during the years leading up to the Parĕgrĕg war shows us that the tensions between the two courts were very much on the minds of the East Javanese nobility. The *Sudamala* tale in this context can be read as a guide to the "healing" of the divided kingdom through the intervention of a twin nobleman with divine ancestry, guided by an enlightened sage.

The *Sudamala* tale relates the story of Śiva's cursing his auspicious wife Umā to take on a demonic form as Durgā for twelve years before she is eventually restored to her auspicious state by Śiva, who in the East Javanese period was known as Batara Guru, "the divine guru." The potential sacrifice of the twin Sadewa by Kuntī, his own mother, strongly suggests that the tale grew out of the continuing anxieties that plagued the East Javanese polity after Erlangga's division of the realm.[18] A summary of the tale can tell us much about these anxieties and the importance in East Javanese religious practices of exorcisms carried out by the god Śiva or by his representatives among the high priests (*empu*) of the East Javanese form of Hinduism focused on the god Śiva.

Summary of Batara Guru and Umā in the *Kidung Sudamala*

The three great deities Sang Hyang Tunggal, Sang Hyang Asihprana, and Sang Hyang Wisesa once gathered together in the dwelling place of Batara Guru, the Supreme Deity. They were discussing the misdeed of Śrī Umā, wife of Batara Guru, whom they heard had "shared her betel-nut quid and face-powder" with Sang Hyang Brahma—that is, she had committed adultery with Lord Brahma. Batara Guru was furious upon hearing that news and so cursed Umā to become Durgā, a terrifying demoness. Umā then transformed into a demonic figure with long, disheveled hair: her eyes were like twin suns, her mouth was like a cavern with protruding fangs, her two nostrils were like the holes of twin wells, and her entire skin was covered with spots and blemishes. In that form she was called Ra Nini and was sentenced to reside in a cremation ground called Setra Gandamayu. She had to dwell in that cemetery for twelve years together with her followers until the time came when Batara Guru himself would exorcize her with the assistance of Sadewa, one of the twin sons of Pāṇḍu and Mādrī, and half brother to Yudhiṣṭhira, Arjuna, and Bhīma of the five Pāṇḍawa brothers, famous from the *Mahābhārata* epic.

It is said that at the time, there were also two celestial beings named Citrāṅgada and Citrasena, who committed the misdeed of flying above the head of Batara Guru while he was with Umā in their bathing place. They, too, were cursed by Batara Guru to become twin demons, named Kālañjaya and Kālāntaka, and were sentenced to serve the Korava, the evil cousins of the five Pāṇḍawa brothers, for a period of twelve years, identical to the period of Umā's punishment to take the form of Ra Nini. They are said to reside with Ra Nini in the Setra Gandamayu cremation grounds.

Kuntī, the mother of the Pāṇḍawa brothers, heard the news about those two powerful demons and grew worried about the safety of her sons. Without the knowledge or permission of her sons, Kuntī planned to pay homage to Ra Nini at her shrine in the cremation ground of Setra Gandamayu. She entered the cremation grounds and worshiped Durgā or Ra Nini. The terrible goddess Durgā then appeared to Kuntī, who implored her to help her sons destroy those two demons. But Durgā refused Kuntī's request because those two demons were none other than Ra Nini's own sons.

However, Ra Nini said that she would fulfill Kuntī's desire if she were willing to offer her the sacrifice of a "red-goat," or in other words, a human being. She specifically asked that the victim be Sadewa because Sadewa was a "hot person" who jeopardized every person who was close to him, because he was the second born of a pair of twins. At first, Kuntī refused Ra Nini's request because Sadewa was not her biological son, and instead she offered her own sons, Yudhiṣṭhira, Bhīma, and Arjuna, as a sacrifice to Ra Nini. But then Kālikā, a loyal disciple of Ra Nini, "entered" Kuntī (possessed her), and so she immediately came under Ra Nini's power and went home to bring Sadewa back as a sacrificial victim.

When they arrived at the Setra Gandamayu, Kuntī tied Sadewa to a *randu* tree, a large, tall tree with flowers that are red as blood and commonly found near cemeteries or cremation grounds. Sadewa was assaulted and tempted by many types of ghosts and demons of the cremation ground. When Ra Nini/Durgā saw Sadewa, she was ecstatic and immediately tried to eat him but found she could not do so. Then Ra Nini/Durgā took out her long sword and tried to kill Sadewa, but still in vain. Ra Nini/Durgā could not consume Sadewa because Batara Guru had given him the power to be invulnerable. Durgā then asked Sadewa to exorcize her, so that she could return to her form as Umā, but Sadewa refused, explaining that he lacked the ability to do so. Then Batara Guru entered Sadewa's body in order to exorcize Durgā. After being exorcized by Batara Guru through Sadewa, Ra Nini/Durgā turned back into the gentle and auspicious goddess Umā. To show her appreciation to Sadewa, Durgā/Umā blessed him in two ways. First, she gave him the name "Sudamala," which means "purified or released (*suda, śuddha*) from sin or stain (*mala*)." Second, she advised Sadewa to go to a hermitage in Pĕrangalas to propose marriage to the daughter of the sage Tambrapetra. Sadewa and his twin brother Nakula then journeyed to Pĕrangalas and wed the two daughters of Tambrapetra. Nakula and Sadewa then waged war on the twin demons Kālañjaya and Kālāntaka, killing them both and so ensuring their final release from the curse of Batara Guru and allowing them to assume their original form as two celestial beings.

The *Sudamala* in Context

The idea that the role of Sadewa in the *Sudamala* tale can be linked to anxieties around Erlangga's division of the East Javanese polity has been proposed by the Balinese scholar and coauthor of this chapter, Ni Wayan Ariati, in a work (2016) on transformations of images of Durgā in Java and Bali. In the same work, she proposes that the twelve-year period of the curse of Umā—her taking on a demonic form as Durgā and being forced to live in the Setra Gandamayu cremation grounds—can be linked to the period of twelve years between the death of a member of the high nobility of East Java, that person's funerary rites, and his or her apotheosis as the cult image of his or her mortuary shrine. She particularly notes the possibility that the tale may have a specific link to the funerary rites of the powerful queen mother, Rājapatnī, whose apotheosis as Prajñāpāramitā, the Buddhist goddess of wisdom, in 1365 CE is recounted in detail in *The Description of the Countryside* (*Deśawarṇana*) of Mpu Prapañca.

As discussed in the next section, there are crucial links between the *Sudamala* legend and the *Calon Arang* tale: both accentuate the role of Durgā as the patron of dark forces; both feature the cremation grounds as the natural habitat of these dark forces; and both feature an exorcism/purification, either by Śiva or by a high priest who represents or embodies him in the human world.

Flower: The Calon Arang *Tale, Right-Hand and Left-Hand Magic, and the Path to Salvation*

In the further development of the themes first explored in the *Kidung Sudamala*, the place of Ra Nini has been taken over by Rangda, a human practitioner of black magic who battles the sage Baradah in a contest of magical power that eventually leads to her release from the painful cycle of human existence. In the *Kidung Sudamala*, it is Batara Guru, the divine guru himself, who effects the exorcism of Durgā/Umā. However, in the later part of that story, the sage Mpu Tambrapetra plays the central role of guiding the twins, Sadewa and Nakula, into their marriages and the unification of the country. The religious figures of East Java called *empu*, or *mpu* appear to prefigure the "high priests," or *pedanda*, of Bali. As in the case of the *pedanda*, an *empu* could be affiliated with either a Buddhist or Śaiva stream of the East Javanese religion, yet still play identical roles in ritual and guidance of the community. The practice of both streams during this period was Tantric, with an emphasis on the rituals invoking the presence of the deity in the body and consciousness of the officiating priest. It is in this context that the supreme deity is identified in the *Kidung Sudamala* as Batara Guru, the divine counterpart of his representatives in the ritual system of the East Javanese and Balinese realms.

The earliest of the literary works based on the *Calon Arang* tale is the prose version written in the Middle Javanese language in sixteenth-century Gelgel, during a time when Balinese authors of the courts and priestly households were especially active in composing works in the Middle Javanese language, or Kawi, as it is known in Bali. The political tensions that had marked the history of the eastern and western courts of East Java were no longer prominent when the Balinese court of Gelgel built a unified polity during the rule of Watu Renggong and his spiritual adviser, the famed priest and author Dang Hyang

Nirartha. Even so, the legend of Mpu Baradah's division of the realm at his hermitage in Lĕmah Tulis remained prominent in Balinese eyes. This is because the same legend tells of Mpu Baradah's journey to Bali with the intention of installing one of Erlangga's sons as king of Bali. However, upon meeting the Balinese sage Mpu Kuturan and learning that he intended to coronate his grandson as king, Mpu Baradah was forced to turn back and to divide East Java among the two contending sons of Erlangga. This legend was important enough that the composer of the prose *Calon Arang* makes it the focus of the second part of his narrative, not translated here, which takes place after the confrontation of Mpu Baradah and Calon Arang, the widow from Girah.

The first half of the prose *Calon Arang* focuses on the battle between Mpu Baradah and Calon Arang. This can be read as a struggle between the life-giving forces of right-hand and left-hand magic (*panĕngĕn* and *pangiwa*). Of crucial note here is the fact that Mpu Baradah establishes his hermitage in a cremation ground, which for Calon Arang is the natural habitat of her magical dances aimed at bringing pestilence and death to the realm. A full seven leaves of the prose text, abridged in this translation, are given over to an elaborate explanation of Mpu Baradah's choice of a cremation ground for his hermitage: after the death of his first wife, Baradah's daughter Wedawatī flees twice to the cremation ground to be near the spirit of her mother and to assuage her grief over the loss of her mother and her own mistreatment at the hands of her stepmother. But this literary device masks a more important underlying similarity: the practices and texts of the path of spiritual release were Tantric in character, concerned with methods for overcoming the finality of death that often used the imagery of skulls and the cremation ground. Mpu Baradah's choice of a cremation ground for his hermitage can thus be read as a sign of his having qualified for higher levels of Tantric practice and thus the ability to remain tranquil even in the face of death.

When Mpu Baradah, with the help of Bahula and Ratna Manggalī, succeeds in reading the book of Calon Arang, he sees that it is no different from any other work of the Tutur tradition of Javano-Balinese metaphysical texts, but it is used by Calon Arang with evil intent rather than to provide a means for release from the painful cycle of existence. The benevolent aspect of Mpu Baradah's teaching in the prose *Calon Arang* is further underscored by the union of Baradah's son and pupil, Mpu Bahula, with Ratna Manggalī. This brings Baradah and Calon Arang into the relationship of in-laws, or *warang* (Ind.: *besan*). Marriages in premodern Java and Bali were just as much about uniting two lineages through the parents as about bringing together the bride and groom. Both Calon Arang and Mpu Baradah call attention to this important bond, which is ultimately Baradah's basis for bringing Calon Arang back from death and bestowing on her the secret of achieving spiritual liberation at the moment of death, one of the central practices taught in the Tutur literature.

If read in historical context, the prose *Calon Arang* appears to be a defense and glorification of the role of the Śaiva and Buddhist high priests of Bali, who in the personage of Mpu Baradah are portrayed with the greatest respect for their high spiritual status and magical power, even over life and death. This is contrasted with representations of ritual dancing and music that go back to Tantric roots but have been demonized through the portrayal of Calon Arang and her students. What may once have been ecstatic rituals aimed at invoking the presence of the goddess are portrayed in the prose *Calon Arang* as performances aimed at inviting the presence of demonic forces, then controlling them as harbingers of pestilence and death. This chapter does not attempt to offer an explanation of how female practitioners of Tantrism came to be identified with witchcraft and black magic, except to say that these may have to do with continuing anxieties around widows and mothers without sons in the patriarchal structure of Balinese society. These anxieties appear in the *Kidung Sudamala* in the queen mother's seeming willingness to sacrifice her own son for the sake of the safety of the realm, while in the prose *Calon Arang*, they are explicitly attached to a widow, Rangda of Girah.

Fruit: Barong-Rangda and the Further History of Rangda in the Balinese Performing and Ritual Arts

The final transformation of Rangda into a divine figure commonly associated with the goddess Durgā may best be explained by considering the importance of masks in Balinese culture, in particular the masks of Rangda and the playful Chinese lion called Barong. These masks are sacred to the Pura Dalĕm, the temple located at the "southern" end of a town, separating the space of human habitation from the cemetery and cremation ground. Postmortem rituals aimed at converting the soul of the deceased from a "restless spirit" (*pirata*) to a protective ancestor (*pitara*) are associated with the Pura Dalĕm, associated in theological theory with *pralīna*, the stage of dissolution that follows upon creation (*utpatti*) and the continuity of life (*sthiti*).

As Balinese have become more attuned to contemporary Indian representations of deities and myths, the Pura Dalĕm and the mask of the Barong have come to be associated with Śiva. A long history of demonic images of Durgā from the visual arts and literature of East Java and Bali supports the popular identification of the mask of Rangda with Durgā. This is not a new association, for we can see in Rangda/Calon Arang a line of descent stretching back to Ra Nini, who is herself very likely an autochthonous female deity merged in the Hindu-Buddhist period with images of Umā and Durgā. The shift back and forth between auspicious and inauspicious aspects of the goddess that is evident in the *Kidung Sudamala* is less common in the Indian tradition. What we see in the dynamic confrontation of Rangda with her rivals rather parallels the cyclical nature of Javano-Balinese rituals that convert potentially malevolent "lower world" spirits (*bhuta-kāla*) into their auspicious, divine counterparts (*dewa*). The presence of a benign male figure representing priestly powers is crucial to this configuration. Played in literature and the visual arts by the religious figures known as *empu*, in the masks and performances of the Pura Dalĕm this role is played by the Barong.

While performances of the *Calon Arang* drama are still common in Bali, they rarely include an enactment of Baradah's division of the realm, or indeed a depiction of Baradah's killing and reviving Calon Arang in order to send her on the path of spiritual liberation. Instead, as in the Tĕktĕkan performances of Tabanan district, the play ends with an attack on Rangda by the armed followers of the Barong, who takes the place of Mpu Baradah in the drama at that point. Since Rangda is considered invulnerable even to divine attack, as the followers of the Barong charge with their *keris* blades stretched out before them, they are forced to retreat, while turning their blades upon themselves. In the case of yearly events of this type in Jimbaran and Kesiman, these dramatic displays trigger deep trances among many of the followers of the Barong. The mask of the Rangda is kept covered with a white cloth until it is time to take it off its stand and put it on the head of a specially trained dancer considered capable of "containing" the spirit of Rangda. In villages with a mask that is considered especially powerful (*tĕngĕt*), it is not uncommon to see members of the temple congregation falling into deep trance as soon as the white cloth is removed from the mask of Rangda.

Images of deities are not a focus of traditional Balinese Hindu practices. Their place is rather taken by the elaborate presentations of offerings that mark a religious ceremony, the shrines that serve as "seats" of the deities when they "visit" their temples, and masks. Like the empty "lotus seats" of Balinese temples, masks are considered receptacles for divine energies. As such, they serve as both symbols of metaphysical forces and artifacts that play important roles in ritual life. Masks of Barong and Rangda are among the most potent of these ritual artifacts, often triggering trance events that are said to return a village to an auspicious state after a time of tension. When the ancient confrontations of Batara Guru and his wife Umā, or of Mpu Baradah with Rangda/Calon Arang, merged with the tradition of the Barong and Rangda masks of the Pura Dalĕm, it completed a process that today has led to a common identification of Rangda as Durgā, rather than a witch seeking the blessing of Durgā. Well-read Balinese understand that this identification is incorrect, and that Rangda and Durgā are separate characters in the story. But the identification has a strong element of common sense supporting it: If Rangda is invulnerable to even divine attack, as she is in the performances, is she not also divine?

SOURCE

The tale of sorcery translated here takes up about 30–40 percent of the *Calon Arang*, whether in the original prose form or later versions in verse. The remainder, not translated here, concerns Erlangga's decision to abdicate and divide the kingdom between his two sons and the important role played by Mpu Baradah in (magically) dividing the realm into two parts, the "eastern realm" of Janggall/Kahurpian and the "western realm" of Daha/Kaḍiri. According to the date given at the end of the Middle Javanese text of Poerbatjaraka, the work was composed in 1462 Śaka (1540 CE).[19] It is thus a product of the Gelgel period in Balinese literary history. While the language is recognizable as within the range that falls under the rubric of Middle Javanese, it is quite distinct from the older language of works like the *Kidung Sudamala* or of prose works of the East Javanese tradition like the *Pararaton*, or *Tale of the Line of Kings*. The language of the prose *Calon Arang* has more in common with that of several later works in *gĕguritan*, or *Sĕkar Alit*, form that were produced in the two centuries following the composition of the prose text. Yet it retains discourse features found in the earlier Kakawin literature that served as the ultimate model for all later composition in traditional genres.

There is a great deal of variety among the works of the Middle Javanese tradition. Some of these variations may be tied to developments within the history of the language, while others may reflect local styles or even the idiolects of particular composers. A proper historical study surveying the various forms taken by Middle Javanese in metrical and prose works from roughly 1400 to 1900 CE should be a desideratum for the next generation of scholars working in the Javano-Balinese literary tradition.

The translation in this chapter is based on I Made Suastika's romanized edition (1997) of the prose *Calon Arang*. Suastika's text is based in turn on the manuscripts LOr 5387 and LOr 5279, two closely related manuscripts in the collection of the Library of Leiden University. These two manuscripts were earlier used by Poerbatjaraka in his edition of 1926, in addition to LOr 4562, which he describes as being written in "very well-formed Balinese letters." Although Poerbatjaraka did not provide details on the choices he made in selecting among variants in the composition of his edition, he appears to have taken the reading of LOr 4562 as his primary source.

FURTHER READING

Ariati, Ni Wayan Pasek. 2016. *The Journey of the Goddess Durga: India, Java, Bali*. Satapitaka Series no. 621. New Delhi: Aditya Prakashan.

Belo, Jane, ed. 1970. *Traditional Balinese Culture*. New York: Columbia University Press.

Geertz, Hildred. 1994. *Images of Power: Balinese Paintings Made for Gregory Bateson and Margaret Mead*. Honolulu: University of Hawaii Press.

Hobart, Angela. 2005. "Transformation and Aesthetics in Balinese Masked Performances: Rangda and Barong." In *Aesthetics in Performance: Formations of Symbolic Construction and Experience*, edited by Angela Hobart and Bruce Kapferer, 161–82. New York: Berghahn.

NOTES

The authors and editor thank Dr. Charles Li for his assistance with the Balinese script sample.

1. The short first paragraph summarizes folios 1–6a. The full translation commences thereafter, and other abridged sections are flagged in the notes. For a recent study that brings out the importance of Baradah's hermitage at Lĕmah Tulis, see Sidomulyo (2011, 123–42). Poerbatjaraka (1926, 1975) uses the spelling "Bharaḍah," which reflects the orthography of the original. However, it is more common in the literature on East Java to use the spelling "Bharāda," which is found in the fourteenth-century work *Description of the Country Side* (*Deśawarṇana*). See Robson, Wibisono, and Kurniasih (2002) and Zoetmulder (1982). We standardize to the more common spelling "Baradah" throughout.

2. The translation opts for the spelling "Calon Arang" for ease of reading. The original text uses the more archaic form *Calwanarang*.

3. The Javano-Balinese script makes no distinction between capital and lowercase letters, and spelling conventions vary. Thus, Śrī Bhagawatī is sometimes also transcribed as *sri bagawati*.

4. In the Javano-Balinese literary tradition, people frequently express humility toward those of higher status by addressing their feet or, even more humbly, "the dust of their feet." We also find metonymous references to oneself as "the head" (*ng-hulun*), which refers to the custom of bowing low at the feet of a respected elder, or even "tasting" the dust of the feet of an honored elder.

5. Balinese ideas about the sacredness of the head and torso relative to the abdomen and feet are very strong. If you put your foot above someone's head it is said you will be *tulah*—cursed to walk upside down in the next life. These ideas are so strong that there are no traditional Balinese dances that allow the movement of the feet above the torso or head. When Rangda or one of her students stands on her head, or even turns a garment upside down, this is uncanny, transgressive behavior that would only be resorted to by those involved in witchcraft or black magic.

6. A *tumpĕk* is the coincidence of a Saturday of the seven-day week with Kajeng of the Balinese three-day market week and Kliwon of the Javanese five-day market week, both days of power in traditional reckoning.

7. Cf. Tvaritā's story in the next chapter, in which *caru* or "rice pudding" has a similarly transgressive meaning.

8. This paragraph abridges folios 13a–14a5.

9. This paragraph abridges folios 14b7–15a9.

10. Mpu Bahula addresses his wife Ratna Manggalī as "sister," reflecting the cultural importance of the sibling bond in insular Southeast Asia. The older sibling is expected to look out for the welfare of the younger, and both prosper from the mutual affection of the relationship. The sibling bond then becomes the model for the ideal behavior of the couple in a marriage.

11. The *añjali* gesture is made by forming a cup with the two outstretched hands, as if to receive an offering of food, and respectfully raising it to the forehead.

12. Betel nut is a common stimulant used in South and Southeast Asia. The time indicated is perhaps twenty to thirty minutes.

13. Balinese religion was still called Agama Tirta, the religion of holy water, in the early twentieth century. One of the most important daily ritual acts of a Balinese "high priest" (*pedanda*) involves consecrating spring water so that it becomes holy water, which is still known as *tirta* in Bali. In the ritual process the great rivers of India are invoked through mantras, especially the Gangga, or Ganges River.

14. The previous two sentences abridge lines 20b4–9.

15. It is not entirely clear whether the woman is asking to follow her husband in his death or for Baradah to bring him back to life so that she can follow him in this life. Baradah's reply makes plain that he understood the request in the latter sense. This is

consistent with Balinese beliefs about the inseparability of the body (*raga*) and its motivating force (*urip, jiwa, atma*) so long as it is in this world.

16. The "in-breath and out-breath" of the world refers to one of the basic tenets of the metaphysical Tutur literature of Bali: a path for achieving spiritual liberation (*mokṣa*) at the moment of death is developed around yogic control of the inhalation and exhalation. The internal process of controlling the breath (called *prāṇāyāma* in the Indian tradition) is then likened to cycles of creation and dissolution in the physical world. It is based on the Balinese idea of the equivalence of the "inner" world (*buwana alit*) and the "outer" world (*buwana agung*).

17. For a detailed study of the *Sudamala* in Dutch, see Stein Callenfels (1925).

18. Sadewa is the Javano-Balinese spelling for the Sanskrit Sahadeva. Many characters in this tale derive from the *Mahābhārata* epic.

19. Poerbatjaraka (1926, 45).

FIGURE 19. Tvaritā, by Laura Santi

CHAPTER 10

Tvaritā

The Swift Goddess

MICHAEL SLOUBER

The Tantric tale told in this chapter is known to survive only in manuscripts from the Kathmandu Valley of Nepal, where the moderate climate has helped ancient libraries preserve copies of many rare texts. As discussed in the essay, Tvaritā does not appear to be native to Nepal; we have good reason to believe she was brought there from the Deccan plateau region of India between the eleventh and twelfth centuries and later adapted as Nepal's celebrated royal goddess, Taleju Bhavānī. Fragmentary manuscripts that include Tvaritā's mantras and rituals, but not the narrative, are widely represented in Indian archives. Several active temples in the central Indian state of Maharashtra are dedicated to her, although their icons now depict her as Durgā in the act of slaying the buffalo demon, an episode that plays no part in the ancient lore presented here.

The source selected for translation is the first chapter of *Tvaritā's Basic Teaching* (*Tvaritāmūlasūtra*), a Tantra in hybrid Sanskrit whose earliest surviving manuscript dates to the late twelfth century. It declares itself an abridged version of the forgotten classic, the *Troṭala Tantra*. The *Troṭala* itself is a lost member of the so-called Poison Tantras or Gāruḍa Tantras, named after the divine bird and archenemy of snakes, Garuḍa. A conversation between Śiva and Tārkṣya, another name of Garuḍa, frames the present narrative.

The Gāruḍa Tantras as a whole are a branch of Tantric medicine concerned with rituals and herbal antidotes for treating snakebite. The current text, however, makes only passing reference to healing snakebite. Rather, it tells the story of Tvaritā's origin as a goddess generated by Pārvatī in an outburst of anger at Śiva's participation in a secretive ritual with other goddesses. Tvaritā goes on to become a goddess on whom Tantric sorcerers can call at a moment's notice for effecting various supernatural interventions in mundane life. Readers should watch for the themes of divine anger and pacification, neglect, and the satisfaction that comes from adulation. Consider, too, how the story constructs the origin, management, and application of the power behind Tantric sorcery, and how it advertises this power to potential royal patrons.

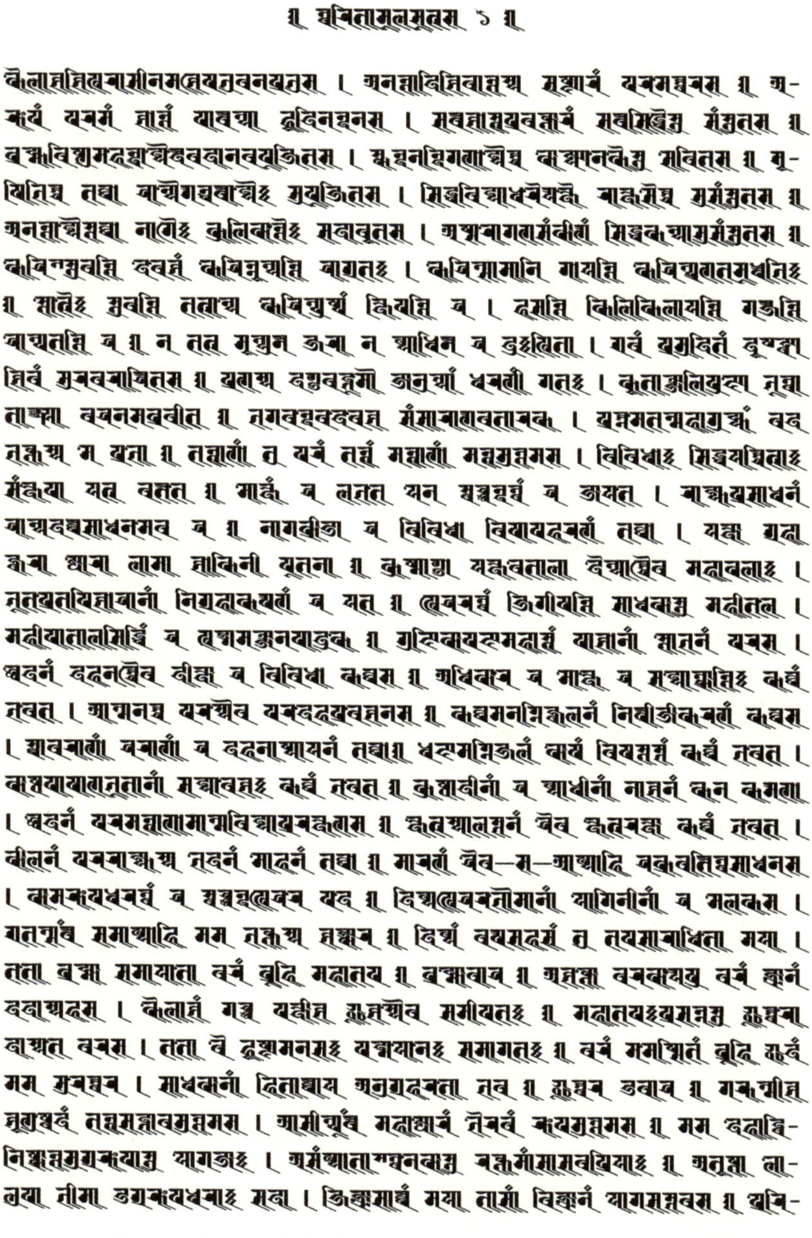

FIGURE 20. *Tvaritāmūlasūtra,* a hybrid Sanskrit work in the Ranjana script. Font "Ranjana Unicode 2.0" © Saneer Karmacharya.

THE STORY OF TVARITĀ'S CREATION

All the perfected beings praised the supreme Lord seated atop Mt. Kailash's peak. Master of all the worlds, he is the creator of the universe from bottom to top. He is formless and supremely calm, a delight to the heart of the mountain's daughter, Pārvatī. As the original teacher of all knowledge systems, all the perfected beings honored him, as did the gods—Brahmā, Viṣṇu, and Indra the great, to mention a few—and the demonic descendants of Danu. Many tens of millions of servants waited upon him, including Skanda, Nandi, and the rest. In the same way, the ancient seers honored him fully, as did many others—celestial singers and the like. Perfected sorcerers, *yakṣa* demigods, and demons all praised him highly. He is always surrounded by the eight divine serpents headed by Ananta and ending with the one named Kulika. Crowds of celestial women flanked him, and perfected girls thoroughly honored him. Some praised the Lord of the gods, some danced before him, some sang religious songs, and some respectfully bowed their heads. Others lauded him there with tributary poems, while some threw flowers toward him, laughed, shouted with joy, whooped, and jumped. As a result of all this, there was no death there, nor aging, nor disease, nor suffering.

Seeing that Śiva was in a good mood from all of this praise by the best of gods, the divine eagle Tārkṣya fully prostrated on the ground, then kneeled and joined his palms in reverence and addressed these words to him: "My lord, you are supreme over the highest gods! You ferry all beings across the ocean of existence! O lord, please explain to me, your devotee, this very secret matter: I want to know the highest teaching among all the Tantras, the highest mantra among mantras, and about the various wonderful powers, if it is possible to explain briefly. Please tell me how to attain autonomy, so that one is released from the cycle of suffering. And also, please tell me how to acquire a kingdom and procure wealth. Please teach me the various snake charming powers and the removal of poison. And teach me how to attract and subjugate *yakṣa* nature spirits, aggressive spirits, fierce fever demons, lusty *lāmā* temptresses, vampire-like *śākinīs*, foul-smelling *pūtanā* demons, demonic *kuṣmāṇḍas*, dryads, vampires, mighty descendants of Diti, spirits, ghosts, and flesh-eating demons.[1] Tell me about Tantric initiates on earth who seek to become skywalkers, and the power to travel anywhere on earth or in the underworlds, and about magical swords, ointments, and sandals. I also want to know about magical pills, cloths, and weapons, and about the excellent ability to disable spiritual traps.

Please tell me about rites to effect cutting and burning, and how the various types of Tantric initiation work. How can one immediately leave the body at will, or at the time of spiritual liberation? And how does it work to enter another's body for one's own sake or to help someone else? How can one attain the power of not being burnt by fire, rendering impotent, and purifying and strengthening plants and animals? How can one render immobile a scale, fire, water, treasure, or poison? And how to instantly possess living beings, or wood, or a stone? By what ritual can one destroy diseases like leprosy and its ilk? How can one intercept the mantras of an enemy, and protect one's own spells? How can one use mantras to take possession of land and to protect it? How to magically restrain a hostile kingdom, and sow dissension and confusion there? And please tell the techniques for murdering with mantras, for achieving the status of an emperor, for shapeshifting while flying about at will, and for consorting with divine, sky-faring, and earthly *yoginīs*. Tell all of that to me, your devotee, O Śiva.

"For a thousand divine years I propitiated Brahmā with severe austerities. Then he approached and said, 'Name your boon great ascetic!' Following my request, Brahmā said, 'I am unable to give these types of boons, but I will give a boon of knowledge: go to Kailash, O lord of birds, to the presence of Lord Śiva himself. Śiva will be pleased with your great austerities and will grant the boon.' Then indeed, overjoyed, I took leave of lotus-born Brahmā. You said, 'Tell me the boon you desire.' This is it, O Lord of the gods. For the sake of Tantric power-seekers, please be gracious!"

The Lord said, "Lord of birds, listen to this: it is the highest essence of the Tantras! Once upon a time, I issued forth from my body a very horrible, unrivaled form of myself known as Bhairava. From his esoteric practices (yoga) fierce-looking *yoginīs* came into being. They were numerous, indeed innumerable, and they craved blood, flesh, and liquor. Never sated, they are always famished, terrible, and frightful to behold. I wanted to test their knowledge gained from the esoteric practices. They urged me to serve as a 'sacrificial male,' respectfully requesting, 'O Lord of the gods, please take part in our "rice pudding" rituals in the maṇḍala.' I said, 'I will do it,' and I went to the summit of Mt. Meru. There, I fashioned the Diamond Rod maṇḍala with five colored powders. In the middle I made a lotus with eight petals, shining with a yellow central receptacle. I put Diamond mantras in the four cardinal directions, and enclosed diamond mantras in the intermediate directions. I made doors and pathways there, and an exit at the southern gate. There I stationed myself in the middle of the lotus, which was full of the strength of feminine energy. I meditated on the supreme form of that feminine energy which is immovable, supremely steadfast.

"At that moment, on the slopes of Mt. Kailash, Pārvatī asked Śiva's servant Nandi, 'Where is the blessed lord Rudra?' Nandi answered, 'He is serving as a sacrificial male, O goddess. The *yoginīs* asked him to take part in their "rice pudding" rituals, and he is standing in the maṇḍala.' Then Pārvatī became enraged, blazing with anger like millions of lightning bolts. Instantly (*tvaritaṃ*) she uttered the Tvaritā spell, consisting of three-times-three seed syllables. She blazed like ball lightning, pervading the whole world of moving and nonmoving things with untold billions of light beams pulsing out to the ten directions. She paralyzed the gods, Brahmā and so on, with a fiery ball of light.

"They cried out in desperation, and said, 'Save us, O goddess, beloved of Śiva!' They came and fell at her feet and lauded her with excellent hymns of praise. She was pleased by these various complements to the qualities of her head, feet, and so on. That each syllable of the goddess's spell stands for a pair of her arms is well known. The eighteen-armed goddess is seated upon a lion that represents the throne of righteousness (*dharma*).[2] The lion is a lovely white like cow's milk, shining with a long tail. It has a large face with lolling tongue, its long, sharp teeth glittering. It is very fearsome with blazing eyes and looks fierce with its upright ears. Roaring, it is powerful and wild and has a blazing mane. It is menacing with sharp, bared claws capable of tearing the worlds asunder. It stood facing east, blazing as if devouring the whole world of mobile and immobile things.

"Tvaritā was seated on it with her left leg hanging down and her right doubled back, resting her heel on her other thigh. The goddess's toenails sparkle like twinkling stars and her lotus-red feet have the same qualities as a lotus. The soles of her feet shine and she has lovely, long, and symmetrical toes. She has round and full calves and thighs, with wide hips and buttocks. She has a deep navel and a belly with three folds beautified by a streak of abdominal hair. She has broad loins and breasts like golden pitchers. Her neck resembles a shell, lips red like ripe ivy gourd, a gorgeous nose, eyes resembling the petals of blue lotuses, bow-like curved eyebrows, lovely ears, and a shining crown. She glitters, bright with jewels and snake earrings, and the king of snakes as a necklace, brilliant with a thousand hoods. The goddess's arms shine, beautified with snake bracelets, and adorned with a large snake serving as a sash over her loin area. On the feet of the goddess are two terrible snake anklets, and her left foot is placed in the middle of a lotus with a thousand petals. One garment, adorned with flowers, looks like forked lightning in the sky. Another garment is like a rainbow draped across her breasts. It is studded with numerous flowers and tied tightly with a great serpent. The goddess's hands carry weapons, and the tips of her shell-like nails are sharp. On her right she holds a thunderbolt weapon, staff, sword, discus, mace, shining spear, arrow, and javelin, and she displays the gesture of granting boons. On her left she holds a bow, noose, plow, bell, a threatening finger, conch, and a goad, and she also displays a gesture of goodwill and holds a lotus. Abounding with shimmering rays of light, her radiance is like thousands of lightning bolts. Encompassing the whole universe, from the level of Śiva down to the earth, she covers everything with her brilliance.

"All of this happened the instant the Tvaritā spell was uttered. The inclusion of the sound HŪṂ made her fierce. Dreadful to behold, she threatened all the directions and the unapproachable gods. The circle of *yoginīs* was bewildered and fainted on the slope of Mt. Meru. Fallen, being burned up, they cried 'Save us O goddess, queen of the gods.' Praising her with various hymns of praise, I said Oṃ and offered her water. I honored that goddess, prostrated to that *yoginī*, and said, 'O goddess, check your anger toward me and the circle of *yoginīs*.[3] O lady of blazing light, stand here in the middle of the maṇḍala.' The goddess entered the maṇḍala and seated herself in the center of the lotus. She was worshiped with various garlands, fragrant powders, incense, and gifts. Being praised with many hymns along with mantras and sacred hand gestures, the goddess was established in the observance: that any Tantric aspirant who remembers her will acquire the power he seeks. She will give it quickly. Those *yoginīs* who roam the earth, who grant all desires, wealth, and powers, will be his. Gods, demigods, celestial musicians, nature spirits, demons, divine snakes, and celestial damsels—all will give the desired power after your worship, O Tvaritā. He who always worships you in his home with devotion and according to his own ability, will have his enemies, who shun good people, destroyed. One who worships you can easily conquer the kingdoms of his enemies. And he gains powers such as lordship over the earth, freedom from disease, and long life. For such a Tantric practitioner, all the various spiritual and mundane works come to fruition.

"At that moment, Brahmā came to the slope of Mt. Meru. He worshiped her according to the prescriptions, praising her with numerous hymns of praise. And so did Viṣṇu, king Indra, the fire god Agni, and Yama, god of death. And so the chaos god Nirṛti, lord of the seas Varuṇa, the wind-god Vāyu, and Kubera, giver of wealth. Śiva himself worshiped the goddess Pārvatī, along with the perfected beings, the legions of titans, and the heavenly dancers. Worshiped and praised, the goddess was satisfied, and goodheartedly said, 'I will do this, O Lord of the gods, for whatever man remembers me. I will quickly grant his desired power.' Then Brahmā made this request of her: 'Tell us how to practice the spell.' Then, they were all dismissed and the ultimate Tantra was told: the *Troṭala*—supreme, secret, and surpassing 125,000 stanzas, O bird. Thus, drawing on that, I tell you nothing but the essence of the essence, the supreme secret; now listen attentively.

"Many spells are found there, Tārkṣya, and the foremost consist of nine seed syllables. This Tvaritā spell is supreme and esoteric, secret even among secrets. She is the highest of the esoteric spells and accomplishes all desires. Deadly to all snakes, she also destroys the ranks of one's enemies. And moreover, she is well known as the destroyer of all obstacles. She brings about the sexual arousal of all women, divine and otherwise.[4] She is revered in the form of a vulva which gives birth to all seed syllables.[5] She is the heart of all goddesses and is dear to *yoginīs*. This spell, pervading the endless worlds, is good for any purpose. She grants perfection in all rites, in this world and the next. Knowledge of her is difficult to obtain, even for all the gods, seers, yogis, sages, sorcerers, and so forth who were perfected in various ages. Nature spirits, demons, flesh-eating demons, ghosts, and indeed any spirit—this single Queen of Spells terrifies them all instantly.

"The 'tala' element of her name 'Troṭalā' signifies the seven underworlds whose names all end in *tala*, reaching as far down as the level of the Rudra who burns everything at the end of time. The phonemes of the spell, starting with Oṃ, stand for the levels of reality from heaven to the Egg of Brahmā, which is to say the created world. With the sound Oṃ, she protects (*trāyate*) everyone, and moreover sows terror (*trāsate*) everywhere. Because of that she is called Troṭalā. This is the established meaning of the title of the Tantra. This ancient spell is perfected without recourse to observances and offerings. It gives magical powers even when one lacks knowledge and has not done the normally obligatory worship of their guru. Hostile sorcerers do not pay heed as to whether the rite should be done or not, or whether the victim deserves to be harmed or not. They could perform fearsome rites, even against the gods.

"In this world, people get discouraged by the excessive repetition of rituals that their guru requires for them to become accomplished. They suffer with the good and bad outcomes of prior deeds (karma). But with the Tvaritā spell, those who were previously not successful will quickly succeed in their goals and sooner or later attain liberation. Those who want to become accomplished sorcerers or universal emperors likewise quickly succeed. People whose goal is the performance of marvels can play with snakes without being harmed. Those who want to be able to move in the sky along with perfected yoga masters are able to. Those who desire a self-chosen death can extend their life as long as the god Sadāśiva. They are able to produce powers of royal dominion, not to mention mere material powers. They would certainly be able to perform the various magical rites with the mind alone—attraction and so on—thus killing, causing panic, subjugation, cutting, burning, sowing dissension in an enemy army, striking down adversaries, bewildering all nefarious forces, and protection for those afflicted with fear. In the body of one who repeats this spell—or rather of one who would utter it only once—the Goddess, God, and Garuḍa exist as a triad. Thus, she is called 'three-pointed' and manifests in the form of a triangle. She also signifies other triads, such as the Left, Right, and Siddhānta schools of Tantric revelation. This 'three-pointed' spell grants all desires. She brings about success quickly; thus she is called Tvaritā."[6]

So ends the first chapter in "Tvaritā's Basic Teaching," part of the original *Troṭala*.

THE GODDESS IN CONTEXT: THE LIVES AND AFTERLIVES OF A TANTRIC GODDESS

"The Swift One" (*tvaritā/tūrṇā/śīghrā*) is a fitting name for a goddess called on in times of urgent need. She first appears in the textual record as a goddess invoked to cure snakebite, in medical Tantras dedicated to treatment of poisoning and the like. These Tantras are known as Gāruḍam for their connection to the divine eagle and enemy of snakes, Garuḍa. While he is best known today as the servant and mount of the great Hindu god Viṣṇu, other religious sects have also long claimed Garuḍa as their own. Indeed, he has existed as an independent figure since the Vedic period, some three thousand years ago.[7] In the passage translated in this chapter, Śiva is in conversation with Garuḍa, here referred to by the alias Tārkṣya. He asks Śiva for a summary version of the supreme Tantra, which the narrative later identifies with Tvaritā's own scripture, the lost *Troṭala*. Titled after the goddess's nom de guerre (combat name), the *Troṭala* was one of the oldest and most-cited Gāruḍa Tantras, known since at least the tenth century CE.[8] Ostensibly, it was a massive work. The *Mṛgendra Tantra* calls it the chief scripture of the very extensive "eastern" stream of revelation.[9] Despite her illustrious past, today the name Tvaritā is not well known. Later tradition refers to her as merely one among many in the retinue of another goddess or identifies her as a form of Durgā. Her own story has been forgotten, until now.

Seed: From the Soil of Obscurity

Since the text translated here, *Tvaritā's Basic Teaching*, is the oldest surviving source, identifying the goddess's earlier origin is based on guesswork and deductions. We know that her most famous scripture, the lost *Troṭala Tantra*, was an important part of the Gāruḍa Tantras. Given that curing snakebite is mentioned but is not central to the source translated here, it is reasonable to suppose that she had a tighter association with curing snakebite in the *Troṭala*. The visual form she takes in the translated passage supports this theory, since she is described as being adorned with snake ornaments, a feature that has little to do with the facets of sorcery, royal dominion, and sexuality this story presents as her areas of specialization.

Other epiphanies of Tvaritā survive that allow us to take this question of origins somewhat further. Mark Dyczkowski surveyed numerous sources on Tvaritā in the introduction to his massive fourteen-volume study of one section of the *Manthānabhairava Tantra*. He notes that in addition to the eighteen-armed form, she is also commonly depicted as a four-armed Śavara tribal woman adorned with snakes and holding peacock feathers.[10] The same two versions appear in the *Agni Purāṇa*, and I have demonstrated elsewhere that *Tvaritā's Basic Teaching* is the basis of the eighteen-armed form in the Purāṇa.[11]

The question, therefore, is how the simpler four-armed form of Tvaritā as a Śavara woman fits into the puzzle of her origin. The Sanskrit word *śavara* was a generic way to refer to a number of tribal communities in classical and medieval India, but it also denotes a specific tribe that stills exists and is now better known under the name Saora. A study of this tribe by mid-twentieth-century anthropologist Verrier Elwin describes numerous snake gods and the tribe's prominent female shamans.[12] Drawing on this and other sources, Miranda Shaw argues that the Buddhist goddess Parṇaśavarī is modeled on the type of the tribal female shaman.[13] Parṇaśavarī is similar to Tvaritā in several respects: they are both associated with healing and adorned with snakes, and in the case of the *Manthānabhairava Tantra* epiphany mentioned previously, they are both linked to the Śavara tribe and hold peacock feathers; peacocks had long been associated with healing snakebite in earlier traditions. Moreover, they both appear in the artistic and textual records around the tenth century. These similarities are not enough to conclude that Tvaritā was the model of Parṇaśavarī, or vice versa, but they do suggest that the Śavara tribe was well known for its female shamans and their healing powers, and that goddesses based on this motif became popular in early medieval India.

It is thus likely that the eighteen-armed form of Tvaritā described here is not her original form, but that is not to say that *Tvaritā's Basic Teaching* elaborates its vision of Tvaritā on the basis of the *Manthānabhairava Tantra*. The latter Tantra, like the *Agni Purāṇa*, includes both the simpler tribal-woman form as well as the elaborate eighteen-armed form. In both cases, both visual forms are likely to have been derived from the lost *Troṭala Tantra* itself. The number of arms corresponds two-by-two with the nine syllables of Tvaritā's spell. By all surviving accounts, she is defined by these nine syllables. Given that the *Troṭala* was reputed to have been a voluminous source, the presence in it of multiple forms of the goddess is to be expected.

That a hypothetical tribal goddess who heals snakebite was incorporated into mainstream Tantric traditions in the first millennium CE is both logical and consonant with the patterns apparent throughout the history of Indian goddesses. Popular goddesses are not invented out of nothing; they are modified or unmodified epiphanies of local goddesses who become associated with deities and mythological structures of transregional Hinduism.

Flower: A Goddess Who Commands All the Gods

If Tvaritā did, in fact, emerge into the Tantras from a humble tribal origin as a snakebite goddess, the narrative as we have it takes her in several new directions. The seven hundred verses of *Tvaritā's Basic Teaching* and the two hundred verses of the related *Tvaritā's Wisdom Spellbook* (*Tvaritājñānakalpa*) present a grand and complex Tantric system in which Tvaritā is the central goddess surrounded by nine attendant goddesses of her own. In several respects, she has been thoroughly incorporated into the Śākta Tantric fold. She is described in terms of her feminine power (*śakti*), and she is propitiated with standard Tantric techniques.[14]

To understand the inner logic of Tvaritā's story, one must closely examine what led to her creation. Śiva was engaged in some sort of ritual with a band of *yoginīs*—a polysemous word that can include human women, but which here refers to divine women. Learning about Śiva's involvement in such a ritual made Pārvatī furious, which resulted in her creating Tvaritā by uttering the syllables of her spell. The interpretation of this scene hinges on how we understand the key line: "They urged me to serve as a 'sacrificial male'. . . in our 'rice pudding' rituals" (*preritaś ca paśutvena aham . . . carukāryeṣu*). The most basic meaning of *carukāryeṣu* is "rice pudding" rituals. However, such an innocent literal meaning is unlikely in this context, since the *yoginīs* were just described as craving nonvegetarian food. In some Tantric contexts, *caru* is a euphemism for bodily fluids, including sexual fluids, and given Pārvatī's extreme anger upon hearing about it, such a meaning appears probable. On the other hand, a text called the *Pārameśvarīmata* preserves a condensed version of this narrative that supplies a few additional details. It says:

> They begged you, O god, saying "give us a piece of your own body—a piece of your body mixed with rice and liquor." They were all satisfied, standing in the maṇḍala and they played. Then you spoke again, O god, and said "Take! Take!" without doing anything to protect yourself there in the middle of the Diamond maṇḍala. When I heard about such goings-on while standing on Mt. Kailash, a great anger arose and exited my body. With the light of twelve suns, it terrified the whole world. I said, "I am definitely going to eat the circle of *yoginīs*!"[15]

Therefore, in the *Pārameśvarīmata*'s account, Pārvatī is angry that her husband is essentially feeding himself to the *yoginīs* and not to her. Her own hunger is being ignored. Śiva's self-sacrifice and the hunger of Pārvatī and the *yoginīs* do not necessarily imply sexuality, but given the double entendres of mouths, feeding, and eating in Sanskrit (and in English slang for that matter), the involvement of sexual practices here cannot be ruled out. Indeed, it would make the basis of Pārvatī's fury more clear.

All of this begs the question of what normally happens at such encounters of a male with a group of *yoginīs* (*yoginīmelaka*). What transpires is rarely stated overtly. Olga Serbaeva, the author of chapter 12, wrote an excellent article analyzing the varieties of these sorts of encounters in the *Jayadrathayāmala*, another early, unpublished Śākta Tantra. While the eleventh-century polymath Abhinavagupta identified two varieties—a more violent type called *haṭhamelaka*, wherein the male's life is in danger from supernatural *yoginīs*, and a more pleasurable type (*priyamelaka*) that might involve sexual contact between the male and human *yoginīs*—Serbaeva clarifies that most passages do not fit such a simple division of types.[16] Shaman Hatley, the author of chapter 4, kindly provided me with a collection of additional passages on *yoginīmelaka* from early Tantras. In some of these sources, the *yoginīs* provide the male with "rice pudding," which may be a reversal of what is happening in our text.[17] Another Tantra, the *Kaulajñānanirṇaya*, specifies that the rice pudding is made of "the five nectars," which elsewhere are specified as bodily fluids.[18] The *Jayadrathayāmala* also uses the term *melaka* to refer to physical ritual encounters between male and female practitioners that are suggestive of sexual ritual, while later Tantras, such as the *Kulārṇava Tantra*, describe such rituals as unambiguously sexual.[19] It is thus *possible* that in our narrative Śiva and the *yoginīs* were planning a ritual encounter wherein sexual fluids would be exchanged as power substances, and given Pārvatī's reaction, I consider it probable.

Following this interpretation, the word *paśu* (translated as "sacrificial male") probably does not imply the usual Śaiva metaphor for a soul that is spiritually "bound," that is, not yet liberated, but follows from the more basic meaning of an animal offered as sacrifice to a deity. If we understand the encounter as sexual in nature, *paśu* may be a technical term for a male who offers himself and his bodily fluids, specifically his sexual fluids, to a band of *yoginīs*.

Interpreting Śiva's encounter with the *yoginīs* as sexual also fits the reference later in the story to Tvaritā having the ability to sexually arouse all women.[20] If her anger represents a transformation of her unaddressed sexual needs, it makes sense that such anger would revert to a potent sexuality upon Śiva acknowledging and ameliorating her emotional state. All of this also fits with the reference to Tvaritā taking the form of a vulva (*yoni*), a practice that connects her growing cult with ideas about the spiritual power of sexual energy that were gaining traction in many Tantric movements of the late first millennium. Tvaritā's sexual nature in the present text also makes her incorporation into the Tantras of the goddesses Kubjikā and Tripurasundarī a natural fit, as both became connected with sexual energy, as Anna Golovkova discusses in the next chapter.[21]

The picture that emerges is of a tribal snakebite goddess, or a goddess modeled on a female tribal shaman, who leapt to popularity in the last few centuries of the first millennium as part of the burgeoning field of the Gāruḍa Tantras. Her growing following attributed to her all sorts of other associations, as sects vied for patronage and followers. With *Tvaritā's Basic Teaching*, a later generation of Tantric specialists sought to reinvigorate her fame by bidding for new recruits seeking an easy path to the powers of sorcery. They likewise appealed to potential royal sponsors with their promises of universal sovereignty and abilities to conquer enemy armies, with Tvaritā's divine backing.

Fruit: A Goddess in Decline, a Goddess Reborn

The identification of Tvaritā with Pārvatī and other major Tantric goddesses appears to have been responsible for both her fame and her decline. If Tvaritā is simply a form of the Great Goddess, then any number of cults growing in popularity can absorb her unique qualities into their own version of the Goddess or make space for Tvaritā as simply a member of another goddess's entourage. Thus, the goddess Kubjikā comes to have Tvaritā as an epithet and incorporates her spell into its scriptures.[22] Thus, the Jain Śākta Tantra *Bhairavapadmāvatīkalpa* opens by saying Tvaritā and Tripurā and its own Padmāvatī are all one and the same. Thus, Tvaritā becomes a Nityā goddess in the retinue of Tripurasundarī.

Little of Tvaritā's grandeur in the translated passage survives in later Tantric traditions. But Tvaritā has not been entirely forgotten in practice. Several temples in India continue to actively worship her. In the Beed district of Maharashtra, the village of Talwada has two temples to Tvaritā: one under the name Śrī Tuḷjā Bhavānī Mandir—referring to Tvaritā's local name Tuḷjā Bhavānī—and the other a colorful temple called simply Tvaritā Devī Mandir. In the city of Pune, also in Maharashtra, there is another temple to Tvaritā (Shree Twarita Mata Mandir).

In *Heroic Shāktism*, Bihani Sarkar (2017) studied various historical linkages of kings with clan goddesses who supported their lineages. Included are some references to another prominent Tvaritā temple, that of Tuḷjā Bhavānī at Tuljapur near Osmanabad in southern Maharashtra state, near the border with Karnataka.[23] Significantly, this form of Tvaritā was the patron goddess of the famous Maratha king Shivaji, who waged war on the Mughal empire. Sarkar notes that Shivaji's sword was kept near the goddess's altar when not in use.[24] The implication is that the sword's power, and thus Shivaji's own military success, derived from his relationship with the goddess—evidently, the sort of marketing of the goddess toward a royal clientele that we see in the story was highly effective. Sarkar reports that the temple icon identifies her with Durgā, shown slaying the buffalo demon. The local text called *Turajā Māhātmya*, however, describes the goddess arriving at this site with a retinue of *yoginīs* and a fierce entourage, which points to a Tantric genealogy, since non-Tantric visions of Durgā do not typically associate her with *yoginīs*. By contrast, *Tvaritā's Basic Teaching* makes her association with *yoginīs* central to her identity.[25] Roland Jansen also studied the Tuljapur site and the *Turajā Māhātmya*, in *Die Bhavani von Tuljapur* (1995). Though unaware of Tvaritā's history in the Gāruḍa Tantras, Jansen indirectly outlines her most significant survival: her migration to Nepal and related identity with the royal Newar goddess Taleju Bhavani.

Taleju is famous as the protector of the former kings of Nepal and is therefore among Nepal's most important goddesses. She is thought to possess selected virgin girls (*kumārī*) of the Shakya caste, known as living goddesses, even today. In Nepal, her name is also spelled Tulajā, which corresponds to the Marathi spelling Tuḷjā. Jansen argues that she was brought to the Mithila region of southern Nepal and northern Bihar by a military officer of the Pālas from Karnataka named Nānyadeva, who broke away and established the Karṇāṭa dynasty there in the eleventh century.[26] According to Newar royal histories (*vaṃśāvalī*), her statue was brought from India to Bhaktapur in Nepal by one Harisiṃhadeva in the early fourteenth century.[27] This window of time between Nānyadeva and Harisiṃhadeva corresponds to the date of the oldest surviving manuscript of *Tvaritā's Basic Teaching* (*Tvaritāmūlasūtra*; 1197 CE).[28] Mary Shepherd Slusser references a chronicle in which the sixteenth-century king Trailokyamalla of Bhaktapur in Nepal installed a diamond-studded *yantra* in honor of Taleju.[29] Such a *yantra* may very well be based on Tvaritā's signature "diamond-rod maṇḍala," referenced in the story translated in this chapter.

The origin of the name Taleju has long eluded scholars, but in light of her connection to Tvaritā, a derivation based on Tvaritā's alternate name Troṭalā (also commonly spelled Totalā) appears probable.[30] Further research is sure to uncover more details in this early history of Tvaritā-Tulajā's migrations and influence. This chapter presents just one example of the exciting discoveries that await future scholars who will take into account unpublished sources.

SOURCE

The Sanskrit text of *Tvaritā's Basic Teaching* (*Tvaritāmūlasūtra*) is available in two complete paper manuscripts from Nepal, microfilmed on NGMPP reel numbers B126/9 and H170/3. They are independent witnesses to the text, since neither copies from the other, as can be deduced by a close examination of variant readings. A few palm-leaf folios of another manuscript dating to

1197 CE also survive.[31] The present translation covers the first of the nine chapters only and is based on a draft edition using the two paper manuscripts.[32] The language of the *Tvaritāmūlasūtra* is a hybrid-Sanskrit register that medieval commentators called *aiśa*, "divine," because its peculiarities are understood as the way that Śiva speaks in many early Tantras.

FURTHER READING

Dyczkowski, Mark. 2009. *Manthānabhairavatantram: The Section Concerning the Virgin Goddess of the Tantra of the Churning Bhairava*. New Delhi: Indira Gandhi National Centre for the Arts.

Sarkar, Bihani. 2017. *Heroic Shāktism: The Cult of Durgā in Ancient Indian Kingship*. The British Academy Monograph Series. Oxford: Oxford University Press.

Slouber, Michael. 2017. *Early Tantric Medicine: Snakebite, Mantras, and Healing in the Gāruḍa Tantras*. New York: Oxford University Press.

Stainton, Hamsa. 2019. *Poetry as Prayer in the Sanskrit Hymns of Kashmir*. New York: Oxford University Press.

NOTES

A special thanks to Somadeva Vasudeva, who originally encouraged me to work with this text and who offered extensive feedback on several early drafts of my translation. Thanks also to Shaman Hatley, Mark Dyczkowski, Harunaga Isaacson, Jessica Vantine Birkenholtz, and Alexis Sanderson for sharing their expertise and weighing in on various issues concerning the textual history of Tvaritā. I am grateful that the staff at the Kaisher Library in Kathmandu allowed me to photograph several leaves of what turned out to be the oldest manuscript available of part of the *Tvaritāmūlasūtra*.

1. The long list of demonic beings given here is not exhaustive. My translations of many of their names either convey a quality associated with the type or, in the case of more obscure demons, make conjectures about their nature by etymology.

2. On the visualization of righteousness (*dharma*) as a throne in Tantric practice, see Goodall and Rastelli (2013, vol. 3), s.v. *dharmādi*.

3. The fact that here Pārvatī/Tvaritā herself is referred to as a *yoginī* is significant. It suggests that her reaction involved anger at being ignored in favor of these other *yoginī*s.

4. The word translated as "sexual arousal" (*kṣobha*) has a range of possible meanings, such as disturbance, shaking, excitement, stimulation, and even orgasm in some contexts. Here the negative sense of disturbance or agitation at first seems preferable, because of Tvaritā's earlier jealous anger. However, the text is about to state that she is the heart of all goddesses and dear to *yoginī*s, and thus a negative interpretation is inappropriate. The specification of women in particular suggests that the meaning is

sexual, since practitioners using spells to attract and seduce women is a recurring topic in many Tantras, which sometimes use *kṣobha* in this sense. Consider, for example, the Jain Tantra *Vidyānuśāsana* (p. 155): "All the best women from a town or village see the true mantra master and run about. They become aroused and then come [to him]" (*dravanti vanitāḥ sarvā dṛṣṭvā sanmantravādinam. kṣobhaṃ gatvāgamiṣyanti puragrāmavarastriyaḥ*). Here the verb "run about" could possibly have a secondary meaning of "become wet," but that may be reading too far into the language choice. Even more clear examples can be seen in many passages describing Tantric sexual rituals. For example, Abhinavagupta says in *Tantrāloka* 29 that "*Kṣobha* is characterized by kissing, embracing, and pounding each other, etc." (*parasparāhananāliṅganaparicumbanādilakṣaṇaḥ kṣobhaḥ*). Similarly, *Brahmayāmala* 45.321 says, "Respectfully addressing her as a goddess, the mantra master should then begin to arouse her" (*deviṃ vijñāpya tāṃ mantrī tato kṣobhaṃ samārabhet*).

5. A parallel ritual text, the *Īśānaśivagurudevapaddhati*, says, "The mantra reciter should duly project the mother goddess (Tvaritā) in a fire built in a vulva-shaped pit" (2.22.34: *kuṇḍe tu yonipratime tu māntriko [em., māntrike Ed.] vahnau samāvāhya yathāvad ambikām*).

6. I interpret the "thus" in this last verse as inclusive of the previous verse as well, for it appears to be playing on the phonetic similarity of the "triadic" (*tritaya*) nature of Tvaritā and the name "Tvaritā" itself.

7. See Slouber (2017, 19–23).

8. The spelling of *Troṭala* varies: *Trotala, Trottala, Trotula, Totula,* and *Totala,* etc.

9. *Mṛgendra Tantra* 3.35 (*Caryāpada*): *prācyaṃ trotalādi suvistaram*. The earliest known reference to the *Troṭala* is Vairocana's *Lakṣaṇasaṃgraha*, which Alexis Sanderson dates to the tenth century (2014, 28–29).

10. Dyczkowski (2009, 2:83–94).

11. For the evidence that the *Agni Purāṇa* depends on Tvaritā's Tantric sources, and the *Tvaritāmūlasūtra* in particular, see Slouber (2017, 96–98).

12. See Elwin (1955).

13. See Shaw (2006, 188–202).

14. My reasoning here is based on an idea of Alexis Sanderson conveyed to me in person in 2010, which he later published in Sanderson (2014, 43n161).

15. *Pārameśvarīmata* 39.1–6.

16. Serbaeva (2016, 51–73).

17. *Brahmayāmala* 85.13cd–14ab.

18. *Kaulajñānanirṇaya* 11.7cd–10. See also Goodall and Rastelli (2013, vol. 3), s.v. *pañcāmṛtākarṣaṇa*.

19. *Jayadrathayāmala* IV.76, *Vīratāṇḍavavidhikramapaṭala* vv. 5–30b, and *Kulārṇava Tantra* 8.73, cited by Biernacki (2007, 42).

20. *Tvaritāmūlasūtra* 1.77: *divyādivyā[ḥ] striyo yās tu tāsāṃ kṣobhakarī*. On the interpretation of the word *kṣobha*, see note 4.

21. Slouber (2017, 98–100) and Dyczkowski (2009, 2:83–94).

22. Heilijgers-Seelen (1994, 258–59 and notes).

23. Sarkar (2017, 173).

24. Sarkar (2017, 195).

25. Sarkar (2017, 191).

26. Jansen (1995, 85–91).

27. Jansen (1995, 85–91). See also Manandhar (1988). She argues that Taleju is, in part, an adaptation of the older Licchavi royal goddess Māneśvarī. Slusser (1982, 317–19) likewise discusses this connection with Māneśvarī at length.

28. The colophon of the manuscript identifies the ruling king as Lakṣmīkāmadeva. This must be the second king by this name, whom H. C. Ray (1931, 209) identifies through several other colophons, noting that he is entirely omitted in the traditional histories. The *Tvaritāmūlasūtra* manuscript notes the date it was copied as NS 317, *śrāvaṇaśuklatṛtīyāyāṃ śaniścaravāre* (Saturday, July 19, 1197 CE).

29. See Slusser (1982, 316).

30. The *ju* element of her name is an honorific suffix, and the *tale* element might be conjectured as a shortening of T(r)otalā influenced by the Sanskrit feminine vocative *totale*. Slusser discusses the history of Taleju and briefly reflects on the origin of her name (1982, 316–20). She suggests that the *tala* element is a Tantric reference to genitalia, which would link her with the most important goddess of Nepal, Guhyeśvarī. Note that Tvaritā's story says that she is revered in the form of a vulva, which is one of several interpretations of Guhyeśvarī's icon at her main temple near Kathmandu.

31. The fragment shows part of the ninth chapter of the *Tvaritāmūlasūtra* and is located as the final three folios grouped with the *Matasāra* manuscript filmed as NGMPP reel C6/7. This bundle is housed at Kaisher Library in Kathmandu.

32. Researchers unable to access the microfilmed manuscripts can consult Mark Dyczkowski's digital transcription of the manuscript that was filmed as NGMPP reel B126/9, published on the Muktabodha website in 2014 as *Troṭalātantra*; it was not consulted for this translation.

FIGURE 21. Kāmeśvarī, by Laura Santi

CHAPTER 11

Kāmeśvarī

Visualizing the Goddess of Desire

ANNA A. GOLOVKOVA

The Tantras selected here give few clues about geographical locations. Of the six short passages, the third alone mentions a place called the "Garlanded" (Mālinī) Mountain and a ravine or cave named Kokila, which may refer to sites in the far northeast of India, in the state of Arunachal Pradesh, such as the ruined temple site called Malinithan in the Siang Hills. This area borders Tibet, Myanmar, and Bhutan and is home to numerous tribal communities speaking dozens of languages and hundreds of dialects. Its green forests and high mountains host some of the most biodiverse wilderness in India, with over 750 species of birds and hundreds of mammals, including snow leopards, red pandas, and gibbon apes.

These six short passages translated from the Sanskrit depart from the narrative format and instead present Tantric-guided visualizations and hymns of praise to the so-called goddess of desire, Kāmeśvarī. They are all about vivid description, characteristics of the practitioner, and praise for the goddess's power. The first two pieces are from the *Nityākaula*, a previously untranslated Tantra predating the eleventh century and the sole surviving representative of the Nityā cult, as described in the essay. This important early Tantra has barely reached the present, for it survives in a single damaged palm-leaf manuscript from Nepal. The frequent ellipses (. . .) in the first passage flag places where the text is damaged and unreadable. The passage from the *Ciñciṇīmatasārasamuccaya* serves as a midpoint that elaborates on the nature and power of Kāmeśvarī. The latter three passages are from the *Vāmakeśvarīmata*, a Tantra of slightly later origin that expands the goddess's retinue and links her to the famous diagram of nine interlocking triangles, called the Śrīcakra. The passages are thus arranged sequentially to illustrate the historical flow of religious influence from the Nityā cult to that of Tripurasundarī, who is still actively worshiped today in the popular Śrīvidyā tradition.

Readers should analyze several themes in these passages: the portrayal of female sexuality and the way it is incorporated into a religious tradition, the importance and symbolism of colors in visual analogies, the role of sacred sounds and ritual speech in Tantric ritual, and the use of metaphors from the natural world. Each of these themes could be fruitfully compared with its role in other religious traditions.

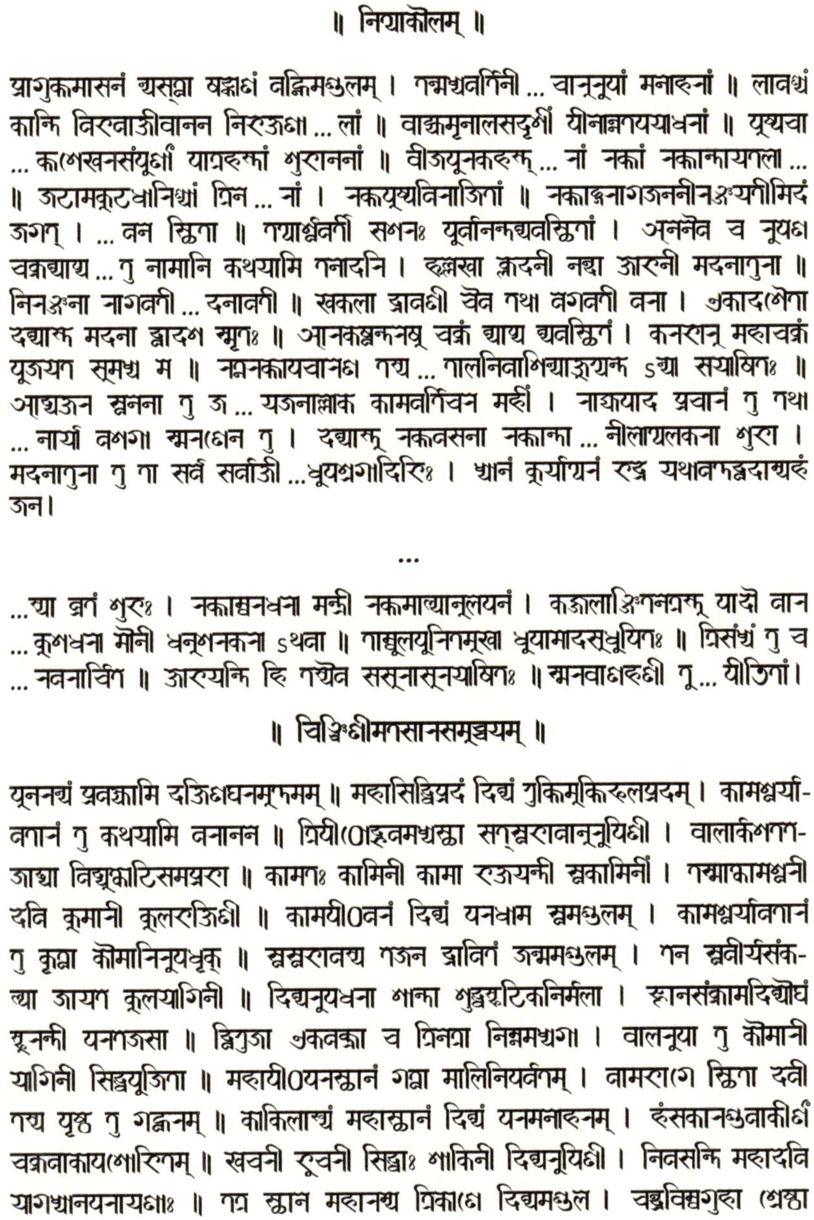

FIGURE 22. *Nityākaula* and *Ciñcinīmatasārasamuccaya,* hybrid Sanskrit works in the Newar script. Font "Nepal Lipi Unicode" © Nepal Lipi Online.

VISUALIZATIONS OF THE GODDESS

Visualizing Kāmeśvarī and Her Retinue (from the Nityākaula*)*

Bhairava spoke to the goddess about the ritual and its benefits: "The person performing the ritual should install a seat in the manner previously described, and then draw the hexagonal fire maṇḍala, a Tantric ritual diagram.[1] In the middle . . . he should visualize the goddess holding a flower bow, a cup, and a citron, . . . beautiful, charming, and lovely, with intoxicated eyes reddish in the corners, . . . heavy breasts, and arms slender as a lotus filament, adorned with a resplendent diadem, her face shining with a reddish complexion, bearing a crest of matted hair, three-eyed, . . . resplendent with red flowers, her limbs rubbed with reddish ointment, . . . radiant like a red firefly, the creatrix of passions reddening this world with desire. . . . At her side is the Archer (the god of love), established at the end of the eastern spoke, and the goddesses who look just like her are established in the entire maṇḍala. Their names, O slender-waisted lady, are Hṛllekhā (the Heart's Furrow), Kledinī (the Moist), Nandā (the Rejoicer), Kṣobhanī (the Agitator), Madanāturā (Afflicted with Love), Nirañjanā (Beyond the Passions), Rāgavatī (Enamored), Madanāvatī (Intoxicating), Khekalā (Skillful in Flight), Drāvaṇī (Putting to Flight), and Vegavatī (Swift).[2] These goddesses are eleven, and Madana (Maddening, i.e., the god of love) is visualized as the twelfth. Together they pervade the entire diagram, occupying the spokes and the intermediate places.

"The adept should worship this great *cakra*, O fair-waisted goddess, O lady with lovely thighs, with offerings of red jewels. . . .[3] Women of the subterranean regions and other females will tremble, falling under his spell, just by being thought of. . . . And he will roam the earth, like the god of love Kāmadeva himself, . . . traversing on foot the entire kingdom. . . .

"He should visualize the subordinate goddesses dressed in red garments, with eyes reddish in the corners, . . . beautiful, with blue lotuses in their hands, . . . all of them intoxicated and lovesick. . . . Having worshiped them with perfume, incense, and garlands, he should perform a visualization of the principal goddess, O auspicious one, just as I will tell you."

The Practitioner of Love Magic (from the Nityākaula*)*

The reciter of mantras, clad in red clothing, wearing garlands of red flowers and smeared with red unguent, eyes outlined with collyrium and feet tinted red, silent, bearing the goad and noose, or the bow and arrows in his hands, mouth full of betel and spices, and perfumed with fragrance and incense . . . during the three junctions of the day, O goddess honored by the best. . . . Excited for him alone, all women, human, divine, and demonic, are immediately pierced by the bow of Smara (Memory, i.e., the god of love).

Introducing Kāmeśvarī, the Goddess of Desire (from the Ciñciṇīmatasārasamuccaya*)*

I will tell you of another excellent teaching—that of the Southern order. Divine, it grants great supernatural powers and gives the fruit of enjoyment and liberation. I will also tell you of the incarnation of Kāmeśvarī, O lovely faced one.[4] She stands in the middle of the triangle made by the three sacred seats of the Goddess, her form corresponding to the true nature of reality. Radiant like hundreds of newly risen suns, splendorous like millions of lightning bolts, she arises from desire. Desirous and desirable herself, she causes the world to consume desire. Thus, she is the Goddess of Desire. Taking the form of a young girl, she consumes *kula*, the material reality.[5] Her maṇḍala is the supreme divine abode, the excellent Kāmarūpa, a seat of the Goddess.[6] Having made the descent, Kāmeśvarī appears as a young girl, her birth maṇḍala moist with the power of ultimate reality.[7] In this way, of her own power and volition, the *yoginī* of *kula* emerges with a heavenly form, peaceful, flawless like a pure crystal, manifesting the divine flood of transmission of knowledge by her supreme power.[8] A face, three eyes, two arms, and a slender waist—as a virginal girl, worshiped by *yoginīs* and perfected *siddhas*, she goes to the supreme place, a great seat of the Goddess, the Mālinī Mountain.[9] The Goddess stands on the left side of that mountain, on the slope of which there is a ravine known as Kokila, an extraordinary place, divine and supremely delightful, full of geese and ducks, ruddy shelducks among them.[10] There dwell flying *khecarī* women, earthly women, perfected *siddhā* women, and the powerful *śākinīs* of celestial form, intent on yoga and meditation, O Great Goddess.[11]

In that exceedingly delightful place within the triangle of the divine maṇḍala, abides the virgin goddess Śukravāhinī (Awash with Sexual Fluids). She eclipses the moon in splendor, and is the first perfected lady among sages and ascetics. My dear, the angry and capricious sage, accompanied by other ascetics, performed exceedingly fierce austerities to propitiate the Goddess for a thousand divine years, growing emaciated and old, fasting, passing beyond the mind, gazing upward, with his thoughts turned inward.[12] Having seen the Goddess of the gods, the Goddess of Sexual Transmission, ascetics reel from her divine power, O goddess. With her divine transmission of knowledge, O lovely faced one, they obtain divine bodies, having become Kāmadeva (the god of love) personified. By the power of Kāmeśvarī, they become rejuvenated. With the two seeds fused as one, the *Rudrayāmala*, bright with divine splendor and granting divine pleasure, arises.[13] Having thus extracted the highest knowledge, meditation, and power, O lovely faced one, the sage is joined for more than a hundred thousand verses with the *Rudrayāmala*, containing the power of eloquence with the radiance of the ultimate reality, O goddess.[14] O Great Goddess, O lovely faced one, his son, Kaulīśa, propagated this great knowledge, which is so hard to obtain, to men bound by the state of karma and *saṃsāra*, as I have told you, my love.[15]

Now I will also tell you about the goddesses of Kāmeśvarī's retinue, who descend together with her: Hṛllekhā (the Heart's Furrow), Kledinī (the Moist), Nandā (the Rejoicer), Kṣobhanī (the Agitator), Madanāturā (Afflicted with Love), Nirañjanā (Beyond the Passions), Rāgavatī (Enamored), Madanāvatī (Intoxicating), Khekalā (Skillful in Flight), Drāvaṇī (Putting to Flight), and Vegavatī (Swift). The goddesses are eleven, and the twelfth is said to be Madana (the Maddening One, i.e., the god of love). O Great Goddess, having honored the goddesses pervading the *cakra* within the spokes and the intermediate spaces of the six-cornered fire maṇḍala, O lovely faced one, the adept should worship Madana, established in the eastern spoke, and, in the middle of that celestial maṇḍala, the goddess Kāmeśvarī, whose eleven-syllable *vidyā* is extracted according to the thunderbolt grid.[16] And the secret worship of lovely Madana should be learned only from verbal instructions of a guru.

In Praise of the Sacred Sounds of the Goddess (from the Vāmakeśvarīmata*)*

I praise the goddess, who has the form of the lords of the planets, constellations, and zodiac signs, who contains all the mantras, the Mother-of-Speech, who abides in the seats of the goddess.[17] I bow to the Great Goddess, the mother, the supreme ruler who brings about the cessation of the rushing waves of the force of time. If one masters even one of her sounds, he will rival the Sun, Garuḍa, the Moon, Kāmadeva, Śiva, Fire, and Viṣṇu. I honor the Goddess, the moonlight of whose letters adorns the three worlds, who is the ruler of all, the great venerable Siddhamātṛkā.[18] . . . I bow to the Great Goddess who possesses the groups of phonemes of the Sanskrit alphabet, beginning with *"a," "ka," "ca," "ṭa," "ta," "pa," "ya," "śa,"* residing in the head, arms, heart, back, hips, and feet, whose highest substratum is in the extraction of the syllable *"i,"* who is both transcendent and immanent, and the embodiment of the highest bliss. . . . I honor that goddess who has the form of the undecaying *"kṣa"* sound, who shines forth in the waves which are the constitutive powers of totality, who arises from the highest transmission of knowledge. I praise her, presiding over the eight great supernatural powers which arise from the eight groups of phonemes, whose eight alphabet goddesses are established through the association with her sequence of phonemes. I praise the venerable Tripurā, who is the treasure-house of the four teachings, the one who resides within Kāma[rūpa], Pūrṇa[giri], that which is named by the letter *"ja"* (Jālandhara), and the Śrīpīṭha (Oḍḍiyāna).[19]

Visualizing Tripurasundarī as the Goddess of Desire (from the Vāmakeśvarīmata*)*

Then visualize the goddess: she resembles a lotus, reddish as the rays of an early-morning sun, like a hibiscus or pomegranate flower, a ruby, and saffron water, adorned with glittering crown-rubies and a string of bells, with a mass of curls like a swarm of black bees, the orb of her face-lotus shining like the new dawn, with a delicate circlet on the round forehead, slightly curved like a half-moon, the Supreme Goddess, the arch of whose beautiful eyebrows mimics the bow of Śiva the Bow-Bearer himself, her eyes playfully agitated, like waves of bliss and delight, whose large golden earrings are radiant ray-clusters, the round curve of her lovely cheekbone—a nectarine orb surpassing the moon, with a nose straight as the measuring chord of Viśvakarma, the creator, with lips the shade of copper, coral, and the bright red *bimba* fruit, equal to ambrosia, by the sweetness of whose smile the taste of sweetness itself is surpassed, whose chin is without compare and whose neck is like a conch shell, large eyed, with arms lovely like the soft and shiny lotus fiber, her tender hands—the likeness of red lotuses, her nails filling the sky with their brightness, with strings of pearls reaching for her high breasts, her waist adorned with three undulating folds, her navel resembling a whirlpool in the river of beauty, her hips endowed with a girdle made from priceless jewels, a line of hair—a goad for the elephant in the shape of her buttocks, with thighs delicate as quivering plantain trunks and calves equal to plantain branches in their beauty, her lotus-like feet scraped by the crest jewels of the bowing down

Brahmā, the flow of her laughter is bright, like the light of hundreds of moons, reddish like vermilion, hibiscus, and pomegranate, even surpassing redness itself, dressed in red garments, resting on a red lotus, adorned with red ornaments, her hands lifting up the goad and noose, four-armed, three-eyed, and also bearing five arrows and a bow, her mouth filled with betel mixed with flecks of camphor, her body ruddy like saffron, unrestrained and passionate like a great elephant, endowed with every variety of seductive garb, and decorated with all the ornaments, the mother of the world's delight, she excites, attracts, and embodies the cause of the world's existence, encompassing all the mantras, beautiful by virtue of every type of auspiciousness, containing all kinds of wealth, she is the eternal Nityā, rejoicing in supreme bliss—the best of adepts should then remember the Mahātripurā gesture (*mudrā*), having summoned with the *vidyā* of summoning as stated above, O auspicious one, having bowed, and having regarded Mahātripurasundarī in the middle of the Śrīcakra, the adept should then begin the worship.[20]

In Praise of Tripurasundarī as the Supreme Divinity (from the Vāmakeśvarīmata*)*

Listen, O goddess, to the great knowledge, supreme and highest among all types of knowledge, by the mere practice of which one will never again be immersed in the ocean of worldly existence. Tripurā is the supreme *śakti*, my dear, born first from the primal Goddess; she is the Mother distinguished by gross and subtle forms, in whom the three worlds originate. One in whose nature the entire multitude of elemental principles (*tattvas*) without remainder have been dissolved; when she is fully developed, no higher (deity) is sought. Devoid of *śakti*, the Supreme Lord would not be able to accomplish anything, but, united with her, he would indeed be capable. Without *śakti*, name and form would not exist in Śiva, given his transcendent nature.[21] And if it were known, O Great Goddess, no action or refuge of any kind would be possible. At the time of resorting to meditation, there is no desire and no stability of mind. After entering within the supreme path, she abides in a transcendent form. The primal Goddess by whom all seeds were swallowed, becomes the first sprout. Vāmā is the tip, Jyeṣṭhā forms a triangle, and Raudrī, O Supreme Goddess, swallows the world. Thus, she is indeed the only supreme *śakti*. Tripurā is the threefold Goddess in the form of Brahmā, Viṣṇu, and Rudra; her nature is the potentiality of knowledge, action, and desire, my love! She emits the three worlds; therefore, she is celebrated as Tripurā.[22]

THE GODDESS IN CONTEXT: FROM THE ASHES OF SENSUALITY

The translated passages are from the Śākta Tantras, which is to say Hindu scriptural texts on goddess worship, framed as private conversations between Bhairava and the Goddess that the reader is fortunate to "overhear."[23] The Tantras contain instructions for propitiating deities, acquiring supernatural powers, achieving liberation from mundane reality, or a variety of other specific purposes. Such instructions often include encoded descriptions of mantras and *vidyās* (condensed ritual formulas for male and female divinities, respectively), and ritual hand gestures called *mudrās*, ritual diagrams known as *yantras* and maṇḍalas, as well as visualizations of deities and speculation on the nature of the universe.[24] The passages translated here are examples of guided visualizations of the goddess Kāmeśvarī (the Goddess of Desire) and the famous Tripurasundarī (the Beauty of the Three Cities). The latter is still actively worshiped today in the popular transregional Śrīvidyā tradition.[25]

Although Tantric traditions are associated with the use of practices that violate rules of purity, they have in fact occupied various locations along the continuum between the heterodox and the orthodox. The extent to which transgressive practices were used has differed according to time, geographic location, and lineage. At the heterodox fringe of this continuum were the so-called left-handed Tantrics of the Kaula movement, named for the religious families or clans (*kula*) that considered their secret worship with impure substances to be the highest level of Tantric Śaivism. The Kaula cults discussed here include the Nityā cult, a unique sect within the larger religious movement of Śākta Śaivism, in which the principal goddess Kāmeśvarī was surrounded by a group of subordinate goddesses called Nityās (lit. Constant, Eternal). The Nityā cult is related to a later Kaula cult of the goddess Tripurasundarī.[26] Other Tantric movements that came to be classified as Kaula included the Trika, named for its worship of a triad of goddesses; the Krama; the cult of Kālasaṃkarṣaṇī, the Devourer of Time, also known as Kālī, the Dark One; and the cult of Kubjikā, the so-called Crooked goddess who was identified with the coiled serpent power of *kuṇḍalinī*, made famous in later yoga traditions. The cult to Kubjikā contained, among others, the *Ciñciṇīmatasārasamuccaya*, an excerpt of which is translated in this chapter. It describes four Kaula traditions, with the Nityā cult classified as the transmission of the Southern order.[27] A later classification according to the *Vāḍavānalīya Tantra* elevated the worship of Kāmeśī (or Kāmeśvarī), Tripurasundarī, and other related goddesses—such as Lalitā, Bālā, and Tripurabhairavī—to the upper tradition, superseding all other Kaula systems.[28]

Kaula adepts, referred to as "heroes," used secret practices that defied Brahminical rules of ritual purity and rejected the very dichotomy between "pure" and "impure" by offering to a deity supposedly impure substances like fish, wine, and, in some traditions, even bodily excretions, then consuming them as part of a Tantric ritual. While the Nityā cult and the cult of Tripurasundarī discussed in this chapter were classified among the Kaula traditions, their unorthodox methods were "cleaned up" as the cult was brought to southern India and made to conform to the customs of orthodox Brahminism.

Seed: The Nityā Cult

The Nityā cult and the related cult of Tripurasundarī were among the latest Tantric traditions to emerge.[29] Although not much is known about the former due to scant textual evidence, it appears that this form of worship was practiced in the north and/or northeast of the Indian subcontinent prior to the eleventh century CE.[30] Although Tantras typically avoid giving specifics of geography, the *Ciñciṇīmatasārasamuccaya* passage translated in this chapter refers to the Mālinī Mountain and a ravine named Kokila, which may be linked to sites in the far northeastern area now part of Arunachal Pradesh in India. Worship of the Nityās was known to the famous Kashmirian polymath Abhinavagupta, who cited a variety of scriptural texts and authors in his masterpiece, *Light on the Tantras* (*Tantrāloka*).[31] Unlike most of the earlier Tantric cults, in the Nityā cult we find no ferocious goddesses and, surprisingly, no mention of Śiva outside of the framing dialogue, since the consort of the principal goddess here is the god of love, Kāmadeva. Mythology pertaining to Kāmadeva is well known in Hindu lore, but his worship did not survive to the present. Similarly, ritual practices of the Nityā cult ceased to flourish, and even the evidence of its existence has all but disappeared. In addition to the *Ciñciṇīmatasārasamuccaya* mentioned previously, another Kubjikā Tantra called the *Manthānabhairava* preserves a variant of the Nityā cult in its fourth volume, the *Siddhakhaṇḍa*. The only text from within the Nityā cult itself is the *Nityākaula*, which has come down to us in a single damaged and incomplete manuscript.[32] The study of these texts illuminates the practice of a Tantric tradition that has fallen out of use and also allows us to trace parallels between this form of worship and the later cult of the goddess Tripurasundarī.

The *Nityākaula* passage translated here describes the Goddess as red, wearing red garments, and holding in her four hands the weapons of Kāmadeva: the goad, noose, bow, and arrows of flowers.[33] All of these elements have been adapted into the cult of Tripurasundarī.[34] The color red here is the color of passion and desire, not anger or blood as is the case elsewhere. The use of red imagery is consistent with the use of red for Tantric rituals aimed at producing amorous attraction and with visualizations of the god of love.[35] The Goddess of the *Nityākaula* is lovely and sensual, and her propitiation promises the adept success in love, eloquence, and all the courtly graces. In the *Ciñciṇīmatasārasamuccaya*, Kāmeśvarī's complexion is compared to the color of hundreds of newly risen suns (i.e., reddish), but this metaphor is an isolated example of the use of imagery associated with the color red. The dominant metaphor for desire in this text is rather sexual fluids, which serve as the medium for the transmission of knowledge.[36] Kāmeśvarī is described in the *Ciñciṇīmatasārasamuccaya* as emerging from a triangle of her "birth maṇḍala," made up of locations associated with Śākta worship (*pīṭhas*).[37] In this context, the triangle symbolizes the *yoni*, the female organ of procreation, and the descriptions of the birth of the Goddess, her appearance, and the results of her propitiation ooze with liquid metaphors. Despite the palpable sexuality of the language, the *Ciñciṇīmatasārasamuccaya* amalgamates the physical, sexual, and worldly in descriptions of the Goddess, along with the transcendent and sublime. The association of Kāmeśvarī with desire and enjoyment (*bhukti*), as well as knowledge—including that of the transcendent kind (*mukti*)—is further articulated in the next phase.[38]

Flower: The Classical Cult of Tripurasundarī

The classical cult of Tripurasundarī is described in the *Vāmakeśvarīmata*, a text of the early eleventh century CE or earlier, before the Śaiva nondualism of Abhinavagupta and Kṣemarāja had become widely influential.[39] Whereas the Nityā cult had its principal goddess accompanied by a retinue of eleven—or sometimes nine—Nityā goddesses, the classical cult envisioned Tripurasundarī surrounded by an expansive retinue of subordinate goddesses, arranged in nine groups along the concentric levels of the intersecting triangles of the Śrīcakra diagram. The complexity of the Śrīcakra is without parallel in the Hindu Tantric traditions. The new ritual system included fifteen Nityā goddesses. Tripurasundarī, as the sixteenth and foremost among them, was placed in the most elevated location—the dot in the middle of the ritual diagram. Just as the eleven Nityās of the *Nityākaula* corresponded to the main eleven-syllable mantra in that text, the new number of Nityās matched the number of syllables in the principal mantra of the classical cult of Tripurasundarī. One of the new features of this later ritual system was a connection of numerology with the sixteen lunar phases, a feature that was explored in the later texts of this tradition.

In the new ritual system of the classical cult, Tripurasundarī's consort was Śiva, not Kāmadeva. However, references to the god of love as well as to love and desire proliferated in the names of subordinate goddesses, in the sensuality with which the physical appearance of the principal goddess was depicted, and in the descriptive metaphors associating her with red, the color of desire.[40] Consistent with the Nityā cult, in addition to success in love and amorous attraction, propitiation of the Goddess in the classical cult also promised mastery over snakebites and poisons and control of various supernatural beings. Practices for knowledge and eloquence were included, just as in the antecedent cult, and liberation was mentioned among the results of practice. But it was not until a later text of the cult of Tripurasundarī, the *Yoginīhṛdaya*, that salvation began to play a significant role.[41]

Fruit: Śrīvidyā

The ritual system of the classical cult of Tripurasundarī has remained virtually unchanged to the present day. The shape of the Śrīcakra and the location of deities within its nine intersecting triangles, two rows of petals, and a borderlike enclosure with four doors facing the cardinal directions have been preserved unaltered. However, while this complex structure was originally constructed with colored powders for the duration of the ritual, permanent two- and three-dimensional forms have since become more common. Typically they are created from metal (such as a five-metal alloy with or without gold plating), though some are made from semiprecious stones, and occasionally one might still find a temporary *yantra* fashioned with colored powders or flower petals on special occasions. The ritual hand gestures (*mudrās*) described in the *Vāmakeśvarīmata* are still practiced by Tantric adepts; however, two slightly different versions of the main mantra have crystallized over time: the so-called *kādi* and *hādi*, that is, beginning with *ka* or beginning with *ha*. To my knowledge, only the *kādi* mantra is presently transmitted in initiation lineages.

Although the ritual system recorded in the *Vāmakeśvarīmata* just about a millennium ago has come down to the present time relatively unchanged, its interpretation has undergone several transformations. During the first significant wave, the worship of the goddess Tripurasundarī was reinterpreted according to nondual Śaivism. This process of reinterpretation is apparent in the *Yoginīhṛdaya* composed after the mid-eleventh century, as well as in the thirteenth-century commentary by the Kashmirian Jayaratha on the *Vāmakeśvarīmata*.[42] While the authors of the *Vāmakeśvarīmata* did not take a position on philosophical dualism, Jayaratha's commentary on that text, as well as the *Yoginīhṛdaya* itself, used a new interpretive language: that of a philosophical system called Pratyabhijñā (divine recognition). Śrīvidyā scriptures and commentaries composed after the mid-eleventh century included an explicitly nondual view of the universe pervaded by consciousness. They proclaimed the unity of Śiva, the guru, and the self, as well as the Śrīcakra, the Goddess, and the mantra. This divine consciousness was understood to manifest from the undifferentiated cognition within the dot in the central triangle of the Śrīcakra in three stages, corresponding to the knower, the object known, and knowing itself—that is, the central conceptual triad of Pratyabhijñā. In addition to a new philosophical interpretation, the *Yoginīhṛdaya* also included innovative practices. In this text, the adept visualizes the nine levels of the Śrīcakra as superimposed onto the subtle body and mapped to its energy centers. These energy centers, referred to in this text as lotuses and later on as *cakras*, were to be meditated upon using auditory and visual practices. The expected result was that *kuṇḍalinī* (the feminine serpentine energy in the body) would rise up and pierce three "knots" on the way to the uppermost energy center, corresponding to the dot within the innermost triangle in the Śrīcakra. The ultimate goal of these practices was liberation while living, by means of yogic awareness.

A second wave of reinterpretation took place in the southern part of the Indian subcontinent as the Brahminical Smārta orthodoxy adapted the practice of the Śrīcakra ritual. The thirteenth-century south Indian exegete Śivānanda, who distanced himself from his Kaula counterparts, developed a new interpretive paradigm in his commentary on the *Vāmakeśvarīmata*. While preserving in his interpretation the nondual Śaiva language of Pratyabhijñā inherited from the earlier exegetes, Śivānanda aligned the worship of Tripurasundarī with the scriptural world of the Vedas and Upaniṣads. The elucidation of Śrīvidyā, as the cult of Tripurasundarī came to be known, in light of the Vedic corpus and

Advaita Vedānta has become the standard interpretive model since that time. And Tripurasundarī came to be seen as the esoteric essence of local goddesses in south Indian *śakti pīṭhas* (seats of the Goddess) in Tamil Nadu, Andhra Pradesh, and Karnataka.[43] Tripurasundarī is still widely worshiped in contemporary south India and the diaspora. For example, many devotees still chant hymns to the goddess, under her popular name Lalitā (the Playful One). What came to be forgotten is the history of Tripurā's worship, which connects her with Kāmadeva, the god of love.

SOURCES

The first two passages translated here are from the *Nityākaula*, the only extant text from within the Nityā cult. They reach us in a single damaged palm-leaf manuscript in Nepal, microfilmed by the Nepal-German Manuscript Preservation Project on reel B26/21.[44] It is the only manuscript of the *Nityākaula* to survive. These excerpts contain a visualization of the principal goddess, whose name is not preserved in the manuscript, as well as visualizations of the subordinate goddesses and the adept performing the visualizations as part of the ritual. The manuscript is badly damaged, and in my translation an ellipsis indicates a part of the sentence where some text is missing due to damage in the original. Because of the missing fragments and idiosyncratic language, a number of changes to my original translation have been made to aid general readers in understanding the meaning of the cited passages. Specialists can refer to my more technical translation and detailed notes on these passages elsewhere.[45]

The third excerpt translated is a section of the *Ciñciṇīmatasārasamuccaya* that describes Kāmeśvarī's emanation into the earthly realm, where she appears in the form of a young girl. The passage translated here ends with Śiva's conclusion of his exposition on the principal goddess, before he proceeds to the section on the subordinate goddesses. Both the *Nityākaula* and *Ciñciṇīmatasārasamuccaya* were likely composed prior to the early eleventh century. Both texts use a register of Sanskrit called *aiśa* (i.e., divine, belonging to Śiva), which does not conform to standard grammatical conventions. Its frequent use of incorrect inflections and lack of subject-verb agreement may have been meant to emulate the archaic language of the earlier Tantras. Texts of the classical cult of Tripurasundarī did not use *aiśa* Sanskrit and examples of it in the *Vāmakeśvarīmata*, from which I translate the last set of passages here, are rare. My translations do not reflect this peculiarity, aiming instead for maximum intelligibility and accessibility for nonspecialists. There is no published edition or translation of the *Ciñciṇīmatasārasamuccaya*, but Dyczkowski (1988) contains a discussion and synopsis of the text.[46]

The final three passages are excerpted from the earliest extant text of the classical cult of Tripurasundarī, the *Vāmakeśvarīmata*, also called the *Nityāṣoḍaśikārṇava*. Several Sanskrit editions of the *Vāmakeśvarīmata/Nityāṣoḍaśikārṇava* are available. For my translation, I used the 1945 edition of the Kashmir Series of Texts and Studies with a commentary by Jayaratha.[47] Of the three passages from the *Vāmakeśvarīmata* translated here, the first is a selection from the opening section of this text (1.1–4, 7–8, 10–12), which praises Tripurasundarī as a cosmic goddess controlling the universe, time, supernatural powers (*siddhis*), seats of the Goddess, and in particular, speech in all its manifestations.

The second passage from the *Vāmakeśvarīmata* is taken from later in the first chapter. It follows a detailed discussion of powers granted by the worship of the Śrīcakra, the practice of principal and supplementary *vidyās*, and the adept's preparation for performance of the ritual. The adept must emulate the physical form of Tripurasundarī by rubbing his body with saffron and camphor, chewing a betel leaf, and adorning himself with red garments, ornaments, and fragrance. Having dressed as the goddess, the adept also visualizes his body as the goddess herself, having divinized it by mantras and touch in a Tantric practice called *nyāsa*, which prepares one for ritual performance. The adept then prepares the ground, draws the Śrīcakra, and meditates on the goddess. This is where the second passage from the *Vāmakeśvarīmata* (1.113–33) picks up, with a detailed description of how the goddess is to be visualized from head to toe, giving minute particulars of her appearance beginning with her complexion, hair, jewelry, and eyes, going down to her hands, navel, thighs, and feet, and concluding with garments, weapons, ornaments, and so forth. The entire section, which spans twenty verses, forms a single sentence, most of which consists of a string of compounds modifying the word "goddess" (*devīṃ*). The final passage is excerpted from the beginning of the fourth chapter (4.3–12 ab) and describes the goddess as the supreme *śakti* (the divine feminine potentiality), who contains the seeds of everything, manifests the three worlds, and grants even Śiva his ability to act.

FURTHER READING

Golovkova, Anna A. 2012. "Śrīvidyā." In *Brill's Encyclopedia of Hinduism*, Vol. 4, edited by Knut Jacobsen, H. Basu, and A. Malinar, 815–22. Leiden: Brill.

———. 2019. "From Worldly Powers to *Jīvanmukti*: Ritual and Soteriology in the Early Tantras of the Cult of Tripurasundarī." *Journal of Hindu Studies* 12, no. 1 (May): 103–26.

———. 2020. "The Goddess's Forgotten Consort: Desire in the Nityā Cult and the Cult of Tripurasundarī." *International Journal of Hindu Studies* 24, no. 1 (April).

Lidke, Jeff. 2017. *The Goddess Within and Beyond the Three Cities: Śākta Tantra and the Paradox of Power in Nepāla-Maṇḍala*. Tantra in Contemporary Researches 5. New Delhi: DK Printworld.

NOTES

I am grateful to Lawrence J. McCrea, Alexis G. J. S. Sanderson, and Somadeva Vasudeva for their encouragement, inspiration, and advice for my work on the early textual tradition of Śrīvidyā.

1. The original, which is incomplete, does not include the statement "Bhairava spoke to the goddess about the ritual and its benefits," which has been added for clarity. The phrase "a Tantric ritual diagram" has also been added. The original does not specify the relationship between the hexagram and the fire maṇḍala (*ṣaṭkoṇaṃ vahnimaṇḍalam*). However, a sentence that follows the list of subordinate goddesses states that the eleven goddesses and Madana (another name for the god of love, the consort of the principal goddess) pervade the entire *cakra* (wheel/maṇḍala), occupying the spokes and the intermediate places, which suggests that the entire configuration is contained within a six-cornered figure. Cf. *Ciñciṇīmatasārasamuccaya* 125: *cakravyāptaṃ mahādevi ṣaṭkoṇaṃ vahnimaṇḍalam, arakair antarālaiś ca pūjayitvā varānane.*

2. All of these are proper names, for which I provide approximate translations to give the reader a sense of the implied meanings. Some names have a number of possible meanings, which are not reflected in this translation. The names of Rāgavatī and the first syllable of Madanāvatī are missing in the original and have been supplied from *Ciñciṇīmatasārasamuccaya* by Alexis Sanderson in his transcription of the *Nityākaula*.

3. "O lady with lovely thighs" glosses *karabhoru*, which more literally means "O lady with thighs like the [gently sloping] trunk of an elephant."

4. Many Tantras, including this one, are framed as a dialogue between Bhairava and the Goddess. Therefore the text contains a number of epithets of the latter, whom Bhairava addresses. These epithets, which are in the vocative case in Sanskrit, are capitalized here.

5. The word *kula* has a range of meanings. In nontechnical usage it refers to a family or clan and, in the esoteric "Kaula" traditions, to an initiatory lineage. I take *kula* here to refer to material reality.

6. *Maṇḍala* in Sanskrit refers to a disk or an orb, as well as a realm (e.g., the land belonging to a king), and, in the Tantric context, a ritual diagram which is considered

to be coequal with the deity and the mantra. In this latter meaning, it is synonymous with *cakra* (used later in the text) and *yantra*. Here, I understand it to mean "abode," a place in which the deity manifests in the earthly realm, described here as a triangle and formed by the principal seats of the Goddess (see note 37). The mention of the seat named Kāma alludes to Kāmarūpa.

7. Birth maṇḍala refers to the triangle in the middle of which the Goddess appears, as well as the female organ of generation (*yoni*), which is symbolized by a downward-pointing triangle.

8. Kulayoginī, the presiding *yoginī* of the *kula*, the initiatory "family," is an epithet of Kāmeśvarī, the principal goddess in this section of the text.

9. *Yoginīs* are powerful and attractive supernatural female beings. The term can also describe human female adepts. *Siddhas* are a class of semidivine "perfected beings," that is, adepts who have acquired supernatural powers and liberation in the body.

10. The ruddy shelduck (*cakravāka*) is known in India as the *brāhmanīya* duck and is prevalent in the Himalaya region. The *Rāmāyaṇa* tradition describes *cakravāka* birds as cursed by Rāma to remain separated from their mates at night.

11. See note 9. This list includes various groups of semidivine female beings. Śākinī literally means "enabler."

12. The Angry Sage (*krodhamuni*) is an epithet of the sage Durvāsa, famous for his fiery temper. Stories of Durvāsa are found in one of the two great Sanskrit epics, the *Mahābhārata*, and in Kālidāsa's drama *Abhijñānaśākuntala*.

13. The two seeds refers to semen and menstrual blood. The blissful state that arises from the union of Rudra and Rudrāṇī is the source of all manifestations, such as the material universe and also the *nāda* (the divine sound), the latter including the highest scripture, that is, the *Rudrayāmala*.

14. This appears to be a pun on the name of the text, *Rudrayāmala*, and its meaning: the union of Rudra and Rudrāṇī (a form of Śiva and his consort).

15. Kaulīśa (a middle-Indic form of Kauleśa, i.e., the Kaula Lord) is named as the first guru of this tradition.

16. A *vidyā* is a condensed ritual formula for a feminine Tantric deity. *Vidyās* are rarely spelled out in the texts. Instead, they are either encoded using words frequently used to stand in for specific letters (i.e., "fire" for "*ra*" and "god of love" for "*ka*"); their location in the alphabet (i.e., the third letter for "*i*" and the one after "*sa*" for "*ha*"); or using specific grids (*prastāras*), such as the thunderbolt grid mentioned here.

17. The "seats" of the Goddess, which form the triangle mentioned in the passage, are Uḍḍiyāṇa (Oḍḍiyāna), Jālandhara, and Pūrṇapīṭha; Kāmarūpa is located in the center of the triangle. For a discussion of the locations of Uḍḍiyāṇa and Pūrṇapīṭha, see Sanderson (2007, 265–67, 298–99). For a discussion of the triangle of *pīṭhas* in the cult of the goddess Kubjikā, see Dyczkowski (2009, vol. 1, 290–91).

18. Siddhamātrikā refers to a north Indian post-Gupta script used to write many Tantras. In Tantric traditions, both the sounds and the way they were recorded in writing were venerated.

19. See note 17.

20. This sentence, while certainly long, is by no means unprecedented in Sanskrit, since this language follows different rules and conventions than English.

21. Although the original reads "name and place" (*nāma dhāma*), I am following Alexis Sanderson's conjecture by translating it as "name and form" (*nāma rūpa*).

22. Brahmā, Viṣṇu, and Śiva are the three principal male deities of post-Vedic Hinduism and are associated with creation, maintenance, and destruction. Rudra (Terrible, Dreadful) is an epithet of Śiva, which dates back to the Vedic hymns.

23. Śākta is an adjective referring to religious traditions focused on Śakti, a name for the Goddess and the feminine power she represents. Śākta traditions are closely allied to, indeed often explicitly a part of, the broader Tantric movement with Śaivism (the strand of Hinduism focused on the god Śiva).

24. On encoded mantras and *vidyā*s, see note 16. The distinction between male and female mantras and *vidyā*s is specific to the medieval Tantric context and is no longer in use.

25. *Śrīvidyā* is a compound consisting of two parts: *śrī*, an honorific, which conveys the meaning of "auspiciousness," and *vidyā*. Typically the word *vidyā* is translated as "knowledge," but elsewhere I argue that in this context it refers to the Tantric mantras used to propitiate female deities and specifically to the fifteen-syllable root mantra (*vidyā*) of this tradition, famous for its unusual length.

26. On the relationship between earlier Śaiva/Śākta traditions and the Nityā cult, see Sanderson (2009, 47–49). For a detailed analysis of continuities and differences between the Nityā cult and the cult of Tripurasundarī, see Golovkova (2017, 19–65; 2020).

27. For more details, see Sanderson (2009, 48–49) and Golovkova (2017, 17–18 and 148).

28. *Vāḍavānalīya* in *Puraścaryārṇava* (Jha 1985). The transcription of the relevant portion of the text was kindly provided to me by Alexis Sanderson in email correspondence on May 17, 2010. See also Golovkova (2017, 17–18 and 149).

29. Sanderson (1988, 689).

30. For the chronology, see Golovkova (2017, 13).

31. *Tantrāloka* 28.123 and 124ab, *Parātriṃśikāvivaraṇa* (Gnoli 1985, 238).

32. Sanderson (2009, 48). For a detailed discussion of the *Nityākaula*, see Golovkova (2017, 19–37; 2020).

33. See Golovkova (2017, 35–36).

34. Golovkova (2017, 19–65).

35. Golovkova (2017, 26–27).

36. For more on this subject, see White (2003, xii–xv, 94–122).

37. See note 17.

38. See Golovkova (2019).

39. For a discussion of the dates of Abhinavagupta and Kṣemarāja, see Sanderson (2007, 411).

40. See Golovkova (2017, 19–20, 25–37; 2020).

41. See Golovkova (2019).

42. For discussion of the date of the *Yoginīhṛdaya,* see Golovkova (2012, 819). For Jayaratha's date see Sanderson (2007, 418–19).

43. See Golovkova (2017, xi; 2010, 12–14).

44. The passages translated are on folios 2r–2v (up to line 8), and 7r (lines 1–4) respectively.

45. See Golovkova (2017, 2020).

46. For a brief retelling of the section of the *Ciñciṇīmatasārasamuccaya* on the southern transmission, see Dyczkowski (1988, 71). For my translation, I used a scan of the manuscript microfilmed by NGMPP on reel B157/19. Alexis Sanderson provided his own transcription of this manuscript for our reading session in the fall of 2013, during my dissertation research at Oxford University. The passage translated corresponds to folios 18r–20r (up to line 8). In Mark Dyczkowski's draft digital edition on the Muktabodha Digital Library, the passages translated here can be located in the section numbered 7.100–154. He references this manuscript with the siglum "K."

47. Louise M. Finn's (1986) translation of this Tantra with Jayaratha's commentary is also available. Furthermore, Jeffrey S. Lidke (2017, appendix A) includes translations of *maṅgala* verses with commentaries.

FIGURE 23. Avyapadeśyā Kālī, by Laura Santi

CHAPTER 12

Avyapadeśyā

Indefinable Kālī

OLGA SERBAEVA

Our final selection is a very unique passage on Kālī from a little-known, yet fundamentally important, Tantra called the *Jayadrathayāmala*. Its four massive volumes each contain about six thousand stanzas and survive in manuscripts from Nepal and elsewhere. Scholars disagree about the text's provenance, but it is north Indian, possibly compiled in part in Kashmir, and dates to the ninth or tenth centuries. It belongs to the Kālīkula branch of goddess-centered Tantras and details mind-blowing visualizations and secret invocations for over 150 forms of Kālasaṃkarṣaṇī Kālī: Kālī as the Destroyer of Time.

The passage selected is a fine example of apophatic thealogy, the so-called path of negation (*via negativa*) that describes a divine being by foregrounding what she is not, rather than what she is. Readers should keep in mind that the passage comes toward the end of the *Jayadrathayāmala*'s third volume; at this point around one hundred different goddesses have already been revealed and explained with their *vidyā*s and practices, and some fifty more are to come in the fourth volume. It thus represents a culmination and mystical completion of the diverse goddesses of the earlier sections. It has many features in common with a related tradition known as the Krama (the Sequence). Instead of worshiping a particular form of a singular Great Goddess, the Krama taught the sequential worship of multiple series of goddesses, who ultimately were identified as the phases of the cyclical pulse of cognition. In other words, these goddesses were understood to be symbolic expressions of one's own ultimate awareness, to be realized through ritual worship and contemplation.

The passage is challenging with its frequent references to Tantric technical concepts and figures. The detailed notes and essay that follow helpfully explain many of the esoteric ideas and words. As you read, consider the broader significance of the various things that this passage asserts the Goddess is not and try to discern the underlying logic of describing the divine in this way.

॥ जयद्रथयामलम् ३.३५ ॥

एवमाकर्ण्य सा देवी वरवीरेन्द्रवन्दिता । परं संतोषमापन्ना पुनः प्रोवाच
शङ्करम् ॥ तृप्तास्मि परमेशान प्रसादात्तव सांप्रतम् । आदितः सकलं ज्ञानं
तन्त्रराजानमुत्तमम् ॥ अधुना श्रोतुमिच्छामि कथं सा परमेश्वरी । मन्त्र-
मन्त्रेश्वरी सुष्का सिद्धयोगेश्वरेश्वरी ॥ सिद्धिदा रिद्धिदा या सा मोक्षदा पा-
पनाशनी । आसहस्राक्षरारम्भाद्यावत्सप्तादशाक्षरा ॥ एकाक्षरान्तिका देव
कथं सा परमाकला । एका सती अनेका सा बहुरूपा कथं स्थिता ॥ अ-
थवाबहुभेदैव तवाख्याहि महेश्वर । येन संशयनिर्मुक्ता भवामि परमेश्वर ॥
एवमाकर्ण्य सहसा साट्टहासमुवाच ह । भैरवो भीमसंसारशमनैकतरः परः
॥ शृणुष्व कथयिष्यामि यथाहं चोदितस्त्वया । महारहस्यमतुलं दुर्लभं त्रि-
दशेश्वरैः ॥ या सा सर्वगता सूक्ष्मा शक्तिर्भैरवकारणम् । न सा वर्णत्मिका
देवी न स्वरैरपि रञ्जिता ॥ न परा न च पश्यन्ती मध्यमा वैखरी न च ।
न कूटस्फोटभेदाख्या वचसं तु स्वरूपिणी ॥ न व विद्यात्मिका देवी न च
नादमया हि सा । न च बिन्दुकला सैव न व्याप्ती न निरर्थका ॥ न चक्रा-
धारसंरूढा न च नाडिमुखारणी । न च शून्यत्रयाधारा न च धामत्रयीमयी
॥ न सिता नाप्यसौ रक्ता न पीता न व कृष्णिका । न कपोता न कपिला न
च कर्बुरिता हि सा ॥ शबला नैव सा देवी न च तेजःकलाकुला । न शब्दं
न च सा स्पर्शं नैव रूपं रसं न हि ॥ न च गन्धं नेन्द्रियाणी करणानि न
सा परा । नापरा परमेशानी परात्परतरा न हि ॥ न सा भासा न सा वीर्यं
न सा व्यक्तिः कला न सा । न प्रधानं न पुम्स्तत्त्वं न विद्या नागमे व सा
॥ कालं न साकला नैव नियतिर्न नियामिका । न सा माया महामाया न
विद्या शुद्धसंज्ञिका ॥ नेश्वरं सा न सादाख्यं न शक्तिर् न शिवं च सा । न
सुप्ता नोत्थिता देवी न जडा न च मन्थरा ॥ न दिङ् मूर्त्तिर्च नाभा सा न
भूता न विनायकाः । न सा जातिर्न सा देशं न सा देहं न भासुरा ॥ न
कामक्रोधरूपा सा न मृता न च जीवति । न सा जाग्रन्न सा स्वप्नं सुषुप्तं
नैव सा प्रिये ॥ न सा तुर्यं तदन्तं वा पिण्डस्थं नैव सा सदा । पदस्थं न
च रूपस्थं न रूपातीतमेव सा ॥ बुद्धा प्रबुद्धा संबुद्धा न कदाचिद् इहेश्वरी
। प्रचया नैव देवी सा न मया प्रचया हि सा ॥ परनिवृतिनिष्पन्ना न वा
ह्यज्ञानरूपिणी । न †शून्यानामिसा† हौत्री न वागेशी त्रयीमयी ॥ न सा
भर्गशिखा प्रोक्ता न खशोल्का महेश्वरि । न वा हंसी न वानन्दा निरानन्दा
न चैव हि ॥ न योगिनी न देवी सा न शक्ति न करङ्किणी । न काली नैव क-

FIGURE 24. *Jayadrathayāmala*, a hybrid Sanskrit work in the Devanagari script. Font “Free Serif” © gnu.org.

KĀLĪ THE INDEFINABLE (*JAYADRATHAYĀMALA* 3.35)

After hearing the previous teaching, the goddess praised by heroes was highly pleased, and spoke again to Śiva. The goddess said, "O Great Lord, I am now content—you graciously imparted complete knowledge: the supreme King of Tantras. Now, I wish to hear about *Her*, the highest Goddess, the Mistress of all mantras called Śuṣkā, shriveled, and Siddhayogeśvarī, the queen of magic female spirits—the one who gives supernatural powers and worldly prosperity (*siddhi* and *ṛddhi*), bestows liberation and destroys sins, the one whose mantra-forms span from one thousand syllables down to seventeen syllables, and even to a single syllable—O God, how is she the supreme root of creation?[1] Being singular, how does she become many and of multiple forms? Or rather, O Great Lord, speak of the one who does not take many forms, so that I become liberated from doubt." On hearing that, supreme Bhairava, the only one capable of pacifying this terrible ocean of existence (*saṃsāra*), suddenly laughed loudly and said, "Listen—just as you requested, I will tell you that great and peerless secret that is hard to know, even for the highest gods.

"This subtle Power (*śakti*) is all pervasive, the originator of Bhairava.[2] The Goddess does not consist of letters and is not affected by the vowels. She is not the highest level of speech, nor visionary speech, nor the middle type, nor common speech; her essence is that speech that cannot be defined by the separations related to gross and subtle qualities of sound. This Goddess is not the embodiment of knowledge, nor does she have the nature of the subtle sound or vibration (*nāda*) that underlies existence. She is not an aspect of the primal vibration called 'drop' (*bindu*), nor is she the pervasions—and yet she is not meaningless.[3] She does not arise from the foundational energy center (*cakra*), nor does she serve to inflame the mouth of the vital channels.[4] She is not the basis of the three voids, nor does she have the nature of the three luminaries.[5] She is not white, not red, not yellow, and not black, not gray, not brown, and not of mixed color. This Goddess is not mottled, nor is she fiery in appearance. She is not sound, not touch, not form, nor taste. She is not smell, nor the sense organs, nor their subtle forms.[6] She is not the non-supreme goddess of the Trika school Aparā, not the supreme goddess Parā, and not Parāparā who is supreme-cum-non-supreme.[7] She is not pure light, nor power, nor the manifest, nor an aspect.[8]

"She is neither primordial matter, nor spirit, nor the limited knowledge found in the scriptures.[9] She is not time, nor limited agency, nor the limited view of causation, nor that passion that derives from karmic necessity. She is neither illusion, nor the great illusion called pure knowledge. She is not Īśvara, and not Sadāśiva, not Śakti and not Śiva.[10]

"She is not sleeping and not standing, neither inert nor sluggish. She is not a personification of space, nor light, nor is she a ghost, nor an obstructing spirit. She has no caste, nor place; she has no body, and neither is she shining. She does not take the form of desire and anger; she is neither dead nor living.

"She is not the wakeful state, nor dream, nor deep sleep, my beloved.[11] She is not the fourth state of pure consciousness that underlies the prior three, nor what is beyond that.[12] She is not eternally abiding in the Body, nor the Word, nor in Form, nor in the Transcendence of Form.[13] In this tradition, the Goddess is never characterized as the state of being awake, wide awake, nor fully awake. She is not the mystical state known as Accumulation, nor is she the Great Accumulation beyond that.[14] She neither arises from supreme bliss, nor does she take the form of ignorance. She is not related to the priesthood, and she is not the goddess of Speech consisting of the triple Veda. She is not the one called Bhargaśikhā, nor is she the great sun goddess Khaśolkā.[15] She is not the goddess Haṃsī, embodying the *haṃsa* mantra, nor is she bliss or devoid of bliss.[16] She is not a *yoginī*, not a goddess, and not a female spiritual power (*śakti*). She is not the skull-bearing goddess Karaṅkiṇī, nor the dark goddess of time Kālī, nor skeleton-like Kaṅkālī.

"She is not the seventeen-syllable *vidyā*, nor a single-syllable *vidyā*, nor one consisting of many syllables, nor does she have the nature of a network of powers.[17] She is not running, nor standing still, nor crying, nor speaking. She is neither the endpoint of the supramental state, nor true consideration, nor is she the blowing out of a lamp (i.e., the Buddhist *nirvāṇa*). She is not Brahmā, not Viṣṇu, not Rudra, not Īśvara. This Goddess is not the eternal Sadāśiva, nor does she have an independent form.[18] She is not the goddess in the central channel, and she is not the magic female spirit Siddhayogeśvarī. She is not Cāmuṇḍā, nor is she the great parching goddess Mahocchuṣmā. She is not the gaping Karālā, buck-toothed Danturā, Raktā the Red, or the fierce-eyed Caṇḍākṣī. She is not Viccā and not the frightful Bhairavī.[19] She is not the Queen of Horror Ghoreśī, and not the Queen of the Universe (Viśveśī), nor is she the non-horrific leader of the universe, Viśvāghoranāyikā. She is not Hāraudrī who screams 'hā,' not smoky-lipped Bhaṃbhoṭṭhā, not the bone goddess Haḍḍā, and not Haḍḍāyudhā who bears bone weapons.[20] She is not 'bear-eared' Ṛkṣakarṇī, nor the fierce goddess Caṇḍeśī, nor the Queen of Dancers Naṭṭeśvarī. She is not the mothers, the female powers behind the gods Brahmā, Maheśvara, Kumāra, Viṣṇu, Varāha, and Indra, nor the mothers Viccā and Caccikā.[21] She is not the power of Yama, god of death, nor of Kubera, god of treasure. She is not the power of the water god Varuṇa, nor that of the wind, Samīraṇa. She is not the power of Agni, god of fire, nor that of lord Īśāna, nor of the chaos god Nairṛti, the sun, or the moon. She is not the power of the skull-bearing Kapālī, nor that of Garuḍa or Bharūṭika. She is not the power of Narasiṃha, not that of Rudra, and she is not the beloved of Bhairava.[22] She is not to be known as the singular Ekatarā, and neither is she Jvālāmukhī, the fire-breathing goddess. She is not Khiṃkhiṇī, nor the mother of heroes Vīramātā, nor Śivadūtī, the messenger of Śiva.[23] She is not the goddess who takes the form of weapons, Astrarūpiṇī, nor is she the tumultuous Ḍāmarikā. She is not the victorious goddesses Jayā, Vijayā, and Jayantī, nor their sister the invincible Aparājitā. She is not a messenger goddess (*dūtī*), nor a servant goddess (*kiṃkarī*), nor is she Kāmeśvarī, the one with an elephant-goad.[24] The Goddess is not the Queen of Speech Vāgeśvarī, nor is she the coiled one called Kuṇḍalā. She is not the auspicious Maṅgalā, nor the eternal Nityā, nor indeed Ratneśvarī, the Queen of Jewels.[25] She is not to be found in the Dakṣiṇa Tantras of the right side, nor the Vāma Tantras of the left. She is not in the Eastern (Gāruḍa) Tantras nor the Western (Bhūta) Tantras. She is not in the Upper revelation, nor the Lower, nor is she doctrine or discipline. She is not in Kula or Kaula Tantra, nor the Atimārga or Lākula. She is not in the Siddhānta, nor what is beyond it, nor is she in the Kāruka and Vaimala traditions. She is not in Vedānta, nor in the Veda, nor its auxiliary literature.[26]

"She is called Nameless, Waveless, and Without-a-Clan.[27] Manifesting in that expansive domain of reflexive awareness, she is that true nature that encompasses the true nature of each individual. She is it. It is she. That is exactly how she is. She is that consciousness which shines forth on its own by virtue of her supremacy over unconsciousness. Everything that was named before is colored by her. Truly, she is never colored by anything. For without her there is nothing in this world of animate and inanimate things characterized by distinctions and nondistinctions, O Great Goddess. That is her true nature, which was taught from the guru's mouth. That person who ascertains this firmly is said to be Bhairava; otherwise, my beauty, his state of being bound does not change. For this reason, O goddess, she is called the 'Seal' (*mudrā*). All of this bears her impression, from Śiva down to the earth. O Great Goddess, she is unchangeable, waveless, beyond the mind, without divisions, without dependencies, having a true nature that cannot be reached by any paths.[28] Her form encompasses the entire cosmic orb, resembling a full, brimming ocean. O goddess, everything that was named above springs forth from her. O lady with beautiful eyebrows, in this world, she is to be known as located inside the bulb.[29] She is infinite, and all of this is pervaded by her. She takes all forms, is present everywhere, is queen of everything, and is garlanded with everything. She is eternally near, not far away. That formless one is truly one's own true nature.

"Knowing her, one attains liberation while alive. Any other way is useless. By merely knowing her, one may immediately master anything that exists, from Śiva down to the earth. O Supreme Goddess, she is hard to obtain even for Brahmā and other gods. Even if not sought after, blessings come to the aspirant because of her power. Wherever such a mortal lives, be it in the country, in a town, or in a city, he will lead others to liberation instantly by a glance or a touch. Even inanimate things he touches, O Supreme Goddess, become united with Śiva, have no doubt. Such a one is the foremost religious abode and the supreme basis of the mantras.[30] That one is the incomparable womb of *vidyā*s. That one is a purifying fire to the firewood of sin. That one is what the 'rays' praise; the magical perfections always flock to him.[31] Relying on that Lakṣmī of liberation, he always flourishes. One who has this knowledge in his body, acquired by the grace of the guru's mouth, doubtlessly becomes a man who accomplishes everything by resorting to that power. She is the essence of numerous *vidyā*s, possesses numerous forms, and bestows the results of numerous accomplishments. Possessing hand gestures (*mudrā*s) and maṇḍalas, she is singular, yet embodies the universe. She has slipped away from the distinctions of existence.[32] This, which is beyond any quality, has been explained to you in accordance with the essence of the scriptures.

"It has been received like this, from mouth to mouth, and it is never to be written in a book. That essence of various Kula and non-Kula teachings is to be obtained from the mouth of the guru. Free of mantras and so forth, it is ever abundant, quiescent, and extremely bright. O daughter of the mountains, this is the secret of everything, which should be kept from improper recipients. Tell me what I shall tell you now, from among the things stationed in my heart."

Thus ends the chapter on knowledge of Kālī beyond any quality or appellation, in the third hexad of the *Jayadrathayāmala*, the great Tantra of twenty-four thousand verses, belonging to the canon of the Śiraścheda, stationed within the Vidyāpīṭha that belongs to the Bhairava stream of revelation.

THE GODDESS IN CONTEXT: DEFINING THE INDEFINABLE

Today Kālī is among the most important Hindu goddesses, along with Durgā, Lakṣmī, and Sarasvatī. And yet the image and associations that most people have regarding Kālī are often uninformed by the multifaceted traditions that have been dedicated to her down the ages. The Kālī that one thinks of today is a classical form known as Dakṣiṇa Kālī, where she stands on Śiva, holds a sword, and wears a skirt of severed arms and a garland of heads. Yet this originally Tantric image is rather late; it expresses a form of Kālī that rose to popularity in northeastern India, probably after the thirteenth century CE. This famous image is but one of more than a hundred forms of Kālī known around the tenth century in northern India. Each of these Kālīs had her own secret invocations (*vidyā*), was surrounded by a particular clan of *yoginīs*, and was invoked by unique practices. Each came into the visions of Tantric practitioners in hair-raising and mind-blowing forms, which the old visionary passages (*dhyāna*) struggle to capture in words.

These now-forgotten Kālīs belonged to the *Jayadrathayāmala*, the only surviving Tantra that taught such a large variety of goddesses under the umbrella name "Kālī."[33] Despite the number of scholars working on various aspects of Kālī's diverse religious traditions, few writing for general audiences have taken into account the vast and fundamental corpus of early Tantric texts on Kālī. The present chapter offers a translation of a passage from the *Jayadrathayāmala* that elevates Kālī to the highest level in the universe, making even her usual consort Bhairava appear a mere expression of her nature and power. It does so by following the so-called *via negativa* found in many mystical traditions around the world: it enumerates the various things she is *not* in order to emphasize her ultimate transcendence.

Seed: Kālī and the Tantras

It is not possible to locate the precise time and place that Kālī appeared as a Hindu goddess or when she was first an object of Tantric worship. In the Vedic rituals, and further in Śaiva (Śiva-oriented) rituals, the all-important god of fire Agni was said to have seven tongues, which were gendered feminine, and one of which was named "Kālī." In the earliest Purāṇas, Kālī is also the name of a mentally generated daughter of the Vedic forefathers, standing at the very beginning of creation.[34] These same compendia feature Kālī as an independent goddess, incorporated as the darker-complexioned form of

Pārvatī, who, unlike her form as wife of Śiva, participates in various battles and destroys demons. Even though these early instances of Kālī apparently enjoyed great respect within the orthodox Brahminical tradition, they were not originally linked to the Tantric Kālī that so heavily influenced how she is viewed today.

It is not until the second part of the *Liṅga Purāṇa* that Kālī's identity as a Tantric goddess is made explicit to the relatively orthodox audiences of the Purāṇas, and she becomes an object of worship as a deity of personal choice.[35] And it is only in the *Matsya Purāṇa* that she starts to be seen as Śiva's perfect equal, retaining her form even after the destruction of the universe at the end of a cosmic eon.[36] Somewhere around the tenth century we see a major change in the Purāṇas: they start to incorporate whole chapters of the Tantras, and Kālī emerges from the world of esoteric Tantras and transgressive rituals into the orthodox realm without shedding her full Tantric glory.[37] Various other Purāṇas, such as the *Kālikā* and the ritual manuals dedicated to Dakṣiṇa Kālī, came later.

Tracking the earlier rise of Kālī in the Tantras, of course, is a separate and much more difficult task; the Tantric literature is vast, and many voluminous and critically important early sources are only available in unedited manuscripts. The principal gateway into early Tantric literature is the indispensable scholarship of Alexis Sanderson, recommended in the further reading section. Conveying something of the development of the Tantras in a few pages necessitates great simplifications. From the early centuries CE, an array of Śaiva religious groups laid the foundation for what would soon become the Tantric traditions. From its inception, the Tantras constituted a religious movement that promised liberation from the suffering of life in *saṃsāra* through a ritual of initiation by a guru, an authorized religious master. The nature of that initiation (*dīkṣā*), the rituals the aspirant would be required to fulfill, the cosmology of deities, and the means of worshiping them all developed in diverse ways in dozens of distinct Tantric sects. Nevertheless, the sects almost always shared particular features: the use of sacred sounds (male mantras and female *vidyās*) to invoke, evoke, and propitiate the deities that those same sounds embodied; the arrangement of their worship in sacred spaces (maṇḍalas), often circular, in which the deity is elaborately visualized or physically depicted as residing in the center and surrounded by a coterie of attendant powers; and the development of models of the universe distinct from those of earlier Hindu traditions.

Early on, in the Śaiva renouncer traditions of the Atimārga and the early scriptures of the Siddhānta sect, goddesses were hardly visible or played only a secondary role. But parallel to those early traditions, various local cults worshiped numerous wild and dangerous female deities. The early Tantras, especially the texts of the Trika (triad) school and the *Jayadrathayāmala*, preserve numerous goddesses with non-Sanskrit names and sometimes non-Sanskrit *vidyās*; one of the most popular was Cāmuṇḍā, who became largely synonymous with Kālī. The goddesses gradually overtook Śaiva structures, replacing Śiva or Bhairava as the central deity of the maṇḍala and transcending his role as the highest of the high in the cosmology. In philosophical terms, the Goddess becomes that ground from which the consciousness of Bhairava manifests, but which he knows nothing about. That process was gradual and can be seen in transition from the *Brahmayāmala*, the early Trika Tantras (*Siddhayogeśvarīmata* and *Tantrasadbhāva*), to the Kālīkula and Krama schools.

Flower: Kālī's Apogee in the Krama Cult

Kālīkula, or the "clan of Kālī," survives in a number of different scriptures. In his monumental *Light on the Tantras* (*Tantrāloka*), the famed Kashmirian polymath Abhinavagupta represents the Kālīkula as the second major Tantric tradition following the Trika and hints that for him the Kālīkula is synonymous with the *Jayadrathayāmala*.[38] Indeed, the *Jayadrathayāmala* calls itself a part of the Kālīkula.[39]

The *Jayadrathayāmala* is a massive text entirely devoted to rituals and lore for numerous forms of Kālī. It consists of four volumes, called hexads (*ṣaṭka*) because each was reckoned to contain approximately six thousand verses. It was compiled in northern India, before or during the tenth century CE, and was known to and extensively cited by Abhinavagupta and Kṣemarāja in Kashmir, whence the common misconception that it is a tradition unique to Kashmir.[40]

Although the *Jayadrathayāmala* was likely compiled by a single person, the text itself should not be seen as an independent creation; it is an assemblage of pieces of some fifty different texts that have been identified so far, cited directly and indirectly, while the total number of texts, their classes and subclasses, and their traditions known to the compiler at least by name exceed nine hundred.[41]

The typical structure of most of the *Jayadrathayāmala*'s 202 chapters is rather stable and follows the typical logic of the Kālīkula branch of the early Tantras: an introduction; a coded *vidyā* of a particular form of the goddess; and a description of her *dhyāna*, that is, the way she looks when she appears in a spontaneous vision, or sometimes, the way she is to be drawn on a canvas. This is followed by the technicalities of the practice one undertakes to propitiate her (*sādhana*) and the resulting supernatural powers (*siddhis*). In the *sādhana* passages the practitioner is advised which observances (*vrata*) to adopt, which gestures (*mudrā*) to use to activate the power of the goddess, in which places and with which ingredients the worship is to be done, and so forth. However, there is a distinct set of chapters in the third and fourth volumes that propose one more level of esoteric reading.[42] These chapters deny any particular form of the Goddess as being the absolute one, stating that she is the dynamic, all-encompassing consciousness, the source from which everything comes into existence, but also that she is not affected by that creation in any way. She is formless and nameless. These chapters bear clear traces of the Krama tradition, and the passage translated here belongs to that set.

What distinguishes the Kālīkula from the Krama is the latter's sequential worship of a group of Kālīs rather than one particular goddess as supreme or a single set of particular goddesses. Furthermore, adherents regard these sets as representations of four or five phases (*krama*) of the cyclical pulse of cognition.[43] Each goddess represents a particular aspect of consciousness, a particular step (*krama*) in the realization of the absolute, encoded, broadly speaking, by a set of relations between the knower, the object to be known, and the means of knowing. The Kālīs become aspects of the ever-changing functioning of consciousness—not the goddesses with multiple arms—and it was precisely the Krama tradition that laid its imprint on the whole philosophy of Abhinavagupta. In the Krama, the goddesses lose some of their Kula or Kaula features; the external means of worship so critical in the prior systems has little to do with the realization of the absolute nature of consciousness in the Krama. That nature cannot be described in words, which is the reason for the description by negation, or for combining the poles of any scale. For example, she might be described as "the highest of the high, yet present in mundane things."

The reader should keep in mind the following feature of the Krama while revisiting the passage: it tends to represent the usual Tantric procedures, that is, mantra recitation, maṇḍalas, hand gestures (*mudrā*), and other external aspects of worship as useless, having no effect on one who wants to realize the supreme reality. The same is true in relation to deities. The chapter mentions many ancient and otherwise unknown and forgotten goddesses, both reviving and reinvoking them, yet asserting that they are not the complete essence of the Nameless Kālī. The Krama is a way without a way; it is a tradition opting for spontaneous realization in a single instant or, sometimes, in a sequence of powerful and life-changing firsthand experiences. The highest of them is the realization of the true nature of consciousness, and once the state of that realization becomes permanent, the person is then considered to be liberated while alive (*jīvanmukta*) and equal to Bhairava himself.[44]

The translated passage precisely describes that state of consciousness where one identifies with the Goddess here called "Kālī who Defies Definition." It describes by negation, by primarily stating what the Goddess is *not* rather than what she is. In India, this hearkens back to the Vedānta tradition, in which the absolute nature of the self (*ātman*) is characterized by the utterance "not–, not–" (*neti neti*).[45] In other words, it is beyond normal description—beyond mundane human categories. Various interpretations of the Krama school distinguish four or five main phases: creation, preservation, destruction, and the Nameless (*anākhya*), which is the final one in some of the traditions, while in the others it is superseded by the pure light of consciousness (*bhāsā*). Interestingly, the passage translated here reinforces the Nameless approach and denies that light is a fitting identifier for her. Even though it does not use the preferred Krama term "nameless," it clearly points to this concept by describing her as indefinable (*avyapadeśyā*), without name (*nirnāmā*), and so forth.

Fruit: The Jayadrathayāmala *and Later Kālī Traditions*

The vision of Kālī as the perfect embodiment of absolute transcendent and immanent consciousness, beyond which nothing would exist, had a profound influence on the works of Abhinavagupta and Kṣemarāja, both of whom were impacted by the Krama. However, the Krama and the related Kālīkula traditions rather mysteriously vanished from the religious landscape in India, with some exceptions.[46] A case could be made, however, that among all Tantric goddesses known to the early Vidyāpīṭha, it is Kālī who became the Tantric goddess par excellence (in her form Dakṣiṇa Kālī) because—at least in part—of the influence of the *Jayadrathayāmala* and its conglomeration of more than 150 goddesses under Kālī's name. Indeed, the direct influence of the *Jayadrathayāmala* is visible in the various chapters of the *Mahākālasaṃhitā* and in the cult of Guhyakālī, or Secret Kālī, which is still very active in Nepal.

SOURCE

The translated passage is chapter 35 of the third six-thousand-verse volume (*ṣaṭka*) of the *Jayadrathayāmala*, written in Tantric hybrid Sanskrit. It has never before been published, so the translation is made on the basis of the eight surviving manuscripts that include this section, in whole or in part. Archival details of each manuscript are listed under *Jayadrathayāmala* in the "Primary Sources" section in the back of this volume.[47] The translation has supplied English versions of the names of various goddesses so that the flavor of the Sanskrit comes through in the translation. Readers should note, however, that the iconographic descriptions of these goddesses do not regularly reflect the literal meaning of their names. For example, the goddess whose name we render as "the 'bear-eared' Ṛkṣakarṇī" is not actually described as having bear-like ears, despite this being the literal meaning of her name.

FURTHER READING

Dyczkowski, Mark. 1988. *The Canon of the Śaivāgama and the Kubjikā Tantras of the Western Kaula Tradition*. Albany: State University of New York Press.

Sanderson, Alexis. 1988. "Śaivism and the Tantric Traditions." In *The World's Religions*, edited by S. Sutherland, 660–704. London: Routledge and Kegan Paul.

———. 2009. "The Śaiva Age: The Rise and Dominance of Śaivism during the Early Medieval Period." In *Genesis and Development of Tantrism*, edited by Shingo Einoo, 41–350. Institute of Oriental Culture Special Series, 23. Tokyo: Institute of Oriental Culture, University of Tokyo.

Serbaeva, Olga. 2015. "Yoga from Yoginīs' Point of View." *Journal of Hindu Studies* 8: 245–62.

NOTES

Dedicated to Pitājī and Alexis Sanderson. I am also grateful to Michael Slouber and Shaman Hatley for polishing my non-native English and for some important suggestions concerning translation of technical terms.

1. The *vidyās* of Śuṣkā and Siddhayogeśvarī are explained in the third book (*ṣaṭka*); Śuṣkā also occurs throughout *ṣaṭkas* 2 and 4. The name of the root Tantra of the Trika

is *Siddhayogeśvarī*, and this is the first of many references to Trika goddesses in this chapter. For more on the Trika and its early scripture the *Siddhayogeśvarīmata*, see Törzsök (1999). The translation "the queen of magic female spirits" follows Törzsök. The third *ṣaṭka* of the *Jayadrathayāmala* gives three *vidyās* exceeding one thousand syllables in their extracted forms: those of Trailokyaḍāmarī, Matacakreśvarī, and Ghoratarā. The word for "supreme root of creation" (*kalā*) can mean anything from particle to agent; what is important here is the fact that *kalā* is always a limited part of something else. *Paramakalā* often refers to the secret *kalā*, or phase of the new moon, which is invisible itself, but by which the moon changes its phase.

2. The phrase "the originator of Bhairava" (*bhairavakāraṇam*) might alternatively mean "Bhairava's causal body."

3. Regarding the hierarchical levels of speech, see Padoux (1990). The phrase "cannot be defined by the separations related to gross and subtle qualities of sound" translates *na kūṭasphoṭabhedākhyā*. These are technical terms referring to mantras; *kūṭas* are the parts that are effectively pronounced, whereas *sphoṭas* refer to subtle parts of speech, having particular value in the description of the effects that mantras have in the *Jayadrathayāmala*. Monier-Williams's dictionary, citing Patañjali, defines *sphoṭa* as follows: "the eternal and imperceptible element of sounds and words and the real vehicle of the idea which bursts or flashes on the mind when a sound is uttered." The concept of "subtle sound" (*nāda*) refers to a stage in the divine emanation of speech in Tantric cosmology. The phrase "nor is she the pervasions" alludes to the practice of provoked deity possession (*āveśa*), the very essence of the Tantric system upon which the *Jayadrathayāmala* is founded.

4. "The foundational energy center (*cakra*)" refers to the position of *kuṇḍalinī* as dormant at the root of the spine in the *mūlādhāra cakra*, and the preliminary stages of her awakening, when the channels leading upward are getting opened and their mouths "inflamed."

5. The phrase "the three luminaries" (*dhāmatrayī*) may variously be interpreted as yogic states of consciousness marked by particular visionary experiences or may refer to the sun, moon, and fire.

6. Sound, touch, form, taste, smell, and the ten gross and subtle sense organs refer to the lowest fifteen levels of reality (*tattvas*) of the Sāṃkhya philosophical system, which are rejected.

7. Here two of the famous goddesses of the Trika system are invoked using synonyms (Parameśānī and Parātparā).

8. The precise meanings of these terms (*bhāsā*, *vīrya*, *vyakti*, and *kalā*) are not yet clear. The same words define the *śakti* at *Jayadrathayāmala* 3.2.529cd: *vīryavyaktikalāśrayān*. *Bhāsā* and *vīrya* occur as a pair in *Jayadrathayāmala* 2.21. Krama scriptures sometimes identify *bhāsā*, or "pure light," with the Absolute. "Power" (*vīrya*) is given much importance in the *Jayadrathayāmala* as the force behind the *vidyās*.

9. "Primordial matter" (*pradhāna*) refers to the female principle of the Sāṃkhya system that gives rise to the material world, better known as *prakṛti*, the twenty-fourth *tattva*. "Spirit" refers to the twenty-fifth *tattva* of Sāṃkhya, the male principle (*puruṣa*).

10. "Not time . . . not Śiva" The first five principles being negated are the technical terms *vidyā, kāla, kalā, niyati,* and *niyāmika,* which refer to the so-called corset (*kañcuka*), the first five principles of reality (*tattva*) that Śaivas added to the Sāṃkhya set of twenty-five. The text then denies Kālī's identity with the six higher principles up to the thirty-sixth level: *māyā, śuddhavidyā, īśvara, sadāśiva, śakti,* and *śiva.*

11. *Āgamas* are Tantric texts, sometimes referring to the Śaiva Siddhānta scriptures only, and otherwise used generically for all Tantric texts, or even all revelation, including the Vedas.

12. The Upaniṣadic doctrine of five states of consciousness is rejected as the identity of the Goddess: wakeful state, sleeping, deep sleep, the fourth state (*turya*) of pure consciousness, and the mystical state beyond the fourth (*turyātīta*).

13. *Piṇḍa, pada, rūpa, rūpātīta,* and so forth are the classification of bodies from gross to increasingly subtle in the Kula Tantric system. See Vasudeva (2004, 214–33). This classification often runs parallel to the gross, subtle, very subtle, and supreme (*sthūla, sūkṣma, kāraṇa, mahākāraṇa*) sequence of bodies known also in various yoga traditions, but these two classifications related to the bodies are not easily linked. Here the Kula/Kaula way of progress in the practice is being rejected.

14. "Accumulation" and "Great Accumulation" (*pracaya* and *mahāpracaya*) are technical terms for mystical states of consciousness that the *Mālinīvijayottara* (2.38) correlates with the previously referenced states called the fourth state and beyond the fourth (*turya* and *turyātīta*). See Vasudeva (2004, 229–30). I thank Michael Slouber for attracting my attention to the MVT, which supported *mahāpracaya* as a conjecture for *mayāpracaya.*

15. Bhargaśikhā is a reference to Paramārkakālī, whose *vidyā* is taught in *Jayadrathayāmala* 4.52; *khaśolkā* is a likely reference to Mārtaṇḍakālī, in the same chapter. Bhargaśikhā and Paramārkakālī are also linked in the *Kramastotra,* as edited in Silburn (1975, 194).

16. The *haṃsa* is a symbol of the yogic liberation, a goose or swan, here given in the feminine. The major *vidyās* of the *Jayadrathayāmala* mention the goddess Haṃsī.

17. The seventeen-syllable *vidyā* is the root spell of the goddess Kālasaṃkarṣaṇī, the most important *vidyā* of the whole text, encoded and decoded throughout the *Jayadrathayāmala.* The interpretation of *ekārṇā* as "a single-syllable *vidyā*" fits the context. However it is possible that the word *arṇa* alludes to a "wave," which could be a reference to the "waveless" concept of the Krama school; in this case we would understand *jāla* as watery rather than a network of *śaktis.*

18. The previously mentioned Brahmā, Viṣṇu, Rudra, and Īśvara are the highest gods of classical Hinduism. Now the Śaiva upgrades to the normal structures, including all gods, are being rejected. The word "independent" (*anāśrita*) already held great spiritual significance in the earliest surviving Śaiva Tantra, the *Niśvāsatattvasaṃhitā,* in the Vyomavyāpin mantra: *oṃ vyomavyāpine 2 vyomarūpāya sarvavyāpine śivāya anantāya anāthāya anāśritāya dhruvāya* (5.11.2.1, cited from Dominic Goodall's electronic transcript). The *Svacchandabhairava Tantra* gives particular importance to that form in chapters 7, 10, and 11.

19. "Cāmuṇḍā . . . Viccā": these are the most important goddesses of the *Brahmayāmala*, occurring in its various maṇḍalas and the modes of worship throughout the text. See, for example, the third chapter on maṇḍalas, edited and translated by Csaba Kiss (2015, 14, 18, 206, 222). Viccā is a part of early Cāmuṇḍā *vidyās*, sometimes seen as an independent goddess and not just a part of a mantra in the *Jayadrathayāmala*.

20. Hāraudrī is one of the six secret *yoginīs* of the Trika. This demonstrates that the author of this chapter was well aware of even minute details of the Trika. The list of those *yoginīs* is given in *Mālinīvijayottara Tantra* 20.59cd, *Siddhayogeśvarīmata* 28.17cd and 29.13ab, *Tantrāloka* 33.2ab, and *Tantrasadbhāva* 5.25ab and 16.4ab. It is probably a metrical corruption of *mahāraudrī*, which became a true mark of the Trika. Bhaṃbhoṭṭhā, Haḍḍā, and Haḍḍāyudhā are archaic Tantric goddesses who are still invoked in the *Jayadrathayāmala* in various big *vidyās*, such as that of Śabdakālī. The English interpretations of their names are speculative.

21. Ṛkṣakarṇī (Bear-ears) is a goddess taught in the *Jayadrathayāmala*'s *ṣaṭka* 2 and 4. Caṇḍeśī might refer to Caṇḍayogeśvarī's root *vidyā*. Naṭṭeśvarī's *vidyā* is taught in *ṣaṭka* 4. Viccā and Caccikā are sometimes included in lists of the *mātṛs*, and replace Cāmuṇḍā.

22. This extended list of *mātṛs*, including ones associated with the directions, is found in the earliest *yāmala* Tantra, the *Brahmayāmala* (e.g., chapter 56). Many are also found in the earliest Purāṇas. Later on, the list of *mātṛs* gets crystallized at seven. On that, see Serbaeva (2006). Bhāruṭikā/-ḍikā/-ḍhikā is an archaic goddess who is apparently only recorded in the *Jayadrathayāmala*. It preserves some of her *vidyās* incorporated within the bigger ones but does not dedicate any whole chapters to her.

23. The *vidyā* of Ekatarā is given in *ṣaṭka* 4. Jvālāmukhī belongs to the earlier strata of the goddesses. The name "Jvālāmukhī" appears in Cāmuṇḍā-related *vidyās*, which constitute what appears to be the earliest textual strata of Śākta religion. Khiṃkhiṇī and Śivadūtī are early forms of the goddess, who appear in many raised *vidyās* of the *Jayadrathayāmala* but are not invoked independently in this text. Śivadūtī appears in some Purāṇas in the context of killing demons. Vīramātā, described in *Jayadrathayāmala* 2.17, is followed by multiple goddesses having the forms and names of various weapons.

24. Jayā, Vijayā, Jayantī, and Aparājitā are very ancient *śaktis* who became extremely popular in early medieval India, especially when they were presented as Tumburu's sisters in the Vāma Tantras. *Kiṃkaras*, or servants, are lower deities of the maṇḍala, often placed toward its outside in the *Jayadrathayāmala*. *Dūtīs* are the female deities who attend on another goddess, sometimes surrounding her directly in the maṇḍala. "Nor is she Kāmeśvarī, the one with an elephant-goad" (*na ca sāṅkuśarūpiṇī*). The translation supplies "Kāmeśvarī" as a cross-reference to chapter 11, but the goad is a weapon that many goddesses like her hold or that appear in their maṇḍalas.

25. "Vāgeśvarī . . . Ratneśvarī": here Bhairava denies several *vidyās* that he revealed in *ṣaṭka* 3 as being the essence of the goddess. Vāgeśvarī was revealed in *Jayadrathayāmala* 3.16 and Kuṇḍaleśvarī in *Jayadrathayāmala* 3.15. It is tempting to read Maṅgalā as a reference to one of the goddesses of the Krama, but the deities with Maṅgalā in their

names are of secondary importance in the *Jayadrathayāmala*. One would still need to examine all Krama-related *vidyās* in the *Jayadrathayāmala* to be sure about it. Nityā appears as the name of various texts in *Jayadrathayāmala* 1, and we find Nityākālī in *Jayadrathayāmala* 4.50. On the early cult of *nityās* that precedes the Śrīvidyā tradition, see Sanderson (2007, 385n510). Ratneśvarī occurs as the characterization of the Goddess in *Jayadrathayāmala* 3.11, and 4.69, though it can also be an epithet of Kauberī from 4.54.

26. "Dakṣiṇa . . . Lower": these are six classes of Śaiva scriptures linked with the 5 + 1 faces of Sadāśiva. On this schema, see the introduction to Hanneder (1998). "Nor is she doctrine or discipline" (*na nayaṃ vinayaṃ na ca*): these may refer to types of Tantras, sections of Tantric texts, or they may be intended more generically in their usual sense as tentatively translated here. The Śaiva Tantras of the Bhairava stream generally present themselves as a higher revelation than the Siddhānta. On these doctrines and how they fit the total structure of Śaiva revelation, see Sanderson (1988, 2009). On the Lākulas, see in particular Sanderson (2006). On the reference to these doctrines in the context of the Purāṇas, see Serbaeva (2006).

27. "She is called Nameless, Waveless, and Without-a-Clan" (*nirnāmā, nistaraṅgā, nirākulā*): this is notably the first positive characterization of the Goddess in this chapter, although it still consists of lacked attributes.

28. The phrase "from Śiva down to the earth" (*śivādyavanigocara*) is a stable expression in the early Tantras to refer to the whole span of the universe, from its highest to its lowest principle or part. Waveless, *nistaraṅga*, is a Krama term to describe a close to absolute state of consciousness. See Serbaeva (2003).

29. The phrase "inside the bulb" may mean to identify her with Kuṇḍalinī.

30. "He will lead others to liberation instantly by a glance or a touch" refers to the power of a guru who knows the indefinable Kālī to liberate others via touch or eye contact. These and other methods are described in great detail in *Jayadrathayāmala* 3.20.

31. "Rays" is a typical Krama way to talk about *yoginīs*.

32. "from the distinctions of existence": this line is tenuous because of an apparent corruption in the text; namely the word *aroṣṭhataḥ*.

33. There were certainly other important Kālī Tantras that incorporated a wide variety of goddesses, but much of what was produced in medieval India has not survived to the present.

34. For example, *Vāyu Purāṇa* 2.9. Regarding the Purāṇas, by "early" I mean ca. fifth to tenth centuries CE.

35. *Liṅga Purāṇa* 2.6.

36. *Matsya Purāṇa* 172.19.

37. We see clear evidence of a Tantric Kālī in the *Agni Purāṇa*, for example, which dates to around the end of the eleventh to twelfth centuries. Slouber's chapter on Tvaritā in this book also calls attention to incorporation of Tantric goddesses in the *Agni Purāṇa*.

38. *Tantrāloka* 28.15, 29.43, and 35.33. For a general introduction to the Kālīkula and Krama, see Sanderson (1988, 2009). For an overview of the doctrines and structures of

selected texts attributed to the Krama, see Serbaeva (2003). A database of previously unidentified cross-citations in the Vidyāpīṭha texts is being compiled by Olga Serbaeva and will soon be available online.

39. The self-attribution to the Kālīkula occurs especially in its second and third volumes (*ṣaṭka*).

40. There was much misinformation about the Krama prior to Alexis Sanderson's 2007 article, in which he lists and analyzes the eighteen surviving short texts that associate themselves with it (250–52). Before this point, scholarship on the Krama was based on summaries in the works of Abhinavagupta and Kṣemarāja of Kashmir. This lack of primary-source scholarship prior to 2007 led many researchers to think of the Krama as a tradition limited to the region of Kashmir. See, for example, the characterization of "Kashmir Shaivism" and the Krama as linked to Kashmir in the work of Swami Lakshman Joo, Jagadisa Candra Chatterji, Lilian Silburn, Moti Lal Pandit, André Padoux, and Paul Muller-Ortega.

41. The estimate of more than 900 named texts known to the compiler of the *Jayadrathayāmala* is based on the approximately 545 texts listed in Dyczkowski (1988) and my own database, which includes additional texts referenced in the *Jayadrathayāmala*. My view that the text was compiled by a single person differs from that of Alexis Sanderson, who argues for separate authorship of the first volume and that the latter three were compiled in Kashmir (Sanderson 2004, 280–83). The first volume repeatedly cites as a source the *Śiraścheda*, which it describes as a whole class of Tantras (1.40.76–84). A single Tantra by this name is already referenced in the early ninth century in Cambodia (Sanderson 2001, 7n5ff., 31n33ff.). Only a small set of the chapters in the first book of the *Jayadrathayāmala* (chapters 6–8) could be a part of that very ancient compendium, if it was in fact a single text at some point. These chapters represent some rather archaic Tumburu-related structures, in a more archaic register of Sanskrit, stylistically different from the rest. The remaining forty-plus chapters run in rather good coherence with the other volumes (*ṣaṭkas* 2–4). Moreover, all of the volumes use the same codes for *vidyās*, especially the core *vidyā* of Kālasaṃkarṣaṇī. The texts and traditions mentioned in the first volume (1.35–45) are further incorporated into various parts of all four volumes, following the same logic and order of the elements.

42. The Tantric tradition can be seen in its totality as an esoteric interpretation of the "exoteric" Brahminical lore. Each Tantric tradition adds a new layer to the interpretation of the already known things but generally does not reject the previous structures.

43. Sanderson (1988, 683–84).

44. A preliminary study on the concept of *jīvanmukti* in the Tantras can be found in Serbaeva (2010).

45. For example, *Bṛhadāraṇyaka Upaniṣad* 3.9.26.

46. Exceptions include the *Mahārthamañjarī* of Maheśvarānanda, written around the twelfth century near Trivandrum, and a few hints in the literature discovered by Alexis Sanderson (2007, 250–52). Traces of both Kālīkula and Krama texts can be

found only in Nepalese manuscripts that preserved the transmission from the twelfth century onward.

47. The following folios from each manuscript cover the translated passage, in whole or in part: (A) 215r6–217v6; (B) incomplete, 308v3–5; (C) 290v6–294r2; (D) 223r6–226r1; (E) 180r4–182r7; (H) 197r8–199v1; (I) 93r2–94r last line; and (J) 196v3–198v last line. A basic transcript was made using manuscript A, and the variants in the other manuscripts were recorded and taken into account.

GLOSSARY

Cross-references to other terms in this glossary are in boldface type.

ADVAITA VEDĀNTA A prominent orthodox school of Hindu philosophy that emphasizes the nonduality (unity) of God and the world. See also **Nondualism.**

ĀGAMA Tradition. Used to refer to ritual and philosophical texts that are largely synonymous with **Tantras.**

AGAMA TIRTA The religion of holy water. A name for Balinese religion used up to the early twentieth century.

AIŚA Divine, belonging to Śiva. A hybrid register of the Sanskrit language with nonstandard grammar; common in early **Tantras.**

AMARĀVATĪ Capital city of the gods in Hindu mythology.

AMMA Mother. A term of address for goddesses in southern India that is often tagged onto their names; for example, Cāmuṇḍamma, which means Mother Cāmuṇḍā.

AṂŚA Portion. A goddess regarded as a fragment or **avatar** of a more well-known goddess.

AÑJALI A respectful gesture made by forming a cup with the two outstretched hands, as if to receive an offering of food, and respectfully raising it to the forehead.

APOPHATIC THEALOGY Knowledge of the divine obtained through negating concepts that she is not, as opposed to cataphatic, or the use of positive conceptions. See also **mysticism.**

APSARĀ/APSARAS An all-female class of semidivine beings renowned for their beauty, sensuality, and abilities in dance, song, and acting.

ĀRATĪ Offering of a lamp or candle to a deity's icon, as well as accompanying mantras and devotional songs. See also ***pūjā.***

ARECA NUT The fruit of the areca palm (*Areca catechu*). It is chewed as a traditional stimulant throughout southern Asia and the Pacific Islands region.

ARGHA An offering to a guest consisting of water and other, optional items.

ARTHA Economic prosperity as one of the four aims of life (*puruṣārtha*) in classical Hindu thought. See also ***dharma, kāma,*** and ***mokṣa.***

ĀRYA Noble person. Term from the **Veda** denoting a member of the ancient Sanskrit-speaking tribes of northwest India, as opposed to other communities inhabiting different areas and with different cultural practices at the time in question.

ASHRAM Hermitage, home of a **guru.** Literally, "place of [spiritual] striving."

ASURA Anti-god, demon.

AUṂ An alternative spelling of the sacred **mantra** Oṃ. Its three parts are analogized with various other conceptual triads in Hindu mystical literature.

AVATAR/AVATĀRA Crossing down. An incarnation of a deity with a separate apparent identity (e.g., Kṛṣṇa as an avatar of Viṣṇu).

BABA (BĀBĀ) Father. A respectful term of address for elders and especially religious ascetics.

BAL Strength.

BĀLA TANTRAS Early **Śaiva Tantric** medical texts specializing in protecting young children from demonic attack.

BECHARAJI Bahucarājī. Name of the town in northeast Gujarat state where Bahucarā's principal temple is located.

BETEL LEAF The leaf of *Piper betle* used to wrap a quid of **areca nut.**

BETEL NUT See **areca nut.**

BHAKTI Devotion. Associated especially with the devotional current in Hinduism that promises salvation by devotion alone.

BHIL One of the largest tribal groups in India, found across a broad swath of the north and central regions.

BHUJANGA Snake. Technical name for a low-status variety of **Śaiva,** non-**Brahminical** ritual specialist in Bali.

BHUKTI Enjoyment. One of the goals and benefits of the Tantric path. Often paired with ***mukti*** (liberation).

BHŪTA Ghost. May also signify nonphysical entities in general. Spelled *bhuta* in Middle Javanese texts.

BHŪTA TANTRAS Early **Śaiva Tantric** medical texts specializing in curing diseases caused by demonic possession.

BHUTA-KĀLA See ***bhūta.***

BIMBA Scarlet gourd (*Coccinia grandis*) frequently used as an object of comparison for its deep red color.

BRAHMA/BRAHMĀ The four-faced creator god of classical Hindu mythology.

BRAHMAPUTRA A major river flowing from the Tibetan plateau through India and Bangladesh and draining into the Bay of Bengal.

BRAHMIN (BRĀHMAṆA) A Hindu social class traditionally associated with priestly functions and scholarship.

BRAHMINICAL A tradition in Hindu culture associated with **Brahmins.**

BRAHMINISM An umbrella term coined by scholars to describe various religious and social systems of orthodox Hinduism that hold the **Veda** and related literature as authoritative.

BRAHMINIZE To make **Brahmin**-like. See **Sanskritize.**

BUH CITRA The region where Mpu Baradah lives in the ***Calon Arang*** tale.

CAKRA Wheel. A synonym of ***yantra***; may also refer to the energy centers in the esoteric Tantric conception of the body.

CALON ARANG Candidate in sorcery. Also used as the title of Rangda's story and as a proper name for Rangda.

CARU Rice pudding, or any number of other deity offerings referred to as *caru* euphemistically. See the essay section of chapter 10 for a discussion of the euphemistic meanings of *caru.*

CATURBHADRA The four aims of life. It refers either to the classical ***puruṣārtha*** (***dharma, artha, kāma,*** and ***mokṣa***), or an alternative list.

CATURVARGA See ***caturbhadra.***

CHARAN A pastoral and bardic caste group in Gujarat and Rajasthan, from which Bahucarā is said to have originated in some narratives.

CREMATION GROUND An area, usually on the fringes of a settlement, where the dead are burned to ashes. Cremation grounds are regarded with fear and revulsion by many Hindus but are sought out by certain sects of Hindu and Buddhist ascetics, who consider them excellent places to meditate.

DAHA/KAḌIRI The western court of medieval Java.

DAITYA Demon. May be used generically or as the proper name of a particular class of demonic beings descended from a female figure named Diti.

DALIT Oppressed. Modern catchall for a variety of caste groups in South Asia that have historically been excluded from positions of social privilege. Dalits make up about 25 percent of the population of the Republic of India.

DAṆḌAKA Name of a particular forest in southern India that plays an important role in the *Rāmāyaṇa* epic and the *Bhadrakāḷī Māhātmya.*

DEVA See ***devatā.***

DEVATĀ God. Literally "divine" and/or "shining," the *devas* are the primary class of deities in the Hindu pantheon. The word *deva* is gendered male, whereas *devī* is reserved for goddesses, and *devatā* can refer to either (though it is grammatically feminine).

DEVĪ See ***devatā.***

DEWA Middle Javanese spelling of ***deva.***

DHARMA Moral/religious education as one of the four aims of life (*puruṣārtha*) in classical Hindu thought. See also ***artha, kāma,*** and ***mokṣa.*** Also used as a synonym for ***vrata.***

DHYĀNA Meditation. In many Tantric contexts, refers to visualization practices.

DVĀRAPĀLA Door guardian. The figures Chagala and Kumbhakarṇa served as door guardians at the temple of the Seven Mothers in Koṭīvarṣa.

DVEṢABHAKTI Hatred-devotion. The concept that one can have a salvific, intimate relationship with the divine even when the emotional bond is based on hatred.

DVIJA See **Brahmin**.

ELM Acronym for the *Ekaliṅga Māhātmya* in the Rāṣṭrasenā chapter.

EMPU High priest of East Javanese religion, who could be affiliated with either Buddhist or Śaiva sects but still serve the entire community. See also ***pedanda***.

GAṆA A member of Śiva's entourage.

GAṆAPATI Lord among Śiva's ***gaṇas***; an epithet for Śiva's son Gaṇeśa and several other figures in Śaiva mythology.

GANDHARVA A class of celestial beings ranked below gods and associated with music and dance.

GANGA Name of the most religiously significant river in northern India, personified as a goddess of the same name.

GANGES Anglicized spelling of **Ganga**.

GANGGA Indonesian spelling of **Ganga**.

GAṆITRI Dried seeds widely used for prayer beads (Rudraksha/*Elaeocarpus ganitrus*).

GĀRUḌA TANTRAS Early **Śaiva** medical **Tantras** concerned with healing snakebite.

GELGEL A village near the regional capital Semarapura in eastern Java, Indonesia. Gelgel was once the center of a powerful kingdom of the same name.

GOKARNA A major pilgrimage site in Karnataka, with an important Śiva temple.

GRAHA Seizer/grasper. May refer either to astrological planets or to demons in general, which seize/possess people.

GRAHAṆĪ Female ***graha***.

GRĀMADEVATĀ Village deity. Also spelled *grāmadēvate*. An important class of Hindu deities whose members are protectors of particular locales and often have ancient, non-elite origins.

GUHILA Name of a dynasty that ruled the **Mewar** region as vassals from the eighth through tenth centuries CE, then independently from the eleventh to thirteenth centuries.

GUPTA The principal imperial dynasty in classical India (ca. 320–550 CE).

GURJAR Name of a large and diverse ethnic group living primarily in northwest and central India.

GURU Teacher. Used in a wide range of senses. A guru may be one's parent, a religious or nonreligious teacher, or a deity. A respectful term of address in southern Karnataka state.

HAVAN See ***homa***.

HIJRA A community consisting primarily of transgender women in South Asia. See also **Pāvaiyā**.

HINGLAJ A popular Hindu pilgrimage site and ***śaktipīṭha*** in southern Pakistan. Reputed to be the site where the goddess Sati's head fell to earth.

HOMA The ritual offering of ghee (clarified butter) into a sacred fire. *Homa* originates in the **Veda**, and it is a feature of **Tantric** ritual as well.

INDIC Indian. Pertaining to India in a broad sense, or to Indo-Aryan languages narrowly.

JANGGALA/KAHURIPAN The eastern court of medieval Java.

JĪ (SUFFIX) A gender-neutral suffix indicating respect that is commonly added to names in modern Indo-Aryan languages.

JṚMBHAKA Gaper. A class of bloodthirsty spirits that inhabit weapons. Also the proper name of a ***yakṣa*** in the Bahucarā narrative.

KAILASH Kailāsa. A sacred mountain in Tibet that features in many Hindu narratives as the dwelling place of Śiva and Pārvatī.

KALI AGE Name of the current degenerate age in the classical Hindu *yuga* time cycle. Despite the similar appearance in roman letters, there is no connection between *kali* and the name of the goddess Kālī.

KĀLĪKULA Clan of Kālī. Name of an early **Tantric** sect of the Kulamārga variety of **Śākta Tantra**. The *Jayadrathayāmala* is the principal surviving scripture of the Kālīkula.

KĀMA Pleasure as one of the four aims of life (*puruṣārtha*) in classical Hindu thought. See also ***dharma***, ***artha***, and ***mokṣa***.

KAMALIA A Muslim caste group that is associated with the Bahucarā temple in Gujarat.

KĀMARŪPA A historical region in the northeastern Indian state of Assam.

KAṂSĀḶE A musical tradition popular in southern Karnataka state.

KANGSI A type of cymbals used in Bali.

KAPINI A river in Kerala and southern Karnataka near Mysuru, and a tributary to the **Kaveri**. Also spelled Kabini and Kapila.

KAPOK A culturally significant tree of Bali (white silk-cotton tree/*Ceiba pentandra*).

KARAJA (TANK) Arising from the hand. Name of a bathing tank/pond near Ekliṅgjī temple in Rajasthan.

KARMA Action. The theory of karma involves every action (whether good or evil) having a just result, either in this life or in another.

KATHĀ Story.

KAULA An early **Tantric** sect centered on worshiping goddesses through transgressive practices and deity possession.

KAVERI An important river that flows through southern Karnataka near **Mysuru** and through Tamil Nadu.

KEMANAK A type of bronze idiophone (gong) used in the Indonesian gamelan orchestra.

KHECARĪ Female skywalker. A class of semidivine women or human women who have attained the power of flight via **Tantric** ritual.

KIDUNG A genre of lyrical old Javanese poetry.

KIṂNARA A class of celestial beings whose forms combine animal (especially horse) and human features. May alternatively refer to transgender women.

KINNAR See ***kiṃnara***.

KOLI An ethnic group in northern and central India associated with Bahucarā in Gujarat.

KRAMA A highly mystical branch of the early **Tantric Kaula** sect, wherein worship is devoted to a fixed sequence (*krama*) of sets of goddesses, especially forms of Kālī.

KṢATRIYA An archaic Hindu social class traditionally associated with warfare and kingship.

KULA Family, clan, or initiatory lineage. Other technical meanings include material reality.

KULADEVĪ Clan goddess. A goddess who protects a particular clan or royal family.

KŪḶI Name of a class of demons specific to Kerala and involved in Bhadrakāḷī performance traditions.

KUMĀRĪ Girl, virgin. Especially one who has not yet menstruated. Also refers to a few select girls who serve as goddesses throughout their young childhood in Nepal, as well as girls worshiped as goddesses on festival occasions in other Hindu contexts.

KUṆḌALINĪ The Coiled One. A feminine serpentine power coiled at the base of the spine. Early **Tantras** regarded Kuṇḍalinī as a goddess, whereas later texts presented it as a power or energy.

KUSA A grass (*Desmostachya bipinnata*) strewn as ground cover in preparation for ritual or meditation.

KUṢĀṆA An ancient empire (fl. first through third centuries CE) with territory stretching from central Asia and Iran to northern India.

KUTILA RIVER Crooked River. A river in the Mewar region of Rajasthan.

LĀṄGURIYĀ A sometimes bawdy song and dance tradition at the temple of Kailā Devī.

LĔMAH TULIS The field of writing. Name of the **cremation ground** that is home to the sage Baradah in the *Calon Arang* tale.

LĪLĀ Play. Commonly used in reference to divine actions for which no logical explanation is forthcoming.

LIṄGA An emblem of Śiva with an array of interpretations. Originating as a phallic symbol, it has been regarded as aniconic for much of history.

LIṄGĀYAT A popular religious sect in southern India that traces itself back to the twelfth-century saint Bāsava. Also known as Vīraśaiva.

MĀGH, MONTH OF A lunar month in the Hindu calendar system that corresponds roughly to January/February.

MAHĀKĀLA Name of a forest in the *Bhadrakāḷī Māhātmya*.

MĀHĀTMYA Glorification. A genre of religious narrative literature that tells of ancient mythological events, often linking them to a particular locale.

MAHĀVIDYĀ Great Spell. A title for various goddesses. ***Vidyās*** are the feminine equivalent of **mantras**.

MAṆḌALA A sacred geometric diagram inhabited by divine forces and used in Tantric worship to represent the cosmos.

MANDARA Name of a mountain in Hindu mythology used to churn the ocean of milk. Identified with Mt. Everest, which is called Sagarmatha (Ocean's churn) in Nepal.

MAṄGALA Auspicious. May refer to invocatory verses that preface many Sanskrit texts.

MANSAROVAR Lake of Desire. Contraction of *mānasa* (of the mind, of desire) and *sarovar* (large lake). A sacred lake fed by the glaciers on Mt. **Kailash** in Tibet. Regarded as a subterranean source of the **Ganga** River. Also identified with local sites in various regions of India. Name of a pond connected with Bahucarā in Gujarat.

MANTRA A sacred sound or series of phonemes with or without lexical meaning that has power to effect change in the world when recited aloud or silently. In early **Śaiva Tantras**, mantras are identified as the sonic forms of deities; therefore reciting them invokes the deity. See also ***vidyā***.

MANTRAMĀRGA The Way of Mantras. The name of the most prolific division of early **Śaiva Tantras**, whose traditions were open to both householders and ascetics.

MĀRI A common title for fearsome local goddesses in south India. In ancient Tamil sources, the word *māri* meant rain. Goddesses called Māri or Māriyamman̲ are connected with rainfall and drought, as well as with infectious disease.

MĀTṚ Mother goddess.

MĀTṚNĀYIKĀ Leader of the Mother goddesses.

MĀTṚ TANTRA A **Tantric** scripture of the cult of the Mother goddesses.

MEDIUM A person who allows a deity to take possession of her or his body and speak through her or him directly to devotees.

MEENA Name of a tribal ethnic group living primarily in Rajasthan and Madhya Pradesh.

MERU Name of a mythical mountain in the Himalaya where the Hindu gods dwell. Regarded as the center of the world in ancient Indian myths.

MEWAR A region of southern Rajasthan state in India.

MOKṢA Spiritual liberation as one of the four aims of life (*puruṣārtha*) in classical Hindu thought. See also ***dharma***, ***artha***, and ***kāma***.

MPU See ***empu***.

MUDRĀ Seal, stamp. Technical word for particular hand gestures applied in Tantric ritual.

MUGHALS A Muslim-led empire in India with central Asian roots that ruled from 1526 to 1857 CE.

MUKTI Release, liberation (synonym of ***mokṣa***). One of the goals and benefits of the **Tantric** path. Often paired with ***bhukti*** (enjoyment).

MUNI Silent one. A sage, seer, wise man, monk, and so forth; especially one who has taken a vow of silence.

MŪRTI Icon; material representation of a deity.

MYSTICISM Theories and practice surrounding ecstatic religious states of consciousness that often involve a sense of union with the divine and direct access to nondiscursive knowledge.

MYSURU A city in the southern part of Karnataka state in south India. Also spelled Mysore.

NĀDA Sound. In **Tantric** cosmology, it may refer to the divine sound of the universe or to a particular sound heard by the Tantric adept during meditation.

NĀGA A divine serpent. May also refer to a cobra or any other snake.

NAGARKOT Old name of a small town in Himachal Pradesh now known as Kangra. The area is home to several important goddess temples.

NAÑJALAGŪḌI/NANJANGUD A town near Mysuru famous for its temple to the local form of Śiva, named Nañjuṇḍēśvara.

NARMADA Delightful (*narmadā* in Sanskrit). Name of a sacred river in north central India that divides the **Vindhya** and Satpura mountain ranges and flows west into the Gulf of Cambay.

NAVAGRAHĀḤ (*NAVAGRAHA*) The nine planets/celestial bodies: the sun, the moon, Mercury, Venus, Mars, Jupiter, Saturn, Rāhu, and Ketu.

NAVARĀTRA See ***Navarātri.***

NAVARĀTRI The nine nights: an important Hindu festival each autumn commemorating Durgā's battle with the buffalo demon.

NAVRĀTRI/NAVRATRI See ***Navarātri.***

NEWAR An ethnic group in Nepal most closely associated with the Kathmandu Valley and surrounding areas.

NIRVĀṆA Blowing out, liberation. A common term for spiritual liberation from the cycle of birth, death, and rebirth (***saṃsāra***). Synonymous with ***mukti*** and ***mokṣa.***

NITYĀ Eternal. Name of a particular class of **Tantric** goddesses and their system of worship. The Nityās form all-female retinues subordinate to a particular high goddess.

NONDUALISM A philosophical position that states that the divine is one with the universe, not inherently separate from creation. The term includes both **Śaiva** and non-Śaiva varieties of this doctrine in Hinduism. See also **Advaita Vedānta.**

NYĀSA Deposition. A common procedure in **Tantric** ritual involving visualization of particular mantra deities on particular parts of the body, and/or touching various parts of the body while reciting those mantras. The result is a sort of temporary self-deification during the ritual.

PĀLAI A landscape of drought and heat, wasteland and war. Particularly associated with fierce goddesses. One of the seven conventional landscapes in classical Tamil literature.

PARAMAGATI Liberation from the cycle of rebirth; literally "the supreme refuge." In devotional religion, liberation is imagined as permanently dwelling in the presence of the supreme deity.

PARBATIYA From the mountains. Refers to various groups of Nepali Hindus.

PAŚU Domesticated animal. Used euphemistically to refer to the soul in its bound state. See notes to chapter 10 for discussion of other uses.

PĀŚUPATA An early **Śaiva** ascetic sect, so called for its focus on Śiva in the form of Paśupati, Lord of the Bound. See also ***paśu.***

PATI Lord, husband.

PATIVRATĀ A faithful/submissive wife; literally, a woman who has taken a vow to support her husband.

PĀṬṬŬ Malayalam ritual song performance that reenacts a narrative to the Goddess.

PĀVAIYĀ A Gujarati term roughly equivalent to **Hijra.** The Pāvaiyās are closely associated with the goddess Bahucarā.

PHĀLGUN, MONTH OF A lunar month in the Hindu calendar system that corresponds roughly to February/March.

PIŚĀCA Flesh eater. Name of a class of demonic beings that possess people and eat them from the inside out.

PEDANDA High priest in Bali affiliated with either a Buddhist or **Śaiva** stream of the East Javanese religion.

PRALĪNA Dissolution. The final stage in the repeating three-stage cycle of Hindu time. See also ***utpatti*** and ***sthiti***.

PRĀṆĀYĀMA Breath control. One of several core practices of **yoga**.

PRASĀD Grace. Food that has been offered to a Hindu deity and returned to devotees as blessed food.

PRASTĀRA Spreading out. In **Tantra**, a grid used for laying out and decoding the syllables of a **mantra** or ***vidyā***.

PRATIMĀ Image. May refer to a small gold or silver plate onto which the image of a deity is impressed.

PRATYABHIJÑĀ Recognition. Name of a school of **Tantric** philosophy centered on the realization that everything in the world is Śiva.

PRETA Departed/ghost. Name of a class of spirit beings who possess people.

PŪJĀ Worship. A broad term covering any type of ritual activity involving worship of a deity in Indian religions. It may involve caring for an icon of the deity; offering food, flowers, incense, money, and so forth; prayer; meditation; or other activities.

PURĀṆAS A large class of Hindu religious texts containing myths and a wide range of other material.

RĀJASŪYA A **Vedic** ritual performed to consecrate Hindu kings.

RAJPUT A large and diverse category of castes prominent in northwest India and traditionally associated with kingship and warfare.

ṚDDHI Worldly prosperity. A possible goal of **Tantric** practice, along with ***siddhi*** and ***mukti***.

RĔSI See ***ṛṣi***.

RICE PUDDING See ***caru***.

ṚṢI Sage, seer, holy man.

RUDRAYĀMALA Pair of Rudras. Refers to the cosmic pairing of the divine male (Rudra) and female (Rudrāṇī) principles, which results in creation. Also the name of a **Tantra**.

RWA BHINEDA Unity in duality. An important doctrine underlying Balinese understanding of the Rangda-Barong performance.

SACRIFICE Food offering for a deity. Vegetarian deities are strictly offered vegetarian food, whereas some deities are "non-veg," meaning they accept or even require the flesh of livestock (usually the male of the species). In either case, the food offered is subsequently returned to the community as a blessing (*prasāda*) and eaten.

SACRIFICIAL MALE See ***paśu***. See also **sacrifice**.

SĀDHANA Practice of religious discipline. Covers a wide variety of **Tantric** and Yogic practices such as meditation, visualization, and mantra recitation.

SĀDHU A renouncer, ascetic, holy man.

ŚAIVA Associated with the god Śiva; a prominent variety of Hinduism.

ŚĀKINĪ A class of semidivine female beings. Often used as a synonym for ***yoginīs***.

ŚĀKTA Associated with the goddess Śakti; a prominent variety of Hinduism that regards a form of the Goddess as supreme.

ŚAKTI Power. In Sanskrit power is gendered feminine and regarded as a force that upholds the universe. It is personified as a goddess called Śakti or other names associated with the goddess regarded as the wife of Śiva.

ŚAKTIPĪṬHA/ŚAKTIPĪṬH Seat of power. A pilgrimage site connected with the body of the goddess Satī.

SAṂSĀRA The world as a cycle of birth, death, and rebirth that is regarded as full of suffering and something to escape.

SAṂSKĀRA A life-cycle ritual. The word has a wide range of other meanings not relevant here.

SANSKRITIZE/SANSKRITIZATION A process of social change that involves adoption of practices and language more characteristic of higher castes and the ideas and terms commonly represented in orthodox Sanskrit texts.

SAPTAMĀTARAḤ The Seven Mothers.

SAPTAMĀTṚKĀ See ***saptamātaraḥ***.

SATĪ Good woman. The British made this phrase refer instead to the rare and long-illegal practice of a widow burning with her deceased husband on the funeral pyre. Satī is also the proper name of a goddess.

SEED SYLLABLE A single-syllable **mantra** that represents the essence of a deity.

SEIZER Demonic being who possesses people. See also ***graha***.

SETRA GANDAMAYU Name of an important **cremation ground** in the *Sudamala* tale (summarized in chapter 9).

SIDDHA A perfected being. Either a perfected human or a member of a semidivine group of beings believed to have supernatural powers.

SIDDHĀNTA A major **Śaiva Tantric** sect characterized by its dualistic philosophy and orthodox character. Compare with **Nondualism**.

SIDDHI Supernatural power. Literally "perfection."

SIWA See **Śaiva**.

SMĀRTA A post-**Vedic** Hindu movement that recognized the authority of **Brahminical** texts and traditions while incorporating a variety of devotional, philosophical, and ritual practices of the classical era.

ŚRĪ An honorific prefixed to the names of many deities and saints.

ŚRĪCAKRA Proper name of the ornate ***yantra*** of the goddess Tripurasundarī.

ŚRĪVIDYĀ A living **Tantric** sect especially prominent in southern India and focused on the goddess **Tripurasundarī**.

STHITI Maintenance, stability. The middle stage in the repeating three-stage cycle of Hindu time. See also ***utpatti*** and ***pralīna***.

ŚŪDRA An archaic Hindu social class traditionally associated with service to the other classes.

SVĀMI Swami, religious ascetic. Also used as a respectful term of address in southern Karnataka.

SVK Acronym for the *Svasthānīvratakathā*, the story of Svasthānī's vow.

TAMBIṬṬU A rice dish combining rice and jaggery sugar, formed into a ball or mound that may be offered to goddesses in southern Karnataka.

TANTRA(S) An important and prolific class of religious scriptures in Hindu, Buddhist, and Jain traditions and their associated values, philosophies, and rituals. Tantric practices may include meditation, ***pūjā***, mantra recitation, deity possession, medicine, and sexual rituals. The varieties of religion found in the Tantras are now collectively referred to as Tantra.

TANTRIC Adjective form of **Tantra**.

TATTVA An element; a truth. Technical term in **Tantra** for a level of reality or principle of existence including, and expanding upon, the standard twenty-five of the ancient Sankhya system.

TĪRTHA A place of pilgrimage, especially a site on a sacred river.

TRIKA Triad. Name of an early **Tantric** sect that worships a set of three goddesses.

TROṬALA TANTRA A canonical **Gāruḍa Tantra**, which *Tvaritā's Basic Teaching* (*Tvaritāmūlasūtra*) summarizes.

TUTUR Genre of Sanskrit and Old Javanese metaphysical literature in Indonesia.

ULTIMATE CAUSE (*KĀRAṆA*) Refers to the initial agent of creation in various schools of Hindu thealogy. In **Śākta Tantras**, it is identified as the supreme form of the Goddess.

UTPATTI Creation. The first stage in the repeating three-stage cycle of Hindu time. See also ***sthiti*** and ***pralīna***.

VĀHANA Vehicle, mount. An animal or other being whom a Hindu deity rides or is otherwise signified by.

VAIṢṆAVA A prominent variety of Hinduism associated with the god Viṣṇu.

VAIŚYA An archaic Hindu social class that contained the majority of the population and traditionally associated with a range of agricultural and mercantile occupations.

VEDA A large and important body of religious scripture, most parts of which date from approximately 1200 to 500 BCE.

VEDIC Associated with the **Veda**.

VIDYĀ Knowledge. In the **Tantras**, *vidyā* refers most commonly to a female **mantra** and the goddess it represents.

VINDHYA Name of a mountain range in central India that divides the Indo-Gangetic plains of northern India from the Deccan plateau in the south. These mountains are home to several goddesses featured in this book.

VIPRA See **Brahmin**.

VRATA A vow or votive rite to honor a deity, often with a specific goal in mind.

VRATA-KATHĀ A story that explains the background of a particular ***vrata***. Here it refers to the Svasthānī story in chapter 5.

WARANG The culturally significant relationship between parents of a married couple in Bali, that is, in-laws.

WAYANG Shadow-puppet theater of Bali and Indonesia.

YAJÑA An act of worship, especially a **Vedic** fire offering.

YAKṢA A class of nature spirits that is often associated with trees.

YAKṢIṆĪ A female nature spirit. See also ***yakṣa***.

YĀMALA [TANTRA] Union Tantras. An important branch of early **Śaiva Tantras**.

YAMUNA RIVER A major river west of the Ganga in northern India that meets up with the latter in Allahabad/Prayagraj.

YANTRA A portable **maṇḍala**. See also ***cakra***.

YOGA In the **Tantras**, yoga refers to a range of meditative and ritual practices. In other contexts, yoga has a wide range of other meanings.

YOGEŚVARĪ Mistress of yoga. Leaders of bands of ***yoginī***s.

YOGI A male practitioner of **yoga**, in any sense of the word. Also spelled in English as *yogin* or *yogī*.

YOGINĪ A class of goddesses related to the Mothers. Literally meaning "female practitioners of **yoga**," this title blurs the line between human female practitioners and goddesses.

YONI The female genital organ.

LIST OF DEITIES AND CHARACTERS

Cross-references to other names in the list are in boldface type.

ĀDYAŚAKTI MAHĀMĀYĀ YOGAMĀYĀ A set of epithets for **Bahucarā** that identify her as the Supreme Feminine Energy, Great Goddess of Illusion, and Magic of Yoga, respectively.

AGASTYA A Vedic seer said to be born from a jar. He is famous for going to the south of the Vindhya Mountain, asking the Vindhya to remain lowered only until he came back north; he never did, so the Vindhya had to remain lowered.

AGHORĪ A fearsome goddess whose name literally means "non-fearsome." Sometimes included as an eighth goddess among the **Seven Mothers**.

ĀGNEYĪ The female form of the god **Agni**.

AGNI The god of fire in the Vedic pantheon and later Hinduism, and guardian of the southeastern direction in Tantric contexts.

AISĀSURA Brother of the demon **Mahiṣāsura** in the *Beṭṭada Cāmuṇḍi* ballad.

AMBIKĀ Mother. A common name for many goddesses.

AMṚTEŚA Lord of Nectar. An epithet for **Śiva**.

ARJUNA A famous heroic prince from the Indian epic *Mahābhārata*. Referenced in the **Bahucarā** narrative for an episode in which he lived as a transgender woman for a period of time.

ARUṆ Name of a demon who is killed by the goddess avatar **Bhramarī**.

ĀŚAVA A sage in the **Svasthānī** tale, sent by **Śiva** to instruct **Gomā** and others in the performance of the vow.

AṢṬAMĀTRIKĀ A group of eight fierce Mother-goddesses important in Nepal and originating from an expanded Tantric list of the earlier **Seven Mothers**.

BABA KEDARGIRI See **Kedargiri**.

BAHORA Name of a Gujur devotee of **Kailā Devī** who served as a medium. A temple to Bahora faces that of Kailā Devī.

BAHUCARĀ/BAHUCARĪ Much movement/She who roams widely. Name of a prominent goddess in the state of Gujarat.

BAHULA Son of the sage **Baradah**; fiancé, then husband, of **Ratna Manggalī**.

BAHUMĀṂSĀ One of the Seven Mothers in the *Skanda Purāṇa* narrative. She is generated by **Śiva** and takes the place of **Cāmuṇḍā** in the narrative. Her name, "Much flesh," may either refer to her having a corpulent appearance or be a euphemism for her appetite for sacrificial offerings.

BĀLĀ The Girl. An epithet for **Tripurasundarī**.

BĀLĀTRIPURĀSUNDARĪ The goddess **Tripurasundarī** appearing in the form of a young girl.

BARADAH Name of the principal sage in the *Calon Arang* tale. He is also called "Lord of Life" and "Lord of Yogis," and his name is often prefixed with the respectful title *Mpu* or the honorific *Śrī*.

BARBARIAN Name of a demon (*barbara*) in the **Kauśikī** narrative.

BARONG A lion-like figure in masked performance traditions of Bali. A counterpart to **Rangda** thought to represent Śiva.

BĀṢPA (BAPPĀ RĀVAL) Mythico-historical progenitor of the Mewar royal lineage and purported founder of the **Ekaliṅga** temple.

BATARA GURU The Divine Guru. An epithet for **Śiva** in the *Sudamala* tale.

BHADRĀ Auspicious/Good Lady. A shortened form of **Bhadrakāḷī**.

BHADRAKĀḶĪ Good **Kālī**. A name of the goddess in the Tantras that remains popular as a regional identity in Kerala.

BHAGAWATĪ Goddess, Blessed One. Refers to the goddess **Durgā** in the *Calon Arang* tale.

BHAIRAVA Frightful. A fierce form of **Śiva** common in the Tantras. Also a name for any firmly resolved spiritual aspirant in the Indefinable **Kālī** passage.

BHAIRAVĪ Frightful. An epithet for several fierce goddesses. See also **Bhadrakāḷī**.

BHAVA A name of **Śiva**.

BHRĀMARĪ Female bee. An avatar the Goddess took to defeat a demon.

BRAHMĀ A Hindu god associated with creation and granting boons to those who perform severe austerities. Also spelled Brahma.

BRAHMA DĒVA See **Brahmā**.

BRĀHMĪ The female form of the god **Brahmā**.

CALON ARANG (CHARACTER) Candidate in sorcery. Came to be used as a proper name for **Rangda of Girah**.

CĀMARĀJA WOḌEYAR Name of many kings of the Woḍeyar dynasty that ruled the kingdom of Mysuru for centuries.

CĀMUṆḌĀ A fearsome goddess often depicted as emaciated. Frequently identified as a form of **Kālī**, or sometimes **Durgā**.

CĀMUṆḌAMMA See **Cāmuṇḍā**. See also ***amma*** in the glossary.

CĀMUṆḌĪ/CĀMUṆḌI See **Cāmuṇḍā**.

CĀMUṆḌĒŚVARI See **Cāmuṇḍā**.

CAṆḌĪ/CAṆḌIKĀ Fierce One. A common epithet for **Kālī**.

CANDRASENA Name of the king in the frame narrative of the **Bhadrakāḷī** story who listens to the tale narrated by the sage **Sutīkṣṇa**.

CANDRAVATĪ The sinful daughter-in-law of **Gomā** in the **Svasthānī** tale. Wife of **Navarāj**.

CARCIKĀ A name of **Cāmuṇḍā**.

CHAGALA Goat. The name of one of **Śiva**'s attendants and a door guardian.

DĀNAVA Descendant of **Dānu**; demon. Proper name of a demon in the **Bhadrakāḷī** narrative. Son of **Dānavatī**.

DĀNAVATĪ Mother of the demon named **Dānava**.

DAṆḌHĀSUR Name of a demon who is both antagonist and devotee in the **Bahucarā** narrative.

DANU A demon king and father of **Rambha** and **Karambha**. See also **Dānava**.

DĀRIKA/DĀRUKA Name of the demonic adversary of **Bhadrakāḷī**.

DĀRUMATĪ Mother of the demon **Dārika**.

DHŪMRALOCANA Smoky eyed. Name of a demon killed by **Durgā**.

DUNDUBHI Kettle drum. Name of a demon in the **Kauśikī** narrative and other myths.

DURGĀ Difficult to Approach. Important Hindu warrior goddess famous for fighting and slaying a buffalo demon. Sometimes considered to be the wife of **Śiva**.

EKALIṄGA/EKLIṄGJĪ Solitary *liṅga*. Name of a local form of **Śiva** connected to **Rāṣṭrasenā**, north of Udaipur in Rajasthan state.

ERLANGGA Regnal name of king who ruled the eastern half of Java in the eleventh century. Features in the *Calon Arang* tale.

GAṆEŚA Lord of **Śiva**'s Divine Entourage. In early Śaivism the title referred to several figures. Most common is the son of **Pārvatī** and **Śiva**, pictured with an elephant head and a human body. Commonly worshiped in order to remove obstacles in one's life.

GANGA The goddess Gaṅgā and the major north Indian river named after her (anglicized as "Ganges").

GARUḌA A divine eagle associated with **Śiva** in Śaiva contexts, **Viṣṇu** in Vaiṣṇava contexts, the Goddess in Śākta contexts, and various enlightened beings in Buddhism.

GAURĪ Light complexioned. An epithet for **Pārvatī**.

GĀYATRĪ A goddess who personifies the **Vedic** Gāyatrī mantra.

GOMĀ A character in the **Svasthānī** tale and the first woman to perform the Svasthānī vow and receive its benefits.

GOMĀ BHAṬṬINĪ See **Gomā**.

GOMAYAJU See **Gomā**.

HĀRAVA Name of an *asura* demon; the son of Diti and Kaśyapa. He figures in the Kauśikī narrative and in various accounts of the war between the gods and the demons.

HĀRĪTARĀŚI A sage of Mewar and devotee of **Ekaliṅga** and **Rāṣṭrasenā**.

HETUKEŚVARA Causal Lord. An epithet for **Śiva** in the Seven Mothers narratives.

INDRA King of the gods in the archaic Vedic pantheon. Guardian of the eastern direction in Tantric contexts.

ĪŚĀNA A name of **Śiva**. He is guardian of the northeastern direction in Tantric contexts.

ĪŚĀNĪ One of the female forms of **Śiva**.

ĪŚVARA Lord. An epithet for **Śiva** and the technical designation of a *tattva* in Tantric cosmology.

-JĪ (SUFFIX) A gender-neutral suffix indicating respect that is commonly added to names in modern Indo-Aryan languages.

JṚMBHAK Name of a nature spirit (*yakṣa*) who guards the area of Mansarovar.

JVALAJJIHVĀ Flaming Tongue. An epithet for **Uttanahaḷḷi**.

JVĀLĀMUKHI Having a Mouth like Fire. An epithet for **Uttanahaḷḷi**.

JYEṢṬHĀ The Eldest. Name of one of **Śiva**'s three principal *śakti* goddesses, along with **Vāmā** and **Raudrī**.

KAILĀ DEVĪ Name of a goddess popular in northeastern Rajasthan, worshiped as a pair with her sister, **Cāmuṇḍā**.

KAITABH Name of a demon killed by **Durgā**.

KĀLASAṂKARṢAṆĪ Devourer of Time. See **Kālī**.

KĀLĪ/KĀḶĪ An important Hindu warrior goddess popularized in the Tantras. Her name means both "The Dark One," referring to her skin complexion (as opposed to the fair-complexioned **Gaurī**), and more esoterically, "Lady of Time," referring to Kālī's association with time and death. In Malayalam-influenced Sanskrit works, Kāḷī may be a shortened name for **Bhadrakāḷī**.

KĀLIKĀ See **Kālī**.

KĀMADEVA The God of Love.

KĀMEŚVARĪ The Goddess of Love.

KAṆṆAKI AND KŌVALAṈ Names of the main characters in the classical Tamil *Tale of the Anklet* (*Cilappatikāram*), a literary work that influenced the tradition of **Bhadrakāḷī** worship in Kerala.

KAṆṬHEKĀLĪ Dark-throat Lady. Another name for **Bhadrakāḷī**.

KANURUHAN See **Ken Kanuruhan**.

KAPILA In the Svasthānī tale, name of a brahmin sage who instructs **Candravatī** in the performance of the **Svasthānī** vow.

KARAMBHA Demon brother of **Rambha**. Killed by **Indra** in the **Kailā Devī** narrative.

KAUBERĪ The female form of the god **Kubera**.

KAULĪŚA Lord of the Kaula sect. Name of the first guru of the Tantric Kaula sect.

KAUMĀRĪ The female form of the god **Skanda**.

KAUŚIKĪ Born from a sheath. A form of the goddess **Durgā** whose name alludes to the myth of her arising from the cast-off skin of the goddess **Pārvatī**.

KEDĀREŚVARA Lord of the Kedara region (in Uttarakhand, India). An epithet for **Śiva**.

KEDARGIRI Name of an ascetic holy man closely associated with **Kailā Devī**.

KEN KANURUHAN Nobleman who helped arrange the marriage of **Bahula** and **Ratna Manggalī**.

KHINCHI See **Mukund Das Khinchi**.

KOṞṞAVAI A fierce goddess of ancient southern India whose iconography and lore informed the development of **Kālī** in southern India, and **Bhadrakāḷī** in Kerala in particular.

KṚṢṆA Dark, referring to complexion. Name of one of **Viṣṇu**'s most celebrated avatars.

KUBERA A god of wealth in classical literature, and guardian of the northern direction in Tantric contexts.

KUBJIKĀ The Crooked/Hunchback. An important early Tantric goddess who is identified with the coiled serpent power of **Kuṇḍalinī**.

KUJAMBHA Name of a demon mentioned in the Kauśikī narrative and other mythological stories. His battle chariot is drawn by mules who wear demonic masks.

KULAYOGINĪ Yoginī of the Family. An epithet for **Kāmeśvarī**.

KUMBHAKARṆA Pitcher Ears. Name of a door guardian at the temple of **Bahumāṃsā** and **Hetukeśvara** in the *Skanda Purāṇa*.

KUṆḌALINĪ The Coiled One. A feminine serpentine power coiled at the base of the spine. Early Tantras regarded Kuṇḍalinī as a goddess, whereas later texts presented it as a power or energy.

KUNTĪ Devotee of **Ra Nini** and mother of **Sadewa** in the *Sudamala* story.

LAKṢMĪ The goddess of fortune and wife of the god **Viṣṇu**.

LALITĀ The Playful One. An epithet for **Tripurasundarī**.

LOHITĀKṢA Red Eyes. The name of a male companion to an archaic group of Mother-goddesses.

LOHITĀYANI Name of a Mother-goddess in the epic *Mahābhārata* who is associated with the Brahmaputra River. She may be an earlier form of **Bahumāṃsā**.

LORD OF LIFE, LORD OF YOGIS Epithets for the sage **Baradah** in the *Calon Arang* tale.

MĀ/MA Mother. Shortened form of **Mātā**.

MADANA The Maddening One. Name of the god of love, **Kāmadeva**.

MĀDHAVA Sweet. An epithet for **Viṣṇu**.

MAHĀDEVA The Great God; an epithet for **Śiva**.

MAHĀDEVĪ A title meaning "The Great Goddess" that is applied to any goddess whom a devotee regards as supreme. Typically this is reserved for goddesses associated with **Śiva**.

MAHĀKĀLĪ The Great **Kālī**. An honorific name of **Kālī**.

MAHĀLAKṢMĪ Great **Lakṣmī**. Mahālakṣmī is sometimes included as an eighth goddess among the **Seven Mothers**.

MAHĀTRIPURĀ/MAHĀTRIPURASUNDARĪ The Great Lady of the Three Cities. An honorific for **Tripurasundarī**.

MĀHENDRĪ The female form of the god **Indra**.

MĀHEŚVARĪ One of the female forms of the god **Śiva**.

MAHIṢA Buffalo. See also **Mahiṣāsura**.

MAHIṢĀSURA Buffalo demon. A demonic enemy of the Goddess in myth cycles from about the fourth century CE onward.

MAHIṢĀSURAMARDINĪ Slayer of the buffalo demon. An epithet for **Kauśikī-Durgā**.

MAHIṢAWADANA Pupil learning sorcery from **Rangda of Girah.**

MANGGALĪ See **Ratna Manggalī.**

MANODARĪ Daughter of the demon architect **Maya** and wife of **Dārika.**

MĀRAMMA/MĀRIYAMMĀ See **Māriyammaṉ.**

MĀRIYAMMAṈ Mother Māri (see *māri* in glossary). An important fierce goddess, and class of goddesses, of southern India. Like **Śītalā**, she is associated with curing smallpox and related infectious diseases.

MĀRKAṆḌEYA Name of an ancient sage who narrates, or serves as a stock figure in, many Sanskrit Purāṇas.

MĀTĀ Mother. An appellation of the goddess that is frequently added to another name (e.g., **Bahucarā** Mātā) or used alone. Sometimes compounded with **-jī** suffix (Mātājī) to mean "Honored Mother."

MAYA Famous *asura* (demon) architect who built lavish palaces and cities for various demons in Hindu mythology.

MPU BARADAH See under **Baradah.**

MPU KEBO BAHULA See under **Bahula.**

MUKUND DAS KHINCHI (MUKUND DĀS KHĪṂCĪ) Name of a Rajput king and devotee of **Kailā Devī** reported to have ruled the Khinchi dynasty in the twelfth century.

NANDA Joy. Name of the foster father of the god **Kṛṣṇa.**

NANDI/NANDĪ/NANDIN Joyful. In early Tantras and other literature, Nandi is often an ectype of **Śiva** and an important figure in his entourage, who is often said to have the face of a monkey. Also a name for Śiva's vehicle that takes the form of a bull.

NANDIMAHĀKĀLA Name of the general of **Bhadrakāḷī**'s army.

NAÑJUṆḌĒŚVARA A local form of **Śiva** in the town of Nanjangud near Mysuru.

NĀRADA Name of an ancient sage who serves as a stock figure in myths as a messenger for the gods.

NAVARĀJ The son of **Gomā** in the **Svasthānī** tale.

NIRṚTI The god of chaos in the **Vedic** pantheon, and guardian of the southwestern direction in Tantric contexts.

NIŚUMBHA/NISUMBHA Name of a demon slain by **Durgā.** Brother of **Śumbha.**

PĀÑCĀLA A particular *yakṣa* king and servant of **Durgā** in the **Kauśikī** narrative.

PARĀ Supreme. Name of one of three goddesses collectively regarded as the highest divinity in the Trika sect of Śākta Tantra.

PARAMEŚVARA The supreme Lord; an epithet for **Śiva.**

PARAMEŚVARĪ "The supreme Goddess; an epithet for **Svasthānī.**

PĀRVATĪ "Mountain's Daughter"; a major Hindu goddess regarded as the wife of **Śiva** and daughter of the Himalaya mountain range. See also **Svasthānī.**

PAVANDEVA See **Vāyu.**

RA NINI The great Hindu Goddess in the *Sudamala* tale (**Pārvatī/Durgā**). Served as the prototype for **Rangdā** in the *Calon Arang* tale.

RAKTABĪJA Blood-seed. A demon referenced in many Hindu goddess myths. Every drop of his blood instantly generates a clone of the original demon upon touching the ground.

RAKTĀSURA See **Raktabīja.**

RAMBHA Name of the demon who practiced austerities and fathered **Mahiṣāsura** and produced **Raktabīja** in the **Kailā Devī** narrative.

RANGDA OF GIRAH The widow of Girah. Rangda came to be used as a proper name for this character.

RĀṢṬRASENĀ/RĀṢṬRAŚYENĀ Army of the Kingdom/Hawk of the Kingdom. Names of the hawk-goddess who protects the kingdom of Mewar.

RATNA MANGGALĪ Auspicious Jewel. Name of **Rangda**'s daughter.

RAUDRĪ Wrathful. Name of one of **Śiva**'s three principal *śakti* goddesses, along with **Vāmā** and **Jyeṣṭhā.**

RUDRA A name of **Śiva**, and the name for a class of gods created by Śiva to rule over various realms.

RUDRĀṆĪ One of the female forms of **Śiva.**

RUKMAṆI Name of **Kṛṣṇa**'s principal wife. Also spelled Rukmiṇī.

SADĀŚIVA "Eternal **Śiva**"; a name for Śiva and a particular form of him in the Śaiva Tantra hierarchy of *tattvas*.

SADEWA The son of **Kuntī** and an intended sacrificial victim to **Ra Nini** in the *Sudamala* tale, which heavily influenced the *Calon Arang* tale.

ŚAKRA A name of the god **Indra**, or possibly another god in the **Seven Mothers** narrative of the *Skanda Purāṇa*.

ŚAKTI The Goddess as the source and embodiment of the animating power behind all life (*śakti*).

SANATKUMĀRA Name of one of the ancient ancestors of humankind; sometimes identified with **Skanda**. Narrator of the "Glorification of Koṭīvarṣa" in the **Seven Mothers** chapter.

SANG HYANG Revered God. An honorific prefixed to the names of many deities in Balinese Hinduism.

ŚAṄKARA A name of **Śiva.**

ṢAṆMUKHA Six-faced. An epithet for **Skanda.**

SAPTA MĀTARAḤ/SAPTAMĀTṚKĀ See **Seven Mothers.**

ŚĀRADĀ/SĀRADA Autumnal/modest/clever. An epithet for **Sarasvatī.**

SARASVATĪ The goddess of learning, music, and the arts.

ŚARVĀṆĪ Another name for the goddess **Rudrāṇī**, one of the female forms of **Śiva.**

SATĪ A past-life identity of the goddess **Pārvatī**. In the **Svasthānī** tale, name of **Gomā**'s mother.

SATYAVRAT Vow of truth. Name of a sage who encourages **Daṇḍhāsur** to die at the hands of the Goddess in the **Bahucarā** narrative.

SEVEN MOTHERS A group of seven goddesses who show up in a variety of Hindu goddess myths. See especially chapter 4.

SHIVAJI Name of a famous Maratha king and goddess devotee who revolted against Mughal rule in the seventeenth century.

SI GAṆḌI, SI GUYANG, SI LARUNG, SI LĔNDĔ, SI LĔNDI, AND SI LĔNDYA Pupils learning sorcery from **Rangda of Girah**. See also **Wĕkśirṣa; Mahiṣawadana.**

SIDDHAMĀTṚKĀ Perfected Alphabet. Name of a goddess who embodies the sacred sounds of the Sanskrit alphasyllabary.

SIDDHAYOGEŚVAREŚVARĪ Queen of magic female spirits. Name of a goddess who represents the Trika sect of Śākta Tantra.

ŚIKHAṆḌĪ Name of transgender man in the classic *Mahābhārata* epic.

ŚĪTALĀ A form of **Mahādevī** that is particularly associated with causing and curing the smallpox disease.

ŚIVA A major Hindu god visualized as an ascetic who meditates high in the Himalayan Mountains with his wife **Pārvatī** and children **Gaṇeśa** and **Skanda.**

ŚIVA BHAṬṬA/ŚIVABHAṬṬA He whose lord is **Śiva.** Name of the elderly brahmin father of **Gomā** in the **Svasthānī** tale.

ŚIVA ŚARMA/ŚIVAŚARMAN He who takes refuge in **Śiva.** The elderly brahmin mendicant who became the husband of **Gomā** in the **Svasthānī** tale. Name of a sage serving as **Mārkaṇḍeya**'s interlocutor in the *Bhadrakāḷī Māhātmya*. Father of **Bappā Rāwal** in the **Rāṣṭrasenā** narrative.

ŚIVAŚAKTI The combined form of **Śiva** and **Pārvatī** visualized as each making up half of a single body, or the philosophical idea that Śiva and his female consort together make up the supreme godhead.

SKANDA A major Hindu god regarded as the son of **Śiva** and **Pārvatī** whose cult declined in popularity after approximately 500 CE. In southern India the god Murugan was identified with Skanda and remains popular today.

SMARA Nostalgia. An epithet for **Kāmadeva.**

ŚRĪ An honorific prefixed to the names of many deities and saints. See specific names.

SUKHDEV/SUKHCHAND PATEL Names of a devotee of **Kailā Devī** who served as a medium.

ŚUKRAVĀHINĪ Awash with sexual fluids. An epithet for **Kāmeśvarī.**

ŚUMBHA/SUMBHA Name of a demon killed by **Durgā.** Brother of **Niśumbha.**

ŚUṢKĀ Shriveled/emaciated. An epithet for **Kālī.**

SUṢUMĀṆA A king of Mewar mentioned in the *Ekaliṅga Māhātmya*.

SUTĪKṢṆA Very sharp. Name of the sage living in the Daṇḍaka forest who narrates the **Bhadrakāḷī** story to the king, **Candrasena.**

SVASTHĀNĪ Goddess of One's Own Place. A form of **Pārvatī.**

TĀRKṢYA A name of the bird deity **Garuḍa.**

TEJPĀL Name of a transgender prince whose female body was transformed into a male.

TILOTTAMĀ Name of a goddess created by **Brahmā** to delude and destroy two demon brothers in the *Mahābhārata*. She was so beautiful that when she circumambulated Śiva, the god created four heads for himself to be able to see her in all directions.

TRIPURĀ Lady of the Three Cities. A shortened form of the name **Tripurasundarī.**

TRIPURĀ BĀLĀSUNDARĪ See **Bālātripurāsundarī.**

TRIPURABHAIRAVĪ Fierce Goddess of the Three Cities. An epithet for **Tripurasundarī.**

TRIPURASUNDARĪ The Beauty of the Three Cities. An important goddess in early Tantra who is still actively worshiped in the Śrīvidyā tradition.

TROṬALĀ A name of **Tvaritā,** used particularly for her fearsome form.

TUNGGAL Also known as Acintya; a supreme deity in Balinese Hinduism that is equivalent to the concept of *brahman* in the Hindu scriptures called the Upaniṣads.

TVARITĀ The Swift One. A form of **Pārvatī**.

UMĀ A name of the goddess **Pārvatī**.

UTTANAHAḶḶI Name of **Cāmuṇḍi**'s sister, whose temple is located on a hillock near Cāmuṇḍi hill next to the city of Mysuru.

VAIṢṆAVĪ The female form of the god **Viṣṇu**.

VĀMĀ Lady Contrary. Name of one of **Śiva**'s three principal *śakti* goddesses, along with **Raudrī** and **Jyeṣṭhā**.

VĀRĀHĪ The female form of Varāha, boar avatar of **Viṣṇu**.

VARUṆA The lord of oceans, descended from the Vedic god of the same name. The guardian of the western direction in Tantric contexts.

VĀSUKI Name of one of the eight divine serpents who play roles in many Hindu myths and rituals.

VĀYU The god of wind in the Vedic pantheon, and guardian of the northwestern direction in Tantric contexts.

VEDAGARBHA The royal priest and interlocutor of king **Suṣumāṇa** in the **Rāṣṭrasenā** narrative.

VETĀLĪ Vampire. Name of a bloodthirsty goddess who aids **Bhadrakāḷī** on the battlefield.

VINĀYAKA The elephant-headed general of **Śiva**'s attendants. The son of **Pārvatī** and Śiva better known as **Gaṇeśa**.

VINDHYAVĀSĀ/VINDHYAVĀSINĪ She who dwells in the Vindhya Mountains. An epithet for **Durgā**.

VĪRABHADRA Auspicious hero. A name of the fierce form of **Śiva** or a god generated by Śiva.

VIṢṆU A major Hindu god visualized as a king who reclines on a divine serpent and periodically comes to earth to support the righteous.

VIŚVAKARMA The All-maker. Name of the architect of the gods in the **Vedic** pantheon. Name for any creator god.

VYĀSA A famous sage in classical Indian literature and the interlocutor in the "Glorification of Koṭīvarṣa" narrative in the chapter on the **Seven Mothers**.

WEDAWATĪ Daughter of the sage **Baradah** who flees to a cremation ground to escape her wicked stepmother.

WĚKŚIRṢA Pupil learning sorcery from **Rangda of Girah**.

YAMA The god of death in the **Vedic** pantheon, and guardian of the southern direction in Tantric contexts.

YĀMĪ The female form of the god of death, **Yama**.

YOGIRAJ An ascetic holy man who reportedly brought the image of **Kailā Devī** to its present location in Rajasthan.

PRIMARY SOURCES

Titles are listed in Indic alphabetical order. Full references for edited texts are provided in the References under the editor's or editors' name(s) and year. The acronym NGMPP stands for the Nepal-German Manuscript Preservation Project.

Agni Purāṇa. Ed. Joshi and Dutt (2001).

Abhijñānaśākuntala. Ed. Vasudeva (2006).

Amarakāvyam. Ed. Kothari, Sarma, and Bhatanagara 1985.

Īśānaśivagurudevapaddhati. Ed. Shastri (1990).

Ekaliṅga Māhātmya. Ed. Sharma (1976) and Juganu (2016).

Aiśānayāmala. Not known to survive.

Kaliṅkattupparaṇi. Ed. Civananam (1979).

Kālikā Purāṇa. Ed. Pratap and Shastri (2008).

Kidung Sudamala. Ed. Stein Callenfels (1925).

Kumārayāmala. Not known to survive.

Kumārasambhava. Ed. Smith (2005).

Kulārṇava Tantra. Ed. Vidyaratna (1965).

Kaulajñānanirṇaya. Ed. Bagchi and Magee (1986).

Kramastotra. Ed. Silburn (1975).

Gaüḍavaho. Ed. Pandurang Pandit (1887).

Gāndhārayāmala. Not known to survive.

Guhyasūtra. See *Niśvāsatattvasaṃhitā*.

Calon Arang. Ed. Poerbatjaraka (1926).

Cāma Celuve. Contemporary play; Akki (2012).

Cāmarājokti Vilāsa. Ed. Odeyar (1894–1896).

Ciñciṇīmatasārasamuccaya. Unpublished. Manuscript filmed as NGMPP B157/19. Digital transcript available at Muktabodha.org.

Cilappatikāram. Ed. Cinivasarakavacari (1872).

Jayadrathayāmala. Unpublished. The following manuscripts filmed by the NGMPP contain the translated chapter: (A) A152/9, (B) B26/09, (C) A1312/25, (D) B122/03, (E) C72/01, (H) B122/13, and (I) C47/03. Also utilized: (J) Berlin MS HS. OR.8535.

Jvālāmālinīkalpa. Ed. Shastri (1964).

Tantrasadbhāva. Ed. Dyczkowski (2008).

Tantrāloka. Ed. Shastri and Shastri (1918–1938).

Turajā Māhātmya. Ed. Jansen (1995).

Troṭala Tantra. A canonical Gāruḍa Tantra. Partially survives in the *Tvaritāmūlasūtra* and *Tvaritājñānakalpa*.

Tvaritājñānakalpa. Unpublished. Manuscripts filmed as NGMPP A59/15, A59/17, B26/14, and B126/15.

Tvaritāmūlasūtra. Unpublished. Manuscripts filmed as NGMPP B126/9, H170/3, and C6/7. Mark Dyczkowski produced a rough digital transcript of B126/9, available at Muktabodha.org under the title *Troṭalātantra*.

Tvaritāvidhānasūtra. Unpublished. Manuscript extract of the *Manthānabhairava Tantra* filmed as NGMPP A59/13.

Dārikavadham See *Bhadrakāḷī Māhātmya*. Also name of performative tradition.

Devī Purāṇa. Ed. Tarkaratna (1895–1896) and Sharma (1976). Translation based on provisional critical edition by Shaman Hatley. For manuscripts, see Hatley (2018, 621).

Devī Bhāgavata Purāṇa. Ed. Shrikrsnadasa (1986).

Devī Māhātmya. See *Mārkaṇḍeya Purāṇa*.

Deśawarṇana. Ed. Robson (1995).

Nandiyāmala. Not known to survive.

Nityākaula. Unpublished. Manuscript filmed as NGMPP B26/21.

Nityāṣoḍaśikārṇava. See *Vāmakeśvarīmata*.

Niśvāsatattvasaṃhitā. Edition and translation of the *Mūla*, *Uttara*, and *Naya-sūtra* by Goodall, Sanderson, and Isaacson (2015). Edition and translation of the *Niśvāsamukha* by Kafle (2015). For the *Niśvāsaguhya* and *Niśvāsakārikā*, contributors used digital transcriptions from the EFEO team in Pondicherry.

Nainsī rī Khyāt. Ed. Jinavijaya Muni (1960).

Padma Purāṇa. Not consulted for this book, but the *Svasthānīvratakathā* is spuriously attributed to it.

Pararaton. Ed. Brandes (1896).

Parātriṃśikāvivaraṇa. Ed. Gnoli (1985).

Pārameśvarīmata. Unpublished. Digital transcript published at Muktabodha.org.

Puraścaryārṇava. Ed. Jha (1985).

Pratiṣṭhālakṣaṇasārasamuccaya. See *Lakṣaṇasaṃgraha*.

Bahucarmānī Utpatti Kathā. See *Śrī Bahucarā Ārādhanā*.

Bṛhatkālottara. Unpublished. Manuscripts filmed as NGMPP B24/57 and B24/59.

Bṛhatsaṃhitā. Ed. Kern (1865).

Bṛhadāraṇyaka Upaniṣad. Ed. Olivelle (1998).

Beṭṭada Cāmuṇḍi. Ed. Rajasekhara (1972).

Brahmayāmala. Partially edited in Hatley (2007, 2018) and Kiss (2015). An electronic transcription of the entire text is available from https://muktabodha.org. The unpublished electronic transcription of Shaman Hatley and Alexis Sanderson is preferred.

Bhadrakāḷī Māhātmya. Ed. Girija and Visalakshy (1999–2000). Translation based primarily on T697 at Oriental Manuscript Library, University of Kerala.

Bhāgavata Purāṇa. Ed. Shastri (1965).

Bhairavapadmāvatīkalpa. Ed. Jhavery (1944).

Matasāra. Unpublished. Manuscript filmed as NGMPP B28/16.

Matsya Purāṇa. Ed. Mora (1954).

Manthānabhairava Tantra. Partially edited and translated in Dyczkowski (2009).

Mayadīpikā. Ed. Juganu (2008).

Mahākālasaṃhitā. Ed. Jha (1976–1979).

Mahābhārata. Ed. Sukthankar (1927).

Mahāyāgakrama. Ed. not available. Digital transcript published at Muktabodha.org.

Mahārthamañjarī. Ed. Shastri (1919).

Mātṛsadbhāva. Unpublished. Oriental Manuscript Library, University of Kerala, T.792.

Mārkaṇḍeya Purāṇa. Ed. Pargiter (1969).

Mālinīvijayottara. Ed. Vasudeva (2004) and Shastri (1922).

Mṛgendra Tantra. Ed. Bhatt (1962).

Yoginīsaṃcāraprakaraṇa. Section of the *Jayadrathayāmala*.

Yoginīhṛdaya. Ed. Dviveda (1988).

Rāmāyaṇa (Vālmīki). Ed. Bhatt and Shah (1975).

Rudrayāmala. Not known to survive. Published texts circulating under this title date to a later period.

Lakṣaṇasaṃgraha. Ed. Sharman and Sharman (1966 and 1968).

Liṅga Purāṇa. Ed. Sharma (1969).

Vāḍavānalīya Tantra. Ed. in Jha (1985).

Vāmakeśvarīmata. Ed. Shastri (1945).

Vāyu Purāṇa. Ed. Singh (1995).

Vārāhī Tantra. Unpublished. Digital transcript published at Muktabodha.org.

Vidyānuśāsana. Ed. Gunadharanandi (1990).

Śiraścheda. See *Jayadrathayāmala*.

Śrī Kailādevī Itihās. Pilgrim's religious booklet in Hindi language. Scan available on Archive.org.

Śrī Bahucarā Ārādhanā. Pilgrim's religious booklet in Gujarati language. Scan available on Archive.org.

Śrīmatottara. Unpublished. Manuscript filmed as NGMPP A194/3.

Śrīmanmahārājavara Vaṃśāvaḷi. Ed. Row (1916).

Śrīvidyārṇava. Ed. Sharma (1966).

Sarasvatī Purāṇa. Ed. Dave (1940).

Sārasvatayāmala. Not known to survive.

Siddhayogeśvarīmata. Ed. Törzsök (1999).

Sudamala. See *Kidung Sudamala*.

Solanki-no Garba. Unpublished. Manuscript held at British Library under shelf number VT2592.

Skanda Purāṇa. Ed. Adriaensen, Bakker, and Isaacson (1998–2018).

Svacchanda Tantra. Ed. Shastri (1921–1935).

Svacchandabhairava Tantra. See *Svacchanda Tantra*.

Svasthānī Kathā. See *Svasthānīvratakathā*.

Svasthānīvratakathā. Translation based on unpublished version in manuscript filmed as NGMPP B13/42.

Svāyambhuvayāmala. Not known to survive.

Haracaritacintāmaṇi. Ed. Shivadatta and Parab (1897).

Harivaṃśa. See *Mahābhārata*.

REFERENCES

Acri, Andrea, Roger Blench, and Alexandra Landmann. 2017. *Spirits and Ships: Cultural Transfers in Early Monsoon Asia*. Nalanda-Sriwijaya Series 31. Singapore: ISEAS.

Adriaensen, Rob, Hans T. Bakker, and Harunaga Isaacson, eds. 1998–2018. *The Skandapurāṇa*. Vols. 1–4. Groningen: E. Forsten.

Aiyar, Indira S. 1997. *Durgā as Mahiṣāsuramardinī: A Dynamic Myth of Goddess*. New Delhi: Gyan Publishing House.

Akki, Sujatha. 2012. *Cāma Celuve*. Mysore: Vismaya Prakashana.

Ariati, Ni Wayan Pasek. 2016. *The Journey of the Goddess Durga: India, Java and Bali*. Śata-piṭaka Series 651. New Delhi: International Academy of Indian Culture and Aditya Prakashan.

Aubert, L. 2004. *Les feux de la déesse: Rituels villageois du Kerala (Inde du Sud)*. Lausanne: Payot.

Bagchi, Prabodh Chandra, and Michael Magee, eds. 1986. *Kaulajñānanirṇayaḥ*. Varanasi: Prācya Prakāśana.

Bakker, Hans T. 2014. *The World of the Skandapurāṇa*. Leiden: Brill.

Belo, Jane. 1970. *Traditional Balinese Culture*. New York: Columbia University Press.

Bennett, Lynn. 1983. *Dangerous Wives and Sacred Sisters: Social and Symbolic Roles of High-Caste Women in Nepal*. New York: Columbia University Press.

Bhatt, G. H., and U. P. Shah, eds. 1975. *The Vālmīki Rāmāyaṇa: Critical Edition*. Baroda: Oriental Institute.

Bhatt, N. R., ed. 1962. *Mṛgendrāgama, Kriyāpāda*. Pondicherry: Institut français d'indologie.

Bhattarai, Krishna Prasad, ed. 1988. *Skandapurāṇasya Ambikākāṇḍaḥ*. Kathmandu: Mahendraratnagranthamālā.

Biernacki, Loriliai. 2007. *Renowned Goddess of Desire: Women, Sex, and Speech in Tantra*. New York: Oxford University Press.

Birkenholtz, Jessica Vantine. 2013. "Seeking Svasthānī: The Politics of Gender, Location, Iconography and Identity in Hindu Nepal." *Journal of Hindu Studies* 6, no. 2: 198–227.

———. 2016. "From Text to Internet, Aniconic to Statuesque: Modern Textual and Performative Innovations in a Nepali Goddess Tradition." In *Religion and Modernity in the Himalayas*, edited by Megan Adamson Sijapati and Jessica Vantine Birkenholtz, 85–106. New York: Routledge.

———. 2018. *Reciting the Goddess: Narratives of Place and the Making of Hinduism in Nepal*. New York: Oxford University Press.

———. 2019. "On Becoming a Woman: *Shakti*, Storytelling, and Women's Roles and Rights in Nepal." *Signs: A Journal of Women in Culture and Society* 44, no. 2: 433–64.

Bisschop, Peter. 2009. "Śiva." In *Encyclopedia of Hinduism*, edited by Knut A. Jacobsen, 741–54. Leiden: Brill.

Biswas, Arun Kumar. 1994. "Vaidūrya, Marakata and Other Beryl Family Gem Minerals." *Indian Journal of History of Science* 29, no. 2: 139–54.

Brajendrapal, Maharajkumar. 1990. *Shri Kailadevi*. Karauli, Rajasthan: Bhumendra Vilas.

Brandes, Jan Laurens Andries, ed. 1896. *Pararaton, Ken Arok, of Het Boek der Koningen van Tumapĕl en van Majapahit*. The Hague: M. Nijhoff.

Brooks, D. R. 1992. *Auspicious Wisdom: the Texts and Traditions of Śrīvidyā Śākta Tantrism in South India*. Albany: State University of New York Press.

Brunner-Lachaux, Hélène, Gerhard Oberhammer, and André Padoux, eds. 2000. *Tāntrikābhidhānakośa: Dictionnaire des termes techniques de la littérature hindoue tantrique = A dictionary of technical terms from Hindu tantric literature = Wörterbuch zur Terminologie hinduistischer Tantren*. Vol. 1. Wien: Verlag der Österreichischen Akademie der Wissenschaften.

Brussel, Noor van. 2016. "Revenge, Hatred, Love, and Regret: the Use of Narrative Empathy in a Regional Purāṇa." *Religions of South Asia* 11, no. 1: 193–213.

———. In progress. "Bhadrakali and the Bhadrotpatti: A Comparative Study of a Regional Goddess and Her Narrative Tradition." PhD thesis, University of Ghent.

Bühler, Georg. 1877. *Detailed Report of a Tour in Search of Sanskrit Manuscripts Made in Kaśmîr, Rajputana, and Central India*. Bombay: Society's Library.

Bühnemann, Gudrun. 2003. *The Hindu Pantheon in Nepalese Line Drawings: Two Manuscripts of the Pratiṣṭhālakṣaṇasārasamuccaya*. Varanasi: Indica Books.

Caldwell, S. 1999. *Oh Terrifying Mother: Sexuality, Violence, and Worship of the Goddess Kāḷi*. New York: Oxford University Press.

———. 2001. "Waves of Beauty, Rivers of Blood: Constructing the goddess in Kerala." In *Seeking Mahādevī: Constructing the Identities of the Hindu Great Goddess*, edited by T. Pintchman, 93–114. Albany: State University of New York Press.

Campbell, J. M. 1883. *Gazetteer of the Bombay Presidency*. Vol. 7, *Baroda*. Bombay: Government Central Press.

———. 1890. *Gazetteer of the Bombay Presidency*. Vol. 9, pt. 2, *Gujarat Population, Musalmans and Parsis*. Bombay: Government Central Press.

———. 1901. *Gazetteer of the Bombay Presidency*. Vol. 9, *Gujarat Population: Hindus*. Bombay: Government Central Press.

Chakrabarti, K. 2001. *Religious Process: The Purāṇas and the Making of a Regional Tradition*. New Delhi: Oxford University Press.

Cinivasarakavacari, Ti. Ca., ed. 1872. *Cilappatikāram*. Chennai: Kalviviḷakka Accukkūṭam.

Civananam, M. P., ed. 1979. *Kaliṅkattupparaṇi*. Chennai: Pūṅkoṭi Patippakam.

Coburn, Thomas B. 1991. *Encountering the Goddess: A Translation of the Devī-Māhātmya and a Study of Its Interpretation*. Albany: State University of New York Press.

Craddock, Elaine. 2012. "The Half Male, Half Female Servants of the Goddess Aṅkāḷaparamēcuvari." *Nidan: International Journal for Indian Studies* 24: 117–35.

Dave, K. N. 1985. *Birds in Sanskrit Literature*. Delhi: Motilal Banarsidass.

Dave, Kanaiyalala Bha, ed. 1940. *Sarasvatīpurāṇa*. Mumbai: Śrī Phārbasa Gujarātī Sabhā.

De, Sushil Kumar. 1923. *Studies in the History of Sanskrit Poetics*. London: Luzac.

Dehejia, Vidya. 1986. *Yoginī Cult and Temples: A Tantric Tradition*. New Delhi: National Museum.

Dempsey, Corinne. 2006. *The Goddess Lives in Upstate New York: Breaking Convention and Making Home at a North American Hindu Temple*. New York: Oxford University Press.

Donaldson, Thomas E. 2002. *Tantra and Śākta Art of Orissa*. Vols. 1–3. New Delhi: D.K. Printworld.

Dviveda, Vrajavallabha, ed. 1988. *Yoginīhṛdayam: Amṛtānandayogikṛtadīpikayā Bhāṣānuvādena ca Sāhitam*. Delhi: Motilal Banarsidass.

Dyczkowski, Mark S. G. 1988. *The Canon of the Śaivāgama and the Kubjikā Tantras of the Western Kaula Tradition*. Shaiva Traditions of Kashmir. Albany: State University of New York Press.

———. 2008. "Tantrasadbhāva Partially and Provisionally Edited (etext)." *Digital Library of Muktabodha* (http://muktabodha.org). Based on MS K 1-1985 śaivatantra 1533, NGMPP A188/22; MS Kh 1-363 śaivatantra, NGMPP A44/1, MS G 5-445 śaivatantra 185, NGMPP A44/2.

———. 2009. *Manthānabhairavatantram: Kumārikākhaṇḍaḥ: The Section Concerning the Virgin Goddess of the Tantra of the Churning Bhairava*. Vols. 1–4. New Delhi: Indira Gandhi National Centre for the Arts.

Elwin, Verrier. 1955. *The Religion of an Indian Tribe*. Bombay: Oxford University Press.

Entwistle, A. W. 1983. "Kaila Devi and Lamguriya." *Indo-Iranian Journal* 25, no. 2 (March): 85–101.

Erndl, Kathleen. 1993. *Victory to the Mother: The Hindu Goddess of Northwest India in Myth, Ritual, and Symbol*. New York: Oxford University Press.

Finn, Louise M. 1986. *The Kulacūḍāmaṇi Tantra and the Vāmakeśvarīmata Tantra with the Jayaratha Commentary*. Wiesbaden: Otto Harrassowitz.

Fischer, Eberhard, Jyotindra Jain, and Haku Shah. 2013. *Temple Tents for Goddesses in Gujarat*. New Delhi: Niyogi Books.

Fleet, J. F. 1992. "The Kaliyuga Era of B.C. 3102." In *Time in Indian Cosmology: A Collection of Essays*, edited by Hari Shankar Prasad, 359–400. Delhi: Sri Satguru Publications.

Forbes, Alexander Kinloch. 1973. *Ras Mala: Hindu Annals of Western India*. New Delhi: Heritage.

Freeman, R. 2003. "Genre and Society: The Literary Culture of Premodern Kerala." In *Literary Cultures in History: Reconstructions from South Asia*, edited by S. Pollock, 437–502. Berkeley: University of California Press.

———. 2016. "Śāktism, Polity and Society in Medieval Malabar." In *Goddess Traditions in Tantric Hinduism: History, Practice and Doctrine*, edited by Bjarne Wernicke Olesen, 141–73. London: Routledge.

Geertz, Hildred. 1994. *Images of Power: Balinese Paintings Made for Gregory Bateson and Margaret Mead*. Honolulu: University of Hawaii Press.

Gellner, David. 1986. "Language, Caste, Religion and Territory: Newar Identity Ancient and Modern." *European Journal of Sociology* 27, no. 1: 102–48.

Gentes, M. J. 1992. "Scandalizing the Goddess at Kodungallur." *Asian Folklore Studies* 51, no. 2: 295–322.

Gilmartin, David, and Bruce B. Lawrence, eds. 2000. *Beyond Turk and Hindu: Rethinking Religious Identities in Islamicate South Asia*. Gainesville: University Press of Florida.

Girija, R., and P. Visalakshy. 1999–2000. "Bhadrakālīmāhātmya." *Journal of Manuscript Studies* 34, nos. 1–2: 5–82.

Gnoli, R., ed. 1985. *Parātriṃśikātattvavivaraṇam: Abhinavagupta; Il commento di Abhinavagupta alla Parātriṃśikā*. Roma: Istituto italiano per il Medio ed Estremo Oriente.

Golovkova, Anna A. 2010. "The Cult of the Goddess Tripurasundarī in the *Vāmakeśvarīmata*." MA thesis, Oxford University.

———. 2012. "Śrīvidyā." In *Brill's Encyclopedia of Hinduism*, Vol. 4, edited by Knut Jacobsen, H. Basu, and A. Malinar, 815–22. Leiden: Brill.

———. 2015. "The Cult of the Goddess Tripurasundarī in the *Nityākaula*, the *Vāmakeśvarīmata* and the *Yoginīhṛdaya*." In *Proceedings of the Fifteenth World Sanskrit Conference, Tantra and Āgama*, edited by R. Torella, 162–86. New Delhi: D.K. Printworld.

———. 2017. "A Goddess for the Second Millennium: Transgression and Transformation in the Hindu Tantric Worship of Tripurasundarī." PhD thesis, Cornell University.

———. 2019. "From Worldly Powers to *Jīvanmukti*: Ritual and Soteriology in the Early Tantras of the Cult of Tripurasundarī." *Journal of Hindu Studies* 12, no. 1 (May): 103–26.

———. 2020. "The Goddess's Forgotten Consort: Desire in the Nityā Cult and the Cult of Tripurasundarī." *International Journal of Hindu Studies* 24, no. 1 (April).

Goodall, Dominic, and Marion Rastelli, eds. 2013. *Tāntrikābhidhānakośa: Dictionnaire des termes techniques de la littérature hindoue tantrique = A dictionary of technical terms from Hindu tantric literature = Wörterbuch zur Terminologie hinduistischer Tantren*. Vol. 3. Wien: Verlag der Österreichischen Akademie der Wissenschaften.

Goodall, Dominic, Alexis Sanderson, and Harunaga Isaacson, eds. 2015. *The Niśvāsatattvasaṃhitā: The Earliest Surviving Śaiva Tantra.* Vol. 1, *A Critical Edition and Annotated Translation of the Mūlasūtra, Uttarasūtra and Nayasūtra.* Pondicherry: Institut français de Pondichéry; Paris: École française d'Extrême-Orient; Hamburg: Asien-Afrika-Institut, Universität Hamburg.

Granoff, Phyllis. 2003/2004. "Mahākāla's Journey: From Gaṇa to God." *Rivista Degli Studi Orientali* 77, nos. 1/4: 95–114.

Grodzins Gold, Ann. 2008. "Deep Beauty: Rajasthani Goddess Shrines above and below the Surface." *International Journal of Hindu Studies* 12, no.2: 153–79.

Gunadharanandi, Yuvacarya Munisri, ed. 1990. *Vidyānuśāsana.* Jaipur: Śrī. Di. Jaina Divyadhvani Prakāśana.

Haberman, David L. 2013. *People Trees: Worship of Trees in Northern India.* New York: Oxford University Press.

Hanneder, Jürgen. 1998. *Abhinavagupta's Philosophy of Revelation: An Edition and Annotated Translation of Mālinīślokavārttika I, 1–399.* Groningen: E. Forsten.

Harper, Katherine Anne. 1989. *Seven Hindu Goddesses of Spiritual Transformation: The Iconography of the Saptamatrikas.* Lewiston: Edwin Mellen.

Hart, G. L. 1975. *The Poems of Ancient Tamil: Their Milieu and Their Sanskrit Counterparts.* Oxford: Oxford University Press. Originally published by University of California Press, Berkeley.

Hatley, Shaman. 2007. "The Brahmayamalatantra and Early Saiva Cult of Yoginis." PhD thesis, University of Pennsylvania.

———. 2012. "From Mātṛ to Yoginī: Continuity and Transformation in the South Asian Cults of the Mother Goddesses." In *Transformations and Transfer of Tantra in Asia and Beyond,* edited by István Keul, 99–129. Berlin: Walter de Gruyter.

———. 2013. "What Is a Yoginī? Towards a Polythetic Definition." In *"Yogini" in South Asia: Interdisciplinary Approaches,* edited by István Keul, 21–31. New York: Routledge.

———. 2014. "Goddesses in Text and Stone: Temples of the Yoginīs in Light of Tantric and Purāṇic Literature." In *Material Culture and Asian Religions: Text, Image, Object,* edited by Benjamin Fleming and Richard Mann, 195–225. New York: Routledge.

———, ed. 2018. *The Brahmayāmalatantra or Picumata.* Vol. 1, *Chapters 1–2, 39–40, & 83: Revelation, Ritual, and Material Culture in an Early Śaiva Tantra.* Collection Indologie 133; Early Tantra Series 5. Pondicherry: Institut français de Pondichéry; Paris: École française d'Extrême-Orient; Hamburg: Asien-Afrika-Institut, Universität Hamburg.

Hazra, R. C. 1963. *Studies in the Upapurāṇas.* Vol. 2, *Śākta and Non-sectarian Upapurāṇas.* Calcutta Sanskrit College Research Series 22. Kolkata: Sanskrit College.

———. 1984. "Purāṇa Literature as Known to Ballālasena." *Purāṇa* 26, no. 1: 41–59.

Heilijgers-Seelen, Dory. 1994. *The System of Five Cakras in Kubjikāmatatantra 14–16.* Groningen: E. Forsten.

Hobart, Angela. 2005. "Transformation and Aesthetics in Balinese Masked Performances: Rangda and Barong." In *Aesthetics in Performance: Formations of Symbolic Construction and Experience*, edited by Angela Hobart and Bruce Kapferer, 161–82. New York & Oxford: Berghahn.

Humes, Cynthia Ann. 1996. "Vindhyavāsinī: Local Goddess, Yet Great Goddess." In *Devi: Goddesses of India*, edited by John Stratton Hawley and Donna M. Wulff, 49–77. Berkeley: University of California Press.

Iltis, Linda. 1985. "The *Swasthani Vrata*: Newar Women and Ritual in Nepal." PhD thesis, University of Wisconsin-Madison.

———. 1996. "Women, Pilgrimage, Power, and the Concept of Place in the Swasthānī Vrata." In *Change and Continuity: Studies in the Nepalese Culture of Kathmandu Valley*, edited by Siegfried Lienhard, 303–20. Alessandria: Edizioni dell'Orso.

Jadaun Bhagirathwale, Moolsingh. n.d. *Shri Kailadevi Itihas* [The history of Kailadevi]. Mathura: Shri Vandana Book Depot.

Jansen, Roland. 1995. *Die Bhavani von Tuljapur*. Stuttgart: Franz Steiner Verlag.

Jha, Kisoranatha. 1976–1979. *Mahākālasaṃhitā*. Vols. 1–3. Prayāga/Ilahabad: Gaṅgānāthajhākendrīyasaṃskṛtavidyāpīṭham.

Jha, Muralidhara, ed. 1985. *Puraścaryārṇava*. Delhi: Chaukhamba.

Jhavery, Mohanlal Bhagwandas, ed. 1944. *Comparative and Critical Study of Mantra Śāstra (with Special Treatment of Jain Mantravada): Being the Introduction to Sri Bhairava Padmavati Kalpa*. Ahmedabad: Sarabhai Manilal Nawab.

Jinavijaya Muni, Acharya, ed. 1960. *Muṃhata Nainsī rī Khyāt by Muhaṇota Naiṇsī*. Vol. 1. Jodhpur: Rājasthāna Prācyavidyā Pratishṭhana.

Joshi, K. L., and M. N. Dutt, eds. 2001. *Agnimahāpurāṇam*. Delhi: Parimal Publications.

Joshi, N. P. 1986. *Mātṛkās: Mothers in Kuṣāṇa Art*. New Delhi: Kanak.

Juganu, Srikrsna, ed. 2008. *Sacitra Mayamatam*. Chaukhamba Samskrta Granthamala 127. Varanasi: Chaukhamba.

———, ed. 2016. *Śrīmad Ekaliṅgamāhātmyam: Mohanabodhinī nāmnī ṭīkāsamupetam*. Delhi: Parimala.

Kafle, Nirajan. 2015. "The *Niśvāsamukha*, the Introductory Book of the *Niśvāsatattvasaṃhitā*." PhD thesis, Leiden University.

Kane, Pandurang Vaman. 1974. *History of Dharmaśāstra: Ancient and Mediaeval Religious and Civil Law*. 2nd ed. Vol. 2, no. 1. Government Oriental Series Class B 6. Pune: Bhandarkar Oriental Research Institute.

———. 1991. *History of Dharmaśāstra*. Pune: Bhandarkar Oriental Research Institute.

Kapur, Nandini Sinha. 2002. *State Formation in Rajasthan: Mewar During the Seventh-Fifteenth Centuries*. New Delhi: Manohar.

Kassebaum, Gayathri Rajapur. 1998. "Communal Self and Cultural Imagery: The Katha Performance Tradition in South India." In *Self as Image in Asian Theory and Practice*, edited by Roger T. Ames, Thomas P. Kasulis, and Wimal Dissanayake, 260–79. Albany: State University of New York Press.

Kern, H., ed. 1865. *The Bṛhat Sañhitá of Varáha-mihira*. Calcutta: Asiatic Society of Bengal.

Kinsley, David. 1988. *Hindu Goddesses: Visions of the Divine Feminine in the Hindu Religion*. Berkeley: University of California Press.

Kiss, Csaba, ed. 2015. *The Brahmayāmalatantra or Picumata*. Vol. 2, *The Religious Observances and Sexual Rituals of the Tantric Practitioner: Chapters 3, 21, and 45*. Collection Indologie 130; Early Tantra Series 3. Pondicherry: Institut français de Pondichéry; Paris: École française d'Extrême-Orient; Hamburg: Asien-Afrika-Institut, Universität Hamburg.

Kothari, Deva, Saktikumara Sarma, and Rajendraprakasa Bhatanagara, eds. 1985. *Amarakāvyam*. Udaipur: Sāhitya Saṃsthāna, Rājasthāna Vidyāpīṭha.

Krishnaswamy, Subashree, and K. Srilata, eds. 2008. *Short Fiction from South India*. Delhi: Oxford University Press.

Lidke, Jeff. 2017. *The Goddess Within and Beyond the Three Cities: Śākta Tantra and the Paradox of Power in Nepāla-Maṇḍala*. Tantra in Contemporary Researches 5. New Delhi: DK Printworld.

Lyons, Tryna. 1999. "The Changing Faces of Ekliṅgjī: A Dynastic Shrine and Its Artists." *Asiae* 58, no. 3/4: 255–56.

Mahalakshmi, R. 2011. *The Making of the Goddess: Korravai-Durgā in the Tamil Traditions*. New Delhi: Penguin Books India.

Manandhar, Sushila. 1988. "The Royal Devotion to Deity Taleju." *Ancient Nepal* 107: 6–9.

McDaniel, June. 2003. *Making Virtuous Daughters and Wives: An Introduction to Women's Brata Rituals in Bengali Folk Religion*. Albany: State University of New York.

McDermott, Rachel Fell, and Jeffrey Kripal. 2003. *Encountering Kālī: In the Margins, At the Center, In the West*. Berkeley: University of California Press.

Meister, Michael W. 1986. "Regional Variation in Mātṛkā Conventions." *Artibus Asiae* 47: 233–62.

Mora, Nandalal, ed. 1954. *Matsyapurāṇa*. Calcutta: Gopal Printing Works.

Nanda, Serena. 1990. *Neither Man nor Woman: The Hijras of India*. Belmont, CA: Wadsworth Publishing Company.

Odeyar, Camaraja. 1894–1896. *Śrī Cāmarājōkti vilāsa eṃba Kannaḍa Rāmāyaṇa*. Vols. 1–6. Bengaluru: Cāmuṇḍēśvarī Mudrākṣaraśāle.

Olivelle, P. 1998. *The Early Upaniṣads: Annotated Text and Translation*. New York: Oxford University Press, USA.

Onishi, Yoshinori. 1997. *Feminine Multiplicity: A Study of Groups of Multiple Goddesses in India*. Sri Garib Dass Oriental Series 207. Delhi: Sri Satguru.

Padma, Sree. 2013. *Vicissitudes of the Goddess*. New York: Oxford University Press.

Padmaja, V. T. 1982. "Shakti Cult in Gujarat with Special Reference to Shakta Pithas." PhD thesis, Maharaja Sayajirao University, Baroda.

———. 1986. "Three Sakti Pithas of Gujarat." *Journal of the Oriental Institute* 35: 241–47.

Padoux, André. 1990. *Vāc: The Concept of the Word in Selected Hindu Tantras.* Translated by Jacques Gontier. SUNY series in the Shaiva traditions of Kashmir. Original title: *Recherches sur la symbolique et l'énergie de la parole dans certains textes tantriques.* Albany: State University of New York Press.

Pal, Pratapaditya. 1988. "The Mother Goddesses According to the *Devīpurāṇa.*" *Purāṇa* 30, no. 1: 22–59.

Pandurang Pandit, Shankar, ed. 1887. *The Gauḍavaho: A Historical Poem in Prākrit.* Bombay: Government Central Book Depot.

Panikkar, Shivaji K. 1997. *Saptamātṛkā: Worship and Sculptures.* New Delhi: D. K. Printworld.

Pargiter, F. E., ed. 1969. *Markaṇḍeya Purāṇa.* Delhi: Indological Book House.

Parthasarathy, R. 2004. *Cilappatikāram: The Tale of an Anklet.* New Delhi: Penguin India.

Pasty-Abdul Wahid, M. 2010. "Au plaisir de la déesse: Le muṭiyēttu' du Kerala (Inde du Sud): étude ethnographique d'un théâtre rituel entre tradition et modernité." PhD thesis, Université de Paris.

Pearson, Anne Mackenzie. 1996. *"Because It Gives Me Peace of Mind": Ritual Fasts in the Religious Lives of Hindu Women.* Albany: State University of New York Press.

Pintchman, Tracy. 1994. *The Rise of the Great Goddess in the Hindu Tradition.* Albany: State University of New York Press.

Poerbatjaraka, Raden Mas Ngabehi. 1926. "De Calon-arang." *Bijdragen tot de taal-, land- en volkenkunde van Nederlandsch-Indië* 82, no. 1: 110–80.

———, ed. 1975. *Calon Arang: Si Janda Dari Girah.* Translated by by Suwito Santoso. Jakarta: Balai Pustaka.

Pollock, Sheldon. 2003. *Literary Cultures in History: Reconstructions from South Asia.* Berkeley: University of California Press.

Pratap, Surendra, and Biswanarayan Shastri. 2008. *The Kālikāpurāṇa: Text, Introduction and Translation in English Verse with Shloka Index.* Delhi: Nag.

Rajasekhara, P. K., ed. 1972. *Beṭṭada Cāmuṇḍi.* Mysore: Ta. Vem. Smaraka Grantha Male.

Ramanujan, A. K. 2011. *Poems of Love and War: From the Eight Anthologies and the Ten Long Poems of Classical Tamil.* New York: Columbia University Press.

Rao, C. Hayavadana. 1946. *History of Mysore.* Vol. 1. Mysore: Government Press. Republished as *Epigraphia Carnatica.* Vol. 3. Mysore: Institute of Kannada Studies, University of Mysore, 1974.

Ray, Hemchandra. 1931. *The Dynastic History of Northern India: Early Mediaeval Period.* Vol. 1. Calcutta: University Press.

Reddy, Gayatri. 2005. *With Respect to Sex: Negotiating Hijra Identity in South India.* Chicago: University of Chicago Press.

Robson, Stuart, ed. 1995. *Désawarnana.* Leiden: KITLV Press.

Robson, Stuart, Singgih Wibisono, and Yacinta Kurniasih. 2002. *Javanese-English Dictionary.* Singapore: Periplus.

Rohlman, E. 2011. "Geographical Imagination and Literary Boundaries in the Sarasvati Purana." *International Journal of Hindu Studies* 15, no. 2: 139–63.

Row, Ramakrishna, ed. 1916. *Maisūru Saṃsthānada Prabhugaḷu Śrīmanmahārājaravara Vaṃśāvaḷi*. Mysore: Government Branch.

Roy, Jeff. 2017. "From Jalsah to Jalsa: Music, Identity and (Gender) Transitioning at a Hijra Rite of Initiation." *Ethnomusicology* 61: 348–418.

Sanderson, Alexis. 1986. "Maṇḍala and Āgamic Identity in the Trika of Kashmir." In *Mantras et Diagrammes Rituels dans l' Hindouisme*, edited by A. Padoux, 169–214. Paris: CNRS.

———. 1988. "Śaivism and the Tantric Traditions." In *The World's Religions*, edited by S. Sutherland, 660–704. London: Routledge and Kegan Paul.

———. 2001. "History through Textual Criticism in the Study of Śaivism, the Pañcarātra and the Buddhist Yoginītantras." In *Les Sources et le temps/Sources and Time: A Colloquium, Pondicherry, 11–13 January 1997*, edited by François Grimal, 1–47. Publications du département d'Indologie 91. Pondicherry: Institut Français de Pondichéry/École Française d'Extrême-Orient.

———. 2004. "Religion and the State: Śaiva Officiants in the Territory of the Brahmanical Royal Chaplain (with an appendix on the provenance and date of the *Netratantra*)." *Indo-Iranian Journal* 47: 229–300.

———. 2006. "The Lākulas: New Evidence of a System Intermediate between Pāñcārthika Pāśupatism and Āgamic Śaivism." *Indian Philosophical Annual* 24: 143–217.

———. 2007. "The Śaiva Exegesis of Kashmir." In *Mélanges tantriques à la mémoire d'Hélène Brunner*, edited by Dominic Goodall and André Padoux, 231–442 and 551–82. Pondicherry: Institut français d'Indologie/École française d'Extrême-Orient.

———. 2009. "The Śaiva Age: The Rise and Dominance of Śaivism during the Early Medieval Period." In *Genesis and Development of Tantrism*, edited by Shingo Einoo, 41–350. Institute of Oriental Culture Special Series 23. Tokyo: Institute of Oriental Culture, University of Tokyo.

———. 2014. "The Śaiva Literature." *Journal of Indological Studies* (Kyoto), nos. 24 and 25: 1–113.

Sarkar, Bihani. 2017. *Heroic Shāktism: The Cult of Durgā in Ancient Indian Kingship*. The British Academy Monograph Series. Oxford: Oxford University Press.

Sarkar, Sir Jadunath. (1948) 2006. *The History of Bengal*. Vol. 2, *Muslim Period, 1200–1757*. Dhaka: University of Dacca.

Schaflechner, Jürgen. 2018. *Hinglaj Devi: Identity, Change, and Solidification at a Hindu Temple in Pakistan*. New York: Oxford University Press.

Serbaeva, Olga. 2003. "L'aspect féminin dans l'école Krama du Śivaïsme non-dualiste du Cachemire." Diplôme de spécialisation en Sciences des Religions, University of Lausanne.

———. 2006. "Yoginīs in Śaiva Purāṇas and Tantras: Their Role in Transformative Experiences in a Historical and Comparative Perspective." PhD thesis, University of Lausanne, Switzerland.

———. 2010. "Liberation in Life and after Death in Early Śaiva Mantramārgic Texts: The Problem of Jīvanmukti." In *Release from Life—Release in Life. Indian Perspectives on Individual Liberation,* edited by Andreas Bigger et al., 211–33. Welten Süd- und Zentralasiens. Bern: Peter Lang.

———. 2015. "Yoga from Yoginīs' Point of View." *Journal of Hindu Studies* 8: 245–62.

———. 2016. "The Varieties of *Melaka* in the *Jayadrathayāmala*: Some Reflections on the Terms *Haṭha* and *Priya*." In *Goddess Traditions in Tantric Hinduism: History, Practice and Doctrine,* edited by Bjarne Wernicke Olesen, 51–73. Routledge Studies in Tantric Traditions. Oxford: Routledge.

Shah, A. M. 1961. "A Note on the Hijadas of Gujarat." *American Anthropologist* 63, no.6 (December): 1325–30.

Sharma, Aishwaryadhar. 2001 (V.S. 2057). "Śrī Svasthānī Vrat Sadhana ra Paramparā." *Madhuparka* (January–February): 21–22.

Sharma, Bhadrasheel, ed. 1966. *Sri Srividyarnava Tantram.* Prayaga: Kalyana Mandira.

Sharma, Premlata, ed. 1976. *Ekaliṅgamāhātmyam: Ekliṅg Mandir kā sthalpurāṇ evaṃ Mevāḍ ke rāj-vaṃś itihās.* Delhi: Motilal Banarsidass.

Sharma, Puspendra Kumar, ed. 1976. *Devī Purāṇam (First Critical Devanāgarī Edition).* New Delhi: Śrīlālbahādurśāstrīkendriyasaṃskṛtavidyāpīṭham.

Sharma, Shrirama. 1969. *Liṅgapurāṇa.* Bareilly: Saṃskriti saṃsthana.

Sharman, Damodara, and Babu Krishna Sharman, eds. 1966 and 1968 (Vikrama 2023 and 2025). *Lakṣaṇasaṃgraha: Pratiṣṭhālakṣaṇasārasamuccaya of Vairocana.* 2 pts. Kathmandu: Nepāla Rāṣṭrīyābhilekhālaya.

Shastri, Chandra Shekhar, ed. 1964. *Śrījvālāmālinīkalpa.* Surat: Digambara Jaina Pustakālaya.

Shastri, Ganapati, ed. 1919. *The Mahārthamañjarī, with the Commentary Parimala.* Anantaśayanasaṃskṛtagranthāvaliḥ 66. Trivandrum: Superintendent, Government Press.

———, ed. 1990. *Īśānaśivagurudevapaddhati.* Vols. 1–4. Delhi: Bharatiya Vidya Prakasan.

Shastri, Krsnasankara, ed. 1965. *Śrīmadbhāgavatapurāṇam.* Varanasi: Samsar Press.

Shastri, Madhusudhan Kaul, ed. 1922. *Śrī Mālinīvijayottara Tantram.* Kashmir Series of Texts and Studies 37. Bombay: Tattva Vivechaka Press.

———, ed. 1945. *The Vāmakeśvarīmatam with the Commentary of Rājānaka Jayaratha.* Kashmir Series of Texts and Studies 66. Srinagar: Mercantile Press.

———, ed. 1921–1935. *Svacchandatantra.* Kashmir Series of Texts and Studies 31, 38, 44, 48, 51, 53, 56. Bombay: Nirnaya Sagar Press.

Shastri, Madhusudhan Kaul, and Mukund Ram Shastri, eds. 1918–1938. *The Tantrāloka of Abhinavagupta, with the Commentary (-viveka) of Rājānaka Jayaratha.* Kashmir Series of Texts and Studies 23, 28, 30, 36, 35, 29, 41, 47, 59, 52, 57, 58. Bombay: Nirnaya Sagar Press.

Shaw, Miranda. 2006. *Buddhist Goddesses of India*. Princeton, NJ: Princeton University Press.

Sheikh, Samira. 2010. "The Lives of Bahuchara Mata." In *The Idea of Gujarat: History, Ethnography and Text*, edited by Edward Simpson and Aparna Kapadia, 84–99. Hyderabad: Orient Blackswan.

Shibazaki, Maho. 2007. "The Role Played by Goddesses in the *Haracaritacintāmaṇi*." *Journal of Indian and Buddhist Studies* 55, no. 3 (March): 1035–42.

Shivadatta, Mahamahopadhyaya Pandit, and Kasinath Pandurang Parab, eds. 1897. *Haracharitachintamani*. Kāvyamālā 61. Bombay: Nirnaya Sagar.

Shrikrsnadasa, Ksemaraja, ed. 1986. *The Devībhāgavatapurāṇam*. Delhi: Nag.

Shulman, David. 1980. *Tamil Temple Myths: Sacrifice and Divine Marriage in the South Indian Śaiva Tradition*. Princeton, NJ: Princeton University Press.

Sidomulyo, Hadi. 2011. "Kṛtanagara and the Resurrection of Mpu Bharāda." *Indonesia and the Malay World* 39, no. 113 (March): 123–42.

Silburn, Lilian. 1975. *Hymnes aux Kālī, La roue des énergies divines, traduction et introduction*. Publication de l'Institut de Civilisation Indienne, fasc. 40. Paris: Institut de Civilisation Indienne.

Simmons, Caleb. 2014. "The Goddess on the Hill: The (Re)Invention of a Local Hill Goddess as Chamundeshvari." In *Inventing and Reinventing the Goddess: Contemporary Iterations of Hindu Deities on the Move*, edited by Sree Padma, 217–44. Lanham, MD: Lexington Books.

———, ed. 2018. *Nine Nights of the Goddess: The Navarātri Festival in South Asia*. Albany: State University of New York Press.

Singh, Nag Sharan. 1995. *Śrīvāyumahāpurāṇam*. Delhi: Nag.

Singh, Upinder. 2004. "Cults and Shrines in Early Historical Mathura (c. 200 BC–AD 200)." *World Archaeology* 36, no. 3: 378–98.

Slouber, Michael. 2017. *Early Tantric Medicine*. New York: Oxford University Press.

Slusser, Mary Shepherd. 1982. *Nepal Mandala : A Cultural Study of the Kathmandu Valley*. Princeton, NJ: Princeton University Press.

Smith, David. 2005. *The Birth of Kumāra*. New York: New York University Press.

Stainton, Hamsa. 2019. *Poetry as Prayer in the Sanskrit Hymns of Kashmir*. New York: Oxford University Press.

Stein Callenfels, P. V. van, ed. 1925. *De Sudamala in de Hindu-Javaansche kunst*. Verhandelingen van het Koninklijk Bataviaas Genootschap van Kunsten en Wetenschappen, vol. 66. Batavia: Albrecht & Co.

Suastika, I Made. 1997. *Calon Arang dalam tradisi Bali: Suntingan teks, terjemahan, dan analisis proses pembalian*. Yogyakarta: Duta Wacana.

Sukthankar, V. S., ed. 1927. *The Mahābhārata (Critical Edition)*. Poona: Bhandarkar Oriental Research Institute.

Tachikawa, Musashi. 2004. *Mother-Goddesses in Kathmandu*. Delhi: Adroit.

Tamot, Kashinath. 1991 (V.S. 2047). "Svasthānī Vratkathā Paramparā: Ek Simhāvalokan." *Madhuparka* (January–February): 5–16.

Tanaka, Masakazu. 2000. "Sacrifice Lost and Found." *Zinbun* 34, no. 1: 127–46.

Tarabout, G. 1986. *Sacrifier et donner à voir en pays Malabar—Les fêtes du temple au Kerala (Inde du Sud): Etude anthropologique*. Paris: école Française d'Extrême-Orient.

Tarkaratna, Pancanan, ed. 1895–1896 (Bengali Samvat 1302). *Devīpurāṇa*. Kolkata: Baṅgavāsī Steam Press.

Taylor, M. C. 2008. "What Enables Canonical Literature to Function as 'True'? The Case of the Hindu Purāṇas." *International Journal of Hindu Studies* 12, no. 3: 309–28.

———. 2012. *The Fall of the Indigo Jackal: The Discourse of Division and Purnabhadra's Pancatantra*. Albany: State University of New York Press.

Tiwari, Jadagisa Narayana, and A. L. Basham. 1985. *Goddess Cults in Ancient India (with Special Reference to the First Seven Centuries A.D.)*. Delhi: Sundeep Prakashan.

Tod, James. 1914. *Annals and Antiquities of Rajasthan: Or the Central and Western Rajpoot States of India*. London: Routledge and Sons.

Törzsök, Judit. 1999. "The Doctrine of Magic Female Spirits: A Critical Edition of Selected Chapters of the *Siddhayogeśvarīmata(tantra)* with Annotated Translation and Analysis." PhD thesis, Oxford University, Merton College.

Trautmann, Thomas R. 2011. *India: Brief History of a Civilization*. New York: Oxford University Press.

Tsuchida, Ryutaro. 1997. "Remarks on the Kāvyamālā Edition of Jayadratha's *Haracaritacintāmaṇi*." *Studies of Buddhist Culture* 7 (March): 5–22.

Vasudeva, Somadeva. 2004. *The Yoga of the Mālinīvijayottaratantra*. Publications du Département d'Indologie. Pondicherry: Institut français de Pondichéry/École française d'Extrême-Orient.

———, ed. 2006. *The Recognition of Shakúntala*. New York: New York University Press.

Vidyaratna, Taranatha, ed. 1965. *Kulārṇava Tantra*. Madras: Ganesh.

White, David. 1996. *The Alchemical Body*. Chicago: University of Chicago.

———. 2003. *Kiss of the Yoginī: "Tantric Sex" in its South Asian Contexts*. Chicago: University of Chicago.

Yokochi, Yuko. 1999a. "The Warrior Goddess in the *Devīmāhātmya*." In *Living with Śakti: Gender, Sexuality, and Religion in South Asia*, edited by Masakazu Tanaka and Musashi Tachikawa, 71–113. Senri Ethnological Studies 50. Osaka: National Museum of Ethnology.

———. 1999b. "Mahiṣāsuramardinī Myth and Icon: Studies in the Skandapurāṇa, II." *Studies in the History of Indian Thought (Indo Shisōshi Kenkyū, インド思想史研究)* 11: 65–103.

———. 2004. "The Rise of the Warrior Goddess in Ancient India: A Study of the Myth Cycle of Kauśikī-Vindhyavāsinī in the Skandapurāṇa." PhD thesis, Rijksuniversiteit Groningen.

———, ed. 2013a. *The Skandapurāṇa*, Vol. 3, *Adhyāyas 34.1–61, 53–69: The Vindhyavāsinī Cycle*. Groningen: Brill.

———. 2013b. "The Development of Śaivism in Koṭīvarṣa, North Bengal, with Special Reference to the *Koṭīvarṣa-Māhātmya* in the *Skandapurāṇa*." *Indo-Iranian Journal* 56: 295–324.

Zoetmulder, P. J. 1982. *Old Javanese-English Dictionary*. The Hague: M. Nijhoff.

Zvelebil, Kamil Veith. 1975. *Tamil Literature*. Handbuch der Orientalistik, zweite Abteilung, 2 Band, 1 Abschnitt. Leiden: E. J. Brill. Originally published by Otto Harrassowitz, 1974.

CONTRIBUTORS

NI WAYAN PASEK ARIATI (Ary) has been the academic director of the SIT Study Abroad Program: Indonesia—Arts, Religion and Social Change since 2005. She completed her doctoral studies in 2010 at Charles Darwin University of the Northern Territory, Australia, with a dissertation entitled "The Journey of the Goddess Durga: India, Java, and Bali," which was published in India in 2016. She received a Fulbright Grant in 1996 to teach Indonesian language at Arizona State University's Southeast Asian Summer Studies Institute. Her published articles include "Theodicy in Paradise," *South and Southeast Asia: Culture and Religion* 3 (June 2009).

JESSICA VANTINE BIRKENHOLTZ is associate professor of women's, gender, and sexuality studies and Asian studies. Her book *Reciting the Goddess: Narratives of Place and the Making of Hinduism in Nepal* (Oxford University Press, 2018) earned the 2019 American Academy of Religion Award for Excellence in the Study of Religion (Textual Studies). It presents an archival and ethnographic study of Nepal's local goddess Svasthānī, the widely read *Svasthānīvratakathā*, and the role both goddess and text have played in the construction of Nepali Hindu identity and practice. She is currently preparing an English translation of the modern, Nepali-language *Svasthānīvratakathā*, a project funded by a National Endowment for the Humanities Scholarly Editions and Translations Grant.

DARRY DINNELL received his PhD from McGill University. His research, made possible by the Joseph-Armand Bombardier Canada Graduate Scholarship from the Social Sciences and Humanities Research Council (SSHRC), encompasses history, textual analysis, and ethnography of goddess sites in Gujarat. His article "Can Tantra Make a Mātā Middle-Class? Jogaṇī Mātā, a Uniquely Gujarati Chinnamastā," appeared in *Society for Tantric Studies Proceedings* (2016) and was the "cover story" of volume 8 of *Religions*. He is a coeditor of the forthcoming volume *Intersections of*

Religion and Astronomy. He has lectured at McGill and at St. Thomas More College, University of Saskatchewan.

ANNA A. GOLOVKOVA is a historian of Hindu Tantric traditions. She is assistant professor of religion at Lake Forest College. Golovkova completed her PhD in Asian studies at Cornell University and holds a BA in linguistics and intercultural communication from Moscow State Linguistics University, an MA in the Middle East and Asian languages and cultures from Columbia University, and an MSt in Oriental studies from Oxford University. Her forthcoming monograph is the first comprehensive study of the early history of worship of Tripurasundarī in a popular transregional goddess tradition now known as Śrīvidyā.

SHAMAN HATLEY is an associate professor of Asian studies and religious studies at the University of Massachusetts Boston. He completed an interdisciplinary liberal arts degree at Goddard College in 1998, then studied Indology and religious studies at the University of Pennsylvania. His doctoral thesis on the *Brahmayāmala* and Śaiva *yoginī* cults was completed in 2007, under the direction of Harunaga Isaacson, after which he taught at Concordia University, Montréal (2007–2015). His research mainly concerns early Tantric Śaivism, goddess cults, and yoga. Recent publications include *The Brahmayāmalatantra or Picumata*, Volume 1, *Chapters 1–2, 39–40, & 83: Revelation, Ritual, and Material Culture in an Early Śaiva Tantra* (Pondicherry, 2018).

THOMAS M. HUNTER lectures in Sanskrit and South-Southeast Asian studies in the Department of Asian Studies of the University of British Columbia. He has been a fellow of the National Endowment for the Humanities (1996), the Institute for Advanced Study at the Hebrew University of Jerusalem (2003–2004), the Wissenschaftskolleg zu Berlin (2006–2007), and the Neubauer Collegium for Culture and Society at the University of Chicago (January–May 2020). His publications focus on the ancient literature of India and Southeast Asia, especially literary and didactic works in the Old Javanese language.

ADAM NEWMAN received his PhD from the University of Virginia and is assistant professor at the University of Illinois at Urbana-Champaign. He concentrates on the religious traditions of South Asia, specializing in the study of Hinduism in Rajasthan, and in particular the Mewar region, during the medieval period. Broadly, his research focuses on the study of Purāṇic literature, sacred landscapes and the politics of space, and representations of the body and embodiment in Hindu narratives. Presently he is working on a translation and study of the fifteenth-century Sanskrit Purāṇa known as the *Ekaliṅga Māhātmya*.

R. JEREMY SAUL (PhD, University of Michigan) is a lecturer in Asian religions at the College of Religious Studies, Mahidol University, Bangkok. He has published articles on miraculous folk deities of Rajasthan and northwestern India and is currently working on a book manuscript on the recent popularization of local deities related to

Hanuman, Krishna, and several goddesses, within urban merchant communities and in the Rajasthan countryside. His most recent publication is the forthcoming "Navaratri as a Festival of Hanuman and Male Asceticism," in *Nine Nights of Power: Durga, Dolls, and Darbars*, ed. Ute Hüsken and Astrid Zotter (Albany: State University of New York Press).

OLGA SERBAEVA is an academic associate in Indian studies at the Institute of Asian and Oriental Studies, University of Zurich. After obtaining her PhD from the University of Lausanne in 2006 ("Yoginīs in Śaiva Purāṇas and Tantras: Their Role in Transformative Experiences in a Historical and Comparative Perspective"), she has published numerous articles, mostly dealing with the Krama elements and *yoginī*s in the *Jayadrathayāmala*. She is currently working on a digital edition and translation of the same Tantra. Her present interests in the digital humanities include the application of computational corpus linguistics to Sanskrit texts, especially the automatic search for textual parallels.

CALEB SIMMONS is an associate professor of religious studies at the University of Arizona, specializing in religion in South Asia, especially Hinduism. He is the author of *Devotional Sovereignty: Kingship and Religion in India* (Oxford University Press, 2020) and numerous journal articles and book chapters. He also edited (with Moumita Sen and Hillary Rodrigues) and contributed to *Nine Nights of the Goddess: The Navarātri Festival in South Asia* (State University of New York Press, 2018). He is currently completing a second monograph titled *Singing the Goddess into Place: Folksongs, Myth, and Situated Knowledge in Mysore, India* (State University of New York Press).

MICHAEL SLOUBER researches and teaches the religious and medical traditions of early medieval India. He is associate professor of South Asian studies at Western Washington University and the author of *Early Tantric Medicine* (Oxford University Press, 2016). He earned graduate degrees in South Asian languages and literature at the University of California at Berkeley under the supervision of Robert and Sally Goldman, Alexander von Rospatt, and Somadeva Vasudeva, and at Universität Hamburg in Germany under Harunaga Isaacson. He won the DK Award for the best dissertation on Sanskrit 2012–2014 and is an honorary fellow of the International Association of Sanskrit Studies.

JUDIT TÖRZSÖK is professor (directeur d'études) in Śaiva studies at the Religious Studies section of the EPHE, PSL University, Paris. After earning her master's degree in Indian studies at ELTE University, Budapest, she studied for her DPhil on an early Śākta text at the University of Oxford, supervised by Alexis Sanderson. She worked at the University of Cambridge and the University of Groningen and was lecturer in Sanskrit at the University of Lille between 2001 and 2018. She obtained her "habilitation" in 2011. In addition to Śaiva and Śākta literature, she has also published on classical Sanskrit poetry and the *Skanda Purāṇa*.

NOOR VAN BRUSSEL has worked as a lecturer of Sanskrit and Prakrit languages at the University of Ghent (Belgium) since 2016. In addition to her teaching responsibilities, she is writing a PhD dissertation on the *Bhadrakāḷī Māhātmya*, a regional Purāṇa from Kerala dealing with the fierce goddess Bhadrakāḷī and her triumph over the *asura* king Dārika. She has written extensively on the varied use of narrative strategies in this regional Purāṇa, in view of processes of authority creation and religious identity building.

INDEX

Note: illustrations and maps are indicated by page numbers followed by *fig.* and *map*.

Bahucarā Mātā (*continued*)
connections and, 173, 177–79; Sarasvati-Sabarmati area and, 178–79; significance of, 2–3; slaying of Daṇḍhāsur, 177–79; sources of, 187–88; as Supreme Feminine Power, 173–78, 188; Tantric dimensions of, 6, 187; Varakhaḍī tree and, 173, 175, 178
Bahula, 224–27, 231
Bahumāṃsā ('Very Fleshy'), 83, 86, 99–101, 105
Bakhtyar Khilji, Muhammad, 105
Bakker, Hans, 98, 107
Bālātripurā, 182–83
Bālātripurāsundarī, 175–77, 179, 186, 189n7
Bali: Baradah legend and, 237; *Calon Arang* (tale), 232, 239; Durgā in, 8, 232, 235, 239; Hinduism in, 217, 239; importance of masks in, 238–40; *Kidung Sudamala*, 232–33; literary tradition and, 241, 242n4; marriages in, 237–38; Pura Dalĕm and, 238–40; Rangda-Barong performances in, 15, 232, 238–40; religious figures in, 236; shadow plays in, 232–33; Tutur literature in, 243n16
Ballālasena, 102
Bāṇa, 28–29
Bappā Rāval, 206–7
Baradah, 223–24, 226–29, 233, 237–38
Barbarian, 65–67, 73
Barong mask, 232, 238–40
Barong-Rangda performances, 15, 217, 239–40
Batara Guru, 233–36
Becharaji: Bahucarā temple at, 180–84; Bālātripurā *yantra* worship, 182–83; non-Brahmin groups and, 183–86; Pāvaiyā community and, 184–86; pilgrimage to, 183; Vallabha and, 185
Beṭṭada Cāmuṇḍi ballad, 44*fig.*; battle with Aisāsura, 45–49; Cāmuṇḍi and Uttanahaḷḷi in, 46–51, 53–54; defeat of Mahiṣa, 43, 45; local and pan-Indic traditions in, 54–55; performance of, 56–57; as "sweet" (*rōcaka*) narrative, 52. *See also* Cāmuṇḍi
Bhadrakāḷī, 18*fig.*; on the battlefield, 25–29; battle with demons, 28–29; as Bhairavī, 26; Dārika and, 26–30; as daughter of Śiva, 21, 25–26; glorification of, 21–26; as Kaṇṇaki, 35; as Kaṇṭhekāḷī, 26; Kodungallur and, 35; Koṟṟavai and, 32; origins of, 30–32; as Rurujit, 106; as savior goddess, 4; significance of, 2, 37; Tantric dimensions of, 6
Bhadrakāḷī Kaḷam Pāṭṭu, 39n16
Bhadrakāḷī Māhātmya, 20*fig.*; attitude of Dārika toward women, 19, 23, 29; battle with demons in, 28–30; Brahmā and, 22–24; demonic characters in, 19, 21–30, 36; *Glorification of Bhadrakāḷī*, 21–26; hunger/gorging theme in, 19, 27; origins of, 30; pan-Indian literary world and, 32, 34–35, 37; Purāṇic tradition in, 33–34; regional connections in, 33–37; ring composition in, 19; slaying of Dārika in, 30, 34, 106; Sutīkṣṇa and, 19, 21–22, 25–26, 28; Tamil culture and, 30; translations and, 38; Viṣṇu and, 22–23
Bhadrakāḷī Māhātmya (Girija and Visalakshy), 37
Bhagavad Gītā, 4
Bhāgavata Purāṇa, 37
Bhagawatī, 219–20, 222, 229
Bhagirathwale, Moolsingh Jadaun, 165
Bhairava: as consort to Kālī, 289; Goddess and, 271, 278n1, 278n4, 291; Gorā Bherujī as local form of, 208; hexagonal fire maṇḍala and, 266; Kailā Devī and, 160; Kāla as local form of, 208; on Kālī the indefinable, 285; Śākta Tantras and, 102, 271, 278n4; as terrible form of Śiva, 88, 102, 208, 248
Bhairavapadmāvatīkalpa, 257
Bhairavī, 26, 97
Bharosee Lal Meena, 154
Bhaṭṭa, Raṇachoḍa, 206
Bhattarai, Krishna Prasad, 107
Bhil people, 202–3
Bhrāmarī Devī, 173, 189n4
bird-headed goddesses, 74, 201–2, 210n8, 212n32
Birkenholtz, Jessica Vantine, 117–40, 259, 341
blood: menstrual, 279n13, 306; as procreative, 23, 29, 34, 45, 47, 49, 54, 73, 88, 105, 143, 147, 166n3, 173; rain of, 22; river of, 28, 38, 68, 86, 101, 109n8; thirst for, 28, 30–31, 34, 92, 94, 164, 173, 176–77, 185, 210n7, 223, 248, 305. *See also* Aisāsura; animal sacrifice; Bahumāṃsā ('Very Fleshy'); Dārika/Dāruka; Koṟṟavai; Raktabīja; Ruru; sacrifice; Vetālī
botanical imagery, 10–11
Brahmā: creation of Tilottamā, 72; Dānava and, 23–24; Dārika and, 23–24, 29; demon women and, 22–23; divine eagle

Tārkṣya and, 248; granting of boons, 22–23, 57n1, 63; Koṭīvarṣa and, 85; lotus birth of, 39n7; mother goddesses and, 25, 74, 86, 88–89; Ruru and, 87; young girls as demon-slayers and, 76
Brahmāṇī/Brāhmī, 68, 82*fig.*, 86, 88–89, 116*fig.*
Brahmayāmala, 100–102, 104, 107
Brahminization, x, 171, 180. *See also* Sanskritization
Bṛhatsaṃhitā, 95
Brussel, Noor van, 19–40, 344
Buddhism, 3–4, 7, 95, 97
buffalo demon: Cāmuṇḍi slaying of, 9, 43, 55; Durgā slaying of, 43, 53; Great Goddess slaying of, 53, 71; Kauśikī slaying of, 68, 71. *See also* Mahiṣa (buffalo-demon)

Caldwell, S., 38, 39n16, 40n18, 40n24, 40n32
Calon Arang (sorceress): Baradah and death of, 229–31, 238; black magic and, 219–24, 226, 229–30, 242n5; book of sacred spells and, 219, 221, 226–27, 237; Goddess Bhagawatī and, 219–20, 222, 229. *See also* Rangda
Calon Arang (tale), 218*fig.*; Baradah and, 223–24, 226–31, 237–38; cultural imagination of Bali and, 232–33; death of Calon Arang, 229–31; Durgā in, 8, 229, 232–36; glorification of high priests in, 238; links with *Sudamala* story, 236; literary works based on, 236–37; Mahārāja Erlangga and, 219–20, 224, 233, 235, 237, 240; marriage of Rangda's daughter, 219, 224–26; origins of, 240; performance of, 239; sorcery in, 219–24, 226–27, 237, 240; Tantras and, 217, 219. *See also* Rangda
Cāma Celuve (Akki), 57
Cāmarājokti Vilāsa, 55
Cāmuṇḍā/Cāmuṇḍī, 142*fig.*; Bhadrakāḷī narrative and, 26–27; blood sacrifice and, 164; etymology of, 110n25; as independent goddess, 97; as Kālī, 291; sister Kailā Devī and, 164–65, 167n11, 169n35; as slayer of Ruru, 106; in *Śrī Kailādevī Itihās*, 145, 155, 157. *See also* Cāmuṇḍi; Caṇḍī/Caṇḍikā
Cāmuṇḍi, 42*fig.*; bathing in the Kapini and Kaveri, 50–51; battle with Aisāsura, 43, 45–49; defeat of Mahiṣa, 43, 45; femininity of, 43; as goddess of place, 9–10; as *grāmadēvate*, 52; help from sister Uttanahaḷḷi, 46–49; identification with Durgā, 9–10, 52–53; as Mother of the Universe, 10; Nañjuṇḍēśvara and, 52; pan-Indian mythology and, 54; place connections and, 52, 54, 59n20; as place-guardian, 43; relationship with Kālī, 52–53; relationship with Śiva, 51–52; significance of, 2–3; as slayer of buffalo-demon, 43, 53, 55. *See also Beṭṭada Cāmuṇḍi* ballad; Cāmuṇḍā/Cāmuṇḍī
Cāmuṇḍi of the Hill (Beṭṭada Cāmuṇḍi). See Beṭṭada Cāmuṇḍi ballad
Caṇḍeśvara, 91–92
Caṇḍī/Caṇḍikā, 26, 110n19, 150. *See also* Cāmuṇḍā/Cāmuṇḍī
Candrasena, 19, 21, 34
Candravatī, 124, 126–28, 131, 134–35
Ceṅkuṭṭuvaṉ, 35
Chagala (the Goat), 87, 99
Cilappatikāram, 19, 31–32, 35, 40n30
Ciñciṇīmatasārasamuccaya, 265*fig.*; cult to Kubjikā and, 271–72; Kāmeśvarī and, 263, 267–68, 273, 276; translations and, 277
colonialism, 6–7, 15n6

Daityas, 23, 39n4, 197, 205, 210n7
Dakṣiṇa Kālī, 289–90, 293. *See also* Kālī/Kāḷī
Damajirao Gaekwar, 182
Dānava (demon), 22–24, 39n4
Dānavatī, 22
Daṇḍaka forest, 21, 34, 39n2
Daṇḍhāsur: Bahucarā Mātā and, 171, 173–78; Bālātripurāsundarī and, 175–77; boon from Śiva and, 174; as Demon-and-a-half, 173, 189n2; thirst and, 176; tyranny over three worlds, 174–75
Danu, 146. *See also* Dānava (demon)
Dārika/Dāruka: attitude toward goddess, 23, 29; bad omens at birth of, 22; Bhadrakāḷī and, 19, 26–30, 106; boons from Brahmā and, 23–24; *Cilappatikāram* and, 19, 35; conquest of Indra's city, 25; as lord of demons, 24–25; slaying of, 30, 34, 36, 106; sympathy for, 36. *See also* Aisāsura; Raktabīja; Ruru
Dārikavadham narrative, 35
Dārumatī, 22
demons: in *Beṭṭada Cāmuṇḍi*, 43; in *Bhadrakāḷī Māhātmya*, 28–30; boons from gods and, 57n1; in *Devī Māhātmya*, 36; in *Devī Purāṇa*, 87–91; in *Ekaliṅga Māhātmya*, 197, 205, 210n7; Haimakuṇḍa

demons (*continued*)
and, 83, 85; in *Haracaritacintāmaṇi,* 63–70; Hindu goddesses and, 30, 61; in *Śrī Kailādevī Itihās,* 145–48, 150. *See also* Barbarian; *Bhadrakāḷī Māhātmya;* buffalo demon; Daityas; Dānava (demon); Daṇḍhāsur; Dārika/Dāruka; Dhūmra; Dhūmrākṣa; Karambha; Kujambha; Mahiṣa (buffalo-demon); Pūtanā; Raktabīja; Rāvaṇa; Ruru
Desai, Rammohanray, 185
Devī Māhātmya (Glorification of the Goddess): date of, 15n2; demonic characters in, 36; Durgā as supreme goddess in, 72–74; Great Goddess in, 71; Hindu goddesses and, 2, 34; Kālī and, 52; pan-Indian influence of, 71; parallels with *Devī Purāṇa,* 104–5; slaying of Raktabīja and, 34, 53–54, 73; warrior goddesses in, 71
Devī Purāṇa, 84*fig.*; *Brahmayāmala* and, 102, 104, 107; compilation of, 102; demon battles in, 87–91; hymn of praise to the Mothers, 92–94; Kālarātri as leader of Mothers, 110n19; mother goddesses and, 101; netherworlds in, 104, 113n76; origin of Brahmāṇī, 88–89; origin of the Seizers, 89–91, 104; parallels with *Devī Māhātmya,* 104–5; rise of Caṇḍeśvara, 91–92; Śāktism in, 101, 103; Seven Mothers origin in, 83, 88–89, 96, 105; slaying of Ruru in, 87–88, 94–95, 101–2, 104, 106; supreme goddess and, 103; Tantric Śaivism and, 103–4; *yoginīs* and, 107
devotional religions, 4–5
Dharmandha Badshah (derogatory), 154
Dhūmra, 28–29
Dhūmrākṣa, 28–29
Dinnell, Darry, 171–91, 341–42
Dundubhi, 68–69
Durgā: Bhadrakāḷī and, 29; birth of, 78n4; *Calon Arang* and, 8, 229, 232–36; Cāmuṇḍi as, 9–10, 52–53; Dark principle and, 75; as Gaurī, 72, 78n4; goddess worship and, 4; as Great Goddess, 52, 70, 72–74; Kālī and, 6; Kāmeśvarī and, 2; Kauśikī and, 2; local identity and, 71; as mother of universe, 75; Nine Nights (*navarātra*) festival and, 104; pan-Indian fame and, 9–10; as patron of dark forces, 236; Rangda as, 217, 238, 240; Śiva mythology and, 72, 75; slaying of Raktabīja and, 34, 43, 53; in southern Asia, 8; as transregional deity, 71; Umā and, 234
Dyczkowski, Mark S. G., 6, 253, 277

Eight Mother Goddesses. *See* Aṣṭamātrikā
Ekaliṅga/Ekliṅgjī, 193, 196, 200–201, 205–8
Ekaliṅga Māhātmya, 195*fig.*; conversation of Nārada and Vāyu, 193, 196–200; founding of Ekaliṅga temple, 200–201; manifestation of Rāṣṭrasenā and, 193, 196–97, 201–2, 205–6; parallels with *Skanda Purāṇa,* 204; rules for worship of Rāṣṭrasenā, 197–200; sacred geography and, 194; sources of, 208–9; *śrāddha* rite in, 196, 210n5; *sthalapurāṇas* genre and, 209; Tantric rituals and, 193
Ekavīrī (Solitary Heroine), 106
ELM. *See Ekaliṅga Māhātmya*
Elwin, Verrier, 253
Erlangga, Mahārāja, 219–20, 224, 233, 235, 237, 240

forgotten (goddesses/texts): Bahumāṃsā as, 100; *Bhadrakāḷī Māhātmya* as, 37; Cāmuṇḍi and Uttanahaḷḷi as, 54–55; fruit section and, 11; Kailā Devī as, 163; the Kālīs of the *Jayadrathayāmala* as, 289, 293; meaning of, x, xi, xii, 1–2; non-elite version of Bahucarā as, 186; Rāṣṭrasenā as, 200; Ruru's tale as, 106; the Seven Mothers as, 95; Svasthānī as, 131; Tripurā's connection with Kāmadeva as, 276; *Troṭala Tantra* as, 245; Tvaritā's original identity as, 257; Tvaritā's story as, 253; Yāmala Tantras as, 107
Foucault, Michel, 35
Freeman, Richard, 32–33, 38

Gaṇeśa, 30, 97
Gangaji, Bhudralal, 185
garlands: as blessings, 92; as decoration, 24, 27, 266; entrails as, 29, 222; Mālinī Mountain and, 263; as marker of victory, 146; meaning in book, x; as metaphor for universe and Kālī, 288; as metaphor of Great Goddess, 32; seed-flower-fruit structure of essays and, 11–12; skulls/heads as, 94, 289; in worship, 199, 208, 250, 266
Garuḍa, 46, 58n6, 89, 93, 245, 247–48, 252, 268, 287. *See also Gāruḍa Tantras*

Gāruḍa Tantras, 94, 104, 110n32, 245, 252–53, 256, 258, 287
Gaurī, 63, 72, 78n4
Girija, R., 37
girls: as demon-slayer, 96; as goddesses, 76; *kumārīpūjā* and, 212n26; *kumārī* worship and, 76–77, 258; marriage contests and, 66, 78n14; *vratas* and, 129, 136
Glorification of Bhadrakāḷī (Bhadrakāḷī Māhātmya), The. See *Bhadrakāḷī Māhātmya*
Glorification of Ekaliṅga, The (Ekaliṅga Māhātmya). See *Ekaliṅga Māhātmya*
Glorification of the Goddess (Devī Māhātmya). *See Devī Māhātmya* (Glorification of the Goddess)
goddess worship: botanical imagery and, 10–11; Brahminization of, x; Indian, 1–4; Krama (the Sequence) and, 283, 292–93; *kumārī* worship and, 76–77, 258; local goddesses and, 9–10; monism and, 9; Mother of the Universe, 10; personal devotion and, 4; sacrifice and, 3; Sanskritization of, x; in southern Asia, 8*map*; Tantras and, 2, 5–6; Tantric cults and, 9, 106. *See also* Hindu goddesses; mother goddesses
Golovkova, Anna, 6, 256, 263–81, 342
Gomā Bhaṭṭinī, 123–25, 131, 134
Goodall, Dominic, 6, 296n18
Gorā Bherujī, 208
grāmadēvate, 43, 52
Great Goddess (Mahādevī): as demon-slayer, 61, 70; as Durgā, 52, 70; as Kālī/Cāmuṇḍī, 52; Kāmeśvarī as, 268–69; as Kauśikī, 70; Krama (the Sequence) and, 283; local goddesses and, 32, 52, 157–58; Śiva's energy (*śakti*) and, 70; as slayer of buffalo-demon, 43, 53, 71; as source of all goddesses, 100; Tripurāsundarī as, 2, 270
Great Spell (*mahāvidyā*), *86*
Guhyakālī, 294
Guhyasūtra, 104
Gujarat, 171, 180, 184–86

Haimakuṇḍa, 83, 85
Hanuman, 160
Haracaritacintāmaṇi, 62*fig.*; demonic characters in, 65–69, 73, 79n18; invocation to Śiva, 74–75; Kashmirian/non-Karshmirian elements in, 72–76; Kauśikī as demon-slayer in, 63–65, 67–70; Kauśikī as young girl in, 61, 63–65, 73, 76; nondualist theological verse in, 61, 72; Purāṇic mythology and, 76; seven mother goddesses and, 74; Śiva mythology and, 61, 71–74; Vindhya Mountain in, 63–65, 67–69, 71, 73, 76. *See also* Durgā; Kauśikī
Hāraudrī, 286, 297n20
Harisiṃhadeva, 258
Hārītarāśi, 207
Hārītī, 97
Hāṭakeśvara, 91
Hatley, Shaman, xiii, 6, 83–114, 211n18, 255, 259, 294, 342
Heroic Shāktism (Sarkar), 257
Hetukeśvara, 99, 101
Hijras, 180–82, 184–87. *See also* Bahucarā Mātā; Becharaji; Pāvaiyā community; Tirunaṅkais
Hindu goddesses: colonial interactions with, 7; demonic characters and, 30; diversity of names, 12; feminine divine and, 1; "forgotten," x, xi, 2; as place-guardians, 43, 52; significance of, 2–3; Tantras and, 5–6; transliterations and, 12–14. *See also* goddess worship; mother goddesses
Hinduism: Asian countries and, 7; Balinese, 217, 239; conceptions of time, 139n18; cosmology and, 157; discourse on the divine in, 8–9; Javanese, 233; Kali Age in, 157–58; male deities in, 280n22, 296n18; monism and, 9; monotheism and, 9, 188; Nepali, 117, 129–32; personal devotion and, 4, 36; polytheism as inappropriate label for, 9; *pūjā* in, 58n13; religions of renunciation and, 4; ritual and, xi; Tantric cults and, 4, 7; tensions with Muslims, 6
Hunter, Thomas, 217–43, 342

Indian literature, 30–35. *See also* Purāṇas (ancient lore)
Indian religions: colonialism and, 6–7; goddess worship and, 1–5; historical periods in, 3; Muslims and, 6–7; personal devotion and, 4–5, 9; renunciation and, 4–5; sacrifice and, 3, 5; Southeast Asia and, 7–8. *See also* Buddhism; Hinduism; Islam; Jainism
Indonesia, 7–8, 217
Indra, 86–90, 146. *See also* Indrāṇī
Indrāṇī, 82*fig.*, 86, 90, 116*fig.*

Isaacson, Harunaga, xiii, 6, 259, 342–43
Islam, 6–7. *See also* Muslims

Jagadambā, 145
Jainism. *See* Jains
Jains, 3–4, 31, 95, 97, 139n24, 171, 185, 211n18, 257, 260n4
Jansen, Roland, 258
Java: *Calon Arang* (tale), 217; Durgā in, 8, 217, 239; eastern and western courts in, 233, 235–37; Hinduism in, 233; *Kidung Sudamala*, 232–33, 235; literary tradition and, 240–41, 242n4; marriages in, 237–38; religious figures in, 236; shadow plays in, 232–33
Javanese mythology, 217, 232
Jayadratha, 61, 71–77. *See also* Jayaratha
Jayadrathayāmala, 284*fig.*; apophatic thealogy in, 283; encounters with *yoginīs*, 255; Kālī as supreme mother of the universe in, 5–6, 289, 293; Kālī rituals and lore in, 291; on Kālī the indefinable, 283, 285–88; non-Sanskit goddesses in, 291; as part of the Kālīkula, 291–92; provenance of, 283; ritual encounters in, 256; structure of, 292. *See also* Kālī/Kāḷī
Jayandhara, 28–29
Jayaratha, 71, 275, 277. *See also* Jayadratha
Juganū, Shri Krishnan, 208
Jvalajjihvā, 54
Jvālāmukhī, 54

Kailā Devī, 142*fig.*; animal sacrifice and, 159, 165; ascetics (sādhus) and, 4; Baba Kedargiri and, 148–52, 162; Brahmin boy sacrifice, 156; contemporary worship of, 159–61, 163–65, 168n28; convergence with pan-Indian goddess, 157–58, 160–63, 167n14; as demon-slayer, 150, 158; devotee austerities and, 148; devotee Bahora Gurjar and, 149; fierceness and, 158–59, 164, 168n34; Gurjars and, 160; Hindu mythology and, 157–58; idol and, 152–53, 162; installment of image, 153–54; as local goddess, 157–58, 160–61, 163–64; Meenas and, 159–60, 168n27; merchant devotee and, 150–51; miracle for Khinchi king, 154–56; as nurturing mother, 158, 164; origins of, 158–61, 165–66, 167n11; possession of Sukhchand Patel, 154–55; shrines for, 157, 161–62; significance of, 2–3; sister Cāmuṇḍā and, 164–65, 167n11, 169n35; in *Śrī Kailādevī Itihās*, 143, 145–57; variety of names for, 161, 168n30; Yogiraj and, 151–52, 162–63
Kākī, 202
Kāla, 208
Kaḷam Pāṭṭu, 36
Kālarātri, 90–91, 94, 102–3, 105–6, 110n19
Kālarudra, 90, 102, 110n18
Kālasaṃkarṣaṇī Kālī, 283, 296n17
Kali Age, 157–58, 168n25, 168n30
Kālikā, 148, 290
Kālī/Kāḷī: Bhadrakāḷī as, 26–28; Bhairava and, 289; as Cāmuṇḍā, 52, 291; colonial imagination and, 15n6; contemporary worship of, 106, 294; as Dakṣiṇa Kālī, 289, 293; as destroyer of time, 283; forms of, 289; goddess worship and, 4; the indefinable, 285–88, 293; merging with Koṟṟavai, 32; origins of, 289–91; pan-Indian fame and, 10; significance of, 289; slaying of Raktabīja and, 34; as supreme mother of the universe, 5–6, 289, 293; Tantras and, 2, 5, 289–90, 298n33, 298n37; as warrior goddess, 31; *yoginī* clans and, 289. *See also Jayadrathayāmala*
Kālīkula, 283, 291–93, 298n38, 299n39
Kaliṅkattupparaṇi, 32
Kāmadeva, 272–73, 276
Kamalias, 183–84
Kāmeśvarī, 262*fig.*; depictions of, 273; devotional practices and, 5; emanation as young girl, 276; female sexuality and, 264, 267, 273; as goddess of desire, 267–68, 271; as Great Goddess, 2, 268–69; hymns of praise to, 263, 268–69; Kaula cult and, 271–72; Nityā cult and, 271; practitioner of love magic and, 266–67; red imagery and, 273; retinue of, 266, 268; Tantras and, 6, 263; visualizations of, 266, 271
Kaṃsāḷe musical community, 43, 55–56
Kaṇṇaki, 31, 35
Kaṇṭhekāḷī, 26
Karambha, 146
Karaṅka, 28–29
Karauli Rajputs, 158–59
Karṇamoṭī, 101
Kashmir, 61, 70–71
Kāśmīra, 21
Kauberī, 86

Kaulajñānanirṇaya, 256
Kaula movement, 271–72
Kaumārī, 82*fig.*, 86, 89, 116*fig.*
Kauṇḍika, 26–27
Kauśikī, 60*fig.*; Barbarian and, 65–67, 73; birth of, 78n4; creation of, 147; creation of Brāhmī, 68; demon desire for, 65–68; as demon-slayer, 63–65, 67–70, 79n18; as Gaurī, 63; as Great Goddess, 2, 70; independence and, 61; as Mother of the Three Worlds, 63, 66–67, 77; Pāñcāla and, 65–68, 73, 78n6; place connections and, 71; as savior goddess, 4; seven mother goddesses and, 74, 100; as Śiva's energy (*śakti*), 70, 72, 74; Tantras and, 6; as transregional deity, 76; as warrior goddess, 70–71; as young girl, 61, 63–65, 73, 76. *See also Haracaritacintāmaṇi*
Kauśikī-Durgā. *See* Kauśikī
Kedargiri, Baba: installment of Kailā Devī's image, 153–54; Mother and merchant devotee, 150–51; Mother idol and, 151–53; ritual austerities and, 148–49, 162; worship of Śakti Ma, 145–46; Yogiraj and, 152–53
Ken Kanuruhan, 224
Kerala: Bhadrakāḷī narrative in, 19, 30, 37; composition of *Mātṛsadbhāva* in, 106; cosmopolitan culture in, 19; oral tradition in, 32–33; religious tradition in, 32; ritual traditions in, 36
Kidung Sudamala, 233–36, 239–40
Kiss, Csaba, 101
Kodungallur Bhagavati temple, 35, 168n34
Koṟṟavai, 31–32, 35, 40n18
Koṭīvarṣa (Devīkoṭa): cremation grounds in, 87, 109n11; goddess of, 100; holy water rites in, 106; mother goddesses and, 101; sacking of, 105; *Skanda Purāṇa* glorification of, 83, 85–87, 96, 98–99, 101, 106; Tantric Śaivism and, 99
Kōvalaṉ, 31
Krama (the Sequence), 9, 283, 292–93
Krishnan, Shri, 209
Kṛpāṇa, 28–29
Kṛṣṇarāja Woḍeyar III, 55
Kṣemarāja, 291, 293
Kubera, 97, 99
Kubjikā, 256–57
Kujambha, 70
Kulārṇava Tantra, 256
Kumāra. *See* Skanda
kumārī worship, 32, 73, 75–77, 175, 200, 212n26, 258, 267. *See also* girls
Kumbha, Mahārāṇā, 203, 209
Kumbhakarṇa (Pitcher-ears), 87, 99
Kuntī, 234–35

Light on the Tantras (*Tantrāloka*), 272, 291
Liṅga Purāṇa, 128, 131
local goddesses: Great Goddess and, 32, 52, 157–58; pan-Indian narratives and, 157–58; Sanskritization of, x, 43, 52, 55, 202
Lohitāyani, 100
Lord of the Three Mothers (Tryambaka), 75
Lord of Yogis, 229

Magic Jewel of Śiva's Deeds, The. See *Haracaritacintāmaṇi*
Mahābhārata, 72, 98–100
Mahadēśvara, 56
Mahādeva, 207
Mahādevī. *See* Great Goddess (Mahādevī)
Mahākālasaṃhitā, 294
Mahākālī, 86
Mahālakṣmī, 97
māhātmyas, 34, 209
Māheśvarī, 82*fig.*, 86, 116*fig.*
Mahiṣa (buffalo-demon): in *Beṭṭada Cāmuṇḍi* ballad, 43, 45; in *Devī Māhātmya*, 53; in *Haracaritacintāmaṇi*, 63, 65, 68–69, 73; origins of, 146–47; in *Śrī Kailādevī Itihās*, 146–47. *See also* buffalo demon
Mahiṣāsuramardinī, 53, 55, 148
Mahiṣawadana, 219, 222–23, 228–29, 231
Mahmud of Ghazni, 6, 151, 163
Malayalam language, 38, 38n1
Malaysia, xi, 8, 187, 191n63
Manaji Rav Gaekwar, 182
Mandodarī, 34
Maṇipravāḷam, 32
Manodarī, 29, 34
Mansarovar, 176, 178–79, 181, 190n18
Manthānabhairava Tantra, 253–54, 272
mantras: *aṅganyāsa* rite, 198, 211n17; "heap" (*kūṭa*), 211n18; Śākta Tantras and, 271; sounds and, 285, 295n3; Śrīcakra worship and, 277; Tantras and, 5, 290; Tantric Śaivism and, 109n5; Tvaritā and, 245, 247–48; Vedic, 157
Māramma, 47–48, 50. *See also* Māriammaṉ/Māriyammā/Māriyammaṉ

Māriammaṉ/Māriyammā/Māriyammaṉ, 58n7, 135, 187
Mārkaṇḍeya, 19, 21, 33, 38, 38n1
Mārkaṇḍeya Purāṇa, 25, 29, 33–34, 38, 105
Mātṛsadbhāva (Essence of the Mothers), 106
Mātṛ Tantras (Tantras of the Mothers), 100, 107
Matsya Purāṇa, 73
Mauryan dynasty, 4
Maya, 24
Mā Yogamāyā Śrī Bhavānī, 173
McDermott, Rachel Fell, xi, xiii
Meenas, 159–60, 168n27
Meister, Michael, 98
Mewar region: Bhil tribal people in, 202–3; Ekliṅgjī temple site in, 205–6; goddess worship in, 201–2; Guhila kingdom in, 202–3, 206–7; *Nainsī rī Khyāt* narrative on, 207; Rāṣṭrasenā protection for, 204–6; Rāṣṭrasenā temple site in, 205, 208; Vindhyavāsinī temple site in, 205
Modi, Narendra, 186
Mokal, Mahārāṇa, 206
monotheism and Hinduism, 9, 188. *See also* polytheism (as inappropriate label for Hinduism)
mother goddesses: ancient narratives of, 96–97; bird-headed, 201–2, 210n8; Brahmā and, 25, 74, 86–89; cults of, 95, 97; demon-slaying and, 86; *Devī Purāṇa* and, 101; Koṭīvarṣa (Devīkoṭa) and, 86–87; origins of, 83, 85–86, 88–89, 99–100, 201–2; popular veneration of, 106–7; Śiva and, 86–87, 99, 103; *Skanda Purāṇa* and, 74, 98–99; Svasthānī and, 133; Tantric Śaivism and, 101–2; Ucchuṣma, 91; Viṣṇu and, 86–87, 92, 94; *yoginīs* and, 106–7. *See also* Seven Mothers (*sapta mātaraḥ*)
Mother of the Three Worlds, 63, 66–67, 77
Mothers of the Directions (*diṅmātaraḥ*), 109n6
Mṛgendra Tantra, 253
Mt. Kailash, 25–26, 59n15, 87, 196, 210n1, 247
Muhaṇot Nainsī, 207
Mukund Das Khinchi, 154, 156–57, 159, 163
Muslims, 6–7, 154–55, 162–63, 167n10, 171, 180, 184, 206, 217. *See also* Kamalias
Mysuru, 43, 51–53, 55

Nainsī rī Khyāt, 207
Nandī, 30
Nandimahākāla, 27
Nañjuṇḍēśvara, 51–52, 55
Nānyadeva, 258
Nārada, 76, 193, 196–200
Nārasiṃhī, 105
Naṭeśa (Lord of Dance), 98–99
Navarāj, 124, 126–27, 134
Navarātra/Navarātri. *See* Nine Nights (*navarātra*) festival
Nepal: Hinduism in, 117, 129–32; Newars in, 117, 130–31, 135–36, 258; Secret Kālī cult in, 294; Seven Mothers (*sapta mātaraḥ*) in, 105; Svasthānī vow in, 117, 129–31, 135–36; Taleju Bhavani and, 258; Tvaritā tale in, 245, 258
Newars, 117, 130–31, 135–37, 138n9, 139n31, 258
Nine Nights (*navarātra*) festival, 58n13, 104, 113n77, 208, 212n25
Nine Planets (*navagrahāḥ*), 105, 268
Nisumbha/Niśumbha: in *Devī Māhātmya*, 54; in *Haracaritacintāmaṇi*, 63–65, 68–70, 73; in *Skanda Purāṇa*, 203; in *Śrī Bahucarā Ārādhanā*, 173–74, 176; in *Śrī Kailādevī Itihās*, 147–48
Niśvāsatattvasaṃhitā, 76, 104, 296n18
Nityā cult, 257, 263, 271–74, 276, 287
Nityākaula, 263, 265*fig.*, 266, 272–74, 276
Nityāṣoḍaśikārṇava, 277

Padma Purāṇa, 131
pālai, 31
Pāñcāla, 65–68, 73, 77, 78n6
Parā, 75
Parab, K. P., 77
Pārameśvarīmata, 255
Parṇaśavarī, 253–54
Parthasarathy, R., 31
Pārvatī: Ardhanārīśvara and, 108n2; Bhadrakāḷī and, 26; creation of Durgā, 72; creation of Tvaritā, 245, 249–50, 255–56; discarding of dark aspect, 72, 75, 78n4, 79n28; Mt. Kailash and, 59n15, 87; penance and, 85; Śiva's stained throat and, 39n14; as wife of Śiva, 12, 86–87
Pasty-Abdul Wahid, M., 38
Pāvaiyā community, 180, 184–86. *See also* Bahucarā Mātā; Becharaji; Hijras; Tirunaṅkais
Pintchman, Tracy, 103
Poerbatjaraka, Raden Mas Ngabehi, 241
Poison Tantras. *See* Gāruḍa Tantras
Pollock, Sheldon, 33

polytheism (as inappropriate label for Hinduism), 9
Pratāp, Mahārāṇa, 203
Pratyabhijñā (divine recognition), 275
pronunciation guide, 12–14
pūjā, 58n13
Pura Dalĕm, 238–40
Purāṇas (ancient lore): Bhadrakāḷī narrative as, 33–34; demon-devotee in, 36; demonic characters in, 36; Hindu goddesses and, 2, 6; pan-Indian performances of, 37, 40n34; regional narratives, 33; reweaving of, 106; warrior goddesses in, 71
Pūtanā, 202, 204

Raimal, Rana, 209
Rajasekhara, P. K., 57
Rajasthan, 143, 165, 201
Rajputs, 158–60, 163, 165–66
Raktabīja, 34, 36, 43, 54, 73, 105, 143, 147, 166n3, 173. *See also* Aisāsura; Dārika/Dāruka; Ruru
Raktāsura. *See* Raktabīja
Rāma, 34
Rāmāyaṇa epic, 34, 39n2, 39n3, 58n1, 189n2, 279n10
Rambha, 146–47
Ramesh, Mandya, 57
Rangda, 216*fig.*; Barong and, 232; as Durgā, 217, 238, 240; magic and, 219, 232; masks of, 240; origins of, 232–33, 236–38; Ratna Manggalī and, 219, 224–26; significance of, 2–3; Tantric traditions and, 6. *See also* Calon Arang (sorceress)
Ra Nini, 217, 234–36, 239
Rastelli, Marion, 6
Rāṣṭrasenā/Rāṣṭraśyenā, 192*fig.*; in *Amarakāvyam*, 206–7; animal sacrifice and, 208; as "Army of the Kingdom," 193, 204, 206; as emanation of goddess Vindhyavāsā, 193, 196, 201; as forgotten goddess, 1–2; as "Ladyhawk of the Kingdom," 193, 204, 206; as local goddess, 202–3; manifestation of, 196–97; in *Nainsī rī Khyāt*, 207; origins of, 201–2; place connections and, 205; protection of Mewar region and, 204–6; rules for worship of, 197–200, 212n24; Tantras and, 6; temple of, 205, 208. *See also Ekaliṅga Māhātmya*
Ratna Manggalī, 219, 224–27
Rāvaṇa, 34
renunciation, religions of, 3–4
Revatī, 202, 204
Ṛg Veda, 1. *See also* Vedas
Rudrayāmala, 107, 268, 279n13, 279n14
Ruru: Bhadrakāḷī slaying of, 106; in City of Gold, 91; defeat by Viṣṇu, 87–88; descent through seven netherworlds, 104, 113n76; as ruler of anti-gods, 87; as ruler of Seven Worlds, 87; Seven Mothers and, 83, 90–92, 94–95; slaying in *Devī Purāṇa*, 87–88, 94–95, 101–2, 104, 106. *See also* Aisāsura; Dārika/Dāruka; Raktabīja

sacrifice: demons as, 27, 90; of humans, 156, 222–23, 234, 238; hunger of deities and, 3, 19, 27, 90, 100, 248, 255–56; of self, 23, 255–56; Vedic Age as religion of, 3. *See also* animal sacrifice
Sadāśiva, 75
Sadewa, 234–35
sādhus (ascetics), 4, 143
Śaiva Mantramārga (Path of mantras), 100
Śaiva Purāṇas, 101
Śaiva Tantras, 101, 104–5
Śaivism: animal sacrifice and, 7; Atimārga traditions, 291; comparison of Kashmirian/non-Kashmirian, 73–74; goddesses as Śiva's consort, 9; Kashmirian nondual, 72; Kauśikī as Śiva's energy (*śakti*) and, 70; nondual, 275; Sadāśiva and, 75; Seven Mothers and, 97; Śiva followers as, 4; supreme goddess and, 9; Tantric traditions and, 70, 290
Śākta: animal sacrifice and, 7; girls as goddesses and, 76; religious traditions of, 280n23; *śakti pīṭhas* in, 182; supreme goddess and, 4, 9; *Svasthānī Kathā* (SVK), 131, 133; Tvaritā and, 254
Śākta Purāṇas, 83
Śākta Śaivism, 271
Śākta Tantras, 255, 257, 271
śakti (divine feminine power): Bahucarā as, 188; Bhairava and, 285–86; Cāmuṇḍā and, 173; early medieval period and, 297n24; emanation and localization, 100; ends of human life and, 138n6; Great Goddess (Mahādevī) and, 103, 113n70, 146–47, 156, 161, 174, 277, 295n8, 296n10; *Jayadrathayāmala* and, 296n17; Kālarudra and, 90; Kauśikī-Durgā as, 61, 63, 70; premier

śakti (divine feminine power) (*continued*)
Goddess and, 4; religious traditions of, 280n23; Seven Mothers and, 83, 92, 103–5; Śiva's power and, 72, 74–75, 78n2, 88–91, 95, 113n71; Svasthānī and, 133; Tantric Saivism and, 111n34, 111n35; Tripurā as, 270; Tvaritā and, 254; Yama-Vaivasvata and, 110n30. *See also* Ādyaśakti; Śākta; Śakti Ma; *śaktipīṭha* (goddess seats)
Śakti Ma, 103, 145–46
śaktipīṭha (goddess seats), 54, 100, 174, 178, 182, 267–68, 276–77, 279n6, 279n17
Sanatkumāra, 85
Sanderson, Alexis, 6, 100, 290
Sankhal Raj, 182
Sanskritization, x, 43, 52, 55, 202
Sarasvati-Sabarmati area, 178–79
Sarkar, Bihani, 257
Ṣaṣṭhī, 97, 202, 204
Satī, 122–23. *See also* *śaktipīṭha* (goddess seats)
Satyavrat, 173
Saul, R. Jeremy, 143–69, 342–43
Śaunaka, 193
Secret Kālī cult, 294
Seizers, 89–91, 104
Serbaeva, Olga, 6, 255, 260n16, 283–300, 343
Seven Mothers (*sapta mātaraḥ*), 82*fig.*; battles with demons, 83, 87–90; battle with Ruru, 83, 90–92, 94–95; Brahminical gods and, 97; Cāmuṇḍā and, 52; as creation of Śiva *vs.* of the Goddess, 103; decline in cult of, 1–2, 105; devotional religion and, 4; Durgā and, 74; emergence of, 86, 109n6; granting of boons to, 87, 100; hymn of praise to, 92–94; male guardian figures and, 97–98; origins of, 83, 85–86, 88–89, 96–100, 105; as pan-Indian temple cult, 97–98; sacrifice and, 87; *śakti* (hierarchies of power) and, 88–89, 103; Śiva and, 106; Tantric Śaivism and, 102–3; Tantric traditions and, 6; temple cults and, 95, 102, 106–7; in temple iconography, 105. *See also* Aṣṭamātrikā
shadow plays, 232–33
Sharma, Bhanwar, 208
Sharma, Premlata, 208
Sharma, Pushpendra Kumar, 108
Shaw, Miranda, 15n1, 253
Shibazaki, Maho, 77
Shivadatta, M. P., 77
Shulman, David, 33, 36
Siddhakhaṇḍa, 272. *See also Manthānabhairava Tantra*
Siddhayogeśvarī, 285, 294n1
Si Gaṇḍi, 219, 221–22
Si Guyang, 219, 221–22
Si Larung, 219, 221
Si Lĕndĕ, 219
Si Lĕndi, 219, 221–22
Si Lĕndya, 219, 221
Simmons, Caleb, 43–59, 343
Śiva: Ardhanārīśvara and, 108n2; Barong mask and, 239; Bhadrakāḷī and, 21, 25–26, 30; black throat and, 26, 39n14; Cāmuṇḍi and, 51–52; creation and, 70; creation of Māheśvarī, 86; Daṇḍhāsur and, 174; divine eagle Tārkṣya and, 247–48, 252; Durgā and, 72, 75; energy (*śakti*), 70, 72, 74; female power of, 74–75; goddess cults and, 72; goddesses as consort of, 9; granting of boons to Seven Mothers, 87, 100; Great Spell (*mahāvidyā*) and, 86; Kashmirian myths and, 71–72; as Lord of the Three Mothers (Tryambaka), 75; mother goddesses and, 86–87, 99, 103; myths of, 39n11; names and forms of wives, 12; as Naṭeśa, 98; Pārvatī and, 87; personal devotion and, 4; Pura Dalĕm and, 239; *śakti* (divine feminine power) and, 83, 88–89; slaying of Ruru, 87–88; *yoginī* ritual and, 248–49, 254–56
Śiva Bhaṭṭa, 122–23
Śivānanda, 275
Śivaśarman/Śiva Śarma, 19, 21, 123, 197–98, 211n13
Skanda/Kumāra, 86–87, 89, 96–97, 99, 287
Skanda Purāṇa: demonic characters in, 203; glorification of Koṭīvarṣa in, 85–87, 96, 98–99, 101, 106; local goddesses and, 100; manifestation of goddesses in, 203–4; mother goddesses and, 74, 98–99; original text of, 98; parallels with *Ekaliṅga Māhātmya*, 204; Pārvatī's dark aspect in, 79n28; Seven Mothers origin in, 83, 85, 96; slaying of buffalo demon in, 53, 79n30; Svasthānī narrative and, 131; Vindhyavāsinī and, 203–4; warrior goddess mythology and, 72
Slaying of Dārika (*Dārikavadham*) narrative, 32
Slouber, Michael, ix, x, xi, xii, 1–15, 109n16, 211n18, 212n22, 245–61, 294, 296n14, 298n37, 343

Slusser, Mary Shepherd, 258, 261n27, 261n29, 261n30
Solanki Rajputs, 183
Southeast Asia, 7–8, 8*map*. *See also* Bali; Indonesia; Java; Malaysia
śrāddha rite, 196, 210n5
Śrī Bahucarā Ārādhanā (Adoration of Bahucarā), 172*fig.*, 187. *See also* Bahucarā Mātā
Śrīcakra, 263, 273–75, 277
Śrī Kailādevī Itihās, 144*fig.*; Baba Kedargiri and, 145–46, 148–52; Cāmuṇḍā in, 145, 155, 157; demonic characters in, 145–48, 150; devotee Bahora Gurjar and, 149–50; Kailā Devī in, 143, 145–57; Mahiṣa (buffalo-demon) in, 146–47; Mahiṣāsuramardinī in, 148–53; miracle stories in, 143; Śakti Ma and, 145–46
Śrīmanmahārājavara Vaṃśāvaḷi, 55
Śrīvidyā: religious traditions of, 190n28; Tantric mantras and, 280n25; Tantric movements and, 9; Tripurāsundarī and, 182, 188, 263, 271, 274–75
sthalapurāṇas, 209
Sthūṇa, 28–29
Story of the Ritual Vow to the Goddess Svasthānī, The. See *Svasthānī-vrata-kathā*
Suastika, I Made, 241
Sudamala, 232–36
Sukhchand Patel, 154–55
Śukra, 87
Śumbha: in *Haracaritacintāmaṇi*, 63, 65, 67–69, 73; in *Skanda Purāṇa*, 203; in *Śrī Kailādevī Itihās*, 147–48
Sunda, 72
Supreme Feminine Power, 173–78, 188
Śuṣkā, 285, 294n1
Suṣumāṇa, 193
Sutīkṣṇa, 19, 21–22, 25–26, 28, 34
Svacchanda Bhairava, 104
Svacchanda Tantra, 104
Svasthānī, 116*fig.*; associations with Śiva, 133; Aṣṭamātrikā and, 133; benevolence and, 133–35; description of, 132–33; destructive capacity and, 134; disease and, 135; as goddess of one's own place, 132, 135; granting of boon to Navarāj, 127; Nepali Hindus and, 117, 129–32, 135–36; Newars and, 117, 130–31; origins of, 130, 133; renunciation and, 4; scholarship on, 2; as Supreme Goddess, 133; worship of, 133
Svasthānī vow (*vrata*): Candravatī and, 131, 134; disease in, 135; expansion of worship, 130, 135; Gomā Bhaṭṭinī and, 123–25, 131, 134; month of Māgh and, 117, 129, 134; Navarāj and, 124–28, 131, 134; Nepali Hindu identity and, 130, 132; Newar-language, 130, 135–37; origins of, 131–34; performance of, 120–21, 129–30, 134–36; Purāṇic narrative additions, 131–32, 137; Sanskrit-language, 130, 137; significance of, 117–18; sinful woman and, 126–28; Śiva Bhaṭṭa and, 122–23; story of, 122–28; as women's tradition, 134, 139n35; worship of Pārvatī and, 120
Svasthānī-vrata-kathā, 117, 119*fig.*, 129. *See also* Svasthānī vow (*vrata*)
SVK. *See Svasthānī-vrata-kathā*

Taleju Bhavānī, 245, 258, 261n27, 261n30
Tamil poetry, 30–32, 35
Tāmrākṣa, 28–29
Tanaka, Masakazu, 7
Tantrāloka (Light on the Tantras), 71
Tantras (scriptures): *Bhadrakāḷī Māhātmya*, 30; geographic locations in, 263, 272; goddess worship and, 2, 5–6, 283; Great Goddess in, 9; magic and, 217, 259n4; mother goddesses and, 87; power of mantras in, 5; scholarship on, 6; sexual rituals and, 256; Svasthānī vow (*vrata*) and, 137; *vidyā*s and, 5
Tantric religion/cults: Bhairava and, 102; defining, 5; development of, 4; devotional visualizations and, 5; goddess worship and, 9, 106; Koṭīvarṣa (Devīkoṭa) and, 101; Nityā cult and, 272–73; Southeast Asian spread of, 7
Tantric rituals: *Ekaliṅga Māhātmya* and, 193; hexagonal fire maṇḍala and, 266, 278n1; impure substances and, 272; Kālī and, 2, 5, 289–90, 298n33, 298n37; *Mātṛsadbhāva* and, 106; *nyāsa* and, 277; Parā and violent forces in, 75; Purāṇic narratives and, 106; red imagery and, 273; sacred sounds and ritual speech in, 264, 290; sacred spaces (maṇḍalas) and, 290; *Vāmakeśvarīmata* and, 275
Tantric Śaivism: cosmology and, 111n35; in *Devī Purāṇa*, 103–4; early medieval period and, 15n4; girls as goddesses and, 76; goddess traditions of, 9; initiatory traditions of, 97; Kaula movement and, 271;

Tantric Śaivism (*continued*)
Koṭīvarṣa cremation grounds and, 87, 109n11; Koṭīvarṣa origins and, 99; mother goddesses and, 101–3; sacred sites of goddesses and, 100; Śaiva Mantramārga (Path of mantras) and, 100; Seven Mothers and, 102–3; *vidyās* and, 109n5
Tantric traditions: Brahminical lore and, 299n42; Cāmuṇḍi and, 52; children as deities in, 76; identification of female practitioners with witchcraft, 238; initiation-based religion and, 5; Kālīkula and, 291–92; Śaiva mythology and, 70, 290; Seven Mothers and, 97; Śrīvidyā, 182, 188, 190n28; transgressive practices and, 271; Trika (triad) school and, 9, 75, 271, 285, 291; Tripurāsundarī and, 272–73; Tvaritā and, 254
Tarkaratna, Panchanan, 108
Tārkṣya. *See* Garuḍa
Tejpāl, 181
Thoṭṭam Pāṭṭu (Songs of origins), 35
Tilottamā, 72
Tirunaṅkais, 186–87. *See also* Bahucarā Mātā; Becharaji; Hijras; Pāvaiyā community; transgender
Tod, James, 207
Törzsök, Judit, 6, 61–80, 295n1, 343
transgender, 179–82, 184–88. *See also* Bahucarā Mātā; Becharaji; Hijras; Pāvaiyā community; Tirunaṅkais
transliteration of southern Asian languages, 12–14
Trautmann, Thomas, 3
Trika (triad) school, 9, 75, 271, 285, 291
Tripurāsundarī: Bahucarā Mātā and, 175; as Beauty of the Three Cities, 271; classical cult of, 273–74, 277; contemporary worship of, 271, 276; as goddess of desire, 269–70; as Great Goddess, 270; hymns of praise to, 270; Kaula cult and, 271–72; as local goddess, 276; significance of, 2; Śrīvidyā worship and, 182, 188, 263, 271, 274–75; as Tantric goddess, 182, 188, 256, 272–75; Tvaritā and, 257; visualizations of, 269–71; *Yoginīhṛdaya* and, 274
Troṭala Tantra, 251–54
Turajā Māhātmya, 257–58
Tutur literature, 243n16
Tvaritā, 244*fig.*; contemporary worship of, 257–58; creation of, 247–52, 255–56; depictions of, 249–50, 253; eighteen-armed form of, 249, 253–54; as female shaman, 253–54; migration to Nepal, 258; origins of, 245, 253–54; as a Śavara woman, 253–54; sexual nature of, 256; significance of, 2; as snakebite curer, 252–54; spell, 250–52; Taleju Bhavani and, 258; Tantras and, 6, 245, 257; *Troṭalā Tantra* and, 251–54; *yoginīs* and, 251, 257–58, 259n4
Tvaritā's Basic Teaching (*Tvaritāmūlasūtra*), 245, 246*fig.*, 247–54, 256, 258–59
Tvaritā's Wisdom Spellbook (*Tvaritājñānakalpa*), 254

Ucchuṣma, 91
Umā, 233–36
Upaniṣads, 4
Upasunda, 72
Uttanahaḷḷi, 42*fig.*; battle with Aisāsura, 46–49; birth of, 47, 56; femininity of, 43; as *grāmadēvate*, 52; Jvalajjihvā and, 54; Jvālāmukhi and, 54; pan-Indian mythology and, 54; place connections and, 52, 54; as place-guardian, 43; significance of, 3

Vāḍavānalīya Tantra, 272
vāhana. *See* animal mount (*vāhana*) of goddess/god
Vaiṣṇavas, 4, 7, 9, 95, 131, 133, 185
Vaiṣṇavī, 25, 83*fig.*, 86, 89, 93, 97, 102, 116*fig.*
Vajeshih, 181
Vallabha, 185, 187
Vāmakeśvarīmata, 263, 268–70, 273–75, 277
Varāhamihira, 95, 111n37
Vārāhī, 82*fig.*, 86, 89, 97, 112n65
Varakhaḍī tree, 173, 175, 178, 189n1
Vāruṇī, 86
Vasudeva, Somadeva, xiii, 6, 259, 278
Vāyavī, 86
Vāyu, 87, 193, 196–200
Vāyu Purāṇa, 193, 209
Vedagarbha, 193, 200
Vedas, 1, 94, 103–5, 122, 128, 137, 185, 198, 275, 286–87. *See also* Vedic religion
Vedic mantras, 157
Vedic religion, 3–5, 22, 78n5, 88, 157, 173, 175, 189n5, 223, 252, 289. *See also* Vedas
Vetālī, 27–29, 34
vidyās: as embodiment of the deity, 5; goddess worship and, 283, 288, 291, 294n1; male/

female, 280n24, 290; ritual formulas and, 279n16; in Śākta Tantras, 271; in Tantric Śaivism, 109n5; in *Vāmakeśvarīmata*, 277
Vīṇādhara (Bearer of the Vīṇā-lute), 97
Vinatā, 202
Vināyaka, 97. *See also* Gaṇeśa
Vindhya Mountain: in *Haracaritacintāmaṇi*, 63–65, 67–69, 71, 73, 76; Kauśikī in, 71; lustful depictions of, 67, 73, 76
Vindhyavāsā/Vindhyavāsinī, 193, 196, 201, 203–7
Vīrabhadra (Auspicious Hero), 97
Visalakshy, P., 37
Viṣṇu: Bhadrakāḷī narrative and, 22–23; defeat of Ruru's army, 87–88; goddesses as consort of, 9; mother goddesses and, 86, 92, 94; personal devotion and, 4
Vyanmātā (Bāṇmātā), 207
Vyāsa, 85

warrior goddesses: in *Devī Māhātmya*, 34, 71; Great Goddess (Mahādevī) as, 70; Kauśikī as, 70–71; Koṟṟavai and, 31; local goddesses as, 32; Purāṇas (ancient lore) and, 71; Rāṣṭrasenā as, 204, 206; in the *Skanda Purāṇa*, 72; Tamil poetry and, 31; Vindhyavāsinī and, 204
Wĕkśirṣa, 219, 222–23, 228–29, 231
Woḍeyar dynasty, 58n12

yakṣiṇīs, 1, 201, 203
Yama, 112n65
Yāmala. *See Yāmala Tantras* (Union Tantras)
Yāmala Tantras (Union Tantras), 9, 100–101, 107
Yāmī, 86
Yoginīhṛdaya, 274–75
yoginīs: Bahucarā Mātā and, 177; bird-headed, 210n8; defining, 279n9; *Devī Purāṇa* and, 104; encounters with, 255–56; Kālī and, 289; mother goddesses and, 107; Rāṣṭrasenā and, 197; Śiva and, 91, 248–49, 254–56; Tantric goddess cults and, 106–7, 110n27, 113n87; Tantric rites and, 101; temples for, 106–7; Tvaritā and, 250
Yogiraj, 151–53, 162–63
Yokochi, Yuko, 15n2, 71, 98–100, 107, 109n8, 112n57, 204

Milton Keynes UK
Ingram Content Group UK Ltd.
UKHW012304080124
435686UK00008B/590

9 780520 375758